Mahommah Gardo Baquaqua

PAUL E. LOVEJOY AND
NIELSON R. BEZERRA

Mahommah Gardo Baquaqua

An Enslaved Muslim of the Black Atlantic

The University of North Carolina Press *Chapel Hill*

Set in Arno Pro by Westchester Publishing Services
Manufactured in the United States of America

Library of Congress Cataloging-in-Publication Data
Names: Lovejoy, Paul E., author. | Bezerra, Nielson Rosa, author.
Title: Mahommah Gardo Baquaqua : an enslaved Muslim of the Black Atlantic /
    Paul E. Lovejoy and Nielson Bezerra.
Description: Chapel Hill : University of North Carolina Press, [2025] | Includes
    bibliographical references and index.
Identifiers: LCCN 2024045133 | ISBN 9781469682440 (cloth) | ISBN 9781469682457
    (paperback) | ISBN 9781469682464 (epub) | ISBN 9781469682471 (pdf)
Subjects: LCSH: Baquaqua, Mahommah Gardo. | Enslaved persons—America—Biography. |
    Enslaved persons—Africa, West—Biography. | Enslaved Muslims—Biography. | Free Black
    people—Biography. | Free Black people—Biography. | Black people—Atlantic Ocean
    Region—History—19th century. | Slavery—Atlantic Ocean Region—History—19th
    century. | BISAC: HISTORY / World | SOCIAL SCIENCE / Slavery | LCGFT: Biographies.
Classification: LCC E444.B2 L64 2025 | DDC 306.3/62092 [B]—dc23/eng/20241209
LC record available at https://lccn.loc.gov/2024045133

Cover art: Reprinted from Foss and Mathiews, *Facts for Baptist Churches* (Utica, NY, 1850).

For product safety concerns under the European Union's General Product Safety Regulation
(EU GPSR), please contact gpsr@mare-nostrum.co.uk or write to The University of North
Carolina Press and Mare Nostrum Group B.V., Mauritskade 21D, 1091 GC Amsterdam, The
Netherlands.

Dedicated to the memory

of

Alberto da Costa e Silva

Contents

List of Illustrations ix

Acknowledgments xi

Introduction 1

CHAPTER ONE
Born after Twins in Djougou 20

CHAPTER TWO
Twice Enslaved? 47

CHAPTER THREE
Under Slavery in Brazil 74

CHAPTER FOUR
New York and Freedom 100

CHAPTER FIVE
With the Free Will Baptists 121

CHAPTER SIX
Baquaqua's Narrative of Freedom 153

CHAPTER SEVEN
Return to Africa 170

Conclusion 195

Appendix A. Application for Writ of Habeas Corpus 209

Appendix B. Haitien Mission 1849–50: Annual Reports of the
American Baptist Free Mission Society 215

Glossary 221

Notes 223

Bibliography 255

Index 279

Illustrations

FIGURES

2.1 Slave sale at Ouidah in 1860 65

2.2 Isidoro de Souza 67

2.3 Surf boats with slaves, Bight of Benin 69

3.1 Recife waterfront 78

3.2 Rio de Janeiro 87

3.3 Antiga Sé do Rio de Janeiro on Rua Direita 91

3.4 Rio Grande do Sul in 1852 95

4.1 New York harbor—East River 101

4.2 Colored seamen's home advertisement 104

4.3 New York City Hall 107

4.4 Eldridge Street Jail 111

4.5 Rev. Luther Lee 112

4.6 Luís Henrique Ferreira d'Aguiar 118

5.1 Port-au-Prince, Haiti 122

5.2 Rev. William L. Judd and Baquaqua 126

5.3 McGrawville, New York 133

5.4 New York Central College 140

5.5 Chatham, Canada West 148

5.6 Pamphlet cover, 1854 151

7.1 Baquaqua letter to George Whipple, 1853 183

7.2 Waterlook Docks, Liverpool 188

MAPS

1.1 The Black Atlantic—Baquaqua's Travels 6

1.2 Bight of Benin and Interior 11

3.1 Brazilian Coast 75

5.1 Upstate New York and Canada West 139

TABLES

3.1 Antonio José da Rocha Pereira's ships leaving Rio de
     Janeiro (January/February 1846) 93

3.2 Antonio José da Rocha Pereira's embarkations (1847) 93

3.3 Expenses of voyages between Rio de Janeiro and
     Rio Grande do Sul, 1846 94

Acknowledgments

Mahommah Gardo Baquaqua has truly been worthy of the attention that a large cohort of interested researchers have paid him. Our curiosity stems from two separate tracks. For Lovejoy, Baquaqua holds hidden meaning that was overlooked in his pioneering study of the internal West African trade in kola nuts. A knowledge of Baquaqua, who only came to Lovejoy's attention two decades later when Allan Austin published a preliminary annotated version of Baquaqua's autobiography, would have enhanced Lovejoy's study. For Bezerra, the early fascination was Brazilian. Baquaqua had come to the attention of Brazilian scholars as to what was thought to be the first and only autobiography of someone who was enslaved in Brazil. Bezerra's work on coastal trade in cassava flour and other commodities led him to appreciate Baquaqua's story as someone who was exploited in that trade, rather than the merchants and elite that benefited. Our interest was advanced through numerous discussions with Alberto da Costa e Silva on the role of Muslims in Brazil in the nineteenth century. Paul Lovejoy and Robin Law published an annotated version of Baquaqua's autobiography, together with additional documentation. That initiative only led to more research, particularly in Brazil and North America, and with the assistance of Bruno Rafael Véras, a major focus was on the identity of Baquaqua's editor, Samuel Moore. In the meantime, Riccardo Ciavolella was undertaking additional anthropological research in Djougou, based on Baquaqua's own observations. This book is the result of the scholarly interaction outlined here.

In addition, we would like to recognize and thank the following individuals who have assisted in the research for this study: Shahrzad Parand, Thiago Santo, Carley Downs, Fabio Silva Magalhaes, M. B. Duffill, Feisal Farah, Cheryl Lemaitre, Erika Melek Delgado, Gwen Robinson, Mathew Robertshaw, Ibrahim Hamza, Ibrahim Jumare, Ibrahim Sani Kankara, Mohammed Bashir Salau, N. B. Bako, Guylaine Petrin, Daniela Cavalheiro, Moisés Peixoto, Eliana Laurentino, Juliana Lima, Vinicius Pereira de Oliveira, Gabriel Aladren, Manolo Florentino, Marcus J. M. Carvalho, Brian Prince, Catherine Hanchett, Elisée Soumonni, Sean Kelley, David Bebbington, Allan Austin, and Kardikay Chadha. Several people read all or parts of the manuscript and provided useful advice, including Suzanne Schwarz, Sean Kelley, Henry B.

Lovejoy, Elaine Pereira Rocha, Carlos da Silva Junior, Alexandre dos Santos, and especially Robin Law and Ana Lucia Araujo. We wish to thank Isabella Santos for the maps.

We wish to draw attention to the pioneering work of Allan Austin (ed.), *African Muslims in Ante-Bellum America: A Sourcebook* (New York & London: Garland Publishing, 1984). We would also like to acknowledge Lovejoy's early work with Robin Law, which led to the publication of *The Biography of Mahommah Gardo Baquaqua: His Passage from Slavery to Freedom in Africa and America*, published by Markus Wiener Publishers, Princeton, New Jersey, in 2001 and revised in 2006, and we acknowledge, with thanks, those who aided in the research for that volume. The project could not have been completed without the support of the Social Sciences and Humanities Research Council of Canada and York University.

The book is dedicated to Alberto da Costa e Silva, whose friendship and advice were instrumental over the years and whose continued engagement is dearly missed.

Mahommah Gardo Baquaqua

Introduction

Mahommah Gardo Baquaqua was a Muslim of the Black Atlantic, torn from the interior of West Africa and enslaved in Brazil. He was born into a prominent commercial family in the early 1820s who lived in Djougou, which is an important city in northern République du Benin today. At the time, Djougou was a caravan stop on perhaps the most important trade corridor across West Africa. The town was a caravan stop on the route between the two largest states in Africa at the time. To the west was Asante, which controlled the region inland from the Gold Coast including Gonja, Dagomba, and other areas of the middle Volta River basin. At the other end of the caravan axis to the northeast of Djougou was the Sokoto Caliphate, a Muslim empire founded in *jihād* in 1804–8 and consisting of thirty-two emirates. Sokoto was the largest state in the interior of Africa in the nineteenth century. Its dynamic economy was based on textile production, leather goods, mineral salts, and agricultural commodities.

The reconstruction of Baquaqua's odyssey relies primarily on what he told the Rev. William L. Judd and his wife Nancy A. Lake Judd when he was in Haiti from 1847 to 1849, what the editor of his autobiography, Samuel Moore, understood him to mean in preparing its publication in 1854, and what can be gleaned from Baquaqua's surviving letters. Rev. Judd was the pastor in the Free Will Baptist mission in Port-au-Prince. He and his wife enthusiastically welcomed Baquaqua into the mission and, despite problems of language, undertook to find out as much as they could about Baquaqua's background on the expectation that Baquaqua would be involved in establishing a Free Will Baptist mission in Africa. As for Samuel Moore, whom Baquaqua paid to edit his account, little is known, other than he also was Christian and an abolitionist, apparently British, and knew very little about Africa and therefore misunderstood much of what Baquaqua must have been trying to explain to him. Baquaqua's letters provide an additional gloss on the accounts of the Judds and Moore, but relatively little additional information on his background.

Baquaqua endured a most remarkable odyssey that first took him from Djougou through the powerful slave-exporting state of Dahomey to Pernambuco, a center of sugar cane production in northeastern Brazil. Initially enslaved to a baker in a town near the capital city of Recife in 1845 and subsequently to a ship captain operating between Rio de Janeiro, at the time the capital of the Brazilian Empire, and Rio Grande do Sul, far to the south, he miraculously made his escape from slavery in New York City in 1847 when he jumped his master's ship that was delivering coffee from Brazil. He was therefore able to survive enslavement in the interior of West Africa, the forced march to the coast, the Middle Passage, and slavery in Pernamubuco, Rio de Janeiro, and Rio Grande do Sul, but secured his freedom in New York. Baquaqua's further exposure to the Black Atlantic took him to Haiti, after being broken out of jail in New York. In the Haitian capital Port-au-Prince, he became associated with the Free Will Baptist mission, which arranged for his return to the United States in 1849 to attend New York Central College, a little-known progressive institution in the small town of McGrawville, now McGraw, in preparation for a mission to Africa as a Free Will Baptist. Baquaqua raised funds for his return to Africa through speaking engagements in various Baptist churches in the small towns of Pennsylvania and New York and through the publication of an autobiographical account of his life, which he published in 1854, but which raised little if any money. Thereafter, he went to Britain on a journey that he hoped would take him back to Africa. Despite employment on a ship in the Mediterranean, he does not seem to have been able to sign on to a ship going to West Africa, at least not before 1862 when he managed to reach Liberia. His trail disappears after that. Despite the absence of documentation, unless something happened that prevented his further travel, he could have easily made it from Monrovia to Lagos on the regular steam ships that plied the coast. From Lagos, there was considerable commerce and travel with the far interior cities and towns of the Sokoto Caliphate, including Ilorin, Bida, Zaria, Kano, Katsina, and Sokoto. These are the places that Baquaqua would have known about as a result of living in a major town on the caravan route to the west. Baquaqua's understanding of the geography of the West African interior was considerable because he was born into a commercial family. His trans-navigation of the Atlantic represents an unusual, perhaps unique, journey that went far beyond the caravan trails inland from the Bight of Benin. His journey exposes the layers of the global African experience that amplify the Black Atlantic. Even if he did not attain his ultimate ambition, which was to reach his mother's hometown of Katsina, Baquaqua's odyssey demonstrates that it was possible for someone to return to West Africa and the Muslim centers of the interior.

Baquaqua crossed several political boundaries and thereby was exposed to quite different contexts to which he had to adjust. First, he came from a region affected by four significant historical developments. In Africa, he was affected by Asante and Dahomey politics to the west and south of Djougou, as well as the jihād movement that led to the consolidation of the Sokoto Caliphate and the relative decline of his mother's hometown of Katsina. Second, he arrived in Brazil during the period of empire after the slave trade from Africa had been abolished but still flourished, nonetheless. Despite internal Brazilian political instability, the rapid expansion of coffee cultivation and the continued production of sugar fueled economic expansion and the extension of slave labor. Baquaqua's arrival in New York thrust him into yet another setting, one that was increasingly exacerbated by the issue of slavery and political expansion as represented in the United States' war with Mexico, the annexation of Texas, and plots to intervene in Cuba, Central America, and elsewhere under the inspired slogan of "manifest destiny." Baquaqua's time in Haiti coincided with a final attempt by Haiti to take control of the whole island of Hispaniola, which ended in disaster and an additional burden on the national debt of a country already subjected to annual indemnities imposed by France.

Baquaqua returned to the United States amid the intensifying conflict over slavery that resulted in the Fugitive Slave Law of 1850, which essentially forced abolitionists into a position of violating the law in helping anyone who was Black. Baquaqua was thrust into the thick of the abolitionist movement, dependent on the goodwill of radical, antislavery Baptists and the network involved in the Underground Railroad that had initially freed him from the Eldridge Street Jail in New York. He was at Central College when the notorious Jerry case played out in nearby Syracuse, where one of his liberators from jail was active as a minister and abolitionist. Baquaqua's association with Gerrit Smith, who would run unsuccessfully for president of the United States in 1856, further thrust him into a political situation that by now had assumed an international context.

His time in Britain after 1855 brought him into a society that seemed more tolerant than he had known in North America and Brazil. The enslaved population of British colonies had been emancipated in 1834, despite a subsequent requirement of indenture, and the legal status of slavery was being imposed in territories that Britain controlled. The relative openness of British society further encouraged Baquaqua in his quest to return to Africa filled with lofty ideas of development and transformation. There were others in Sierra Leone and elsewhere who were beginning to expulse ideas of progress and change who were far more articulate than Baquaqua. Nonetheless, his association with many of the leading abolitionists and champions of intervention in Africa makes his story compelling.

We are fortunate in having detailed information on Baquaqua's background, his enslavement, and his subsequent travels across the Atlantic and then around the Atlantic, eventually returning to West Africa. He was un-usual in that he was one of the few people born in Africa who attended col-lege, and he was able to publish his autobiography in Detroit in 1854.[1] Other former slaves also published their personal stories, although there are rela-tively few instances in which those born in Africa and experienced the Middle Passage left personal descriptions. Birth in Africa also signified that in most cases a person was born free.[2] He was unusual in another way as well. He be-came associated with the most radical abolitionists in the United States be-fore the American Civil War. While he was not one of the prominent leaders of the abolitionists, he knew many of the leading activists, agreed with their interventionist strategies in combating slavery, and championed a movement to return to Africa. His autobiography, long neglected, reflects his passionate commitment to ending slavery.

There were numerous autobiographies and biographies available when Baquaqua was preparing his own. A notable example that had considerable political influence at the time and has had enduring interest over the last sev-eral decades is the autobiography of Gustavus Vassa, whose birth name was Olaudah Equiano. Vassa published his "interesting narrative" some sixty-five years before Baquaqua published his. It is even possible that Baquaqua read Vassa's *The Interesting Narrative of the Life of Olaudah Equiano* because of an excerpt that was published in *Voice of the Fugitive* on 18 June 1851. The extract was from "the narrative of Gustavus Vassa, who was stolen from his native land when a boy and made a slave: but who afterwards became enlightened and wrote a history of his life, which was published in England."[3] Baquaqua could also have been inspired by Frederick Douglass, whom Baquaqua must have met, and indeed others.

This study explores Baquaqua's life. In doing so, it adds to the growing cor-pus of accounts of enslaved Africans during the era of trans-Atlantic slavery, and specifically of enslaved Muslims in the Americas, whose accounts are concentrated in Brazil, the United States, and Jamaica. The features of Baquaqua's biography provide insights on the Black Atlantic in the middle of the nineteenth century because he managed to travel from the interior of Africa to Brazil and then to the United States and the Caribbean before re-turning to West Africa.

Baquaqua's description of his time in Africa before his enslavement is un-usual in providing details on Djougou and the area north of Dahomey be-tween Borgu and Gonja/Asante that is astonishing. His account of Muslim commercial life of West Africa amplifies what is known about one of the most important trade routes in the interior. His account is the earliest firsthand ethnographic and historical detail on the complex geopolitical setting of the Djougou region. In an earlier publication, Robin Law and Paul Lovejoy annotated Baquaqua's autobiography and provided additional documentation, including letters and various reports. This study amplifies that earlier exposition, correcting some details and elaborating much more fully on many aspects of Baquaqua's experiences.[4]

Baquaqua provides new insights on the operation of the Underground Railroad through New York City before the passage of the Fugitive Slave Bill in 1850, but his trials and escape from jail in 1847 have been largely overlooked. Although his role in the abolition movement in the United States and Canada was not as prominent as many others, such as Frederick Douglass, Harriet Tubman, and Gerrit Smith, he was associated with all three and corresponded with other prominent abolitionists.

His relationship with the Free Will Baptists deserves to be highlighted. This loose association of Baptist churches from New England to Wisconsin and centered to some extent in upstate New York and neighboring northern Pennsylvania played a particularly radical role in the abolition movement in the United States, which has been largely overlooked as well. That connection helped Baquaqua reach Britain in 1855, and hence his account provides new information on the continued activities of abolitionists in Britain during the 1850s, a decade after emancipation in British colonies, as well as the Baptist movement more broadly. Baquaqua's life is an exceptional example of someone who traversed various parts of the Black Atlantic, from West Africa to Brazil, the United States, Haiti, Canada, and Britain. While there were many other Africans, especially in Brazil and to a lesser extent in Cuba, who returned to West Africa, Baquaqua's journey was more complicated and in some ways was quite different. He was enslaved in West Africa, endured slavery in Brazil, regained his freedom in North America, and actually made it back to Africa at least as far as Liberia.

In recounting the life experience of Baquaqua, we are following an individual from West Africa around the Atlantic in a kaleidoscope of enslavement: Middle Passage, slavery, escape, opportunity, and possibility that took him from Djougou through Dahomey to Brazil, from there to New York City, exile in Haiti, education in the United States, and then Canada, Britain, and Liberia, at last. In less than two years, from 1845 to 1847, he experienced the cruel sale and uncertain relationships of the slave trail. He regained his freedom in 1847 after undertaking back-breaking labor and failing to satisfy his master's need for a trustworthy street vendor. Considered a difficult slave, he was sold to a ship captain who came from the notorious port of Rio Grande

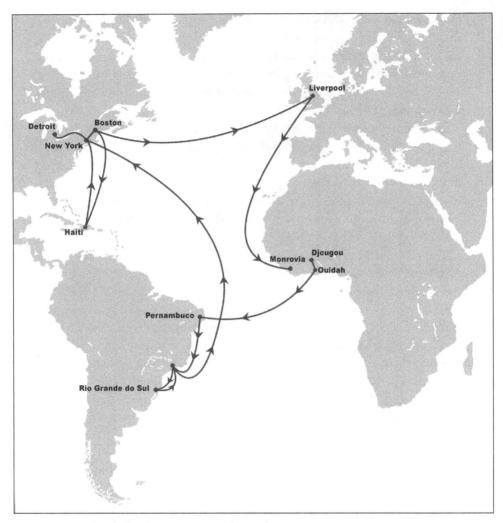

MAP I.1 The Black Atlantic—Baquaqua's Travels

do Sul, known for buying slaves with reputations for resistance, who were punished cruelly. The astonishing achievement of Baquaqua at this time should be emphasized. Not knowing a word of English in 1847, he published his autobiography in 1854.

Once he regained his freedom in 1847, he claimed his identity as Mahommah Gardo Baquaqua, rejecting the name he had been called in Brazil. That he made this declaration to Baptist missionaries in Haiti and later attended college in upstate New York in 1850–53 and published under that name in 1854 attests to this assertion of identity. His autobiography recounts a remarkable

odyssey that took him from the caravan town of Djougou on the route between the Sokoto Caliphate and Asante to slavery in Brazil to freedom in New
York City and conversion to Christianity in Haiti. He identified his mother's
family who came from Katsina in the Sokoto Caliphate, described how he was
first enslaved but freed in the northern Asante province of Gonja and then
enslaved a second time and sent to Brazil via the notorious slave port of Ouidah, spending two years in slavery first to a baker in Pernambuco and then a
ship captain in Rio de Janeiro. As a Muslim, he inevitably met other Muslims
in Brazil, but after his fortunate escape from slavery in New York City seems
not to have known other Muslims before he returned to West Africa in the
early 1860s, after which he would have undoubtedly come into contact with
Muslims. His Brazilian master made the mistake of taking Baquaqua to New
York with a consignment of coffee, which enabled his escape. His association
with the Free Will Baptist Mission in Haiti opened new doors. His incredible
journey then took him to upstate New York where he attended college, and
Canada West, now Ontario, where he completed his autobiography, before
continuing onto Liverpool and eventually back to Africa.

Baquaqua's account is a personalized story of enslavement and freedom. It
is also a remarkable exposition of the transformation that enslavement caused
in his life. After his incarceration near his hometown and his march southward to Dahomey, he still believed that he would be rescued, but when he
reached Abomey, the capital of Dahomey, he knew that his family would not
be able to find him. As he expressed his grief, "I began to give up all hopes of
ever getting back to my home again, . . . and by some means or other of once
more seeing my native place."[5] His autobiography is testimony to the impact
of enslavement when the hope of rescue finally ends. Baquaqua met people
from Djougou in Abomey, and he reports an acquaintance he came across in
Ouidah, the principal slave port on the coast of West Africa, but he was no
longer thinking of liberation or escape, and he was not reassured by these
chance encounters. The encounter with the man in Ouidah, whom he recognized because of his hairstyle, was probably the last time he heard himself
addressed as Gardo, which was the name he would have been called in Djougou. We don't know if he was given a name on the ship that took him to
Pernambuco, but he would have been baptized almost immediately on landing. The first name we have for him is that used by the ship owner who purchased him in Rio de Janeiro, which was José da Costa, where da Costa was
his new master's name. Probably his previous owner in Pernambuco knew
him as José as well, suggesting that this was how he was baptized. His reaction
to being given a Portuguese name became evident when he was in Haiti and

underwent his conversion to Christianity at the Free Will Baptist Mission in Port-au-Prince. He rejected his slave name and chose to call himself Mahommah Gardo Baquaqua, by which he had been known in Djougou.

Biographical accounts of enslaved Africans who experienced their enslavement in the Americas provide insights into the history and legacy of slavery. While a single autobiography or biographical account perhaps reveals little about broader social or economic patterns, such accounts have one very important impact besides chronicling a life history. Biography emphasizes the individual person, not the institution of slavery nor the property dimension of ownership of someone by others. The efforts to come to terms with the slavery past of modern society must confront conflicting interpretations of history. Individuals, and indeed communities that might trace ancestry to enslavement, may want to forget a legacy that is supposedly tainted and categorizes people according to skin color. Those whose ancestors suffered from slavery have had to endure varying degrees of intergenerational trauma that has exacerbated racialized stigmatization. The descendants of those who profited from enslavement have often been glorified with statues and naming of streets and buildings. The effect is the willful, even if not always the obvious, intention to erase complicity and disguise intergenerational benefits that systematically favor those who are descended from slave ownership and thus have reaped the rewards of enslaved labor. Biographical accounts, and especially autobiographies, confront a style of historical analysis that emphasizes broad historical context but avoids personal experiences as episodic. As Baquaqua's autobiography demonstrates, however, personal accounts can inform our understanding of broader historical events by deciphering how individuals fit into context. Life stories can be thought of as situational markers that have to be understood in the difficult task of disentangling historical reconstruction from the blurry legacy of the past. Baquaqua epitomizes this dichotomy separating historical context from personal experience. Born in the interior of West Africa, enslavement took him to Brazil in 1845 and ultimately to the United States, where he was fortunate in reacquiring his freedom in 1847.

Until recently, Baquaqua has been largely overlooked in scholarly discussion. His appearance follows a trend that has been labeled the biographical turn in social history, which began with the early collection of texts in Philip D. Curtin's *Africa Remembered* in 1967 but did not include Baquaqua's account.[6] Thanks to Allan Austin, Baquaqua's unique story came to the attention of scholars in 1984 and then to a wider public emanating outward from Brazil.[7] Biographical and autobiographical accounts of Africans, especially Muslims and males, have become more common, both in Brazil and elsewhere. While many of the accounts of Muslims from the eighteenth century pertain to individuals who came from the Senegambia region and the western savanna, the accounts from the nineteenth century, including Baquaqua's, come from areas further east, specifically in the interior of the Bight of Benin. Abubakar al-Siddiq, whose biography is well documented, came from Buna in the middle Volta basin in the 1790s, and he had a connection with the Hausa through his mother, who came from Katsina, as did Baquaqua's mother. Al-Siddiq came from Jenne, which is on the middle Niger River and is connected via trade with the towns bordering Asante.[8]

Ali Eisami came from a town near Birni Ngazargamu, the capital of Borno, which was destroyed in the jihād and abandoned in 1810.[9] He traveled via Katsina to the Oyo capital of Katunga before being sold to the coast in 1817 in fear that he would join the Muslim uprising emanating from Ilorin in that year. Instead of risking his allegiance, his master, who was an official in the Oyo government, sold him to the coast. The British Royal Navy intercepted his ship, and he was released in Freetown, where he became a key informant for the Church Missionary Society linguist, Sigismund Koelle, whose *Polyglotta Africana, or A Comparative Vocabulary*, published in 1854,[10] the same year as Baquaqua's autobiography, was a major linguistic achievement in identifying African languages among the enslaved captives taken off slave ships by the British Navy. Another of Koelle's informants was Habu—that is, Abu, or Sam Jackson—who was born in Kano but was seized in a raid by Gobir when he was twenty, sometime in the late 1840s, and sold to Lagos. Also, Mohammadu from Katsina was seized by Fulani while working on his farm and then sold to Gobir, taken to Damagaram, and then sold south to Rabba and Ilorin before reaching the coast, probably at Lagos, in the late 1840s. Dan Kano was born in Birnee Yawoori—that is, Birnin Yauri—and was there about sixteen or seventeen years ago before 1821. He had been "seized by Fulani while on a trading expedition" and taken to the Gold Coast, "where he was sold to a Portuguese ship." Similarly, Mohammadu, later known as Jacob Brown, was kidnapped while farming, sold to Damagaram, the western province of Borno, and ultimately reached the coast via Rabba and Ilorin, arriving in Sierra Leone in 1844.[11]

Many of the voices of enslavement from this era are male, and in this regard Baquaqua's account is an excellent representation. There was a predominance of males among enslaved Muslims in particular.[12] Sergeant Frazer of the Second West India Regiment in Sierra Leone was born in Hausaland "and resided there a long time. He was taken prisoner in Goingia [Gonja], and brought to the Gold Coast, where he was sold" sometime before 1821. Frazer was a merchant who dealt in natron, which he had taken to Asante to purchase kola nuts, probably passing through Djougou at about the time that Baquaqua was born. Clapperton's assistant, interpreter, and guide, Abubakar Pasko, is yet another example of an enslaved Muslim who was destined for Brazil, although his ship was intercepted, and Pasko was fortunate in finding employment on the second expedition of Hugh Clapperton in the mid-1820s. He was originally from Gobir and had been "taken in war during the jihad" whereupon a trader took him to Gonja, probably passing through Djougou. He was then sold to "a native of Ashantee" who in turn traded him to a merchant going to Ouidah, who resold him to a Portuguese ship that was intercepted by the British navy, and therefore he was taken to Sierra Leone.[13]

The French naturalist François de Castelnau interviewed Muslims in Bahia in the late 1840s while he was serving as French consul in 1848. Castelnau had earlier completed a botanical survey of the Great Lakes region of Canada and had also conducted extensive botanical research in Brazil, South Africa, and Australia. He interviewed a number of Hausa slaves in Bahia in 1848, including Boue—that is, Bawa—who had come from Zaria, apparently in the 1830s or 1840s, and was taken to Asante, where he was sold to European, probably Portuguese, slavers. Castelnau reports that most Hausa slaves reached the coast at Lagos, but some went via the Gold Coast. Of the twenty-three men he interviewed, all were fluent in Hausa, despite the origins of several men who came from Adamawa, Bagirmi, and Borno.[14] Adamawa was the distant emirate of the Sokoto Caliphate astride the upper reaches of the Benue River and extending into the mountains south of the Mandara Mountains. Bagirmi, a province of Borno, was on the southern shore of Lake Chad in the basins of the Shari and Ubangi rivers.

Although Baquaqua is not included in Philip Curtin's selection of voices from the slavery era, his story conforms to the dominant theme of Curtin's collection, which is entirely male and heavily Muslim.[15] Similarly, Allan Austin's biographical material on enslaved Muslims in the Americas consists entirely of males, and he included Baquaqua.[16] Michael Gomez discusses examples of Muslim women in North America but also notes that almost all enslaved Muslims were men.[17] Sylviane Diouf too has noted that most of the enslaved Africans who came from Muslim areas were males.[18]

These studies confirm a conclusion that the overwhelming majority of enslaved Africans from the central Bilad al-Sudan, including Borgu, were males, most of whom went to Bahia in the early nineteenth century.[19] Baquaqua's journey fit this broader pattern, although he went to Pernambuco, not Bahia, and followed a route to the coast that was further west than most enslaved

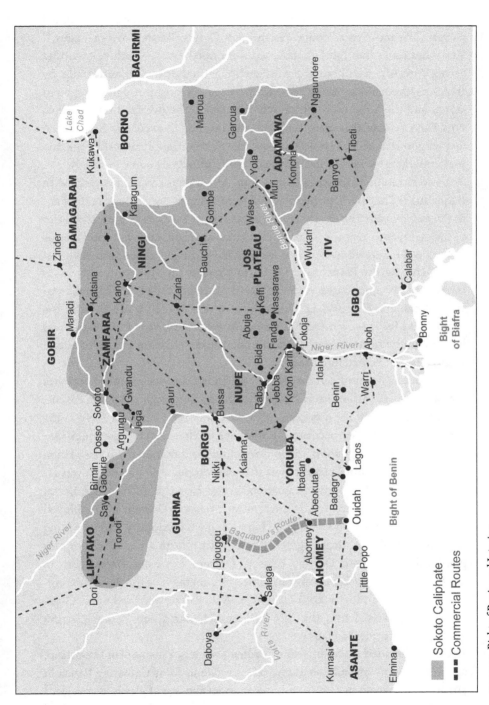

MAP 1.2 Bight of Benin and Interior

Muslims from the interior of the Bight of Benin who ended up in Brazil passed. The more usual route was through Oyo to Porto Novo or Lagos.[20] The main route through Djougou was from northeast to southwest, cutting across West Africa without direct interaction with the trans-Atlantic trade. By the 1820s, there was a vibrant trade from Salaga in Gonja through Djougou to Borgu and the Sokoto Caliphate, which supplied the overland trade in kola nuts from Asante that were sent into the interior in exchange for textiles, leather goods, and other products from the Sokoto Caliphate and Borno, the major markets for kola to the northeast of the principal source of supply.[21]

Various autobiographical and biographical accounts can be compared with Baquaqua's. They perhaps begin with Pierre Tamata, the principal merchant in Porto Novo after its emergence as a major port for Oyo in the last quarter of the eighteenth century. Tamata was of Hausa origin, enslaved and taken as a youth to France, where he was educated. He subsequently became the principal factor for the French trade at Porto Novo in the 1780s and early 1790s because of his connections with the interior through Oyo to the Hausa commercial centers. He survived the collapse of the French trade to head the important Muslim commercial community in Porto Novo.[22] Porto Novo was located on the north side of the lagoon that stretched from Lake Nokoue to Lagos where it flowed into the sea.

Baquaqua's account can be placed alongside other biographical sketches that we have of Muslims from West Africa. Abou Bouker, aka William Pascoe, came from Katsina. He was taken off a slave ship by the British Navy in the early 1820s, thereafter becoming a member of the British expedition into the interior of the Bight of Benin in 1826 under the direction of Captain Hugh Clapperton.[23] Another biography is that of Dorugu, who like Pasko was attached to a British diplomatic mission, in this case that of Heinrich Barth, 1849–55. The missionary J. F. Schon took an interest in Dorugu and employed him as an informant in creating a Hausa–English dictionary and recording detailed stories, historical fragments, and other information, as well as biographical detail about Dorugu himself. Dorugu was from Damagaram in western Borno. He was initially purchased by a member of the British delegation to Borno and the Sokoto Caliphate, Walter Overweg, and upon Overweg's death, passed into the care of Heinrich Barth and became Barth's principal interpreter in Hausa.[24]

Sidi Mahmadee, a Muslim from "Kashna"—that is, Katsina—in Hausaland, apparently wrote his autobiography on an estate in Saint Catherine Parish in Jamaica. He arrived in Jamaica in 1806 at about the age of eleven or twelve.[25] Extracts of his journal were supposedly published in a Jamaican periodical under the title "Sidi" in 1848.[26] Various memoranda are in the office of a former governor, perhaps Charles Edward Grey, governor from 1846 to 1853, or Henry Barkly, governor from 1853 to 1856. The manuscript came into the possession of someone identified as C. M., which appears to the initials for Cora Montgomery, the pen name used by Jane Maria Eliza McManus Cazneau, a journalist and the alleged author of the phrase "manifest destiny" to describe the innate right of the United States to dominate all of the Americas, including the annexation of Mexico, Central America, and Cuba. Cazneau and her husband leased the plantation in Saint Catherine Parish where the Mahmadee manuscript was supposedly found. Cazneau, aka C. M., cut out "some portions which deal rather too freely with certain social relations and family secrets," but otherwise "the editor has literally found nothing to do in the preparation of the work." Sidi Mahmadee was quite accomplished and therefore favored.[27]

Nicholas Said was born in Kukawa, then the capital of Borno after Shehu al-Kanemi successfully repulsed the jihād forces supported by Sokoto that had destroyed the imperial capital at Birni Ngazaragamu on the Komodugu Yo tributary that flowed east into Lake Chad from the Hausa country in the west.[28] He was a victim of the trans-Saharan trade, which took him to the Ottoman capital and ultimately to Russia and travels that mirrored Baquaqua's, only taking him through Ottoman lands to Europe and from there to the Caribbean and North America. He had an ability to learn languages and may have been fluent in as many as eleven, besides publishing his autobiography in Memphis in 1872 in perfectly flawless English. He enlisted in the 53rd Massachusetts all-Black regiment, rising to the rank of sergeant.

Similar accounts survive for Bilali of Sapelo Island,[29] Ayuba ibn Suleiman, who was able to return to Africa in the eighteenth century,[30] and Sambo Makumba, who assisted Muslims in Trinidad in returning to Africa.[31] Numerous biographies can be gleaned from the trial records following the 1835 uprising in Bahia,[32] and there are scattered biographical accounts from the Caribbean, as well as those in North America, that show ongoing connections and attempts at communication with an aim of returning to Africa. Baquaqua's account is unusual in the way he crossed the Black Atlantic. Others were able to return to West Africa from Brazil, Cuba, North America, and Trinidad, but nobody replicated his path of travel in its complexity and diversity.

Egyptian Rose (1719–71) was born in Ouidah, through which Baquaqua traveled only a century later. She arrived in Brazil when she was very young. After a short period in Rio de Janeiro, she was sold to Minas Gerais, where she worked as a prostitute for a long time. At the age of thirty, she sold the few possessions she had gained from prostitution, giving the proceeds to the poor, and became a saint associated with the Catholic clergy. However, she began to have visions and became possessed, arousing the interest of popular followers but also leading to her persecution by the authorities. Rosa then fled to Rio de Janeiro where she was welcomed by the head of the Franciscans, Friar Agostinho de São José, who became her spiritual mentor. Besides the admiration of the Franciscans, the common people in Rio were attracted to her. She was primarily responsible for founding the Recote do Parto, a place of refuge for former prostitutes where services were held that brought together dozens of families who sought her veneration.

During this period, she wrote *Sagrada Teologia do Amor Divino das Almas Peregrinas*, in which she described her life experiences and her ideas on how to position oneself in the world. However, the manuscript was considered heretical, and Father Francisco Gonçalves Lopes destroyed the manuscript with the intention of protecting her from the Holy Office of the Inquisition. Despite this effort, Rosa was arrested for heresy and taken to Lisbon, where she died in the prisons of the Inquisition in 1771.[33]

The life story of Domingos Álvares has also been reconstituted through accounts from his Inquisition trials in the eighteenth century. He was an African healer enslaved in Dahomey and sent to Pernambuco and later Rio de Janeiro, where he achieved his freedom. Like many other Africans, he survived in the streets close to the port in Rio. However, he was accused of sorcery, arrested, taken to Portugal, tried by the Tribunal of the Holy Office, and sentenced to exile in Portugal. When he left Dahomey, King Agaja was extending his power over the territories that surrounded his domains. Domingos Alvares was enslaved during this expansion. His knowledge of healing eased the physical and emotional pain that plagued many people who lived in the context of slavery. His knowledge of Vodun religious practice and his appeals to ancestors fill his biography with episodes and connections that helped people live in captivity. Despite the many gaps in his life story, Domingos Álvares was responsible for curing smallpox among other ills, particularly among those who came from the West African coast.[34]

Domingos Sodré was born in Lagos (Onim) in 1797, and he arrived in Bahia between 1815 and 1820. He was enslaved to Colonel Francisco Maria Sodré Pereira and worked at the Trindade sugar mill, in Santo Amaro, in the Recôncavo region of Bahia. After the death of his master in 1835, his eldest son, Jerônimo Pereira Sodré, freed him, whereafter he split his life between a religious life focused on Yoruba-inspired Candomblé rituals and Catholicism. He was accused of being a soothsayer and a sorcerer, but he was a good businessman. He became a reference for the Black community of Salvador in the second half of the nineteenth century. He married twice, became godfather to fourteen children, and formed an extensive social network. He also became a slave owner, bought real estate, and moved through different levels of Salvador society. He died in 1887, leaving his second wife Maria Delfina da Conceição a considerable sum to ensure the end of her days. They were married for over two decades and experienced the challenges of being freed Africans in a slave-owning city.[35]

There are other personalities who were associated with Yoruba culture in Brazil. Osifikunde came from Ijebu. Purchased by someone from France, he was taken to Paris, where he became the subject of anthropological research. He was the model for a bust that was sculptured. Although technically he was supposed to be free in France, he chose to return to Brazil to be with his family and thereby voluntarily returned into slavery. Nevertheless, his biography stands out as one of the few detailed accounts of an African in Brazil, and indeed in France.[36]

Marcelina da Silva was an African who lived in Bahia in the second half of the nineteenth century. She was of Yoruba origin and became recognized as one of the most important leaders of the Ilê Axé Iyá Nassô Oká terreiro. In fact, she was the second Yalorixá of the oldest Candomblé terreiro in Bahia. Her experience demonstrates how prominent religious leaders were in the African community. It is thought that Marcelina da Silva returned to Africa with her daughter, Madalena, after she was freed. She spent seven years in Ketu before she returned to Brazil. She was accompanied by her daughter and two grandchildren. She immediately resumed her position as the most important religious leader in Bahia.[37] The father of her grandchildren, the African Rodolhpho Manoel Martins de Andrade, also known as Bamboxé Otikô, also returned with her. He is recognized as the most prominent African Babalaô directly responsible for the consolidation of the traditions of Candomblé and Ifá in Rio de Janeiro. Even today, the Bamboxé family plays a central role in Yoruba Candomblé in Bahia and Rio de Janeiro, demonstrating that the impact of the Africans' trajectories in the Black Atlantic spanned generations.[38]

Yet another Muslim who was taken to Bahia was Rufino José Maria, who came from Oyo in the 1820s at age seventeen. His Muslim name was Abuncare, probably a corruption of Abubakari. His story has been well told—from his enslavement in Oyo, his period of slavery in Porto Alegre in Rio Grande do Sul, and his labors on slave ships transporting those who had been enslaved in west central Africa to Brazil, before a British naval vessel seized his ship and took it first to St. Helena and then to Sierra Leone. He learned to prepare medicine while working for an apothecary in Salvador. Like many Muslims, he was sent to southern Brazil after the Male uprising in 1835. He became a cook for a wealthy man in Porto Alegre and became involved in organizing what authorities thought was a club but was probably an association of those who attended the same mosque who met to read the Qu'ran, pray, and keep accounts of the community. He was able to buy his freedom and went to work in the port of Rio de Janeiro where he found employment on ships. Thus, there were parallel circumstances that might have even brought Baquaqua and Rufino into contact, although there is no evidence that they ever met. Nonetheless, the parallels and timing help to substantiate Baquaqua's rendition of his time at sea that would ultimately lead to his freedom. Rufino became a cook on ships serving the transatlantic slave trade, while Baquaqua worked ships plying the Brazilian coast. Freed Africans often found employment in the slave trade, as many were expert sailors and sometimes could interpret, just as enslaved Africans were used in the coastal trade.

Rufino shipped out as a sailor on a slaver bound for Luanda, the main entrepôt of the Angolan slave trade. He was on the coast of Luanda, Ambriz, Cabinda, and elsewhere, and after a British vessel seized his ship, he was taken to St. Helena and then Sierra Leone, the British colony he would visit again after he returned to Brazil. He certainly must have been aware that he was working on slave ships even though the trade was illegal. He was on the *São José* when the British Navy and the Brazilian authorities seized it in Pernambuco. He was a cook on the *Ermelinda* and was responsible for the cargo that was sold in African markets. He was in Sierra Leone after his ship was apprehended by the British navy. His initial stay in Freetown brought him into contact with the large Yoruba community who had been settled there and with whom he would have had no difficulty communicating, and with the Muslim community, particularly that in Fula Town on Fourah Bay. Rufino later returned to Sierra Leone to study with the Muslim scholars whom he had met there. Upon returning to Brazil, he settled in Recife, where he attained considerable recognition within the Muslim community as a diviner, healer, and teacher. He dedicated himself to teaching the Qu'ran and was recognized as an *alufá* in the Muslim community. When he was arrested in 1853 on suspicion of being involved in a plot to stage an uprising, the police confiscated his collection of manuscripts.[39]

As these vignettes make clear, there is a considerable amount of biographical material on Africans, especially Muslims. Nonetheless, Baquaqua's account has often been thought to be the only autobiography of an enslaved person in Brazil, despite the increasing number of biographical accounts not only in Brazil but elsewhere. Over the last few years, biographical accounts of enslaved Africans have expanded the social context of research. The diversity of sources and the biographical methodology have expanded knowledge about the diaspora in the Americas and the many connections that people had with the African continent through the memories they carried throughout their lives.[40] Baquaqua caught the imagination of Brazilians, nonetheless, and since then biography as an historical genre has received more attention in studying the African diaspora. Information on the fate of many people has been emerging and codified for analytical purposes. Scholars in Brazil and elsewhere have been examining police records, Inquisition trials, criminal cases, ecclesiastical documents, baptismal records, marriage certificates, wills, and diaries. The diversity of documentation has enabled the reconstruction of lives in context to a degree that is remarkable.

It is important to highlight that Baquaqua's autobiography documents the fugitive story of an enslaved African and indeed a Muslim who escaped from slavery. Baquaqua's life trajectory is still the only biography written by an African who had been a slave in Brazil, although when he wrote it, he was no longer in Brazil but had since lived in Haiti and the United States. Furthermore, like any other autobiographical narrative, Baquaqua selected what he remembered and denounced slavery to the world, especially with reference to the hard days of captivity in Brazil. Baquaqua's autobiography was also an abolitionist propaganda piece, the harshest experiences in captivity being remembered, so that readers got an overview of the horrors that slavery imposed on the human condition.

A focus on Baquaqua calls into question the nature of slave society in Brazil and the prospects of resistance to slavery in the nineteenth century. His account allows us to contextualize how individuals saw themselves, how they were identified before being enslaved, and the impact of enslavement on self-perception. Baquaqua was able to do things that he never would have conceived in Djougou. After achieving emancipation, he was able to establish an identity that survives in documentation that enables a clearer understanding of names and naming. A wider interest in biographical accounts highlights the importance of Baquaqua's memoirs and his life history, as best as can be reconstructed. In this context, Baquaqua's account is invaluable in reconstructing what his home in Africa was like, Brazilian history in the 1840s at a time its export economy was expanding, and understudied aspects of resistance to slavery in North America at the time of the Fugitive Slave Law of 1850.

This study of Baquaqua's life is discussed in seven chapters, based on an updated annotated version of his narrative, surviving letters that are attributed to Baquaqua or that report directly on his experiences, newspaper

accounts and affidavits of the legal proceedings relating to his quest for freedom in New York City in 1847, and finally a chronology of the events of his
life. Baquaqua traveled extensively in the Atlantic world from the interior of
West Africa and its Muslim-dominated commercial network to the Atlantic
departure points for enslaved Africans in the Bight of Benin, to several parts
of Brazil, from Pernambuco in the northeast to Rio Grande do Sul in the
south. He was in Rio de Janeiro at least twice, and as in Pernambuco and Rio
Grande do Sul, he must have been in contact with the local Muslim community. Although he was in Brazil for only two years, he was deeply exposed to
slavery there. He did not work on a sugar plantation in Pernambuco or live on
a manioc farm in Rio de Janeiro or labor on a coffee estate in the interior, but
he was exposed to the main features of slavery in Brazil. He sold bread in the
countryside outside of Recife and transported stones from quarries in the interior of Pernambuco. He was on ships transporting cassava, dried meat, and
other commodities along the coast as far south as Rio Grande do Sul, and he
was on a ship laden with coffee when he reached New York City in 1847. His
different occupations, from selling bread in the street to cooking on a ship,
were far different experiences than what he had known in Djougou.

His escape from slavery in New York introduced him to the abolitionist
network that ultimately took him to Haiti via Boston, while his sojourn in
upstate New York brought him into contact with abolitionists associated with
the Free Will Baptists and New York Central College, some of the leading
abolitionists of the antislavery movement in the United States and Britain,
including Gerrit Smith, who ran for president of the United States on the Liberty Party ticket in 1856 and was associated with John Brown and Harper's
Ferry. Baquaqua had different ambitions than most abolitionists in North
America because he wanted to return to Africa. In his attempts to do so, he
traveled from upstate New York into Canada West (now Ontario), visiting
Detroit, before returning to central New York and then departing for Liverpool from New York City.

Finally, his attempts to return to Africa connected him with the Mendi
Mission in Sierra Leone, the settlement of African Americans in the newly
recognized Republic of Liberia, and perhaps with Muslim commercial networks that dominated trade in most of West Africa, which would have enabled him to reach Katsina. His relationship to each of these initiatives is far
from clear but does emphasize Baquaqua's determination to return to Africa,
at least to his mother's family's home in Katsina in the Sokoto Caliphate.

This circuitous journey literally took him around the Atlantic in a truly
unusual odyssey. He was a Muslim whose journey extends the view of the

Black Atlantic and the interaction with independent Haiti in the Caribbean. Baquaqua's trajectory is complex in terms of ripples across the Atlantic, following flows of people from specific parts of Africa to Brazil and, in Baquaqua's case, through complex channels also to the North Atlantic. His story provides insights into the complexity of resistance to slavery and the struggle for freedom that challenges the racialized legacy of the past. He experienced a double consciousness of freedom and slavery that pervaded the lives of others forced to cross the Atlantic, which he interpreted through his autobiography. Law and Lovejoy recognize this dichotomy in the subtitle of their edited text, *His Passage from Slavery to Freedom in Africa and America.* He claimed that he was enslaved twice in Africa, initially rescued by his brother, although this is questioned later in this book. His apparent second enslavement took him to Brazil and by chance afforded him the opportunity to regain his freedom once again and even provided him with a network that helped him return to Africa. The complexity of deciphering what we can learn from the available documentation on Baquaqua and what we can learn about the context in which he managed to survive is the challenge that makes his odyssey so interesting.

Considering the narrative he wrote, his story is indeed one of the few detailed biographies of an African enslaved in Brazil, and perhaps the only autobiography. Baquaqua's account can be compared with that of Osifekunde, which was published in the same year that Baquaqua arrived in Brazil and nine years before the publication of his autobiography in 1854.[41] Similarly, the chronology of Rufino's experiences, another Yoruba but who was a Muslim from Oyo, and the travels of Nicholas Said from Borno in the early 1850s also overlap with Baquaqua's story.[42] By comparison, however, the richness of Baquaqua's account is unmatched. It is important to highlight that this is not the only known biography of Africans in Brazil. Over the past few decades, there has been an increasing number of biographical accounts of Africans in Brazil.

Furthermore, like any other autobiographical narrative, Baquaqua selected what he wanted remembered. He denounced slavery to the world, especially with reference to the hard days of captivity in Brazil. Baquaqua's autobiography was an abolitionist propaganda piece, the harshest experiences in captivity being remembered, so that readers were given an overview of the horrors that slavery imposed on the human condition. The autobiography stands out as providing the most detailed information on the African background of enslavement and the structure of society that tolerated slavery in the complex socio-political and religious context that characterized his hometown of Djougou and the caravan route that accounted for its prosperity.

CHAPTER ONE

Born after Twins in Djougou

Baquaqua was born in the early 1820s in the city of "Zoogoo"—that is, Djougou—situated inland from the kingdom of Dahomey, in the region immediately west of Borgu, on one of the most important caravan routes in the interior of West Africa. Borgu included a number of towns, the most important of which were Nikki, Kaiama, and Bussa. The region stretched from the Niger River westward toward the Atakora Mountains. The Niger River above the rapids at Bussa marked the eastern boundary, beyond which were the emirates of the Sokoto Caliphate, the largest state in Africa before 1900, founded in jihād between 1804 and 1810. Borgu itself remained independent of the Caliphate, and despite occasional hostilities, a peaceful détente prevailed that allowed the caravan trade between Asante and the Hausa cities. Djougou was actually immediately west of Borgu, although its history was intricately connected with Borgu.

Baquaqua's family was prominent within the merchant community of Djougou. His father is said to have been a "traveling merchant" who was once "a wealthy man," although he had subsequently lost "the greater part of his property" and was left "comparatively poor."[1] When Mrs. Judd first met Baquaqua in 1847 at the Free Will Baptist Mission in Haiti, she understood that Baquaqua's father had dissipated his wealth through "intemperance and gambling," but this is difficult to square with Baquaqua's later insistence in the *Autobiography* on his father's Islamic piety and is probably a confusion on her part.[2] His mother's family was also involved in craft production and commerce. Her brother, Baquaqua's uncle, is described as "a very rich man, who was blacksmith to the king [presumably of Djougou]." For a time, Baquaqua was apprenticed to him and learned "the art of making needles, knives, and all such things."[3] From Baquaqua's description, this uncle was a generic metalsmith rather than strictly a "blacksmith," because he worked in gold, silver, and copper as well as iron, and made bracelets and rings as well as tools. This also involved him in the caravan trade to Asante, since he used to travel to Salaga, at this time the principal market for foreign merchants trading to Asante, to purchase metals for his craft. His uncle owned property in Salaga, which suggests that he may well have operated a brokerage firm that catered to visiting merchants from the Sokoto Caliphate. In Hausa, he would have been considered a *mai gida*, which in the context would have meant that he was a *dilalli*, or broker, who provided accommodation, food, storage facilities, banking services, and pasture for livestock. Baquaqua's mother inherited this property on her brother's death.[4]

The business activities of his mother's family in Katsina and Salaga and her marital connections into the Dendi community reveal how long-distance trade operated through interlocking social relationships and networks.[5] Moreover, the commercial dimensions of the family were characteristic of Muslim trade in West Africa that depended on a network that connected distant towns in what has been described as an ecologically based economy that crossed geographical zones from the Sahara in the north through the sahel and savanna to the forests in the south along the lower Guinea coast of the Atlantic. His maternal kin were probably one of the important merchant houses of Katsina in the early nineteenth century. As Heinrich Barth reported in the early 1850s, "Almost all the more considerable native merchants in Kátsena are Wangaráwa (Eastern Mandingoes)."[6] Wangarawa was the Hausa term for Wangara, who lived in one of three wards, either Makudawa, Unguwar Madugu, or Masanawa.[7] The commercial sections of all the towns in Borgu, and including Djougou, were known as Wangara.[8] The term also designated the Muslim network in the western Sudan that was otherwise known as Juula or Dioula.

The likelihood that his mother was from a Wangarawa family is increased by its connection with craft production, specifically metalworking, including silversmithing. Settlers in the diaspora communities along the trade routes usually practiced crafts as well as engaged in trade. Usually, one of the sons concentrated on the Islamic sciences, teaching, making charms, and selling amulets, and in Baquaqua's brother's case, serving as a diviner for the local ruler. Hence, the identification with the Hausa commercial diaspora conforms with what we know about the history of this period, but that identification also raises other questions relating to remoter origins. The far-flung links that Baquaqua's mother's family maintained stretched the full length of the "kola route." The family traced its origins to Katsina and presumably maintained its connections there and also operated out of Djougou, with a base in Salaga, the important market center in the Gonja province of Asante in the middle Volta basin; a marriage alliance with another prominent merchant from Nikki, the most important town in Borgu to the west of the Niger River north of the Yoruba states and Dahomey, is characteristic of the way in which this commercial diaspora developed and how it operated.

Baquaqua's family prospered in the economic takeoff following the consolidation of the Sokoto Caliphate and the expansion in trade with Asante, particularly in kola nuts, textiles, salt, and leather goods. These commodities, along with some slaves, were taken overland through Djougou in exchange for kola nuts, specifically *C. nitida,* that were harvested in Asante. Kola is an indigenous West African stimulant with high concentrations of caffeine.[9] The nuts were eaten, usually in small pieces, and had the effect of reducing fatigue, lessening hunger, and sweetening water. In the West African context, the nuts were carefully preserved for up to a year, and the nuts were usually shared because of the strength of the caffeine and because the nuts oxidize rapidly and lose their potency and bitter taste. The nuts were otherwise eaten without any preparation, unlike later alkaloids, including kola, that were carbonated and served as a refreshing drink.

While Islamic prohibitions prevented smoking tobacco and drinking alcohol, there were no restrictions on sharing kola and chewing portions of the two semispheres that formed the nut, which were either red or white. The nuts couldn't be ingested any other way. Sales were bought in bulk for purposes of gifting, but otherwise customers bought a nut one at a time on the street. Price depended on the quality of the nut, with bruised, infected, or decaying nuts being cheapest. The nuts had to be stored in satchels where they could be kept fresh, not exposed to sunlight, and inspected every few days to remove nuts that were starting to go bad. White nuts were more expensive because they did not come from Asante, which was the closest production area to the Sokoto Caliphate and Borno, via trails across Borgu via Djougou, and further north through Mamprussi and Fada Ngurma. Kola was a suitable stimulant for weddings, funerals, naming ceremonies, during Ramadan, and other social occasions and work environments. The *C. nitida* variety was only grown in the forests of Asante and further west as far the interior of Sierra Leone, which determined the direction of trade in the interior of West Africa.

As was common in many parts of West Africa, Djougou was divided into two sections some distance apart. The section known as Kilir was the original town where the royal Djarra dynasty of Sasirou, the court, and the local population resided. The dynasty was of Gurma origin, while the Indigenous inhabitants were Yoowa, also known as Pila Pila, and whose religion and culture were not Muslim. The other part of the town, which was known as Wangara, as were the commercial wards of the various towns in Borgu, was the Muslim quarter, where merchants and craftsmen had settled and where Baquaqua's family lived. Djougou as a town, therefore, had a population of diverse origins, with the Indigenous population speaking Yom, also known as Pila Pila, while the language of the Wangara ward was Dendi, a dialect of the Songhay language that was the commercial tongue of Borgu to the east. To complicate this cultural mosaic even more, the caravans that passed through Djougou came from the Sokoto Caliphate, where merchants spoke Hausa and therefore had to rely on resident Muslims who knew Dendi as well as Hausa.[10]

Baquaqua's description of Djougou and of the countryside around the city provides the first observations of someone who came from the interior of this part of West Africa. His account is fifty years before the earliest European account of the city.[11] Remembering that Baquaqua left Djougou when he was perhaps twenty years old, these early accounts help provide context for Baquaqua's memory. He certainly had a clear memory of the physical environment, the urban landscape, and the diverse ethnic composition of Borgu to the east and the Atakora Mountain region to the west. Borgu consisted of a loose confederation of towns, including Nikki as its nominal liege and Bussa, Wawa, Kaiama, Parakou, and their commercial wards of Dendi merchants were Muslim and who referred to their wards who grew up around the caravansary as Wangara.

The identity of Djougou as his place of birth and childhood is clear, although the location of his homeland has caused confusion among some modern commentators.[12] There are two distinct towns of this name in the general area indicated (both within modern Bénin): Djougou, situated some 185 km north of Abomey, the capital of Dahomey; and Zougou, near Kandi, another 200 km northeast of Djougou. Despite the different spellings nowadays conventional, both names represent transcriptions of the same word, *zugu*, meaning "forest" in Dendi.[13] From the details of Baquaqua's account, especially his route to the coast after enslavement, it is clear that it is the more southerly town (which was also by far the more important of the two) from which he originated. His description of "Zoogoo" also confirms the identification with Djougou, although some aspects of his account also applied to other towns in the region. Some details are more specifically localized, however, notably the titles he gives for the "gatekeepers" of the town, most of which can be identified with the officials of wards at Djougou.[14]

Baquaqua's observations are therefore significant in recording the voice of someone who was enslaved in his late teens or early twenties and hence had a vivid memory of his home country and its broader connections. He certainly had difficulties in explaining details of his experiences to his audience, first the Judds, then his network of Free Will Baptists in the eastern United States, the public to whom he spoke on his lecture tours, and finally his editor, Samuel Moore. Nonetheless, his observations are what he wanted people to know about where he came from. According to what he told people, Djougou was "in the midst of a most fertile and delightful country; the climate, though exceedingly hot, is quite healthy. There are hills and mountains, plains and valleys, and it is pretty well watered. About a mile from the city there is a stream of water, as white as milk and very cool, and not far from that there is a spring of very cold water, also quite white. The residents often go from the city thence for water."[15]

According to his description, "some quite extensive plains" surrounded the town. The countryside was "covered with very tall rank grass, which is used by the people to cover their houses, after the fashion of thatching. On these plains there are but few trees, but what there are, are of great size."[16] His comparison of uncut grass in his home country with what he saw in North America caused him wonder. While he saw grass that was waist high, he remarked that it grew to twice the height of a person where he came from. His sentimental reenactment of images from his youth establishes his underlying pathos, his loss not only of his family, especially his mother, but also his society and its physical surroundings, heightening his isolation.

The region of Djougou, today called Atakora-Donga, was actually little covered by vegetation, the savannah being essentially shrubby with scattered trees. Until recently, despite the relative fertility of the soil, the Djougou countryside was poorly exploited in terms of agricultural development, making the region, over the past two centuries, an area of expansion for farming and a place of refuge for migrant populations from the surrounding areas, notably Borgu but even from the Sahel. It also implies that, although the Indigenous owners of the land considered the whole territory subject to their authority and control, excluding sacred forests, the authority of Djougou was never exercised concretely over large areas, despite the reports of Dupuis and Bowdich, neither of whom went there. In fact, parts of the region around Djougou were not exploited at all.

Memory is often a gauge of subjective interpretation of past events and places because the focus is on what a person wants to remember as well as what is thought best to forget. Baquaqua's description of Djougou is no exception. He suggested that Djougou was comparable in many ways to the cities he passed through before writing his autobiography. His account should be placed in context with his experiences in Dahomey, Brazil, North America, and Haiti. He still thought that "the city itself is large, and surrounded by a thick wall, built of red clay and made very smooth on both sides. The outer side of the wall is surrounded by a deep moat or ditch, which in the rainy season is filled with water. Beyond this, the city is further protected by a hedge of thorns, grown so thickly and compactly together that no person could pass through them; it bears a small white blossom, and when in full bloom looks exceedingly beautiful."[17]

Although he did not specifically compare Djougou with other places that he later knew, he still considered Djougou to be "quite large," which he understood in terms of his later experience in the cities of Brazil and North America. The people who lived in the city were known as the Sartiwa, or "people of the city," while those living outside were referred to as Furatiwa, a derogatory term used to indicate "country people.[18]

Baquaqua's description is the earliest account of the layout of the city, its two wards, and the palace. Baquaqua's description demonstrates a degree of urban planning. "The king's palace (if it may be so called) is within the city wall, at some little distance from the principal part of the city, surrounded by (what in some countries would be called) a park, on a most extensive scale, at the back of which is a dense thicket, precluding the necessity of any protecting all on that side of the royal domain. A broad avenue leads from the city to the king's house, with an extensive market on either side, beautifully shaded with large overhanging trees."[19]

The king (*kpey*) of Djougou was of Gurma or Gourmantché origin and took the Yom title of Sawa for the position of kpey of Kilir, which was the early recorded name for Djougou, referring to the indigenous, non-Muslim town, to be distinguished from the larger commercial twin town that was predominantly Muslim connected with trade. That part of the urban area was known as Wangara, as were the commercial wards in the Borgu towns to the east. The kpey of Kilir—that is, Djougou—was not in fact the senior official in the area; that position was actually filled by the ruler of the tiny, secluded village only a few kilometers from Djougou. Baquaqua tried to explain this political pyramid to the Judds and Samuel Moore, who clearly did not understand what they were being told, which is not surprising since they knew next to nothing about the interior of West Africa.

The center of power was the tiny village of the Soubroukou, where Baquaqua effectively worked as a palace subordinate and retainer. By his own admission, he was charged with harassment, which almost certainly was in the interests of demonstrating the supreme authority of Soubroukou in the region, despite its size. It is likely that his seizure demonstrated resistance to the extreme authority of Soubroukou. Baquaqua also describes the urban complex of Djougou and especially its Muslim quarter of Wangara. The hamlet that became Djougou was originally called Tyilixa by the Indigenous Yowa, which today is the Culcurxu district of the city. According to the historian Yves Person, Gurungu was the kpey at the time Baquaqua was growing up before approximately 1830, after which Gazeri was kpey circa 1830–50. The main part of the town was the Wangara district with its Dendi population. Baquaqua lived in the commercial center of Wangara, which today is near the Zongo market, *zongo* being a Hausa term for caravan rest stop.

According to Marco Aime, the term Kilir originally meant "one who flees," which is evoked locally to explain the foreign origin of the dynasty.[20] The term Wangara implied "outside" as the "place of foreigners"—that is, where itinerant merchants coming from other regions lived—that developed around the Yaramè, the toll station of the Indigenous royalty of the Djarra of Sasirou. The Muslim settlers were mostly Dendi, called Marwa in Yom, who were distinguished from the Indigenous population of the surrounding region, especially the Yowa, but populations that identified as Taneka, Lokpa, and Ditamari. The Yowa spoke Yom, one of the Gur languages, and were close to the Tanéka who occupied the territories north of Djougou. Unlike the latter, the Yowa failed to protect themselves from Bariba incursions from the east, which inserted a strong cultural influence coming from Borgu.[21]

Baquaqua seems to have told Samuel Moore when he was preparing the autobiography that the entrance into the city was through six gates, which bore the names of "their respective keepers," who were supposedly "chosen for their courage and bravery and were generally persons of rank." Baquaqua described them accordingly as: "U-boo-ma-co-fa. 2. Fo-ro-co-fa. 3. Bah-pa-ra-ha-co-fa. 4. Bah-too-loo-co-fa. 5. Bah-la- mon-co-fa. 6. Ajaggo-co-fa. The word cofa means gate, and Bah, means father. Ajagga is the name of a woman whose son was noted for his valor. In times of war, these gates are strongly guarded, hence the necessity of having chosen men of known valor and courage to keep them."[22] Indeed *kofa* ("co-fa") in Hausa does mean gate, but here it seems apparent that Baquaqua's editor, Samuel Moore, did not understand what he was being told. The names actually refer to royal officials at Djougou who were in charge of the various wards of the city. There are no specific names for the gates into Djougou, and the generic term for gate in Dendi is *kpaara wuroyo do*, which literally means the entrance to the city, not the Hausa *kofa*.[23]

Baquaqua was apparently using the Hausa term for gate, but the term in Dendi means "periphery" and can be used in the sense of an entry to the city. Baquaqua refers to guards at these entrances, and the term *"bah"* does mean father as Baquaqua apparently told Moore, but he was using the term in the sense of an official. Baquaqua appears to have been referring to different wards in Djougou, which are sometimes associated with the names of the respective officials. Baquaqua seems to have identified the following quarters: "Bah-too-loo-co-fa" or the quarter of Batoulou; "Fo-ro-co-fa," the quarter of Foromagazi; and "Bah-pa-ra-ha-co-fa," that of *Baparapé*. The last name is probably *Baa Kpaara kpè*, or *baparapéi*, literally the sage or wise man of the city. According to local tradition, the installation of the first Gurma king, *sawa*, at Kilir, appointed a member of the Djarra lineage at Wangara as the official in charge of the caravansary.[24] Baquaqua described this position as follows: "There is a regularly appointed watch to the city, who are paid by the king, he also acting as chief magistrate over the watch."[25] As reported by Person, Kurungu held the title of *bakparakpey* from circa 1810 to circa 1825, his brother Atakora-Kusa from circa 1825 to circa 1830, and their nephew Abdua, or Abudu, from circa 1830 to circa 1860.[26]

Despite sharing a common language and the Islamic religion, the settlers in Wangara, like the itinerant Hausa merchants who dominated the caravan trade, traced their roots to many different origins. This complexity is captured in Baquaqua's account. Jones, who accompanied Baquaqua from Boston to Port-au-Prince in September 1847, understand that "[h]is father and mother were of different tribes,"[27] which Baquaqua also told Moore, stating specifically that his father, who was "not very dark complexioned" because he was "of Arabian descent" from Borgu (Berzoo), and his mother, whose "very dark complexion, was entirely black" was from Katsina (Kashna).[28] The reference to "Berzoo" (i.e., Borgu), almost certainly alludes to Nikki, the most important city in Borgu to the east, whose king was recognized by various other towns, including Djougou, as the capital of a loose confederation. Baquaqua's father's claim to "Arabian descent" suggests that he belonged to the group known as *shurfa*, of North African, most likely Moroccan, origin, claiming descent from the Prophet Muhammad. Shurfa (Hausa: plural Sharifai) merchants were prominent in long-distance commerce in the region.[29] These references further complicate any attempt to pin Baquaqua's identity on a specific ethnicity.

In the late 1820s and 1830s, when Baquaqua was growing up, his family was well recognized both in trade and the scholarly pursuits that coexisted in the same families. As was typical of the Muslim commercial diaspora elsewhere in West Africa, the Muslim quarter known as Wangara was separate from the main town, and when caravans were there, the commercial center became the largest part of the town. Baquaqua described the typical style of housing in Muslim quarters, in which "the houses are built of clay, low and without chimneys or windows." To "give a pretty accurate idea of the generality of the houses of the city," Baquaqua explained:

> A dwelling is composed of a number of separate rooms built in a circle, with quite a space between them; within the outer circle is another circle of rooms, according to the size of the family to occupy them. These rooms are all connected by a wall; there is one large or main entrance in front of the others, in which to receive company. Each family is surrounded by their own dwelling, so that when they are in any apartment, they cannot see any other dwelling, or any one passing or repassing. In consequence of this mode of building, the city occupies a very large space of ground.[30]

The compound that Baquaqua described very well could have been that of his parents. Baquaqua clearly was raised in a large household that had its own discrete compound of rooms. He came from a prominent Muslim family that can be reconstructed to some extent, although there is room for considerable error and there probably are omissions.

The name "Mahommah Gardo Baquaqua" is entirely credible for a person from the background indicated in his autobiography. The first name is, of course, as the Rev. Judd and his wife recognized in Haiti in 1847, a local West African form of the Arabic name Muhammad, which was usually given to the first-born son and advertises his family's allegiance to Islam.[31] In Baquaqua's case, he was not the first-born son, and therefore more likely that he was named after a grandfather, almost certainly his mother's father. It was not uncommon for families to have more than one male in an extended household with the name Muhammad or some variation thereof. In this context, it seems that he was adhering to the customs of his mother—that is, those associated with Hausa society in Katsina. In such cases, the family would not use the name in addressing the boy out of respect for the grandfather, but rather would use a nickname.[32] In Baquaqua's case, he had two nicknames, Gardo and Ba Kwakwa, which he wrote as Baquaqua.

The nickname "Gardo" is a variation on *gado*, used to refer to a son who is born after twins. It is a Hausa name but also is common in both the Dendi and Baatonu languages of Borgu, where it is more properly Gado.[33] The variation in Hausa depends on dialect; in Kano the term is Gado, while in Katsina, where his mother was from, it is Gardo. In Hausa, the term also means "bed" and "inheritance," the implication as explained in Katsina being that the child born after twins inherited the bed of the twins. While Baquaqua does not explain this in the *Biography*, he does note that he was "the next born after twins," although without mentioning the implications for his name.[34] This seems to be the name by which he was usually known in Djougou, assuming the greeting he received from a former acquaintance in Ouidah, who was also enslaved, was typical.[35]

His third name, Baquaqua, was a nickname his mother used for her favorite infant, and the name stuck in his mind. He took it as his surname once he was in Haiti and the United States. The term "*kwakwa*" or the implosive form "*ƙwaƙwa*" does not refer to any known place or ethnic designation, and various meanings of those words cannot be considered plausible. The name "sounds" authentically Hausa but required considerable investigation to pin down. The word *kwakwa* without the implosive "ƙ'" means the oil palm tree. The implosive form means inquisitive. Neither referred to a place or origins, but that only enhances the mystery of meaning. In Hausa, *ba* also means "not," however. Rather than being a prefix, "ba" was the negative. The nickname that his mother used was "not *ƙwaƙwa*," wherein *ƙwaƙwa*, with the implosive phoneme "ƙ," means inquisitive;[36] that is, the mother's nickname for her baby was "[the one who is] not inquisitive," but who was completely dependent on mother with a degree of trust that negated any desire to venture away. In English, the equivalent would be "mother's boy," a term that has positive connotations when a mother referred to her baby as such and negative connotations when children in the school yard later tease a boy. Baquaqua, who repeatedly states his devotion to his mother, reveals the traits of such a relationship. Locally, therefore, he was known by his Gardo nickname, but to his mother he was known as "ba ƙwaƙwa." Did he choose to spell his name with a "q" in some unconscious way to distinguish "qua" from "kwa"? Or was Samuel Moore's untrained ear unable to distinguish between k and ƙ and was confused, despite Baquaqua's efforts to make the distinction. It is hard to imagine this since Baquaqua's command of English was not that good, but he appears to have never spelled his name Bakwakwa, which a native English speaker was just as likely to have done, or probably more accurately to have done as Baquaqua.

The ambiguity does raise the question of what's in a name. When Baquaqua was a child, his grandfather apparently owned the space where "assemblies for public worship are held," probably a reference to the communal prayers held during Ramadan, the Muslim month of fasting.[37] According to Baquaqua, the place of worship was a "large and pleasant yard belonging to my grandfather, my uncle was the officiating priest"—that is, the *imam*.

The people arranged themselves in rows, "the priest standing in front, the oldest people next to him, and so, arranging themselves in order according to age." Baquaqua noted that his father prayed every day at the allotted times of the day. As this testimony makes clear, Baquaqua was brought up in very religious setting that underlay the Muslim community in Djougou. He described what he obviously experienced on a regular basis as follows:

> The priest commences the devotions by bowing his head toward the earth and saying the following words: "Allah-hah-koo-bar," the people responding "Allah-hah-koo-bar," signifying "God, hear our prayer, answer our prayer."[38] The priest and people then kneel and press their foreheads to the earth, the priest repeating passages from the Koran, and the people responding as before. After this portion of the ceremony is over, the priest and people sitting on the ground count their beads, the priest occasionally repeating passages from the Koran.—They then pray for their king, that Allah would help him to conquer his enemies, and that he would preserve the people from famine, from the devouring locusts, and that he would grant them rain in due season.[39]

Baquaqua observed Ramadan, of course, and provides a clear description of the festival of '*Id al-fitr* at the end of Ramadan, which was marked by communal prayers. His observation that the king of Djougou attended Muslim prayers when Ramadan was over indicates recognition of the commercial benefits arising from the caravan trade that was dominated by Muslims.[40] According to Joseph Dupuis, the British diplomat who visited the Asante capital at Kumasi in 1820, the king of Djougou ("Zogho") was "a rigid Moslem," though his evidence was admittedly hearsay, based on information heard at Kumasi, but there is no reason to think that his account is unreliable on the basis of Baquaqua's description of Muslim practice.[41]

> At the close of each day's ceremonies, the worshippers of the prophet go to their respective homes, where the best of everything is provided for the evening's repast. This same worship is repeated daily for thirty days and closes with one immense mass meeting. The king comes to the city on this occasion[42] and great multitudes from the country all round about, who together with the citizens, collect at the place appointed for worship, called Gui-ge-rah [*dyingire*], a little out of the city. This place consecrated to the worship of the false prophet, is one of "God's first Temples." It consisted of several very large trees, forming an extensive and beautiful shade, the ground sandy and entirely destitute of grass, is kept perfectly

clean, many thousands can be comfortably seated beneath those trees, and being upon high ground, the appearance of such a mighty assembly, is imposing in the extreme, the seats are merely mats spread out upon the ground. A mound of sand (this sand differs from the sand of the desert, it is a coarse red sand mixed with earth and small stones and can easily be formed into a substantial mound) is raised for the chief priest[43] to stand upon whilst he addresses the people. On these occasions he is dressed in a loose black robe, reaching nearly to the ground, and is attended by four subordinate priests, who kneel around him, holding the bottom of his robe, waving it to and fro.[44] Occasionally the chief priest will "squat like a toad," and when he arises, they resume the operation of waving his robe. These ceremonies concluded the people return home to offer sacrifice, (sarrah) for the dead and living. Thus ends the annual fast.[45]

"Gui-ge-rah," that is, *dyingire* in Dendi, refers to a public space for collective prayer, including mosques.[46] The place of prayer outside the city used for the public ceremonies is called *idi dyingire*. Its location at the time is unknown, however.

According to the local account of the history of the royal Djarra dynasty of Sasirou, which controlled the land where Kilir (Tylixia) and Wangara (Yarame) developed, the historic mosque of Toukourou was the first in Djougou.[47] Its construction dates to the end of the seventeenth century. Mamane Sare Djarra, alias Maïmaï, was a member of the royal line of Sasirou who built a house on the road used by traders coming from and going to Gonja. The purpose was to collect tolls from passing caravans on behalf of King Djarra of Kilir. These early merchants were practicing Muslims, especially those who came from Borno, which until the jihād of 1804–8 dominated the Lake Chad region, including the Hausa cities of Katsina, Kano, and Zaria. Sometimes visiting merchants stayed several days at what was already considered the "farani" of Maïmaï. This word *farana* is a relic of the Bambara language, the original language of the Djarra, that means "district" or "camp." Mamane Djarra had built the first mosque in Djougou at Yaramè to facilitate the trade to the Hausa cities and Borno to the northeast, and his first son, Abdoulaye Bindiga Djarra, was the first imam who led the daily prayers. This was the social, cultural, commercial, and religious context in which Baquaqua's family subsequently interacted, joining the Hausa trade at Wangara with the Dendi and Yoowa world. The term *sarrah* derives from *salah*, the Muslim term for prayer, which in Djougou also refers to the feast of sacrifice. Baquaqua's description leaves no doubt about his upbringing as a Muslim in a commercial diaspora community.

Baquaqua's editor, Samuel Moore, understood that the "manners of his father were grave and silent; his religion, Mahomedanism . . . but his mother was of no religion at all," although Baquaqua contradicts that statement. Moore misunderstood and thought that Baquaqua told him that "my mother was like a good many christians here, who like to be christians in name, but do not like to worship God much. She liked Mahommedanism very well, but did not care much about the worshipping part of the matter." This may have been Baquaqua's impression, too, but it is hard to verify with what else is known about Baquaqua's family. It is more likely Moore's attempt at understanding. Baquaqua was clear on one point: "[H]is parents were of different countries, his father being a native of Berzoo [Borgu], (of Arabian descent) and not very dark complexioned. His mother being a native of Kashna [Katsina] and of very dark complexion, was entirely black."[48] This gloss on the autobiography raises issues pertaining to Baquaqua's autobiography. It is not always clear what Moore understood, although he generally reported literally what he was told or attempted to paraphrase what he thought he understood. Moore displays a profound commitment to Christianity but does not openly reveal strong anti-Muslim sentiments. He seems to have wanted to record what he thought he understood, but he clearly did not always succeed. Fortunately, the early reports of the Judds in Haiti who had even more difficulty in understanding Baquaqua because of the language barrier, provide variated interpretations of many points, especially in relation to customs, Muslim society, and context.

As far as can be gleaned from this reportage, Baquaqua's parents and broader kin must have been typical of a respectable Muslim merchant family. Although his early Baptist patrons thought Baquaqua's mother was irreligious, he described her as "a woman of rank and wealth."[49] Her family was apparently considered to be Wangara, which in Hausa was referred to as Wangarawa, which designated merchants who originally came from the western Sudan, including those who had settled in the northern provinces of Asante. She came from a prominent commercial family in Katsina, where there were three wards near the market that were associated with Wangara. This nexus of Hausa merchants who claimed ties with the western Sudan through this association appear to have dominated the trade with the middle Volta basin and the kola trade in the eighteenth century and, despite the disruptions of the jihād after 1804, especially in Katsina, continued to dominate trade through diaspora communities such as that at Djougou.

This involvement in trade through Djougou to Salaga, the most important market in northern Asante, is well documented by Baquaqua. His mother's brother owned a compound in Salaga (Sal-gar), suggesting that his business was successful. The uncle's property was "whither he would repair to buy gold, silver, brass and iron for the purposes of his business. The gold and silver he made into bracelets, for the arms, and ear rings and finger rings, the Africans being very fond of such kinds of ornaments."[50] His uncle was "a very rich man, who was blacksmith to the king, and he wanted Mahommah to learn that trade."[51] His father had other ideas: "[H]is father destined him for the mosque, intending to bring him up as one of the prophet's faithful followers. For that purpose, he was sent to school." Nonetheless, Mahommah was not a good student and "not liking schooling very much, he went to live with his uncle and learned the art of making needles, knives and all such kinds of things." His father persisted and insisted that he return to school, but he "soon ran away." According to Moore, Baquaqua "did not like the restraint that his brother (the teacher) put upon him. His brother was a staunch Mahommedan and well learned in Arabic."[52]

Baquaqua had a brother and three sisters, besides twins who died in infancy. Moore misunderstood what he was being told. He thought that Baquaqua was telling him that "Africans are very superstitious about twins." Moore then provides a distorted version of what he thought he understood that he was being told, which was a truncated version of Yoruba practice in relation to twins. Moore generalized his confusion, claiming that Africans "imagine that all twins are more knowing than any other children, and so with respect to the child born next after twins. They are considered to know almost everything, and are held in high esteem. If the twins live, an image of them is made out of a particular wood, one for each of them, and they are taught to feed them, or offer them food whenever they have any; if they die, the one next to them by birth has an image of them made, and it is his duty to feed them, or offer them food."[53] The description applies to *ibeji* figurines in Yoruba culture, not customs in which Muslims were involved. The "little duties ... performed," it was supposed, enabled the image to keep its protector from harm and "preserves them in war."[54]

Despite Moore's projections, Mahommah was clearly telling him that "the next born after twins" had a different meaning in his family and Muslim society. Moore did understand that "he was consequently highly esteemed on account of his birth; it is supposed he never said anything wrong, and everything he wished was done for him on the instant. This no doubt was the reason his mother so fondly loved him, and was the cause of his youthful recklessness. they never crossed or controlled him, his mother was the only person who dared even check him; his love for his mother was exceedingly great."[55] Moore's remarkable psychological insight into Baquaqua's personality highlights the transformation that was inflicted on Baquaqua through slavery. Moore was wrong in confusing Baquaqua's knowledge of Yoruba custom in terms of twins with Baquaqua's own experience, but Moore inadvertently provides information on what Baquaqua knew about social practices relating to twins in the Hausa centers of the Sokoto Caliphate that were applied in Djougou as well as Borgu, which he tried to contrast with Yoruba practice. It is noteworthy that there were communities of Yoruba refugees in the area of Djougou from whom he must have learned about the ibeji figurines and their significance.[56]

After his abortive educational experience under his brother, Baquaqua was apprenticed to his uncle in making needles, which suggests that he was destined for a life in commerce. It was usual for male children to be apprenticed to relatives or to those with whom the family was connected through *asali*—that is, "origins" in Hausa—rather than learning an occupation from the father. Mother's kin were as important in this fostering relationship as the father's family. His educational attainments were modest, but his family's reputation as scholarly was assured because of his uncle's role in leading prayer and his older brother who specialized in divination besides being involved in teaching, not unusual occupations for Muslim clerics. When he was growing up in the 1820s and 1830s, Muslim merchants controlled the trade of this region, and Baquaqua's family was prominent locally, with kinship connections in Borgu, property in the market town of Salaga in the middle Volta basin adjacent to the Asante heartland, and family in Katsina, the Hausa city that had dominated trade of the central savanna regions between the Niger River and Lake Chad in the eighteenth century.

Baquaqua certainly understood the economics of trade as centered on Djougou. Its trade was seasonal. In the rainy season from May to October, few merchants visited the town. During the long dry season, large caravans of one thousand or more merchants and porters, and comparable numbers of donkeys, passed through Djougou, often staying for a short period. They took salt, natron, textiles, spices, leather products, livestock, slaves, and other goods westward to the Volta River basin and returned with kola nuts and gold from Asante, and European imports from the Gold Coast.[57] Some enslaved captives were usually moved as well, although apparently not in considerable numbers, and they were taken in both directions, distance from point of enslavement being a factor in the value of enslaved individuals because of the difficulty of escape.

The connection between his mother's family and Katsina reflects commercial patterns dating to the eighteenth century, when Katsina was far more important than it was when Baquaqua was growing up. The fact that his grandfather owned the prayer ground where Ramadan services were held suggests that he had arrived in Djougou well before Baquaqua was born circa 1824. During that time, the influence of Katsina along the trade route to Asante was well established, and hence his mother's marriage into a Dendi family was not unusual. An earlier example is the case of Abubakar al-Siddiq (born circa 1790), who also had a Katsina mother, although he was born in Timbuktu, the home of his father, and was in Buna visiting an uncle and attending his father's grave. Buna was on the route from Asante northward to Jenne and Timbuktu.[58] Al-Siddiq's father, Kara Musa, who was shurfa in origin and a "tafsir," that is *mufassir*, a specialist in Qur'anic exegesis, had traded to Katsina and Borno, specializing in gold, which he sent to his wife's father, al-hajj Muhammad Tafsir of the countries of Borno and Katsina, both inhabited by her family, who traded in horses, donkeys, mules, silks from Egypt, and probably kola. Al-Siddiq understood that his father traded along a route through Gambaga and Sansani Mango that passed north of Djougou, although he never followed this route himself. His father died in about 1794, a decade before al-Siddiq was enslaved in Buna, when Asante invaded to quell Muslim opposition to the crackdown on Muslims after the ouster of Asantehene Osei Kwame circa 1801 because of "his attachment to the Moslems and, it is said, his inclination to establish the Korannic law for the civil code of the empire."[59] Osei Tutu Kwame, later known as Osei Bonsu, reigned as Asantehene from circa 1801 to 1824, and introduced restrictions on Muslim trade in reaction to resistance in the Muslim-dominated northwestern parts of the empire. Western Gonja and Bonduku, with Kong support and probably Buna, tried to restore Osei Kwame, which led to Asante expeditions to quell opposition that lasted through 1805. One of last campaigns was against Buna when al-Siddiq was taken prisoner and shipped to Jamaica.[60]

Asantehene Osei Bonsu subsequently confined Muslim merchants from the northeast, including those who followed the route through Djougou to eastern Gonja at Kpembe and its commercial ward at Salaga, which rapidly became the major staging point for Asante trade to the north and northeast. The kola trade grew rapidly after that, apparently in large measure because Asante involvement in the trans-Atlantic slave trade withered and the Asante state needed to establish new sources of revenue.[61] The first mention of Salaga in 1804 suggests the town was only a minor settlement at that time, but within the next decade, it became the "grand emporium of Inta [Gonja]."[62] The connection between Djougou and Salaga quickly became important. Alfa Saba emigrated from Djougou and helped tie the new center to the earlier Wangara-Hausa communities to the northeast.[63] There were undoubt-edly other settlers in addition to these. As a result, the town, which was reported to be "twice the size of Coomassy" in 1820, became the focus of commercial activity between Asante and its northern neighbors. Men such as Alfa Saba, who was identified as Wangara—that is, a Muslim—moved from Djougou to Salaga to teach and study and helped transform Salaga into a scholarly center. Alhaji Idrisu had taught in Djougou and Sinende in the early nineteenth century before settling in Salaga.[64]

The caravan route through Djougou supplied kola nuts from Asante to the Sokoto Caliphate in the nineteenth century. Some gold also passed along this route, along with a few other commodities that were relatively unimportant. The main market for kola was the Sokoto Caliphate and especially the princi-pal Hausa cities, including Katsina, Kano, Zaria, Birnin Kebbi, and the twin capitals of Sokoto and Gwandu. The commodities that were sent to the middle Volta basin to purchase kola at Salaga included textiles that were pro-duced locally, especially at Kano and in the numerous towns that surrounded Kano, and also at Zaria and other centers. Indigo dyed cloth, clothing with embroidery, and hats were in particular demand. Cotton was grown extensively in the Hausa region, especially in Zamfara, southern Katsina, Kano, and northern Zaria, and the extensive centers for dyeing cloth em-ployed perhaps fifty thousand workers who were concentrated around dye pits dug deep into the ground and lined with a cement made from the residue of the dyeing process. Some of these dyeing centers had as many as one hun-dred dye pits and resembled factories, although they were out in the open and not in buildings. In addition, leather goods, especially shoes, sandals, and bags, were also manufactured for export, not only to the markets along the route through Djougou but also over a much wider area. Another important export was dried onion leaves, which were easily preserved as a spice in cook-ing. As noted already, various types of salt were important, including salt made in Dallol Fogha to the west of Sokoto, but most important were differ-ent carbonate salts known as *kanwa* from the Mangari and Muniyo districts of Borno north of the Komodugu Yo River that flows eastward from the northern Hausa cities to Lake Chad. The most important salt was *ungurnu*, which was mined on the eastern shores of Lake Chad and brought across the lake and distributed from the port at Baga as far as Yoruba country, Dahomey, and the middle Volta basin. *Ungurnu* was also a carbonate salt, used in cook-ing, as a stomach medicine, and mixed with locally grown tobacco for chewing and snuff.[65]

James Richardson learned in 1851 that there was a trade in enslaved captives southward to the Niger-Benue confluence, who, as he was told, were sold to "America," by which he meant Brazil.[66] The enslaved were also taken north from Katsina across the Sahara. Nicholas Said would pass through Katsina at almost the same time that Baquaqua was finishing his autobiography in 1854.[67] Said had been kidnapped with friends while hunting near the shores of Lake Chad by Tuareg marauders, who took him and his companions to Katsina for sale to merchants crossing the Sahara to Tuat and on to Tripoli. The continued importance of Katsina commercially, despite its decline in population, was its role as a frontier town on the north, with the disposed aristocracies of Gobir and Katsina stationed just to its north, and the route to Zinder in Damagaram and beyond to Agades and the Sahara under the command of forces opposed to the Sokoto jihād. Baquaqua's image of Katsina was favorable, probably because he did not know the political context, which Barth clearly witnessed and described. Baquaqua knew of Katsina largely through the memories of his mother who had grown up there, not from firsthand observation when the city was largely deserted.

The expansion of the kola trade through Djougou, which was known in Hausa as *fataucin Gwanja*, or long-distance trade to Gonja, not only resulted from the adjustments of the Asante economy to the decline in the transAtlantic slave trade and a reorientation of economy inland but also the consolidation of the Sokoto Caliphate after the jihād led by 'Uthman dan Fodio after 1804–8, which created an empire of over thirty emirates and constituted the largest state in Africa in the nineteenth century.[68] The invigoration of Islam following this political expansion effectively expanded the market for kola and promoted the industries that fed the exchange with Asante.

Unfortunately for Katsina, the jihād resulted in its temporary decline. Before the jihād, Katsina was the most important Hausa city, more dynamic than Kano and Alkalawa, the capital of Gobir. Resistance to the jihād was particularly strong in Katsina, resulting in the evacuation of the city and the establishment of a government in exile to the north at Maradi. The jihād began in Katsina under Umarun Dallaji in 1804, and upon his death in 1836, his son, Abubakar Saddiku, became emir but was deposed in 1844 with his older brother, Muhamman Bello, installed in his place. The problems of leadership in Katsina were compounded by the resistance of the pre jihād aristocracy that had retreated north and founded a new city at Maradi, from where they sustained a constant war, known in Hausa as *tawaye*, against Katsina.[69] Dan Mair (circa 1836–43) was able to organize a large-scale revolt that was only crushed with assistance from the caliphate government at Sokoto and neigh-boring emirates. Maradi continued to be a center of resistance, nonetheless.

Katsina was still an important center after being incorporated as an emir-ate in the Sokoto Caliphate after 1808, although commercially the city was largely abandoned by mid-century. Heinrich Barth, who was in Katsina twice in the early 1850s on a diplomatic and geographical mission for the British government, engaged with the merchant community on two occa-sions. Indeed, his landlord was Ahmad Abu al-Ghaith, a resident merchant from Tuat and the wealthiest merchant in Katsina at the time and connected to the trans-Saharan trade. The merchant community could not have been that large; Barth thought that Katsina had a population of only 7,000 to 8,000 people confined in the northeast of the enwalled enclosure that he es-timated once could have had a population of 100,000 or more.[70] Those mer-chants who identified as Wangarawa were associated with trade to the west and especially southwest to the middle Volta basin and Asante. North Afri-can merchants worked through al-Ghaith, whom Barth also had business with, despite some animosity. An account book that belonged to al-Ghaith has survived; given the small size of the population, al-Ghaith's accounts provide an excellent window into the operation of trade and economy at Katsina. Whether or not al-Ghaith had business with Baquaqua's maternal grandparents and uncle is not known, although it is highly likely that there were connections.[71]

The dispersal of merchants from Katsina after the jihād undermined its economic position, leading to not only migration along the trade route to the middle Volta basin but also the relocation of population to Kano. Three groups of Hausa merchants came to dominate the kola trade during the 1830s and 1840s. They were based in several villages southeast of Katsina, in numer-ous villages around Kano, and in several wards in Kano City. They were also found in Sokoto and Jega, as well as the town of Gummi on the Zamfara River. They identified as Kambarin Beriberi, Agalawa, and Tokarawa. Kam-barin Beriberi indicated that the merchants ultimately came from Borno and, hence, in Hausa were referred to as Beriberi. They formed a diaspora within the Sokoto Caliphate, centered on an original point of dispersal from Gummi, south of Sokoto. Associated with a founding father, Dan Toga, the Gummi merchants established homes in Jega near where the Zamfara joins the So-koto River before flowing into the Niger. They also established firms in Sokoto, Dallol Maouri, and especially in Kano. The Kambarin Beriberi had distinct facial markings that resembled Kanuri scarification—numerous long scars from the temple to the mouth.

The Agalawa and Tokarawa families involved in the kola trade were all descended from Bugaje, the term in Hausa that referred to slaves of the Tuareg desert nomads. The Agalawa, at least, were initially found in the rural areas outside of Katsina City at places like Shibdawa and Gabankare, where they engaged in rainy season farming and raised donkeys. As long-distance merchants during the dry season, they came to dominate the import trade in kola nuts from Asante. From Katsina, they were also found in numerous towns around Kano, including Bebeji, Bunkure, and other places, and they were particularly concentrated in Kano City in several wards near the central market. The Agalawa, who were most numerous, also had distinct scarification: three small marks on each temple and three marks close to the corners of the mouth. According to what Baquaqua told the Rev. Judd and his wife when he was in Haiti, his family was heavily involved in the transit trade through Djougou, which would have meant catering to the Agalawa, Tokarawa, and Kambarin Beriberi merchant caravans.

Both the impact of Asante policy on its northern trade and the consolidation of the Sokoto Caliphate affected Baquaqua's family. His father was well placed commercially. He "had been a wealthy man; he was a travelling merchant; carried his merchandise on donkeys and had slaves to accompany him; but by some means he lost the greater part of his property, and at the time of his marriage was comparatively poor; he consequently had but one wife."[72] He was also connected with the Wangara community, especially in Nikki, and as discussed above perhaps identified as shurfa from North Africa and specifically Morocco, claiming descent from the Prophet, in origin. Wangara was the local name for Dendi whose historic network connected them with Songhay, the historic West African empire that collapsed before a Moroccan invasion in the 1590s. Dendi merchants, who spoke the Songhay language, dominated the trade routes to the south and east of the Songhay center along the Niger River from Timbuktu downstream through commercial networks that connected Muslim merchants, who identified as Dyula or Juula, merchants who dominated the trade of the western savanna and sahel, who were known as Wangara, or in Hausa as Wangarawa, with whom his mother must have identified. These merchants in turn connected with trans-Saharan networks but also dominated virtually all of the interior of West Africa. The operation of long-distance trade across sub-Saharan Africa was intrinsic to Baquaqua's life and experience before his enslavement in Brazil.

Baquaqua's reminiscences of his early life in Africa include both memories of particular events in his own individual experience and general observations on the "manners and customs" of his homeland. In reading the text, it is therefore important to make a distinction between the authenticity of specific details in Baquaqua's life and the extent to which his account enhances our understanding of the West African society in which he was born. His recollections come to us, of course, as edited by Samuel Moore, or alternatively, on certain points, as reported by the Judds at the Free Will Baptist mission. Given the various means by which his account was transmitted, therefore, it is not surprising that there is some confusion in his story, especially in relation to his childhood and family.[73] This conclusion is certainly unwarranted, however. Most of his account is not only verifiable but also consistent with the context in which his early life transpired. Allowing for the vagaries of transmission of the reported information, and to the extent that it can be checked, the picture of life in nineteenth-century Djougou that Baquaqua presents seems both plausible and invaluable. Baquaqua's recollections both confirm our general knowledge of trade and politics in the interior of this part of West Africa and add important details that extend our previous knowledge. When put into context, his account of economy and society in Djougou fleshes out the history of the town, the wider networks of long-distance trade in which Djougou's Muslim community was involved, and the role of Islam along the trade routes between the Sokoto Caliphate and Asante.

Baquaqua's account is made more difficult by the limitations of the evidence on Djougou in the first half of the nineteenth century available for comparison. Although Djougou was, as the autobiography makes clear, a partially Islamic society (and Baquaqua himself was from a Muslim family), in which some people were literate in Arabic,[74] no Arabic manuscript material relating to the town during the nineteenth century appears to have survived. Moreover, as the autobiography notes,[75] Djougou itself had not yet been visited by any European traveler, so there are also no contemporary firsthand accounts of the town during Baquaqua's lifetime, other than his own recollections. Its importance within regional commercial and political networks is reflected in references to "Zogho" in material collected from foreign Muslim residents in Kumasi, the capital of Asante, by the British Consul to Kumasi Joseph Dupuis in 1820 and itineraries that mention the town as a center on the caravan trail crossing Borgu to the middle Volta Basin. These hearsay reports are vague and seemingly (at least as regards Djougou's military and political power) exaggerated.[76] The first Europeans to visit Djougou date from the late nineteenth century, the most substantial (and therefore cited here) being that of the German Heinrich Klose in the 1890s.[77]

Djougou was politically and commercially integrated into wider regional networks and was especially closely linked to the region of Borgu to the east and the middle Volta to the west. As Baquaqua notes, the king of Djougou was tributary to the king of Borgu; the reference is probably specifically to the ruler of Nikki, 170 km east of Djougou, which was conventionally regarded as the capital of Borgu.[78] Although no contemporary accounts are available of Nikki itself until the late nineteenth century, Hugh Clapperton and Richard and John Lander traveled through eastern Borgu (visiting the towns of Kaiama, Wawa, and Bussa) between 1826 and 1830 and left extensive descriptions of the area.[79] Given the considerable influence of Borgu on the institutions and culture of Djougou, and the fact that Baquaqua's account deals in part with his family's involvement in the wider world rather than focusing narrowly on Djougou, this material relating to Borgu can also be drawn upon, albeit with caution, in elucidating his text.

As Baquaqua recalled, "[T]he trade carried on between Zoogoo and other parts of the country, is done by means of horses and donkies."[80] Most likely, the reference to horses is really to hinnies, although the kola nut trade depended on donkeys and head loads more than hinnies or mules.[81] Baquaqua also referred to salt, which he learned was "brought from a place called Sabba [sabkha]."[82] This reference to *sabkha*, a term derived from Arabic, is used throughout the region to indicate sources of salt, often saline depressions. The salt trade was fundamental since there were no other sources of salt in the region between the Niger River and the coast where salt was evaporated from seawater, except at Daboya. However, the amount of salt that could be generated from the saline springs in Daboya was limited. It is possible that the term Sabkha refers to coastal areas in the south. Salt was evaporated from seawater in the narrow dune corridor between the ocean and the lagoons behind the coast.

It is more likely, however, that salt came from Dallol Fogha to the north of Borgu across the Niger River.[83] W. B. Baikie, stationed on the lower Niger and Benue, reported in 1862 that Dallol Fogha salt "supplies the whole caravan road to Gonja."[84] At Kumasi in 1820, Dupuis heard that salt sold at the markets of Nikki, Bussa, and Yauri came from a lake two to three days' journey east of Nikki, called "Callio Makaro."[85] Despite the incorrect direction and the too short distance from Nikki, this probably also refers to Dallol Fogha. The salt from Dallol Fogha was produced through the boiling of brine taken from the ponds of water that formed in the valley during the rainy season as water evaporated during the dry season.[86]

Baquaqua's account suggests, however, that salt came from much further inland. He noted: "They exchange slaves, cows and ivory for salt. This journey occupies about two months generally,"[87] which is confirmed in relation to the re-export of natron, a carbonate salt rather than the sodium that came from Borno, most likely the type known as *ungurnu* in Hausa, which came from the eastern shores of Lake Chad and was exported over a wide area as far as Dahomey and the middle Volta basin. *Ungurnu* was used not only in cooking but also as a stomach medicine, and it was mixed with tobacco that was chewed or taken as snuff. Accounts of the kola trade record that *ungurnu* was one of the most important re-exports from Kano and Katsina that was taken to the middle Volta basin in exchange for kola.[88]

Djougou was also a center of production for the local market. According to Baquaqua, "Most of the articles used are of home make. Earthenware is made of clay, they have a nice red and white clay, but the articles they make are very coarse, as they know very little of that kind of manufacture, indeed hardly of any other."[89] Based on what Baquaqua reported, Moore thought that he was being told that manufactures were "very limited; they consist of farming utensils, cotton cloths and silk." Moore mistakenly thought that the cotton came from trees: "The cotton tree grows very large, and the cotton is of good quality," when in fact the trees were silk cotton trees whose fibers were used to stuff mattresses, while the cotton for cloth was grown in fields.[90] Moore did accurately report that "the women do the spinning by a very slow process, having to twist the thread with their fingers; the men do the weaving; they weave the cloth in narrow strips, and then sew it together." Baquaqua also described the nomadic Fulbe cattle herders who roamed the countryside, as they did throughout the savanna and sahel of West Africa, although Moore made his own interpretation of skin color and ethnic origins when Baquaqua was clearly describing Fulbe, who in Hausa were known as Fulani.

> The *Shepherds and Herdsmen of Africa*, are a distinct and subordinate class
> of people, and belong to the government. They have long, straight hair,
> and are as light complexioned as the inhabitants of southern Europe; they
> are nearly white; they take care of the flocks and herds, supply the city
> with milk, butter and cheese, (the butter is quite good and hard, which is
> an evidence of its being cooler in this locality than in most other parts of
> the torrid zone.) They are Mahomedans in their religion, and strictly
> adhere to the rites and ceremonies of that class of religionists. They
> speak the Arabic and Flanne [i.e., Fulani] languages, hence it must be
> inferred that they are of Arabian descent, but of their further history,
> we are in ignorance.[91]

In fact, most Fulbe were not fluent in Arabic, only knowing the Muslim prayers in Arabic, if they had gone to Qur'anic school, which most boys at least would have done.

Baquaqua's family was heavily involved in this trade between Asante and the Sokoto Caliphate in the 1830s and early 1840s, which Baquaqua's account relates. His association with the Muslim merchant community in the Wangara ward of Djougou was the reason he was fluent in Dendi as the first language of the ward.[92] Baquaqua's account does not use either of the terms Wangara or Dendi, but the list of numerals given at the beginning of the autobiography which is presumably what he considered to be his native language, as well as many of the terms given in the text, are identifiable as Dendi. Dendi, it should be stressed, was not the language of the Indigenous inhabitants of the Djougou area, who were Yoowa (Pila-Pila), whose language is Yom.[93] Djougou was in fact a highly multilingual community. Its royal family was of Gurma origin from the area north of the Atakora Mountains,[94] speaking (at least originally) yet another language. As noted earlier, Djougou was also closely linked both commercially and politically with Borgu to the east, where the dominant language was Baatonu (Bariba); and Baatonu linguistic influence is evident in the title system of the town.[95] Moreover, Hausa, as well as Dendi, was widely spoken as a commercial language throughout the Borgu region, including Djougou itself, as noted by Klose in the 1890s, by which time Hausa had long been common along the trade route through Djougou.[96] Arabic was of course the language of literate culture within the Muslim community, and while Baquaqua provides no evidence other than a rudimentary understanding of the language, his brother and uncle appear to have had much more comprehension.

How many of these languages Baquaqua himself might have spoken is uncertain. In a letter in 1854, stressing his qualifications to serve as an interpreter for projected missions to Africa, he mentioned only the Arabic and "Zogoo" languages as those that he spoke.[97] "Zogoo" clearly referred to Djougou, and presumably he meant the Dendi language, but he also could have included Hausa. It is virtually certain that he knew Hausa and probably also some Baatonu, since the former was the ancestral language of his mother's family, as well as being widely spoken in commerce, while his father originated from Borgu, where the latter was the dominant language. Presumably anybody growing up in Djougou also knew Yom; Baquaqua probably did since he was employed in the palace of the ruler of neighboring Soubroukou, where the language in use would have been the local and not the commercial tongue. Although Djougou,

from its commercial and cosmopolitan character, was an extreme case, a degree of multilinguality was common throughout West Africa; this factor has
perhaps been underestimated in considerations of "ethnicity" among African-
born slaves in the Americas, for many of whom, including Baquaqua, a choice
among alternative ethnic identities was evidently available.[98]

On Baquaqua's origins and ancestry, however, there are discrepancies between the autobiography and the earlier statements of the Judds. When he
first arrived in Haiti in 1847, he was understood to claim that he himself was
from Katsina, no mention being made of Djougou: "He is from the city of
Kashina, of the tribe Houssa"; circumstantial corroboration being apparently
provided by the claim that he "remembers well the Yaoors, the next nation
west of the Houssas [i.e., Yauri, on the River Niger]" and "says he is acquainted with the city of Kano," the leading commercial center in the Sokoto
Caliphate at the time.[99] After Baquaqua's conversion in the following year,
when his return to Africa as a missionary was mooted, Judd still understood
that he was "from the city of Kachna," and it was likewise to Katsina that he
was understood to hope to go: he "dreams often of visiting Kachna, . . . and
being kindly received by his mother."[100] The simplest explanation of this
contradiction is that the Judds misunderstood statements about Baquaqua's
mother's origins as referring to himself; that they misunderstood at least part
of what he told them is demonstrated by the fact that in 1847 they thought
that his "native language" was Arabic, whereas the *Autobiography* shows he
was not particularly fluent in Arabic and the vocabulary that is recorded is in
Dendi, which introduces yet another possible misunderstanding among
those with whom he talked and who knew virtually nothing about the interior of West Africa. The Dendi numbers recorded at the beginning of his account may reflect what Moore asked him, which may well have been for
Baquaqua to recount the numbers in Dendi, the language that was used in
Djougou. Moreover, Baquaqua had probably not been to Yauri or Kano; certainly, no such claim is made in the *Autobiography*, although he recounts his
travels to the west of the Djougou region, to Daboya in Gonja, then a tributary
of Asante. His brother had been to Borgu at least, and Yauri was on the Niger
River, adjacent to Borgu. There is no other evidence that any of his family
had been to Kano, although that would not have been difficult since the
family was centered in Katsina. Baquaqua's knowledge of the Hausa region
more probably reflects what was known in his family and more generally in
Djougou. By 1853, it may be noted, Baquaqua's patrons in the American Baptist Free Mission Society had grasped that the home to which he wished to

return may well have been Djougou ("Zougo"), thereby reflecting a confusion among this association between his mother's hometown and where his
mother actually lived.[101] As elsewhere, it is sometimes difficult to understand
what Baquaqua actually told people and what they understood, given that his
associates had virtually no knowledge of the geography or political structure
of the interior of West Africa.

However, Baquaqua's mother seems to have wanted him to identify himself with her family, and hence as Hausa, but what that ethnic labeling meant
at the time in itself is open to interpretation.[102] This identification with his
mother's background was normal and perhaps intensified by the fact that
his father had apparently died before he left Africa; this, at least, was understood by the Judds in 1847, and although not explicitly confirmed in the autobiography, is consistent with the fact that he repeatedly referred to his feelings
of loss with regard to his mother (and sometimes also his brother and sisters),
but never his father.[103] Moreover, concepts of identity were probably misunderstood. Hausa was a language, not an ethnicity. Among the Hausa-speaking
population and at the time, people referred to origins, which is not something that can be considered an ethnicity. For those in the Hausa cities and
the countryside around the city, people claimed identities related to *asali*, origins, which could refer to a city, political entity, or a place from where parents
and ancestors came. Her mother would have said that she was Bakatsiniya
since she was from Katsina, and virtually certainly as Bawangariya, which associated the family with the western Sudan. And she and her family lived in
the Wangara ward of Djougou.

The Judds, Samuel Moore, and others who knew him could not possibly
have understood the complexities of Baquaqua's background. The Judds considered him to be Hausa, and Baquaqua talks a lot about his mother and
about returning to Katsina, not Djougou. Yet the vocabulary that he conveys
in a list of numerals to 1,000 and various terminology are Dendi, not Hausa.
Moreover, those who reported what he said were almost completely ignorant
of West Africa, its political science, and its geography. Baquaqua talked about
his background, but the simplifications inherent in his account and how the
Judds and Moore understood what he said have to be treated with caution. In
light of his father's death, it is conceivable that he believed his mother might
have been intending to move back to Katsina, so he might have thought that
he had to look for her there rather than in Djougou. Moreover, Baquaqua's
self-identification as Hausa also reflected his experience in Brazil, where he
would not have found anybody from Djougou (or even from the Borgu re-

gion more generally),[104] but there was a substantial Hausa (and Muslim) community in Rio de Janeiro with which he probably came in contact. This is indeed suggested by a remark of Judd in 1847, that Baquaqua's recollection of the Arabic language might have been reinforced by "his intercourse with other slaves from the same country," which Judd, as argued here, understood to be Hausaland.[105]

CHAPTER TWO

Twice Enslaved?

Baquaqua gave the impression that he was enslaved twice, the first time being in the northern Asante province of Gonja, at Daboya on the White Volta River, and the second time in a village outside of Djougou where he was in the service of a local official, who like all officials in the area of Djougou was referred to as a king. In the first instance, he claimed that his older brother was successful in securing his freedom so that he could return home, and in the second that he was not freed but hustled to the coast through Dahomey and put on board a ship that took him to Brazil. This remarkable account of enslavement, liberation, and what is described as a second enslavement is unusual in the surviving accounts of enslaved Africans in the nineteenth century. On the surface, his account provides important information on the means of enslavement in Africa, resistance to slavery, and slavery itself in the African context. The problem is that his account is riddled with confusion and improbabilities that require careful analysis. Moreover, he also seems to have told the Rev. Judd and wife in Haiti something that was completely different. However, there is sufficient doubt about what he is alleged to have told them, which leads one to wonder if communication was a problem, since, at the time, Baquaqua was only beginning to learn English, he did not know French, and the Judds did not understand any of the languages that Baquaqua knew.

In October 1847, shortly after he arrived in Haiti, the Rev. Judd and his wife understood that Baquaqua had been enslaved after being kidnapped when he was supposed to be at Qur'anic school, "taken captive when a child, while playing at some distance from his mother's door."[1] Mrs. Judd reported several months later, in March 1848, that "it seems, by what he has informed us lately, that he was several years a slave in Africa" and that he "says he was a slave for some time on the coast of Africa."[2] This account was repeated in 1850, when it claimed that he had been "clandestinely seized upon, and reduced to slavery" at an "early age," and "for some time he was held in this condition in Western Africa" prior to being transported to Brazil.[3] Almost certainly these accounts derive from the difficulty of communication and imagination of the Judds. Baquaqua's fluency in English could not have been very good in late 1847 and even in early 1848, which indicates the efforts of the Judds to adopt Baquaqua as their protégé and new convert to Christianity.

Despite the stereotypical description contained in these reports, they are clearly not accurate since Baquaqua arrived in Brazil when he was an adult. The account says more about the naivety of the Judds and the hopes for recruitment of converts for their mission in Haiti than it does about Baquaqua. The Judds had very little knowledge of Africa, even though the Free Will Baptist movement of which they were a part was committed to the emancipation of slaves in the United States and the ending of slavery. Its mission in Haiti included not only the base in Port-au-Prince but another in Port-au-Paix, on the north coast. It was hoped that Baquaqua could be trained to participate in a similar mission in Africa. Thus, the Judds had a strong reason to know Baquaqua's story, and they were sympathetic to his escape from slavery in the United States, as will be discussed in chapter 7. It is understandable that the early reports were incorrect, and recognizing the room for error introduces a note of caution in the literal interpretation of secondhand accounts of enslavement that might arise from poor communication from inadequate knowledge of Africa and ignorance based on linguistic barriers.

Baquaqua apparently tried to clarify his enslavement in his *Autobiography.* There, he claimed that he had been enslaved twice: the first time when he was a teenager and was freed from captivity, and the second time when he was probably about twenty years old and was sold to the coast and sent to Brazil. The discrepancy between these accounts suggests some confusion on the part of the Judds, who seem not to have understood what they were being told. Moreover, Baquaqua may have had reason to tell his listeners, including not only the Judds but also Samuel Moore and presumably others as well, accounts that they wanted to hear or at least understand. It is necessary, therefore, to analyze at least two different versions of enslavement: first, what the Judds reported that he told them and, second, what he stated in his autobiography. Initially, as published in the annotated version of his text by Law and Lovejoy, it was accepted that he was enslaved twice, although it was admitted that the accounts were confusing and inconsistent.[4]

According to his account in his autobiography, Baquaqua's first enslavement was in Gonja in about 1842 or 1843 when he had accompanied an army from Djougou as a porter that became embroiled in a civil war involving a succession dispute in one of the divisional capitals of Gonja, which owed allegiance to Asante. Asante had conquered the regions north of the Akan heartlands southwest of the Volta River in the eighteenth century. Asante allowed considerable autonomy in Gonja until the death of King Danga in the early 1830s. Safo succeeded Danga but did not secure the support of the various factions in contention. Kali, whom Baquaqua erroneously referred to as

Safo's brother, overthrew Safo, who then committed suicide. Nonetheless, some of Safo's sons and supporters took refuge in the city of Wa, to the north-west, whose ruler was the "neighbouring king" referred to in Baquaqua's account. Kali died shortly afterward, but his successor, Saidu Nyantakyi, in turn faced the continued opposition of the former partisans of Safo, who received outside intervention from Wa. A combined force invaded Gonja and defeated Nyantakyi, who had to abandon his capital at Yagbum. He established a new base at Daboya, at which point Baquaqua accompanied his brother when Djougou troops joined the fray. In response, an Asante army was dispatched to quell the dispute. Asante forces easily occupied Daboya and executed Nyantakyi.[5] Thereafter, Asante imposed tighter control over Gonja. The rival Gonja leaders were not literally "brothers," as reported by Baquaqua, but chiefs of the component divisions of the Gonja kingdom who belonged to the royal dynasty and who in principle succeeded to the paramount kingship in rotation.

In reference to the flight of Nyantakyi from Daboya, in the face of the punitive force from Asante, Baquaqua refers to the use of guns in the battles that ensued. His observation confirms that Asante was better armed than the factions in Gonja. As Baquaqua remembered, "[T]he guns began to boom away, and the war went on in earnest. Guns were used by them on this occasion, much more than bows and arrows. The war was too hot for the king, when he, together with his counsellor, fled for their lives."[6] Although Daboya was in western Gonja, 350 km west of Djougou on the White Volta,[7] soldiers from Djougou became involved in the civil war. Baquaqua was there because he followed his older brother, who was in the service of the Djougou king, whom Nyantakyi recruited after he established himself at Daboya. According to Baquaqua,

> He then went to Da-boy-ya, which was a long way off to the south-west of Zoogoo, beyond a very large river [i.e., the White Volta]. At that place a great many kinds of articles of European manufacture were to be found, such as glass bottles, glasses, combs, calicos, &c, but the buildings were mostly the same as those at Zoogoo, but the city was not surrounded by walls, as at the latter. Here also the king was at war and invited my brother. The cause of this war, was that a king had died, and a dispute having arisen (as is very often the case) between two brothers, which should be the king; they adopted such means to decide who should succeed, and he who could gather the greatest forces was the successor. The unsuccessful candidate placing himself under the protection of a

neighboring king [Wa], until he could gather up sufficient forces to enable him successfully to push on the war, and thus wrest the kingdom from his brother.[8]

After Nyantakyi fled Daboya, the local chief blew up his own palace with gunpowder, killing himself and several Asante officers.[9] As Baquaqua remembered, "It should have been mentioned that the city was destroyed, the women and children having been sent away.—When the wars come on suddenly, the women and children have no means to escape, but are taken prisoners and sold into slavery."[10] Thereupon, Baquaqua recounts that "my companions . . . and myself ran to the river but could not cross it; we hid ourselves in the tall grass, but the enemy [i.e., the Asante army] came and found us, and made us all prisoners. I was tied up very tightly; they placed a rope around my neck and took me off with them."[11]

It is at this point that Baquaqua's account of his enslavement becomes unclear. He reported that his brother subsequently was able to secure his release by purchasing him and then sending him home to Djougou. "Whilst traveling through the wood, we met my brother, but neither of us spoke or seemed to know each other; he turned another way without arousing any suspicion; and then went to a place, and procured a person to purchase me. Had it been known who it was, they would have insisted upon a very great price as my ransom, but it was only a small sum that was required for my release."[12] The difficulty with this explanation is that it is hard to imagine that his brother, in service of the Djougou army, would have been able to have come in contact with the prisoners whom Asante had captured. In similar situations in West Africa, arrangements were made at designated places after battles had finished for opposing sides to meet to exchange or otherwise ransom prisoners. This must have been what happened in Baquaqua's case, if he is to be believed. In this case, however, there is no direct evidence that Asante and the Djougou army had entered into such an agreement to arrange freeing captives. Nonetheless, Baquaqua claimed that "after my purchase and release, my brother sent me home again with some friends," which would mean that he was freed from captivity.[13] Whatever the case, Baquaqua was fortunate not to be taken to Kumasi with the prisoners who were not freed, because an epidemic decimated their numbers, and Baquaqua might very well have died rather than undertake his subsequent adventures.[14]

The reference to possible ransoming is important because the usual practice, if successful, was to arrange the ransom for free-born Muslims, which is well documented in many parts of West Africa where Muslims were found.

The mechanism of ransoming did not always work, of course, as is evident in those cases where Muslims who had been enslaved were taken to the Americas, and Baquaqua would be one such case. Baquaqua was well aware of the practice because his older brother had once been held captive but had been ransomed. As Baquaqua reported, "He at one time went to Bergoo, some distance from [sic: = to] the east of us, where he remained two years. A great war was fought during that time and he was taken prisoner, but was released by his mother paying a ransom, when he returned home again."[15] The incident in Borgu alluded to the period circa 1834–1836.[16] The king of Nikki, Siru Kpera, and other Borgu rulers became embroiled in the jihād emanating from the Sokoto Caliphate in supporting the Yoruba state of Oyo, which had dominated the interior of the Bight of Benin until the Muslim uprising at Ilorin broke out in 1817, whereupon Ilorin became an emirate owing allegiance to the Caliphate in 1823. Oyo's capital at Ile Oyo, also known as Katunga, and the surrounding countryside were abandoned after 1836, with the Yoruba population fleeing south, except for those who were enslaved. Despite early successes, the allies from Borgu who were supporting Oyo were defeated before Ilorin, and several Borgu kings, including Siru Kpera, were killed. According to Nikki tradition, the Borgu captives were set free by the ruler of Ilorin at the request of Kpé Lafia, a rival prince of Nikki who had taken refuge in Ilorin, who conducted the prisoners home.[17] Kpé Lafia himself would subsequently become the king of Nikki. As later in Gonja, Baquaqua's brother was involved because he was a specialist in Islamic divination, or as Moore understood from what Baquaqua told him, "Mahommah's brother was a kind of fortune teller, who when the king was about to go to war, was consulted by him, to know whether the issue of the war would be in his favor or not; this was done by signs and figures made in the sand, and all he predicted, was fully believed would come to pass, so that by his own mysterious power he could either cause the king to wage war or bring the matter to an end."[18] Although not stated explicitly, his brother was probably serving as a diviner-adviser in this war. Tradition names two "diviners" in the service of Siru Kpera, Alfa Salifu and Sibuko, one of whom could have been Baquaqua's unnamed brother.[19]

What has been considered Baquaqua's second enslavement is complicated. He certainly was incarcerated and sold south to Dahomey and ultimately sent into slavery in Brazil. The context of his capture is not entirely clear, however. His account of partying with associates who he thought were friends but who tied him up after he fell asleep in an apparent drunken stupor may well have been true, but the circumstances of this episode require discussion. Based on Ciavolella's anthropological research in Djougou and the outlying villages nearby, it seems possible that Baquaqua was already in a condition of slavery when he was kidnapped according to his own account.[20] While he states that his brother sent him home after freeing him in Gonja, Baquaqua's reference to the "king" is likely to the king of Soubroukou, which is now a small village near Djougou but in the nineteenth century and earlier still was an important political center that had a complicated relationship with Djougou. Baquaqua claimed in his *Autobiography* that "on my return home, I paid our king a visit. He was related to my mother. In a few days after, whilst at home, the king sent for me and said he wished me to live with him entirely, so, accordingly, I remained in his house, and he appointed me a Cherecoo, that is a kind of body guard to the king."[21] The reference to the "king" is not to the king of Djougou—that is, Kilir-Wangara, the two parts of the city of Djougou—but rather, the king in question was the ruler of Soubroukou, which is located about 10 km from Djougou. How Baquaqua's mother might have been related is not explained. Moreover, Baquaqua seems to say that he had reached home in Djougou and went to Soubroukou. Baquaqua did not know the king of Soubroukou before he went there.

Confusion arises from the fact that the heads of villages, land chiefs, and ritual leaders were all referred to as "kings" in the area. As Ciavolella establishes, local terminology indicates the Indigenous "king/chief of the land" was not the king of Djougou, but instead was the "king" of Soubroukou. The "men" who defended his territory were also referred to as "kings," to whom his mother was linked but not his father. Even today, every "chief" or head of a community is referred to in Djougou as "king" not as "village heads" who owe allegiance to the proper king of Kilir—that is, Djougou—whose authority is nominally recognized by all the subjects of Djougou. The "land chiefs" of the village of Sasirou (Culcurxu in Yom) exercised authority over the land around Djougou, under the Gurma aristocracy of Kilir and the Dendi and Hausa "foreigners" who settled in the Wangara ward of the city. To complicate the situation even more, the "king" of Soubroukou claimed authority over the king of Sasirou. This hierarchy of royalty accounts for the confusions of Baquaqua's rendition of his status after he returned home from Gonja.

Baquaqua tried to explain the political system, which the later colonial government had its own difficulty in understanding, but which was later deciphered by Yves Person and finally by Ciavolella. As Baquaqua observed, "The kings are called Massa-sa-ba, and govern several places, and . . . all are called Massa-sa-ba. When the king of the city dies, the Massa-sa-bas are called upon to decide who shall succeed him. If war comes upon them, he [the Massa-sa-ba] is found foremost amongst the brave."[22] The term Massa-saawa (transcribed as "Massa-saba" or "Massa-sawa," the sound ω being a pre-closed rounded and semi-labial vowel typical of the Yom language resembling "b," designates the title of the king of Soubroukou, which indicates that Baquaqua was indeed at the court of Soubroukou. His location is also suggested by other details. The ambiguous use of this term suggests a plurality of "kings," as if the name was a generic title for all the kings of the region, although apparently there is no generic term.[23] Soubroukou was the center of "royal" power that extended over an extensive territory, its authority recognized by "royal" vassals at other villages in the area. In the colonial archives, the title has the form of "Marsa-saba-malou," which seems to be the name of King Sawa Maloum of the Soubroukou dynasty, who reigned in 1870–90.[24] The term *massa* seems to derive from the Mandé-Dyula *mansa*, which is an honorary title for king and which was also the name of the first Wasangaari king of Borgu.

The Massa-sa-bas—in the plural—referred to the "kings" of the various Yoowa villages that were in the territory under the authority of the king of Soubroukou. As Ouorou Komsa Aboubacar explained, succession on the king's death passed to a new "Massa saba" chosen by a body of electors from among three dynastic lineages (Tchallaha, Saw-Monni, and Saw-Sowra), which represented the descendants of the first three kings of Soubroukou. The king normally resided in a dense thicket in a house "built after the manner of the country, but garnished on the outside with marble."[25] There are two kinds of marble in the area, one quite white and the other red. The marble was pounded into a fine dust, and when the mortar used in building houses was still soft, pieces of the marble were pressed into it, in any fantastic shape and figure as might be fancied, which made the wall stronger and gave the building, when finished, a pretty, ornamental appearance. According to Baquaqua, "[T]he king did not reside in the city, but a few miles from it."[26] The "palaces" of the kings were distinguished from other houses by their ornamentation, consisting essentially of paintings (representing scenes from the past) and architectural sculptures (often representing wild animals and symbols of power).[27]

Baquaqua's editor, Samuel Moore, considered that "Africans have a curious way of reckoning distances, they carry their burdens upon their heads and proceed until tired, which is called Loch-a-fau, and in English, means one mile!"[28] The term "mile" should not be taken literally, as "loch-a-fau" is a variable and approximate reference for distances. Soubroukou is 10 km from Wangara. The term probably derives from *lokaci*, which in Hausa and the Dendi languages means "time" or "duration," while *afɔ* means "one" (elsewhere transcribed by Moore as "a-faw"). "Loch-afau" is a transcription of "loka[ci] fɔ," meaning "the time of distance," meaning the distance that one could cover on foot, loaded, during a day's trip. If that is the case, it explains why Moore found it "curious," similarily, the English language has the word "journey," which means, in its medieval origin, almost the same thing.[29]

The implication is that "massa-sa-ba" was a generic title for the rulers of towns subordinate to Djougou, conceivably "the city" here referred to.[30] In Djougou today, however, *masasawa* is explained as the title of one specific town, Soubroukou, southwest of Djougou.[31] Baquaqua's claim that he was a "Cherecoo" is puzzling. This term refers to the notion of *tkiriku*, which was used in Borgu to describe servants in the palace, particularly applicable to Nikki, where the Wasangari aristocracy ruled. The position was normally re-served for a slave or, sometimes, a criminal seeking protection, to the point that historian Jacques Lombard, on whom scholars draw inspiration, consid-ered the *tkiriku* a specific servile category.[32] In Borgu, captives from raids or warfare were settled in villages called *gando*.[33] A very small number of slaves became *tkiriku*, personal servants of the ruling Wasangari.[34] Their position was more desirable than other slaves who were agricultural workers. They dis-played visible symbols of their status such as wearing particular clothing and having partly shaved haircuts. Baquaqua notes that he had such a haircut when he met an acquaintance in Ouidah after being taken to the coast. The *tkiriku* performed a variety of tasks for the Wasangari in Borgu, including be-ing messengers and exercising executive functions. Their power was depen-dent on their relationship with the Wasangari, but their slave status was clear. Baquaqua's description of his role at Soubroukou is very similar. Because Djougou was under the influence of Borgu, it is likely that the term would have had the same meaning there, although it is possible that Baquaqua was comparing his position to the power structure in Borgu. Most likely, the term described the same function for the king of Soubroukou, where a slave as such was described in Yom as *wila*. If Baquaqua had been in Gonja during the Asante campaign of 1841–44 and was taken as a slave to Brazil in 1845, his pe-riod as a palace servant cannot have been more than a few years.

Baquaqua claimed, "I stood only third from the king, Ma-ga-zee and Wa-roo, being the two only in rank above me, next to the king himself. Ma-ga-zee was an old man, and Wa-roo, a youth. I remained with the king day and night, ate and drank with him, and was his messenger in and out of the city."[35] The description of the position of Baquaqua's seat as well attests to the subsidiary function in relation to the king's wives, whose status was considered inferior to men, where in his subordinate position reinforces the hypothesis of his ser-vile status at the court. The king of Soubroukou, Baquaqua continued, "kept nothing from me, but sometimes, when he had very important affairs in hand, he would consult the more experienced Ma-ga-zee."[36] The terms "Ma-ga-zee" and "Wa-roo" were titles associated with specific functions at the royal courts of Djougou and its surrounding villages, including Soubroukou. Alhough it is possible that Waroo or Woroo could refer to a first-born male in Borgu, which is also the case among the Yoowa and the kings of Soubroukou, the term "waru" in *waru kum* ("ouarou-koum") was a name for the "fetish of the earth" within the royal house of Kilir, as well as referring to the main deity venerated by the Yowa, which was a deity of the earth and harvests whose cult was managed by a class of "fetishists" or "priests." The "Woroo" in question here very likely was the "fetishist" of this deity at the court of the king of Soubroukou.[37] The term "Ma-ga-zee" corresponds to "magazin," apparently from the Hausa *magaji*, which in Djougou was a district of the city and a title of nobility. The Hausa term means "heir," referring to the descendants of the first Hausa Muslim merchants and clerics who settled in towns on the route between Gonja and Katsina, as in Salaga, who became notables in the service of the "kings" in charge of markets.[38] In Person's study of the Zarma in the village of Babanzauré, 28 km north of Djougou, the term "Magazi" was the intermediate between the Zarma warrior bands and the indigenous residents along the kola road between the Niger River and Gonja.[39] The term referred to warrior chiefs distinguished according to military values.

> In front of the king's house or palace, was a very large courtyard, beautifully shaded by lofty trees; on one side of this court were three or four trees, under which a rude throne was built of earth thrown into a heap, and covered over with mortar, being joined from tree to tree, which was several feet high, and ascended by steps of the same material. On the throne there was a seat, cushioned, and covered with red leather, made from the skin of the Bah-seh, which was used for no other purpose. On either side, were seats for his two young wives, which was occupied by two of his favorites in their absence. My seat were [sic] at the foot of the throne, on the one side of the steps, and that of Wa-roo on the other; beyond was the seat occupied by Ma-gazee.[40]

Baquaqua claimed that he had a special role in the household of the Soubroukou king.

> Whenever he drank, one of his wives or favorites would kneel before him and place her hands under his chin, so as to prevent any of the drink being spilled upon his person. In their absence, that duty devolved

upon me. Whenever the king required me for anything, he would say Gar-do-wa. I would reply Sa-bee (a term used only in speaking to the king,) and immediately run towards him, falling on my face before him, in an attitude of the most respectful attention. He would then state what he needed, when I would go at full speed to obey his commands, walking not being permitted when about the king's business.—When he desired anything of Ma-ga-zee, he would call me, to communicate to him his will. Thus was I kept running about from morning till night, while his feasts lasted. It was very hard work to attend upon such a king, I can assure you, kind readers. At the king's feasts, all the principal personages would assemble and dine with him, those most of consequence would be entertained at the house of Ma-ga-zee, and those next at other houses, so that the guests were scattered all round about. It is the duty of the women to prepare the food, &c.[41]

Presumably the phrase "Gar-do-wa" includes Gardo, which Baquaqua later used as his middle name and, as explained above, was given to a child born after twins. The suffix "-wa" is emphatic, and "following a command, it takes on the notion of politeness, 'please,'" and therefore "following the name of a person who is called indicates a polite request for attention."[42] This usage confirms that he was known in Djougou by that nickname. "Sabi" written here as "Sa-bee" is a common name in Dendi and in the region more generally, normally given to a second child in the Yoowa context. This name was even given to members of the royal lineage of Soubroukou.[43] As a sign of respect, as suggested in Baquaqua's account. "Sa-bee" is a possible contraction of the expression *sabeni* (majesty) used in addressing kings in the Djougou area.[44] Baquaqua implied that the titles Wa-roo and Ma-gazee were used at the court of Soubroukou, where the "princely" line and its "collectivity" bear the name Magazia. This use reflects the presence of Zarma bands and Hausa merchants on the caravan route from Djougou to Salaga, where the village of Soubroukou was located, and was associated with the court of the local king who had to interact with nearby Djougou and the Kotokoli chiefdoms further to the west. Ma-ga-zee and Wa-roo corresponded to what the French administrators transcribed as Bagazere, the head of the griots or court musicians, and Ba Warakpè, who oversaw the veneration of elders but also collected market taxes by levies on foodstuffs.[45] It seems likely that the titles were used in other places from Borgu to Salaga as well.[46]

Ciavolella recorded important information that informs the importance of Soubroukou when he interviewed its king, Ouorou Komsa Aboubacar, of the

Tchalaha line.[47] The Massa-saba title for vassal "kings" of villages dependent on the authority of Soubroukou literally means "Let's go see the king." The village founders from the Tchalaha lineage arrived in the region from Borgu in the seventeenth century. They first tried to settle in the villages of Biromaté and Passéré but were prevented because they were considered "savages" (*akpanzoho*, literally "headless"). "We were hunters, we lived on sacrifices and we were seers," in the sense of "fetishists," before converting to Islam or later joining evangelical churches.[48] When they arrived in the area, the king of Sasirou already controlled Kilir, which became the heart of Djougou. The Tchalaha chose a secluded and wild area, where the hunter Djatchi was the only inhabitant. The area was difficult to access because of very tall grass, other thick vegetation, and wild animals. The Tchalaha and Djatchi hunted lions, panthers, buffalo, and other animals, and for purposes of security they had to "accompany the women with arrows so that they go to draw water," according to Ouorou Komsa Aboubacar.[49]

The name Soubroukou, whose vernacular version is Tyewelxa, comes from the Gurma expression *subu ku*, which means "high grass." The image was conveyed in Baquaqua's own words as "dense thicket," meaning that it was inaccessible. Other sources indicate that the name comes from the expression *sansané-subuku*, which means "place where one is safe behind the tall grass."[50] According to Ouorou Komsa Aboubacar, "In the beginning there was no king; it is with strength that one becomes king and that is how one founded the dynasty of the lineage of the Tchallaha."[51] The Massa-saba therefore drew his authority from his capacity in this "wild" place to provide refuge to populations fleeing Gurma raids from the north and who "came here to take people and sell them in Abomey," that is, Dahomey.[52] The king of Soubroukou organized the defense and killed the raiders. Soubroukou thereby consolidated its influence over villages south of Djougou, from Soubroukou to Pila, Bodi, and Pélébina toward Pénésoulou and Bassila.[53] Soubroukou never submitted to the authority of Djougou, which developed into the important commercial center, but rather imposed its influence over the dynasty of Sasirou, which controlled Kilir. As Ouorou Komsa Aboubacar claims, "[W]e do not bow to the Djarra of Sasirou; we drove them out and they settled in Bélé-foungou; when we calmed down, some of them came back."[54] The autonomy and power of Soubroukou historically is also attested by the fact that in the "brother village" of Bouloum (Brum in Yom, south-east of Djougou), there is a place where "the king of Kilir goes to make his sacrifices."[55]

The reference to Soubroukou as a city may seem surprising, since today it is a small village outside of Djougou. Baquaqua's reference to the place as a city recalls the centrality of Soubroukou at the time when it referred to the surrounding territory and other villages which recognized its authority. In Baquaqua's time, Soubroukou was a "real city even before the urban core of Djougou developed."[56] It had a market called *sawayaka*, or "king's market" which was even larger than that at Djougou. The Germans in Togo chose Soubroukou, rather than Djougou, as the border outpost with the French colony of Dahomey. Soubroukou became the capital of the canton forming part of the Circle of Djougou in the territorial organization that more or less respected the so-called "native" royalties, while recognizing them as dependent on Djougou. Thereafter, Soubroukou and its influence suffered an inexorable decline in favor of Djougou.[57]

According to what Baquaqua told Moore, "Massa-sa-ba was a generous man and given to hospitality, consequently had a great deal of company."

They love feasting in Africa as well as in any other part of the world, and when the kings give feasts, everything that the country affords is provided. This makes them very popular with the people. . . . Mahommah cannot distinctly state how long he lived with the king, but it was a considerable length of time; whilst he was there he became very wicked. But, (says he,) at that time, I scarce knew what wickedness was; the practises of the soldiers and guards, I am now convinced, was [sic] very bad indeed, having full power and authority from the king to commit all kinds of depredations they pleased upon the people without fear of his displeasure or punishment. At all times, when they were bent on mischief, or imagined they needed anything, they would pounce upon the people and take from them whatever they chose, as resistance was quite out of the way, and useless, the king's decree being known to all the country round about. These privileges were allowed the soldiery in lieu of pay, so we plundered for a living. If the king needed palm wine for a feast, or at any other time, he would send me; and I would take some of his slaves along with me, and knowing by what road the country people laden with wine would come into the city, I would, with the slaves, hide in the long grass, whilst one of our number would climb a high tree, and be on the lookout, for any one coming. As soon as he would espy a woman with a calabash on her head, (women only carry the wine to market,) he would inform us, and we would instantly surround her and secure the wine. If the wine was good, she lost it; if poor, we would return it to her, as the king never drank bad wine, but with the caution, that she was to tell no one that the guards were in ambush, otherwise we should not be enabled to fall upon others, so that the king would have to go without his wine. In this way, toll is levied upon all who bear wine into town, whenever the king needs it. If one woman does not carry sufficient wine for the king's use, others are served in the same way until sufficient is obtained; other articles are also seized upon whenever the king needs them.[58]

This license permitted to palace servants is corroborated by Hugh Clapperton's observations in eastern Borgu in 1826, where he witnessed royal slaves from the Borgu towns of Kaiama and Wawa plundering livestock from villages through which they passed.[59]

Baquaqua was seized and taken south in captivity while he was in the employ of the masasawa or "massa-sa-ba," as Moore understood Baquaqua to say, which now is to be identified with Soubroukou, but his actual imprisonment did not occur at Soubroukou but rather at Yarakéou, which Moore transcribed as Zaracho, located 20 km southwest of Djougou. Baquaqua explained the reason for his enslavement at Yarakéou, attributing the responsibility to a conspiracy based on personal enmity and social envy. His explanation reveals that practices of enslavement by entrapment were part of the economics and politics of slavery that informed the interests of African powers in the Atlantic slave trade.

"Zaracho," or the village of Yarakéou, is southwest of Djougou and 15 km from Soubroukou. The term "Zaracho" is a bad transcription of the actual name, the Victorian calligraphy of Z and Y being quite similar. Substitutions in speech and in transcriptions between the sounds "z" and "dj" are both common, as for the ethnonym Zarma or Djerma, and between "dj" and "y." Dupuis called the village "Yarako" in 1824, while German sources at the turn of the twentieth century called it "Djerakam" and the French called the place Yératiao or Yarakéou.[60] Yarakéou is located on the road that linked Djougou and Soubroukou to the Kotokoli country and Aledjo, 50 km southwest of Djougou, and Krikri (Adjidje) on the Mono River further southwest. The route goes from there south toward the coast or east toward Salaga, as is attested in the Springade map of 1907. German agent Heinrich Klose followed the same route in 1899 during his journey from Djougou through Sasirou, Soubroukou, Djérakam (Yarakéou), and Aledjo-Koura.[61]

The colonial authorities considered Yarakéou as belonging to the area subject to the authority of the Massa-saawa of Soubroukou, which included the area from Soubroukou south to Bodi, but the village was always associated with other places in the Djougou area on the commercial (and religious) route that linked Djougou to Salaga. The village of Yarakéou is on the edge of the Yowa ethno-political sphere, belonging rather to the Temba-Kura group. Kura is spoken there, which is a language related to Yoruba, after refugees from the southwest of Dahomey had moved there to escape slave raids from Dahomey in the eighteenth century. The place is also known in the villages between Soubroukou and Aledjo-Koura as Nyantruku or Oku-Oku.[62] The village depended less on Soubroukou than on Aledjo-Koura, a commercial hub that is on the same Djougou-Salaga axis and, as its name suggests, shares the same Kura language with Yarakéou. The two villages in turn both belong to the political-cultural sphere of the Temba or Kotokoli people. The name may derive from the Dendi expression "give-take back" as pronounced by the people of Djougou, thus attesting to the exchanges between Dendi and Kotokoli. An ethno-political continuity between Soubroukou and the Kotokoli country is attested by the existence of the same Yao lineage with the respective royal lines, even though Yarakéou recognized the authority of the king of Djougou-Kilir.[63]

Baquaqua's account of his enslavement emphasizes betrayal on the part of his "companions." Baquaqua describes the enmity he may have suffered as the result of envy for his rank. He occupied a role that made him responsible for the abuses committed by his companions who "plundered for a living" in the eyes of the population who were victims. American missionaries and politicians who met him in the 1850s described Baquaqua as a man tormented by the sins committed when he was a free man in Africa, which helps explain the "Christian" reading that he offered for his transgressions.

The section of the Djougou-Salaga route between Yoowa country south of Soubroukou and the northeast of the Kotokoli country was deeply affected by the slave trade. During the nineteenth century, the Temba aristocracy based its power on the control of this type of trade on the Djougou-Salaga route and with the coastal zone, exchanging slaves for weapons and salt. The *egom* were groups of Muslim "foreigners" from the merchant communities of the sub-region (similar to the Wangara) and socially and culturally integrated into the Kotokoli world of the "indigenous" Temba. The trade in slaves required the formation of slave militias and therefore, to feed them, the production of an agricultural surplus which could only be ensured by the work of farmers, the "chiefdom slaves," the *uronde yom*.[64] In his passage through Yarakéou, Klose noticed the considerable number of slaves in the fields.[65] Villages south of Soubroukou, such as those around Pélébina and Bogou, remember the instability of the region due to slave raids carried out by Gurma groups.[66] Slaves were sold to merchants coming from the south for money to buy local alcohol called *tukatuka*, which corresponds to the beer of sorghum that Baquaqua mentioned.

According to Baquaqua,

> [W]hen any person gives evidence of gaining an eminent position in the country, he is immediately envied, and means are taken to put him out of the way; thus when it was seen that my situation was one of trust and confidence with the king, I was of course soon singled out as a fit object of vengeance by an envious class of my countrymen, decoyed away and sold into slavery. I went to the city one day to see my mother, when I was followed by music (the drum) and called to by name, the drum beating to the measure of a song which had been composed apparently in honor of me, on account of, as I supposed, my elevated position with the king. This pleased me mightily, and I felt highly flattered, and was very liberal, and gave the people money and wine, they singing and gesturing the time. About a mile from my mother's house, where a strong drink called Bah-gee, was made out of the grain Har-nee; thither we repaired; and when I had drank plentifully of Bah-gee, I was quite intoxicated, and they persuaded me to go with them to Zaracho, about one mile from Zoogoo, to visit a strange king that I had never seen before. When we arrived there, the king made much of us all, and a great feast was prepared, and plenty of drink was given to me, indeed all appeared to drink very freely.[67]

Baquaqua was drinking beer made from sorghum, not realizing that a deception was underway. Baquaqua was about to start his enforced journey to Brazil, ultimately circumventing the Black Atlantic.

> In the morning when I arose, I found that I was a prisoner, and my companions were all gone. Oh, horror! I then discovered that I had been betrayed into the hands of my enemies, and sold for a slave. Never shall I forget my feelings on that occasion; the thoughts of my poor mother harrassed me very much, and the loss of my liberty and honorable position with the king, grieved me very sorely. I lamented bitterly my folly in being so easily deceived, and was led to drown all caution in the bowl. Had it not been that my senses had been taken from me, the chance was that I should have escaped their snares, at least for that time. The man, in whose company I found myself left by my cruel companions, . . . secured

me . . . [in] the following manner:—He took a limb of a tree that had two prongs, and shaped it so that it would cross the back of my neck, it was then fastened in front with an iron bolt; the stick was about six feet long.[68]

Baquaqua was now in the hands of a slave trader. The idea that the task of the latter was "to rid the country of all such as myself" implies that Baquaqua recognized that his destiny was to be exported to the coastal trade, and not held in domestic captivity for local exploitation.[69] We cannot know if it was his conscience at the time of the events or if it was the result of reflection, but everything suggests he understood that being chained had an ominous meaning.

> Confined thus, I was marched forward towards the coast, to a place called Ar-oo-zo, which was a large village; there I found some friends, who felt very much about my position, but had no means of helping me. We only stayed there one night, as my master wanted to hurry on, as I had told him I would get away from him and go home. He then took me to a place called Chir-a-chur-ee, there I also had friends, but could not see them, as he kept very close watch over me, and he always stayed at places prepared for the purpose of keeping the slaves in security; there were holes in the walls in which my feet were placed, (a kind of stocks.) He then took me on to a place called Cham-mah, (after passing through many strange places, the names of which I do not recollect) where he sold me. We had then been about four days from home and had traveled very rapidly.[70]

Unlike his experience earlier in Gonja, on this second occasion he was not ransomed but instead traded southward into Dahomey, changing hands among several successive owners along the way. His route was southward, via towns that he called "Ar-oozoo," "Chir-a-chur-ee," and "Cham-mah."

The first place to be identified is Aledjo, about 55 km southwest of Djougou or about 30 km from Yarakeou, close to the modern Bénin-Togo border.[71] This is the village of Krikri, otherwise known as Ajéidè. This Temba or Kotokoli village is located 15 km (therefore approximately a "loch-a-fau") south of Alejo, with which it had similar sociocultural relations and which included a community of Muslim merchants known as Malwa.[72] The route extended past the mountains that are the source of the Mono River, which flows south to the coast at Grand Popo on the border between what is now Benin and Togo. It was the main trade route that connected the Kotokoli country with the coastal area of the Ewe, Mina, and Xwla between Grand Popo and Aného, in particular for the exchange of slaves for sea salt and alcohol. Baquaqua had "friends" in Krikri but was unable to contact them.

Tchamba was a further 15 km south of Krikri. The four days from "home" presumably included the day spent traveling from Djougou to Yarakeou, prior to Baquaqua's actual imprisonment. The total distance from Djougou to Tchamba is about 80 km, which does not indicate an especially rapid rate of travel. According to Baquaqua,

> I remained only one day [in Tchamba], when I was again sold to a woman, who took me to E-fau; she had along with her some young men, into whose charge I was given, but she journeyed with us; we were several days going there; I suffered very much traveling through the woods, and never saw a human being all the journey. There was no regular road, but we had to make our passage as well as we could. . . . After passing through the woods, we came to a small place, where the woman who had purchased me, had some friends; here I was treated very well, indeed, during the day, but at night I was closely confined, as they were afraid I would make my escape; I could not sleep all night, I was so tightly kept.[73]

The place that Baquaqua called "Efau" probably refers to Ifè, the local term for the Yoruba-speaking communities west of Savalou as far as Aktpamè to the south of Djougou, including Djalloukou in the north of Dahomey, where Baquaqua apparently stayed for "several weeks."[74] Djalloukou was about 40 km northwest of the Dahomey capital of Abomey.[75] He was sold to a man who "was very rich, and had a great number of wives and slaves."[76] He was placed in charge of an old slave, but Baquaqua was clearly nervous. There was a "great dance," and he was "fearful they were going to kill me, as I had heard they did so in some places," and "fancied the dance was only a preliminary part of the ceremony." Although he did not report what he actually did, he did not like the work that was assigned to him, and his new master was "fearful of losing me" and locked him up every night.

Not being satisfied with Baquaqua, the man sold him again, and this time Baquaqua was taken through the countryside to Abomey. As he passed through the city, he noted that they were

> met by a woman, and my keeper who was with me immediately took to his heels and ran back as hard as he could. I stood stock still, not knowing the meaning of it; he saw I did not attempt to follow him, or to move one way or another, and he called me in the Efau language to follow him, which I did, he then told me, after we rested, that the woman we had met was the king's wife, and it is a mark of respect to run whenever she is in sight of any of her subjects.[77]

By implication Baquaqua had picked up some knowledge of the "Efau" language, presumably Yoruba, during his "several weeks" of residence in Djalloukou. The fact that people had to give way and hide at the approach of the king's wives is reported by several European visitors to Dahomey.[78] At the time, Ghezo was king of Dahomey. He had seized power in a coup d'état in 1818 and ruled until 1858. Not only did Ghezo have numerous wives, but he had an elite corps of women soldiers who also had to be avoided.[79]

From Abomey, Baquaqua was taken to the coastal port which he calls "Gra-fe"—that is, Glehue—the local name for the town better known as Ouidah (Whydah), the principal port of Dahomey and the second most important departure point for enslaved Africans taken to the Americas, after Luanda in Angola. As conveyed in the sketch by Frederick Forbes, who was in Ouidah on 16 March 1850, the enslaved were chained together and bound before being paraded before potential buyers. According to John Duncan, who was at Ouidah at virtually the same time as Baquaqua, there were many Muslims at Ouidah, although the *vodun* worship was the dominant religion there and in the interior. Baquaqua may not have known this, but there was a sizable population of returnees from Brazil at Ouidah, most of whom were Yoruba in origin and many of whom were Muslims who had been involved in the Male Uprising ten years earlier in 1835 in Bahia (figure 2.1). According to Duncan,

> [T]he country ten or twelve miles round Whydah [Ouidah] is very interesting, the soil good, land level, and in many places well cultivated by people returned from the Brazils, as I before stated. . . . I learn that many of them were driven away from Brazil on account of their being concerned in an attempted revolution amongst slaves there, who turned against their masters. These people are generally from the Foola [Fula, i.e., Sokoto Caliphate] and Eyo [Oyo] countries. Many, it appears, were taken away at the age of twenty or twenty four years—consequently they can give a full account of their route to Badagry, where they were shipped.[80]

Duncan was on a mission on behalf of the Royal Geographical Society to reach the mythical "Kong Mountains" that were thought to exist in the interior of West Africa, shaping the flow of the Niger River and extending across the interior of West Africa, from Senegambia eastward. Duncan described his journey in two published accounts: first in an article in the *Journal of the Royal Geographical Society* (1846) and at greater length in his 1847 book.

Duncan learned that slaves were not only sent to Badagry to escape the British blockade of Ouidah but also to Petit Popo. The lagoon system enters

THE SLAVE CHAIN AT THE COAST.

FIGURE 2.1 "The Slave Chain" observed on 16 March 1850, in Frederick E. Forbes, *Dahomey and the Dahomans, Being the Journals of Two Missions to the King of Dahomey and Residence at his Capital in the Years 1849 and 1850.* 2 vols. London: Longman, Brown, Green and Longmans, 1851, vol. 1, 100.

the sea at Badagry in the east, which is close to Lagos, and at Petit Popo and Grand Popo to the west. Baquaqua was taken from there along the coastal lagoon that runs parallel to the ocean behind a long sand bar that stretches almost from Lagos in what is now Nigeria to the Volta River in Ghana. As Robin Law has demonstrated, this lagoon system was the internal waterway that enabled communication, trade, and population movement in the region of Africa that is known as the Bight of Benin and was known to Europeans as the Slave Coast. There were no ports. The lagoon system empties into the sea at two places, Lagos in the east and Grand Popo in the west. Otherwise, departures had to occur offshore from the sandy beach via boats that took the people on board to waiting ships through rough surf. The embarkation onto a slave ship here was a difficult process and dangerous. The area is to be contrasted to the Gold Coast in the west, where coastal castles made of stone imported from Europe dominated small inlets that were found between the mouth of the Volta far to the west almost as far as the Bandama River; to the east, the trade emanating from the Niger River delta was concentrated especially at Bonny and, in the nineteenth century, smaller places like Brass or in the Cross River delta slightly inland at Calabar.

Baquaqua's account here is consistent with other contemporary evidence, that the blockade maintained by the British navy's anti-slaving squadron made it difficult to load slaves at Ouidah, and that enslaved cargoes were usually moved along the lagoon either eastward to Porto-Novo or Badagry or westward to Agoué—that is, Grand Popo. Although Baquaqua does not specify in which direction he was moved along the lagoon, it is likely that he was taken westward to Grand Popo 35 km to the west of Ouidah and left from Petit Popo, which is located on the end of the sand bar across from Grand Popo, where the Mono River also empties into the sea. Over 12,000 males left the Bight of Benin in 1844–46, during which Baquaqua's ship had to have made the journey, and based on chronological reconstruction, he must have left in 1845 and hence probably did not go eastward toward Badagry and Lagos.[81]

Considering Baquaqua's movement from Abomey to Ouidah, he would have passed through the da Souza network. Ouidah had long been the principal port of embarkation for enslaved captives in West Africa, and especially from the Bight of Benin. In the nineteenth century, Francisco Felix de Souza (1754–1849) dominated the business of supplying ships. He rose to prominence in 1818 when he supported a coup d'état that enabled Ghezo to become king (1818–58).[82] He was rewarded for his support with the honorific title of Chacha. De Souza even owned ships and invested in others that traded with both Brazil and Cuba.[83] He had originally come from Brazil in the 1790s, establishing his firm at Badagry and Ouidah, and later at Little Popo. The location of de Souza's first business was at Ajido, a few kilometers east of Badagry, although politically subordinate. De Souza established a "factory," which is what the store houses and stockades for slaves were called, when he first went to West Africa in circa 1792–95. He later set up his principal business in Ouidah, which in the early nineteenth century was still sending thousands of enslaved captives to the Americas, especially to Brazil.[84] By the mid-1840s, one of his sons, Isidoro, had taken over the business and was almost certainly involved in the transfer of Baquaqua to a Brazilian ship anchored off Little Popo (figure 2.2).

FIGURE 2.2 Isidoro de Souza; from a painting, circa 1822, in Pierre Verger, *Flux et reflux de la traite des Nègres entre le Golfe de Bénin et Bahia de Todos os Santos du XVIIe au XIXe siècle*, Paris (1968).

The chronology can be worked out because he seems to have arrived in Brazil at the end of March 1845, therefore leaving the Bight of Benin sometime in late 1844. As it happened, Duncan moved along the lagoons west of Ouidah in February 1845, a few months after Baquaqua must have left. Duncan saw slaves being taken westward on 18 February in a manner that Baquaqua must have experienced.[85] By coincidence, Duncan's observations provide an eyewitness account of the conditions under which Baquaqua would have traveled. On 4 March, Duncan noted that he had left Ouidah "by the Lagoon river" and arrived at "Ahguay" [Agoué]—that is, Grand Popo— the following morning. "All was bustle and excitement amongst the slave-merchants. They had, late on the previous evening, shipped five hundred slaves in the short space of an hour, although the surf is always very bad on the coast. Unfortunately two of the slaves were drowned during the shipment. It had been intended to ship six hundred slaves, had the *Hydra* steamer not hove in sight. On the following morning the *Hydra* made the slavery a prize, to the great mortification of all who had slaves on board."[86] The operation of being moved to the slave ship was terrifying, which Duncan observed, and which Baquaqua certainly experienced.

It may be interesting to those unaquainted with slave-shipping to learn something of the mode. When a shipment of slaves is about to take place, the slaves are taken out, as if for their usual airing, perhaps ten or twenty on one chain, which is fastened to the neck of each individual, at the distance of about one yard apart. In this manner they are thus marched in single file to the beach, without any intimation of their fate, about which they seem quite indifferent even when they know it. Every canoe is then put in requisition, and the little piece of cotton-cloth tied around the loins of the slave is stripped off, and the gang on each chain is in succession marched close to a fire previously kindled on the beach. Here marking-irons are heated, and when an iron is sufficiently hot, it is quickly dipped in palm-oil, in order to prevent its sticking to the flesh. It is then applied to the ribs or hip, and sometimes even to the breast. Each slave-dealer uses his own mark, so that when the vessel arrives at her destination, it is easily ascertained to whom those who died belonged. They are then hurried into a canoe and compelled to sit in the bottom, where they are stowed as closely as possible till the canoe reaches the ship. They are then taken on board, and again put into the chain until they reach their destination, where they are given over to their intended masters or their agents.[87]

An illustration in the *Church Missionary Intelligencer* shows "[s]hipping slaves through the surf, West-African coast. A cruiser signalled in sight. (From a sketch by a merchant on the coast)." Slaving operations in the Bight of Benin had to contend with its treacherous surf (figure 2.3).

Baquaqua's description of how the Middle Passage began with terror confirms Duncan's observations, which certainly was the experience of millions of other Africans who could not possibly have known what was in store for them across the Atlantic or what the Atlantic crossing would entail. As Baquaqua recounted,

When all were ready to go aboard, we were chained together, and tied with ropes round about our necks, and were thus drawn down to the sea shore. The ship was lying some distance off. I had never seen a ship before, and my idea of it was, that it was some object of worship of the white man. I imagined that we were all to be slaughtered, and were being led there for that purpose. I felt alarmed for my safety, and despondency had almost taken sole possession of me. A kind of feast was made ashore that day, and those who rowed the boats were plentifully regaled with whiskey, and the slaves were given rice and other good things in abundance.

SHIPPING SLAVES THROUGH THE SURF, WEST-AFRICAN COAST. A CRUISER SIGNALLED IN SIGHT.
(From a Sketch by a merchant on the Coast.)

FIGURE 2.3 *The Church Missionary Intelligencer*. A Monthly Journal of Missionary Information (vol. 7 [1856], frontispiece, facing p. 241).

I was not aware that it was to be my last feast in Africa. I did not know my destiny. Happy for me, that I did not.[88]

It was not whiskey, if that matters, but *gerebita* brought from Brazil, the cheapest *cachaça*, made from slave-produced sugar cane. The irony of imbibing a slave-derived alcohol to entrap more Africans to produce sugar completely escaped the victims of enslavement. Baquaqua could not know that his violation of Islamic prohibitions on drinking alcohol that he knew had assisted his enslavement would be enhanced through the cyclical return of alcohol from slave production in Brazil.

All I knew was, that I was a slave, chained by the neck, and that I must readily and willingly submit, come what would, which I considered was as much as I had any right to know. At length, when we reached the beach, and stood on the sand, oh! how I wished that the sand would open and swallow me up. My wretchedness I cannot describe. It was beyond description. The reader may imagine, but anything like an outline of my feelings would fall very short of the mark, indeed. There were slaves brought hither from all parts of the country, and taken on board the ship.[89]

He experienced the dangers. The rough surf off Petit Popo was as bad or even worse than that off Ouidah, but the risks for the slavers was less because boats could be sent out much quicker to waiting ships off Grand Popo than they could at the beach across from Ouidah and thereby had a better chance of running the British blockade. Ships could not come into the beach because of the shifting sands of the lagoon outlet, but the boats that took the enslaved to the waiting ships could move much faster and at shorter notice than off the beach opposite Ouidah.

In Baquaqua's case, it was still dangerous and deadly. As he recounted, with considerable discomfort,

> The first boat had reached the vessel in safety, notwithstanding the high wind and rough sea; but the last boat that ventured was upset, and all in her but one man were drowned. The number who were lost was about thirty. The man that was saved was very stout, and stood at the head of the boat with a chain in his hand, which he grasped very tightly in order to steady the boat; and when the boat turned over, he was thrown with the rest into the sea, but on rising, by some means under the boat, managed to turn it over, and thus saved himself by springing into her, when she was righted. This required great strength, and being a powerful man, gave him the advantage over the rest.[90]

Baquaqua observed all this, for he was placed in the next boat that was put to sea. At this point, he experienced what must have been his first religious experience of salvation. As he noted, the boat that he was placed in made it to the waiting ship. He later claimed that "God saw fit to spare me, perhaps for some good purpose." However, he was "then placed in that most horrible of all places, THE SLAVE SHIP."

> Its horrors, ah! who can describe? None can so truly depict its horrors as the poor unfortunate, miserable wretch that has been confined within its portals. Oh! friends of humanity, pity the poor African, who has been trepanned and sold away from friends and home, and consigned to the hold of a slave ship, to await even more horrors and miseries in a distant land, amongst the religious and benevolent. Yes, even in their very midst; but to the ship! We were thrust into the hold of the vessel in a state of nudity, the males being crammed on one side and the females on the other; the hold was so low that we could not stand up, but were obliged to crouch upon the floor or sit down; day and night were the same to us, sleep being denied us from the confined position of our bodies, and we became

desperate through suffering and fatigue. Oh! the loathsomeness and filth of that horrible place will never be effaced from my memory; nay, as long as memory holds her seat in this distracted brain, will I remember that. My heart even at this day, sickens at the thought of it.[91]

Slaves were commonly stripped of their clothes prior to embarkation. Another slave who passed through Ouidah, Cudjo Lewis, in 1859 likewise recalled that "the Dahomians avariciously tore their Garments from them, men and women alike were left entirely nude," which he remembered as "a great humiliation."[92] Segregation of the sexes was normal practice on slave ships, the men usually crowded below deck and the women often on the deck.[93] Frederick Forbes, an officer of the British navy's anti-slaving squadron in the 1840s, noted that the height of slave decks for adults ranged from three to four feet, though could be lower for children.[94] Cudjo Lewis, who left Ouidah in 1859, was more fortunate than Baquaqua, recalling that "the hold . . . was deep enough to permit the men of lesser stature to stand erect."[95] The sickening stench of the slave quarters on the Middle Passage is well documented.[96]

Baquaqua's report on what slaves were fed on his ship is worse than normal, which usually consisted of boiled corn, rice, yams, beans, or cassava, supplemented by small amounts of meat or fish and seasoning such as pepper and palm oil.[97]

The only food we had during the voyage was corn soaked and boiled. I cannot tell how long we were thus confined, but it seemed a very long while. We suffered very much for want of water, but was [sic] denied all we needed. A pint a day was all that was allowed, and no more; and a great many slaves died upon the passage. There was one poor fellow became so very desperate for want of water, that he attempted to snatch a knife from the white man who brought in the water, when he was taken up on deck and I never knew what became of him. I supposed he was thrown overboard.[98]

His account of the Middle Passage confirms what we know about the trans-Atlantic crossing.[99] According to the British naval officer Forbes, "[T]he fullest allowance [of water] . . . is one quart each, daily, though seldom more than a pint is given."[100] Mrs. Judd thought that throwing difficult slaves overboard is stated as a fact, rather than a speculation.

When any one of us became refractory, his flesh was cut with a knife, and pepper or vinegar was rubbed in to make him peaceable(!) I suffered, and so did the rest of us, very much from sea sickness at first, but that did not cause our brutal owners any trouble. Our sufferings were our own, we had no one to share our troubles, none to care for us, or even to speak a word of comfort to us. Some were thrown overboard before breath was out of their bodies; when it was thought any would not live, they were got rid of in that way. Only twice during the voyage were we allowed to go on deck to wash ourselves—once whilst at sea, and again just before going into port.[101]

Mrs. Judd thought that Baquaqua's account of pepper being rubbed into wounds referred to the individual slave just mentioned, rather than as here in general terms. If Baquaqua was brought on deck only twice during the crossing, it was not normal practice, slaves being more usually brought on deck daily for feeding and exercise, and to enable their quarters to be cleaned.[102] However, bad weather and fears of rebellion (and, in the nineteenth century, pursuit by the British navy) might lead to slaves being kept below for longer periods.

The torture of the passage lasted a month, which was the average sailing time for slave ships between West Africa and Brazil.[103] For the specific period of Baquaqua's voyage, the average sailing time for ships sailing from the Bights of Benin and Biafra to Brazil in the early 1840s was thirty-two days: This figure relates to Bahia rather than to Pernambuco, where Baquaqua was taken, but presumably sailing times to the latter were similar. An individual voyage might of course be considerably longer, depending on weather conditions and (in the illegal trade) the need to evade British naval patrols.[104]

Baquaqua provides his own assessment of his plight as a slave and the endurance of suffering that was experienced on board a slave ship crossing the Atlantic. His comments are a scathing attack on those who held slaves in bondage and justified their inhumanity by defending slavery.

Let those *humane individuals,* who are in favor of slavery, only allow themselves to take the slave's position in the noisome hold of a slave ship, just for one trip from Africa to America, and without going into the horrors of slavery further than this, if they do not come out thorough-going abolitionists, then I have no more to say in favor of abolition. But I think their views and feelings regarding slavery will be changed in some degree, however; if not, let them continue in the course of slavery, and work out their term in a cotton or rice field, or other plantation, and then if they do not say hold, enough! I think they must be of iron frames, possessing neither hearts nor souls. I imagine there can be but one place more horrible in all creation than the hold of a slave ship, and that place is where slaveholders and their myrmidons are the most likely to find themselves some day, when alas, 'twill be late, too late, alas![105]

Indeed, the hold of slave ships had an extremely unpleasant smell because of the vomit from sea sickness, diarrhea, excrement, and urine, especially when a contagious disease became rampant. Those subordinate to slave owners, ship captains, brokers who handled transactions, and anyone else in a position of power treated enslaved captives in unscrupulous ways and carried out orders unquestioningly. Regardless of the difficulties of interpreting the chain of events from Baquaqua's capture in Gonja through his seizure at Yarakeou and his status at Soubroukou, it is clear that he was indeed enslaved on his trip to the coast, being treated as such at Djalloukou with the apparent expectation that he would remain there and was only sold on when his master was uncertain that he would accept his servitude and might try to escape.

CHAPTER THREE

Under Slavery in Brazil

Baquaqua could not have known that he arrived in Brazil during a complicated era in which the slave trade was technically illegal. A British blockade of the coast attempted to enforce abolition. A Court of Mixed Commission operated in Rio de Janeiro, the capital, handling cases in which ships involved in the slave trade were confiscated and their captains prosecuted for illegal slave trading. Baquaqua's fate would have been far different if a British naval vessel had intercepted the ship he was on as had been done with other ships. Any ships that were detained were conveyed to Rio de Janeiro for trial before a Mixed Commission that condemned the ships and issued papers declaring those on board to be "Liberated Africans" who were technically free but had to serve a period of apprenticeship that could last up to fourteen years. Instead of entering the local market of slaves in Pernambuco, he would have become evidence before the Mixed Commission Court.[1] He would have been then declared to be a Liberated African who technically was no longer a slave but nonetheless was not liberated. Instead, in most cases, he would have been indentured, serving up to seven years, often working on infrastructure projects or in state-run munitions and other factories. The British reports for the mid-1840s allow some comparison with Baquaqua's ship, which seems to have escaped the attention of the British patrol. Hence Baquaqua first arrived in Brazil at an obscure location, but he subsequently traveled along most of the Brazilian coast, from Pernambuco in the northeast to Rio Grande do Sul in the far south on the border with Uruguay.

Because of the illegality of the trans-Atlantic slave trade, the ship that Baquaqua was on had to evade the British patrol of the coast. By 1845, when Baquaqua landed north of Recife, the slave traffic from Africa had been illegal in Brazil for well over a decade, as established by the Law of 28 September 1831. According to a treaty with Britain, the British navy patrolled the coast and intercepted any ships that were thought to be carrying enslaved cargoes from Africa. Baquaqua noted that his ship docked outside "the city" (that is, Recife),[2] but that was the practice at the time to divert the attention of the British navy. As a British agent described the general conditions of the slave trade in Pernambuco in 1846:

> The way in which the African Slave Trade was previously managed in this port now takes on . . . a new characteristic. Instead of the larger types of

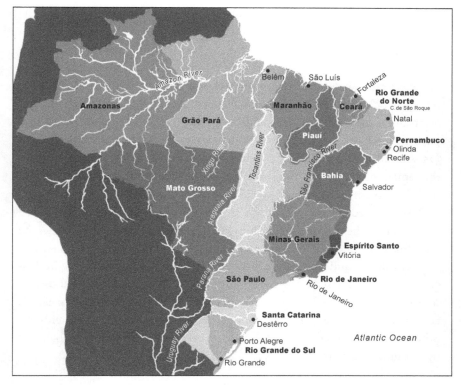

MAP 3.1 Brazilian Coast

vessel, which vary from 150 to 300 tons of weight each, a smaller type is now used, between 45 to 60 tons, namely: "Maria", 52t in size, "Maraquinhas" [Mariquinhas], 52, "Déliberacao" [Deliberação], 54, two "Diligências," 54 and 55, and "San Domingos" [São Domingos], 56t in weight; these insignificant-looking vessels, equipped only with botaló, mainsail and traquette, sail fast, have a small draft, and a low structure, can more easily escape apprehension; the garrison varies from eight to 14 men, who are hired per trip, whose interest is only restricted to making it prosperous, and are always on standby.[3]

These ships carried 150 to 300 slaves in deplorable conditions that are described by Baquaqua in the autobiography and in previous reports made to the Judds.[4]

Most likely Baquaqua was transported by one of the vessels mentioned in that report. Most of the ships that landed slaves in Pernambuco during this period, however, came from Angola or some other place in west central

Africa, not West Africa. Although there are records of six slave ships from the Bight of Benin arriving in Pernambuco in 1844, these voyages seem much earlier than that of Baquaqua.[5] During the year 1845, the only record of slave landings, which may have been that of Baquaqua, was that of a ship whose name is unfortunately not reported, coming from an unspecified location in Africa, which docked on March 31 in Macaro, near Barra de Catuama and not far from the island of Itamaracá, north of Recife. According to the British report, that ship brought 163 slaves: thirty were sold to people in the vicinity (250,000 réis per head), eleven were given to local authorities as bribes, and the remaining 122 people, in principle, were "sold and hidden in nearby sugar mills," although many of them were later taken to Recife.[6]

They arrived on the coast early in the morning, "and the vessel played about during the day, without coming to anchor. All that day we neither ate or drank anything, and we were given to understand that we were to remain perfectly silent, and not make any out-cry, otherwise our lives were in danger." Only at nightfall did the anchor drop and those on board were shown to "our future masters, who had come aboard from the city," which is clearly a reference to Recife and its neighboring suburbs. Baquaqua, along with the others on board, was then "permitted to go on deck to be viewed and handled by our future masters."

> We landed a few miles from the city [i.e., Recife], at a farmer's house, which was used as a kind of slave market. The farmer had a great many slaves, and I had not been there very long before I saw him use the lash pretty freely on a boy, which made a deep impression on my mind, as of course I imagined that would be my fate ere long, and oh! too soon, alas! were my fears realized. When I reached the shore, I felt thankful to Providence that I was once more permitted to breathe pure air, the thought of which almost absorbed every other. I cared but little then that I was a slave, having escaped the ship was all I thought about. Some of the slaves on board could talk Portuguese. They had been living on the coast with Portuguese families, and they used to interpret to us. They were not placed in the hold with the rest of us, but come [sic] down occasionally to tell us something or other.[7]

The transfer of the enslaved to land had to be performed in the context of silence and undercover. The geography of Pernambuco, due to its reefs, beaches, and coves, provided many beaches that served as relatively safe places for the illegal landing of Africans, such as Barra de Catuamá, Itamaracá, Goiana, Pau Amarelo, Cabo de Santo Agostinho, Tamandaré, Porto de Galinhas, among others.[8] The usual landing points were Una to the south of Recife and Catuamá to the north.[9] The British Navy was active along the coast. Because of the likely timing of his crossing, Baquaqua's ship may have been the unnamed Brazilian schooner that missed Catuamá and put in at Macaró, further north, across from the Island of Itamaracá, on 31 March 1845. According to the British report, "30 of the slaves were sold to persons in the neighbourhood at Rs. 250$ per head. To facilitate the debarkation of the remaining negroes 11 were given to the local authorities as a douceur. The rest, about 122 slaves, were disposed of, and secreted in the adjacent Engenhos. On the 3rd of April, the '*Guarapes*,' a schooner of war, was despatched to the vicinity, but arrived too late to find either vessel or slaves."[10] The ship apparently appeared off the coast unexpectedly in the morning and "played about during the day, without coming to anchor," according to Baquaqua. The ship spent the day sitting off the coast waiting until it was safe to land the enslaved on board. Under cover of impending darkness, everyone on board was brought on deck, where they were "viewed and handled by our future masters, who had come aboard from the city" (that is, Recife),[11] and most of the enslaved who were on board were initially "disposed of and secreted in the adjacent Engenhos [sugar estates]," though many of them were later taken into Recife.[12]

Baquaqua was baptized along with everyone else on his ship and given a new name, José. He spent "but a day or two" on the sugar estate (engenho) when he "was again sold to a slave dealer in the city" (that is, Recife). Recife was not only the capital of Pernambuco but also its major port, located at the mouth of the Beberibe and Capibaribe rivers that flowed into the sea behind a reef that ran parallel to the shore. These rivers, the islands they formed, and the flow of several other smaller rivers into the sea behind the reef were the main characteristic of the countryside, which was dotted with numerous towns surrounding Recife during Baquaqua's time in Pernambuco, one of which being where he lived (figure 3.1).

As Baquaqua understood the situation, "When a slaver comes in, the news spreads like wild-fire, and down come all those that are interested in the arrival of the vessel with its cargo of living merchandize, who select from the stock those most suited to their different purposes and purchase the slaves precisely in the same way that oxen or horses would be purchased in a market." He thought that there were many merchants who "make quite a business of this buying and selling human flesh, and do nothing else for a living, depending

FIGURE 3.1 Recife waterfront in 1859; in Gilberto Ferrez, *Photography in Brazil* (Albuquerque: University of New Mexico Press, trans. Stella de Sá Rego, 1984), 160.

entirely upon this kind of traffic."[13] The dealer who purchased him at the engenho "sold me to a man in the country, who was a baker, and resided not a great distance from Pernambuco [Recife]."[14] Thus began his enslavement in Brazil. Clearly, he did not want to be called José. His conscious choice to use names from his youth in Djougou when he was baptized a second time in Haiti in 1848 was a strong statement of defiance against his enslavement, perhaps his rejection of the kinlessness of slavery and his reclamation of his birthright ties.

At the time, Brazil was recovering from a period of political instability after the abdication of Dom Pedro I, who returned to Portugal in 1831, leaving the government in the hands of a regency because his son, Dom Pedro II, was only five years old. Dom Pedro I had become regent of Brazil in 1821 and declared independence from Portugal in 1822, becoming emperor. Therefore, after 1831, Brazil was subjected to a period of regency, with provisional governments commanded by important politicians who were loyal to the monarchy.[15] In 1840, Dom Pedro II was declared of age and was crowned emperor the following year, when he was only sixteen. His regime lasted from 1840 to 1889, which assured sufficient political stability to hold the former Portuguese colony together. The consolidation of the state around the young emperor provoked various reactions in the imperial court in Rio de Janeiro and in the Brazilian Parliament. Pedro II relied heavily on the dominant military figure in the empire, the Duke of Caxias, Luis Alves de Lima e Silva, but the elites in the various provinces were divided between conservatives and liberals who struggled to control local governments and dominate the national government.[16] Despite political instability, the Brazilian economy was vibrant, based on the growth of coffee cultivation and the continued production of sugar cane and gold mining. Under his regime, there was considerable investment in infrastructure, including railroads, telegraph communication, and the shift from sailing vessels to steamships.

Legally, therefore, Baquaqua arrived in Brazil fifteen years after the treaty with Britain had abolished the traffic from Africa. According to the law of 1831, all those from Africa who entered Brazil during the period of illegal trafficking were to be treated as "free Africans," protected by the Imperial state or assigned for apprenticeship for a period of fourteen years. During the period of apprenticeship, the "free Africans" were to work under the illusion that they would learn the ways of living in Brazil. Full freedom only came at the end of that time.[17] The British government had pressured the Brazilian government and Portugal to impose abolition. The infamous Valongo wharf in Rio de Janeiro, where hundreds of thousands of enslaved Africans had landed, was closed in 1831 and was only reopened in 1843 after it was remodeled to receive the grandiose landing of Princess of the Two Sicilies, Teresa Cristina of Bourbon, whom Emperor Dom Pedro II married.

When Baquaqua was in Pernambuco, the political situation was fragile. During the reign of Dom Pedro I and the Regency after 1831, the population of Recife had become dissatisfied with increasing social inequality and the domination of wealthy landowners. A liberal and republican movement led by Pedro Ivo da Silveira opposed the concentration of power in the hands of the Conservative Party, which was controlled by families owning large estates growing sugar that was produced by the enslaved population. The liberal group was called *praieiros* because they met in Rua da Praia in Recife. The newspaper, *Diário Novo*, became the main means of disseminating liberal ideas in Pernambuco. The Conservative government used the local police force to maintain its control and denounced the British Navy whose vessels had begun to blockade the coast to prevent the illegal landing of enslaved Africans, which was the reason that slave ships did not unload their enslaved passengers in Recife but chose instead to divert ships to secluded beaches north of Recife, as in the case of Baquaqua's ship.

Rather than improving conditions through the legal end of the slave trade from Africa, the enslaved population became more restive, which exacerbated an atmosphere of dissatisfaction and insecurity that ultimately led to revolt. When the Antonio Chinchorro da Gama became Conservative governor of Pernambuco in 1845, the population was already expressing its discontent, and the Liberals were organizing the opposition. The Praieiros movement spread throughout Pernambuco, with the greatest repercussions leading to clashes that took place in the cities of Olinda and Recife. Only with the support of central government forces were the Conservatives able to repress the rebel movement, restore stability, and align the Province of Pernambuco with the political guidelines of the Empire. Although he makes no mention of these facts in his autobiography, Baquaqua landed in Pernambuco amid this political turmoil of which he was probably unaware.[18] Armed conflict resulted in open revolt in 1848–49, especially in Recife and Olinda, although by then Baquaqua was no longer in Pernambuco but had attained his freedom in New York and was in Haiti, as discussed below.

The newly arrived persons from Africa, such as Baquaqua, formed a relatively small minority of the enslaved population in Pernambuco. In 1844, Pernambuco had 618,950 inhabitants, of whom 83,854 (13.5 percent) were enslaved and of whom about one-quarter were Africans (22,233, or 26.5 percent, including 13,596 males and 8,637 females). Of the people brought from Africa, it is unlikely that more than 10 percent came from the Bight of Benin and very few from inland locations like Djougou.[19] His identity as a Muslim from a commercial center lying on the route between the Sokoto Caliphate and Asante was lost at the coast where he would have been classified as "Mina," that is from the Costa da Mina. The term "Mina" was widely used in many parts of Brazil, including the coastal provinces and the interior of Brazil, such as Minas Gerais. As James Sweet states, "Mina represented a broad category, ethnic goal, imposed by Europeans on a relatively heterogeneous group of slaves from the so-called Mina coast."[20] More precisely, this was a coastal region east of the Castle of São Jorge da Mina to the Niger River delta. Baquaqua was identified as José da Costa da Mina, or simply José Mina. After all, like other trafficking identities (Angola, Benguela, Mozambique, Mandinga), Mina had become a cultural category used by Europeans to distinguish and conduct surveillance of groups of Africans, considering the region, language, religion, and marks that everyone carried on their bodies.

The Portuguese baker who purchased Baquaqua lived in a town within walking distance of Recife, but apparently not in Recife itself. Although it has not been possible to identify his master, the baking and sale of bread made from cassava flour was an important business in Recife, its suburbs and the various towns surrounding Recife, as it was elsewhere in Brazil, where wheat flour was limited or unavailable. Initially it was thought that the reference was perhaps to Olinda, located along the Capiberibe River a few kilometers north of Recife.[21] Baquaqua's reference to the tide in the river where he tried to drown, as well as the relative proximity to Recife ("Pernambuco"), suggests this possibility. However, neighboring towns, especially Várzea, Poço da Panela, or Monteiro were "*povoados*" (villages) located near the Capiberibe River that flows into the sea at Recife. Other cities in Pernambuco were inland or far from Recife, or both. Igarassu or Cabo de Santo Agostinho, near the Capibaribe river, are also possible. Baquaqua only states that the town was "not a great distance from Pernambuco," which it can be assumed means a distance that one could go by foot, although maybe walking for some time.

According to Baquaqua, the baker's family consisted of his wife, two children, and a "woman who was related to them."[22] He had four other slaves. Baquaqua stated that he tried to gain the trust of his master, seeking to do everything he desired. As an African recently arrived in Brazil, he was also called a "*boçal*"—that is, an ignorant person who did not understand his social functions and was not yet able to understand Portuguese. Baquaqua had already learned some Portuguese on board the ship, however. He was assigned work that newcomers normally performed. During his first months, he had to carry slabs of building stone that were "so heavy it took three men to raise them upon my head, which burden I was obliged to bear for a quarter of a mile at least, down to where the boat lay" because his master was constructing a house. His ease with language and skill with numbers came in handy. He later included in his *Autobiography* numbers from one to a thousand in Dendi. He was familiar with currency, and he came from a family involved in trade. Because his master ran a bakery, Baquaqua soon started selling bread and raising money for his master. In his words: "I soon improved in my knowledge of the Portuguese language whilst here, and was able very shortly to count a hundred. I was then sent out to sell bread for my master, first going round through the town, and then out into the country, and in the evening, after coming home again, sold in the market till nine at night. Being pretty honest and persevering, I generally sold out, but sometimes was not quite so successful, and then the lash was my portion."[23]

This first attempt to be a "good slave" and to raise the opinion of his master was interpreted as an action carried out within the logic of enslavement that Baquaqua knew from Africa. His family would have had slaves in Djougou. Baquaqua would have known how slaves were treated in commercial households, performing tasks from cleaning living quarters, feeding and tending goats and sheep who roamed freely in courtyards, cutting fodder, collecting firewood, carrying water, cooking, and tending children. In Muslim society, it was common practice to manumit a slave as a sign of benevolence during religious festivities or before the master's death.[24] The slaves who were normally freed were those in whom the master trusted the most and was most fond, obviously, because sometimes they performed services requiring trust. However, as Baquaqua found out to his chagrin, this strategy did not work in his case. Life in places like Recife, Olinda, and the surrounding villages was not easy.

A Muslim by origin, he was obliged to observe Christian rituals during family prayers twice a day. As the other enslaved, he had to kneel before Catholic saints, chant some words and prayers twice a day, which he "did not know the meaning of," and make the sign of the cross several times. According to Baquaqua, his master held a whip in his hand during the prayers, ready to relieve any diversion or drowsiness, which "mostly fell on the lot of the female slave, who would often fall asleep in spite of the images, crossings, and other like pieces of amusement."[25] It appears that at first, Baquaqua continued to adhere to his upbringing as a Muslim, although he does not mention praying, which would not have been easy under the circumstances, or dietary restrictions and avoidance of alcohol. By inference, however, it seems that he had learned a lesson from his own captivity after a night of drinking and initially did not drink. "My companions in slavery were not quite so steady as I was, being much given to drink, so that they were not so profitable to my master. I took advantage of this, to raise myself in his opinion, by being very attentive and obedient; but it was all the same, do what I would, I found I had a tyrant to serve, nothing seemed to satisfy him, so I took to drinking likewise, then we were all of a sort, bad master, bad slaves."[26] Baquaqua subsequently claimed that he was drinking whiskey, but it was probably *cachaça*, also known as *jeribita* at the time.

His acts of defiance became more and more pronounced and not only included drinking but escalated into extreme forms of resistance.

Things went on worse and worse, and I was very anxious to change masters, so I tried running away, but was soon caught, tied and carried back. I next tried what it would do for me by being unfaithful and indolent; so one day when I was sent out to sell bread as usual, I only sold a small quantity, and the money I took and spent for whiskey, which I drank pretty freely, and went home well drunk, when my master went to count the days [sic = day's] taking in my basket and discovering the state of things, I was beaten very severely. I told him he must not whip me any more, and got quite angry, for the thought came into my head that I would kill him, and afterwards destroy myself. I at last made up my mind to drown myself; I would rather die than live to be a slave. I then ran down to the river and threw myself in, but being seen by some persons who were in a boat, I was rescued from drowning. The tide was low at the time, or their efforts would most likely have been unavailing, and notwithstanding my predetermination, I thanked God that my life had been preserved, and that so wicked a deed had not been consummated.[27]

Resistance of enslaved people in Pernambuco was common. The attempt by the enslaved to take their own lives suggests a desperate form of resistance to avoid harsh punishment, control through constant surveillance, and the physical and psychological oppression of captivity. The enslaved were forced to deal with situations episodically. What was thought to be ideas of fair and unfair captivity could be violated or altered arbitrarily and without explanation. When punishments were unbearable, the enslaved thought about escape and alternatives such as death itself. Although there were different ways that the enslaved could commit suicide, the most common was drowning, exactly the way Baquaqua tried to take his own life.[28] His attempts at suicide only led to more severe punishment, as he reported: "After this sad attempt upon my life, I was taken to my master's house, who tied my hands behind me, and placed my feet together and whipped me most unmercifully, and beat me about the head and face with a heavy stick, then shook me by the neck, and struck my head against the door posts, which cut and bruised me about the temples, the scars from which savage treatment are visible at this time, and will remain so as long as I live."[29]

The treatment of urban slaves in Pernambuco, as elsewhere in Brazil, was varied. On the one hand, individuals could be given or even assigned considerable mobility, as when slaves moved independently between cities and the countryside involved in commerce or some trade, as with selling bread in Baquaqua's case.[30] The slaves who lived off earnings (*escravos ao ganho*) often did not live with their masters, although Baquaqua did in Pernambuco. It was common for them to rent attics and basements of houses and shops or share

small houses with partners or others. The dwellings were modest, accommo-
dating many people, but they were still better than the slave quarters and the
restricted controls on the coffee farms of the Southeast (Rio de Janeiro, São
Paulo, and Minas Gerais) or the sugar plantations of Pernambuco. It was
common for priests, military personnel, civil servants, and small merchants
to have at least a few enslaved workers.[31] Hence, urban owners of enslaved
people relied on slavery as much as the great landowners, coffee farmers, and
wealthy people of the cities.

On the other hand, the enslaved could be forced to the limit. Running
away was quite common, as reflected in regular advertisements in newspapers offering descriptions of fugitives and offering rewards for their return.[32]
In Baquaqua's case, there was no need for an advertisement because he was
quickly apprehended and returned to the baker. There are two individuals
who worked for bakers that were advertised in *Diário de Pernambuco* in 1845
that demonstrate the desire of individuals to flee slavery and the relative ease
of escape. On 2 October 1845, it was reported that:

> Disappeared from Rua da Cruz to the landfill of Boa-Vista, a black man
> named José, from the Costa Bua nation, with three stripes on his fore-
> head; he has three iron marks on his face; one on the forehead and one
> on each cheek, chest all scratched, with some broken teeth, regular
> stature, full of body, very similar in figure; he took striped cotton pants,
> short-sleeved cotton shirt; having known how to sell bread in the streets,
> with a large panacum, and a new braided cotton towel, with fringe, he fled
> on the 28th of the past, whoever takes him to the landfill of Boa Vista,
> bakery n° 66 will be rewarded.[33]

He left instead of selling bread in the streets, taking his large breadbasket, or
panicum, with him. The location of Rua da Cruz and the Boa Vista district
were along the Capiberibe River, while Rua Brejo da Cruz established his
location in the Ibura district of Recife, which is now on the other side of the
airport. A second advertisement was placed in *Diário de Pernambuco* on
29 October 1845: "On the 23rd of this month, a black man from the coast,
named José, a baker, ran away from his country, whose hands are thick with
calluses, regular stature, full of body, a little pot-bellied, not very black, cuts on
his face, and black marks of wounds, he has a cut middle toe on one of his feet;
it has been seen in plain view at Ponte-de-uchoa and in the apipucos; whoever
catches him, take him to Rua Direita, bakery n° 82, which will be rewarded."[34]
Ponte d'Uchoa was a bridge across the Capibaribe, which had been built after
the expulsion of the Dutch in 1654 by Antônio Borges Uchôa, who owned the

Engenho da Torre. Uchôa wanted the bridge to allow access to the other side of the river to Apipucos, where his relatives lived. The area was originally part of Engenho São Pantaleão do Monteiro and today is located in the Monteiro district. The bakery was located at 82 Rua Direita, which was near the Basilica da Penha in the heart of Recife across from the island behind the reef.

Baquaqua lived and worked in Pernambuco under conditions similar to those reported in *Diário de Pernambuco*. He also lived near a tidal river, as described in the *Autobiography*. As the advertisements suggest, the conditions of slavery for Baquaqua prompted his attempt to flee. Working for a baker was not an easy assignment. The two advertised fugitives who were being sought were described as having facial scarification, which Baquaqua appears not to have had, as revealed in the two images of him that have survived. The Wangarawa of Katsina with whom his mother's family was associated did not practice scarification, and fact that Baquaqua did not have any markings helps confirm the Wangarawa connection. By contrast, most people in Hausa society used scarification as a means of identifying origins, occupation, or status, such as the Agalawa, Tokarawa, and Kambarin Beriberi merchants who passed through Djougou. Moreover, as Feuille documented in elaborate drawings in 1919, virtually all local inhabitants at Djougou, Soubroukou, and other nearby villages displayed elaborate and intricate scarification patterns on their faces and bodies.[35]

Baquaqua was a young man, and his physical condition and age placed him among the most valued enslaved Africans, especially if we consider the context of illegal trafficking in the Atlantic. Moreover, his master could not easily sell him locally, although he tried, because he had attempted suicide and had tried to run away, which did not improve the way he was treated. Eventually, the difficulty of Baquaqua's adjustment to slavery convinced his master to sell him, probably at a loss, and that meant sale out of the province. The practice was common for newly arrived captives from Africa who repeatedly resisted "the horrors of the cruel system of slavery" in one way or another. Baquaqua's case was typical, and as he expressed it, "Yet ignorant and slave as I was, slavery I loathed, principally as I suppose, because I was its victim." After his attempt at suicide, the baker decided to get rid of him, which the baker had already thought about doing. As Baquaqua noted, "After all this cruelty he took me to the city, and sold me to a dealer, where he had taken me once before, but his friends advised him then not to part with me, as they considered it more to his advantage to keep me as I was a profitable slave." "The man to whom I was again sold was very cruel indeed. He bought two females at the time he bought me; one of them was a very beautiful girl, and he treated her with shocking barbarity. After a few weeks he shipped me off to Rio [de] Janeiro, where I remained two weeks previous to being again sold."[36] Thus began his second period of enslavement in Brazil, now in the imperial capital and the center of the coastal trade of Brazil that stretched from the Amazon River in the north to Rio Grande do Sul in the south (see figure 3.2).

The person who purchased him in Rio de Janeiro was Captain Clemente José da Costa, who was based in Rio Grande do Sul but was involved in the coastal trade and hence had business in Rio de Janeiro. As was common in such sales of difficult enslaved individuals, the sale was within Brazil and therefore not subject to the treaty with Britain banning the slave trade. Moreover, enslaved individuals who were considered difficult, as was Baquaqua's case, were often sold to Rio Grande do Sul, which had a reputation for acquiring recalcitrant individuals, in part because they were often less expensive than those who showed less resistance to enslavement.

Although the economy of Brazil was based on slave-produced sugar and coffee for export and the mining of gold, many individuals from Africa, such as Baquaqua, worked in the transport of people and goods on the streets and at the ports. Many others were employed in constructing houses, bridges, and public buildings, or in the manufacture of clothing, soap, hats, and other consumer items. Street vendors became a feature of the towns and cities selling prepared food, cakes, sugarcane broth and other things to eat. It was common to see young children with them, strapped on their backs or, when older, very close by their mothers. Of course, Baquaqua watched that scene many times and remembered being his mother's "dear boy," as the meaning of his nickname reveals.[37]

Baquaqua's new master, Clemente José da Costa, was captain of the *Lembrança*, a ship that plied the coastal waters of Brazil carrying goods between Rio de Janeiro, Rio Grande do Sul, and other places on the coast. From at least 1841, he was captain of the *Lembrança* on trips between Rio de Janeiro and Rio Grande, often with stops in Santos and Santa Catarina.[38] Because Costa now owned Baquaqua, he was now known as José da Costa and worked on the *Lembrança* as a steward. Baquaqua made two trips along the coast of Brazil to Santa Catarina Island as far south as Rio Grande do Sul.[39]

When Clemente José da Costa bought Baquaqua, he inserted his new purchase into a dynamic life of the maritime carrying trade in Brazil. His master traveled to different parts of Brazil. Baquaqua came to accompany him, as he describes in his memoirs. In his biography, he indicated that he started to work as a cook, which allowed him access to the entire crew. It was not uncommon for male Africans to be employed as cooks, both in commercial and

FIGURE 3.2 Rio de Janeiro, as taken in 1850 by F. Pustkov, *Uma cidade em questão I Grandjean de Montígny e o Rio de Janeiro* (Rio de Janeiro: PUC: FUNARTE: Fundação Roberto Marinho, 1979).

domestic activities. In Rio de Janeiro newspapers, advertisements for Africans doing domestic work as cooks were frequent. Besides homes of the wealthy, these enslaved people could be employed in hotels, hospitals, barracks, prisons, and ships, and could receive wages.[40] There was still the possibility of working as a cook on boats and ships, as was the case with Baquaqua. He was a crew member, a slave who served his master directly, in this case the vessel's captain. It is unlikely that Baquaqua had any distinction or prestige relative to other slaves who worked on the crew. However, the fact that he belonged to the ship's captain could allow him to obtain more autonomy or even the possibility of obtaining his freedom.

Baquaqua was young and still inexperienced, but he lived the life of a sailor, which consisted of a daily work regime that required interaction with free, freed, and enslaved workers. In general, the work involved loading and

unloading products in a specific port, navigation, and maritime transport of
these products. Undoubtedly, the job required some specific knowledge. The
life on board required the ability to work collectively, although there were disputes and tensions between crew members.[41] For example, Baquaqua gave a
brief description of his life on the vessel where he was employed:

> I did not at first like my situation; but as I got acquainted with the crew
> and the rest of the slaves, I got along pretty well. In a short time I was pro-
> moted to the office of under-steward. The steward provided for the table,
> and I carried the provisions to the cook and waited at table; being pretty
> smart, they gave me plenty to do. A short time after, the captain and stew-
> ard disagreed, and he gave up his stewardship, when the keys of his office
> were entrusted to me. I did all in my power to please my master, the cap-
> tain, and he in return placed confidence in me.[42]

According to Baquaqua, he assisted the chamberlain and the cook, although
at times he claimed a certain closeness to his master, perhaps because of what
he thought to be his "cleverness" and his ability to perform many tasks.
Because of his promptness, he soon became the steward, taking on a strategic
role in the crew as a whole. In his own words, he was still exposed to the violence of the slave world, as he had been in Pernambuco. His master's wife was
someone capable of purposely provoking him and the others who worked on
board, as he noted and to which he was subsequently exposed when he tried
to jump ship in New York City.

> The captain's lady was anything but a good woman; she had a most
> wretched temper. The captain had carried her off from St. Catharine's
> [Santa Catarina], just as she was on the point of getting married, and I
> believe was never married to her. She often got me into disgrace with my
> master, and then a whipping was sure to follow. She would at one time
> do all she could to get me a flogging, and at other times she would inter-
> fere and prevent it, just as she was in the humor. She was a strange com-
> pound of humanity and brutality. She always went to sea with the
> captain.[43]

His account is probably distorted in that the claim that Costa apparently kidnapped her in Santa Catarina and that they were not married both seem
unlikely.

Rio de Janeiro had a large African population. In its streets Africans were
everywhere. Their work moved commercial activities and daily life from the

port to the most distant regions. According to Mary Karasch, many enslaved Africans sat in front of houses and shops to sing about their African lives and traditions. They recalled their past freedom on the African continent. Despite living in Brazil for a long time, these Africans did not forget the tastes and sounds of their land. Many wished to return to Africa one day, even if it happened only in their beliefs of an afterlife.[44] Carlos Eugênio Soares has discussed the different forms of sociability around the *Zungú*—that is, a place to have coffee and rest—in Rio de Janeiro, to which Baquaqua would have been exposed.[45] Although Baquaqua worked on board a ship, he witnessed the scenes of Rio slavery.

Karasch has estimated that approximately 950,000 Africans landed in Rio de Janeiro, while João Alípio Goulart has estimated that 570,000 Africans lived in the city in the early nineteenth century. Manolo Florentino has suggested that approximately 470,000 Africans lived there by mid-century.[46] Africans of Bantu origin, mainly from Angola and southeast Africa, dominated Rio de Janeiro demographically. There was still a sizable population from West Africa, especially those identified as Mina—that is, people from the Bight of Benin and the coast west of the Volta in what is now Ghana—and those called Nago, which included people who spoke Yoruba, whether or not it was their first language. There were many Muslims, including Hausa, and it would not have been difficult for Baquaqua to come in contact. He would have recognized anyone who spoke Hausa and would have greeted them accordingly. The presence of a discernable Muslim population in Rio de Janeiro came to the attention of 'Abd al-Rahman al-Baghdadi, an imam from Baghdad, who was accompanying several ships from the Ottoman Empire and was unexpectedly in Rio in 1865 when they had to arrange repairs. They were passing from the Mediterranean around Africa on the way to the Indian Ocean. A delegation of local Muslims came on board to greet al-Baghdadi, who at first did not believe that they were Muslims because of a communication problem. He did not understand Portuguese, and they did not speak Arabic. In the end, al-Baghdadi remained in Brazil for some time and wrote a report on his interaction with Muslims not only in Rio but elsewhere in Brazil. His account documents the Muslim community admittedly two decades after Baquaqua was there but nonetheless establishes the likelihood that Baquaqua would have encountered the community.[47] He was familiar with the streets of the Paço neighborhood and the original waterfront before the development of Valongo as the wharf, warehouses, and cemetery of arriving Africans. When Baquaqua was there, the wharf was virtually deserted because Brazil officially abolished the slave trade in 1831.[48]

Although a small minority, those who dominated the commerce of the streets of the city came from the Bight of Benin, and that would have included almost everyone who was Muslim, many of whom would have known Yoruba and some Hausa.[49] Moreover, Mina stood out among those who were arrested and had to appear in court. According to Thomas Holloway, Mina comprised 15.7 percent of Africans arrested by the police in 1850.[50] This preponderance of those tracing origins to the Bight of Benin extended to the Africans who negotiated their manumission. According to Manolo Florentino, 45 percent of slaves who achieved emancipation in the city of Rio de Janeiro were Mina.[51] Sheila Faria has determined that 52 percent were men and 48 percent were women. For the female *liberatos*, 62 percent of those achieving freedom paid for their manumission, which suggests that they had access to the market.[52] Like Baquaqua's mother in Katsina, women who were identified as Mina became street vendors and small shopkeepers in the capital of the Brazilian Empire.

In the days when Baquaqua got to know the city of Rio de Janeiro, the main urban reference was the Church of Candelária, due to its unmistakable position in the city, as well as the building's grandeur. Almost in front of the Church was the Customs building, which, naturally, was very close to the port to facilitate the movement of people and goods that arrived and left through the port and passed through customs control. Considering that the place for contracting the services of the *Lembrança* was located at 20 Rua São Pedro, Baquaqua came to know the main administrative and commercial center of the city. The office for the *Lembrança* was between Alfandega and the Candelária Cathedral on Rua Direita, which intersected with Rua São Pedro (figure 3.3).

A walk along Rua Direita passed African women selling various food and petty goods on the streets. The area also included the Antiga Igreja da Sé, as well as the Paço Imperial, the building where the city's public administration had operated since colonial times. In the opposite direction, Rua São Pedro went toward Porto, crossing Rua das Violas near the imposing structure of the Monastery of São Bento, which was located on one of the few places that had not been leveled and, hence, was one of the highest points preserved in the city. Prainha, Praia do Peixe was another concentration of enslaved and freed workers who contributed to the daily life of the port. By the time Baquaqua was in Rio, the Mercado do Valongo was no longer an active port receiving enslaved Africans. As in Pernambuco, slave traders unloaded their captives at isolated coastal locations. Instead, the Valongo port was being

FIGURE 3.3 *Lembrança's* office was in a street that no longer exists, Sao Pedro Street, which was at the end of Rua Direita, depicted here, from J. M. Rugendas, *Viagem Pitoresca através do Brasil* (Belo Horizonte: Itatiaia, 1986). The church is Antiga Sé do Rio de Janeiro.

renovated in preparation for the arrival of the fiancé of the emperor and had been renamed Cais da Imperatriz (from 1844). However, the sheds where Africans were deposited were still present, and the cemetery of the Blacks was still prominent in the urban scene of that part of the city. Moreover, African-based religious activities were on display everywhere. Urban expansion was concentrated in the parishes of Santa Rita and Santana along the coast of the Recôncavo da Guanabara. The area was located between the hills of Conceição and Livramento, with the Rua do Valongo marking the site of the former slave market that had dictated how the city expanded. The urban landscape of Rio de Janeiro was marked by slavery and the Atlantic traffic. The brigantines, patachos, and galleys anchored in the middle of the bay while smaller boats moved goods to and from the piers and also connected with other parts of the coast and the most distant regions of the Recôncavo da Guanabara. This was a part of the city that Baquaqua knew well. It was common for slaves who belonged to or were put to work by such merchants to walk around the city, so they knew the streets and the main areas of the city.

The owner of the *Lembrança*, who is not mentioned in the *Autobiography*, was Antonio José da Rocha Pereira of Rio de Janeiro.[53] He was born in Porto, Portugal, and came to Brazil at seventeen years of age. According to his entry in the Junta Real do Comércio, he was a merchant who lived on Rua Direita, a street parallel to the waterfront in the center of the city and the location of bustling commerce where people and goods from different parts of the Atlantic world circulated.[54] A postmortem inventory was conducted in 1871 at the request of his wife, Maria Roza Leite Pereira,[55] and their son, José Maria Fernandes. By the time of his death, Rocha Pereira had emancipated three of his slaves who had reached fifty years of age (Januario Angola, Fernando Mina, and Felicidade Mina). It should be noted that two of those emancipated were identified as Mina, as Baquaqua would have been. Rocha Pereira left the remainder of his slaves, whose names are not specified, to his three daughters. According to the *Almanack Laemmentz*, Rocha Pereira was from a family of merchants that included João Antônio da Rocha Pereira, who owned a dry goods and grocery warehouse and store at 20 Rua São Pedro, across from Igreja da Candelaria, the spectacular cathedral in the heart of the city, and within easy walking distance of Rua Direita where José da Rocha Pereira had his office. He was registered with the Junta Real do Comércio.[56]

According to the national registry of coastal and long-distance vessels, in the year 1847, Antônio José da Pereira Rocha was the owner of five vessels, including the *Lembrança*, of which Clemente José da Costa was employed as captain. In January and February 1846, the *Jornal Diário do Rio de Janeiro* noted three ships owned by da Rocha Pereira, the details for which are cited in table 3.1. Rocha Pereira traded in "diverse goods" operating to Port Alegre in Rio Grande do Sul, Santos in São Paulo, and Campos de Goytacazes, north of Rio de Janeiro.

Many people were employed in his business. Baquaqua referred to other members of the crew on the *Lembrança* besides his two fellow slaves, although there are no details on who the rest of the crew was. Because the *Lembrança* was the largest of Rocha Pereira's ships, it could make more extensive trips, like going to New York. The crew had to be trained depending on the size of the ship. As is clear, the work associated with slavery involved the coexistence of free, freed, and enslaved sailors.

Baquaqua's owner handled a significant amount of business for Rocha Pereira. Baquaqua's master was the skipper of the *Lembrança* at least since 1841. The ship traveled regularly between Rio de Janeiro and Rio Grande. It often

TABLE 3.1 Antonio José da Rocha Pereira's ships leaving Rio de Janeiro (January/February 1846)

Ships	Tonnage	Destination	Goods	Date
Beleza do Sul	155	Porto Alegre	Cargo from the north	9 January 1846
Marques de Pombal	168	Santos	Many goods	15 January 1846
Sumaca Leopoldina	92	Campos	Many goods	7 February 1846

Source: Biblioteca Nacional, *Diário do Rio de Janeiro,* Janeiro/Fevereiro, 1846.

TABLE 3.2 Antonio José da Rocha Pereira's embarkations (1847)

Name	Type of Ship	Tonnage
Lembrança	Barque	232
Animo	Brig	192
Marques de Pombal	Brig	161
Conde de Thomar	Patacho	137
Beleza do Sul	Patacho	155

Source: Almanak Laemmert, 1847, 352–357.

stopped in Santos and Santa Catarina.[57] According to the *Almanak Laemmert,* Rocha Pereira owned five vessels in 1847 (table 3.2), including the *Lembrança,* which was the largest ship at 232 tons. It had three masts, of which all but the one at the stern were rigged with square sails. He also owned two brigs, the *Animo* and the *Marques de Pombal,* two masts that were both square-rigged of 192 and 161 tons, respectively, and two pataco, the *Conde de Thomar* and the *Beleza do Sul,* 137 and 155 tons, respectively. There were many cases of captains who managed to acquire a vessel or become partners in the carrying trade or even shareholders in the trans-Atlantic slave trade. The captains of vessels were the representatives of the owner, and they had the authority to command their ships and their respective crews. They were primarily responsible for navigation and administration of each trip.[58] It was possible for maritime captains to acquire a vessel and, in addition to being captain, become owners or partners in the carrying business or even invest in the Atlantic slave trade.

Based on his earnings, Costa was able to accumulate funds sufficient for him to acquire the schooner *Oliveira,* which he bought from Monoel Pereira Jardim, attorney for Lourenço Gomes de Oliveira. The schooner, which was a sailing ship with two or more masts, typically with the foremast smaller than the mainmast, and having gaff-rigged lower masts, was valued at "Dois

TABLE 3.3 Expenses of voyages between Rio de Janeiro and
Rio Grande do Sul, 1846

Expenses	*Amount (réis)*
Payment of captain by voyage	300$000
Payment of Foreman	150$000
Payment of eight sailors	560$000
Payment of four cabin boys	200$000
Purchase of goods by captain	100$000
Purchase of goods by foreman	60$000
Food for twelve people	3$120
Firewood, salt and water to voyage	100$000
Dispatch and Anchorage	200$000
Total	1:673$120

Note: Each 1000 réis is also referred to as "milréis." The exchange rate was 8,000 réis/8 milréis equaled to one pound sterling.

Sources: Almanak Laemmertz 1846, 45; Conrad, "The Contraband Slave Trade to Brazil, 1831–1845," 637.

contos de Réis" (2:000$000 réis, or two million réis), an impressive amount in nineteenth-century Brazil.[59] Between 1848 and 1859, Costa was listed as a "maritime captain" among the people qualified to vote in the city of Rio Grande. He reported that four of his slaves died during that period, therefore after the period when Baquaqua escaped in New York. In 1866, Costa freed Teresa, a seven-month-old, who was the daughter of Rufina, his slave.[60] He was almost certainly the father. He wanted the child baptized as if born from a free womb, a type of manumission that was common in Brazil.[61] Despite the loss of Baquaqua in New York City, Costa nonetheless apparently prospered as a captain and merchant after 1847. As listed in the costs of shipping goods from Rio de Janeiro to Rio Grande do Sul (table 3.3), a captain could earn 300$000, or 300,000 réis per voyage, not including any goods that the captain might buy and sell on his own account.

The city of São Pedro de Rio Grande (figure 3.4), usually referred to as Rio Grande, was the most important port in southern Brazil, trading merchandise such as jerk meat that relied on cattle ranching and whale oil brought in by whaling ships sailing the south Atlantic that provided fuel for street lighting. And there was a transit trade with the Rio de la Plata. The connections with different places in the Atlantic world included people from many parts of the Atlantic world, as well as goods and boats with different origins. As noted in the *Almanack Laemmertz,* ships active on these routes usually carried loads

FIGURE 3.4 Port of Rio Grande do Sul in Pedro Simon, *O Rio Grande do Sul Em 1852—Aquarelas de Herrmann Rudolf Wendroth* (Porto Alegre: Governo do Estado, 1980s).

between 150 and 200 tons (the *Lembrança* carried 200 tons). The vessels left from Rio de Janeiro for Rio Grande do Sul, often stopping to deliver goods and buy cassava flour in Santa Catarina. The cost of such a trip was around 1: 637$120 réis, (1,637,120 réis) and took about three months to be completed, as recorded in table 3.1, which also includes payments for several crew members and different provisions. It is possible that, even as a slave, Baquaqua was remunerated. Surely Baquaqua knew Rio Grande, having spent some of his time there. In any case, he was a person in transit, often on board a ship moving between different ports, as he himself observed,

> Our first voyage was to Rio Grande; the voyage itself was pleasant enough had I not suffered with sea sickness. The harbor at Rio Grande is rather shallow, and on entering we stuck the ground, as it happened at low water, and we had great difficulty in getting her to float again. We finally succeeded, and exchanged our cargo for dried meat. We then went to Rio Janeiro and soon succeeded in disposing of the cargo. We then

steered for St. Catharines to obtain Farina, a kind of breadstuff used mostly by the slaves. From thence, returned to Rio Grande and exchange our cargo for whale oil and put out again to sea, and stood for Rio Janeiro.[62]

According to Naomi Kuniochi, Rio Grande was the third busiest port in Brazil, mostly receiving vessels from Rio de Janeiro.[63] Rio Grande established connections with many places in the Atlantic world, receiving people, goods and vessels from different origins. Rio Grande was a strategic port for trading goods from southern Brazil, also attracting Brazilian traders interested links with Rio Plate. Baquaqua took part in those connections as a slave at Captain Clemente José da Costa's service. Usually, vessels were capable of carrying about 150 or 200 tons (the *Lembrança* carried 200 tons). Ships sailed from Rio de Janeiro to Rio Grande do Sul. They often stopped to load supplies or deliver goods in Santa Catarina. Each voyage cost 1:637,120 réis (1:637$120) and took about three months to be concluded.

Rio Grande also stood out for being the destination of Africans who were considered rebels by their masters. According to Nicolau Dreys, "[W]hen a black man from other provinces in Brazil manifested some vicious disposition, Rio Grande was the destiny that was inflicted as punishment."[64] Baquaqua's behavior in Pernambuco characterized this description, since his escape and suicide attempts, alcohol consumption, and the punishments he suffered while still in Pernambuco make it appear that the sale to Clemente José da Costa was not to change completely. This idea that Rio Grande was a place for difficult slaves satisfied the growing demand for enslaved workers in a city that was expanding steadily.

The economy of the province of Rio Grande do Sul was based on the production of beef jerky, a staple of enslaved food throughout Brazil. The port city of São Pedro de Rio Grande, usually simply referred to as Rio Grande, was at the mouth of Lagoa dos Patos, the lagoon that extends from Rio Grande some 172 km to Porto Alegre, the capital of the province since 1807, where the Riu Jacui enters the lagoon. The workers who produced the beef jerky were mostly enslaved, and their output was exported from Rio Grande to all parts of Brazil. In the first two decades of the nineteenth century, the annual number of slaves that landed at the port of Rio Grande increased from approximately 1,000 Africans (1802) to 1,466 (1817). In 1819, enslaved workers already represented 31 percent of the total population. By the 1840s, when Baquaqua was in Rio Grande, the region already had 40,000 enslaved workers and an identifiable Muslim population.[65]

Baquaqua noted that on his first journey to Rio Grande, "the voyage itself was pleasant enough had I not suffered with sea sickness." The problem was that "the harbor at Rio Grande is rather shallow, and on entering we struck the ground, as it happened at low water, and we had great difficulty in getting her to float again. We finally succeeded, and exchanged our cargo for dried meat, which was taken to Rio Janeiro and soon succeeded in disposing of the cargo."[66] The *Lembrança* then went to Santa Catarina to obtain *farina*, which Baquaqua described as "a kind of breadstuff used mostly by the slaves," which was taken to Rio Grande, where Costa purchased whale oil and "put out again to sea, and stood for Rio Janeiro."[67] The reference to *farina* referred to cassava flour, which was the staple ingredient for the bread that Baquaqua first came to know in Pernambuco when he was enslaved to the baker. Whale oil was used especially as fuel to light street lanterns and the homes of the wealthy.

Baquaqua described another trip between Rio de Janeiro and Rio Grande via Santa Catarina. The voyage started in Rio de Janeiro, where the owner of the *Lembrança* was from. The information presented here points to a possible establishment of Clemente José da Costa, owner of Baquaqua, in Rio Grande. Probably interested in the trade routes of southern Brazil, the owner of the *Lembrança* sought out a captain from southern Brazil to facilitate business access in that region. After working for a long time on those commercial routes, it is possible that the captain chose the square of Rio Grande to establish himself. As noted, Baquaqua described the port of Rio Grande as a place with shallow water where the boats had difficulty in setting sail and docking. Boats were frequently stuck in that port.

While Baquaqua was at Rio de Janeiro one time, he went ashore with his master and one of the men who rowed a small boat from the ship into the harbor. On dry land, Baquaqua drank more than usual. Even though he was already drunk, when he saw his master returning, he went to the place where the boat was moored. Due to his condition, he lost his balance and fell into the sea.[68] He was easily rescued, and after Costa admonished him, nothing else exceptional happened to him that day.[69] However, this scene demonstrates that Baquaqua, despite the harsh treatment he continued to receive, had adjusted to his enslavement. Another time, when he was in Rio de Janeiro, "it was necessary to go to the beach with my master" and again he drank too much.[70]

It is not known when Baquaqua developed a plan to escape. Among the many escapes recorded in Rio de Janeiro, we highlight those carried out by Africans who worked as sailors on the boats that arrived and departed from the port. As the case of Frederico Tapá demonstrates, it was possible to escape by sea. Frederico's name Tapá indicates that he was from Nupe, and almost certainly Muslim. He was a sailor and cook who worked the route between Rio de Janeiro and Rio Grande and escaped.[71] On 26 February 1843, the *Jornal do Comércio* reported that a boy named José, identified as Congo, aged thirteen years old, with an inky, flat nose, a thick pout, and wearing a striped shirt and pants, fled a ship that was also named *Lembrança* and possibly was the same ship under Captain Costa.[72] These two incidents occurred just before the arrival of Baquaqua in Rio de Janeiro. The young José Congo is probably not to be identified with José da Rocha who, together with Baquaqua, escaped in New York in 1847, because Baquaqua's shipmate was described as an older man. Nonetheless, it is possible that Baquaqua knew about the episode. These enslaved Africans who worked on board ships, at least, never lost interest in freedom. Many Africans sang about freedom and lamented their condition outside the shops and houses in Rio de Janeiro. Baquaqua certainly did, as he proclaimed, "I was but a slave, and I felt myself to be one without hope or prospects of freedom, without friends or liberty. I had no hopes in this world and knew nothing of the next; all was gloom, all was fear. The present and the future were as one, no dividing mark, all Toil! Toil!! Cruelty! Cruelty!! No end but death to all my woes."[73] It is highly likely that Baquaqua had dreams of freedom due to his working conditions on board the ship. Many individuals tried to escape, and with the possibilities of freedom worked the crews of different vessels that circulated in the Atlantic world.[74] The constant contact with different places, people, and realities broadened their horizons, interests, and perspectives. This mobility amplified the desire for freedom cultivated by Baquaqua. Baquaqua was young but came from a family that maintained contact with the outside world through its Islamic faith and commerce. He lived for only a short time in captivity and forged an identity as a young African focused on his passage through slavery in Brazil relatively quickly.

After one journey to Rio Grande, he remained in Rio de Janeiro "nearly a month." While there, he admitted that he had taken to drink:

> Whilst there an incident occurred, which I will relate in illustration of the slave system. One day it was necessary for me to go ashore with my master as one of the oarsmen, and whilst there I drank pretty freely of wine, and seeing my master about returning to the boat I made for where it lay, and being rather confused with drink as well as flurried at seeing my master, I fell into the water, but it being only shallow, I suffered nothing

further than a good ducking for my drunkenness. I was easily got out. Whilst rowing my master, my head swam very much from the effects of the liquor I had drank, and consequently did not pull very steadily, when my master seeing the plight I was in asked me what was the matter, I said "nothing sir;" he said again, "have you been drinking?" I answered no sir! So that by being ill used I learned to drink, and from that I learned to tell lies, and no doubt should have gone on step by step from bad to worse, until nothing would have been wicked enough for me to have done, and all this through the grace of God, I was led to abandon my evil ways.[75]

Again, it was almost certainly not wine that he was drinking, but cachaca. Shortly after that, however, his luck seemed to change.

After the cargo was unloaded, "an English merchant having a quantity of coffee for shipment to New York, my master was engaged for the purpose, and it was arranged, after some time that I should accompany him, together with several others to serve on ship board."[76] The shipment of coffee was imported by J. L. Phipps and Co., of New York. On 17 April 1847, the *Jornal do Commércio* in Rio de Janeiro advertised "excellent rooms" on the *Lembrança*: "Interested passengers should obtain information from Rua Direita, 93 / 1°," which was then the main street in the city, later known as Rua Primeiro de Março. On 8 September 1847, the Brazilian consul general in New York, Luiz Henrique Ferreira de Aguiar, wrote to the minister of foreign affairs, Saturnino de Souza e Oliveira: "Having noted in one of the newspapers of that Court the mention made that coffee imported into this country on Brazilian ships would be subject to the 20% duty, I would like to inform you that Brazilian ships and their cargoes enjoy the same privileges in the Union as American ships, with coffee being admitted free of rights as practiced with the shipments of the same article here arrived at the national ships 'Lembrança' and 'Albina'"[77] On 24 April 1847, the *Lembrança* set sail from Rio de Janeiro to New York, with a load of coffee and a few passengers, including an Englishman who, as remembered later in the autobiography, encouraged Baquaqua to think about his freedom.[78] Besides Baquaqua, there were two other slaves on the *Lembrança*: Maria da Costa, who, as her name suggests, also belonged to Captain Costa, and José da Rocha, who belonged to Costa's partner, Antonio José da Rocha Pereira. Maria helped Costa's wife, who accompanied him on his travels, and at the time had just become a mother. On 27 June 1847, the ship arrived in New York.[79]

CHAPTER FOUR

New York and Freedom

The voyage of the *Lembrança* from Rio de Janeiro to New York took a consignment of coffee for Phipps and Brothers, a British firm active in the Brazil trade.
Its agent, Jacob Berrinio, occupied the "excelentes comodos" (excellent accommodations) that the ship had advertised.[1] The ship arrived in the East River of
New York on 27 June 1847 and docked at the foot of Roosevelt Street, opposite
Brooklyn Heights (figure 4.1). Berrinio was on board when it returned to Brazil
on 22 October with a load of pine, softwood lumber that was in demand for
construction in Brazil, and he was certainly ready to receive another shipment
of coffee, thereby participating in the growth in coffee production, which also
increased the demand for enslaved labor in the interior of Brazil.[2]

Phipps and Brothers was the second most important coffee importing
company in New York, and hence in the United States. Despite his business
in distributing slave-grown coffee, Berrinio was complicit in the escape of
Baquaqua and his crew mate, José da Rocha, who belonged to Costa's partner, Antonio José da Rocha Pereira, but who was known later as David. Their
enslaved female companion, Maria da Costa, had the option to escape, too,
but decided not to do so. Maria helped Costa's wife, at the time a new mother,
who accompanied her husband on his voyage to New York, as she had on
other journeys. Perhaps Maria had relatives and children in Brazil whom she
was reluctant to abandon, while the two men had no such attachments or at
least were willing sever them.

The division between the two men and Maria reveals the difficult decisions facing the enslaved who had to survive in a world of subordination and
lack of access to legal and professional support. It may be that Maria had kin
back in Brazil whom she could not abandon. She may have been intimidated
since the conditions of slavery in Brazil relied on fear. Perhaps she was even
promised better treatment if she did not pursue freedom. What we can discern from the experiences of Baquaqua and his companion David is that they
stumbled upon an antislavery network in North America that was intricately
involved in the political confrontation that would lead to the American Civil
War. At the time, the war between United States and Mexico (1846–48) had
heightened the friction over the slavery issue, since the annexation of Texas in
December 1845 and the "Mexican Cession" (California, Nevada, New Mexico,

FIGURE 4.1 New York City: view of the East River in 1852, in "The Renascence of City Hall; Commemorative Presentation Rededication of City Hall," The City of New York, 12 July 1956, 84. The Lembrança docked at the foot of Roosevelt Street, opposite Brooklyn Heights.

and Utah) in 1848 strengthened the proslavery lobby but also invigorated the antislavery forces in the northern states that would benefit Baquaqua. His experiences after landing in New York City thrust him into the abolition movement in a way that those taken off slave ships and defined as Liberated Africans also participated as missionaries, teachers, and traders.

This arrival in New York made Baquaqua "free"—the first word he said that he learned in English. He repeats this moment twice in his autobiography. It clearly had deep emotional meaning. Without explicitly saying so, Baquaqua thought his enslavement was unjust, probably because he was a free-born Muslim. He stated in his *Autobiography*, or at least his editor Samuel Moore attributed as much to him, that the nature of slavery as an institution made few distinctions in terms of who was the enslaver and who was the slave. Before Captain Costa purchased him in Rio de Janeiro, Baquaqua reports,

> There was a colored man there who wanted to buy me, but for some reason or other he did not complete the purchase. I merely mention this fact to illustrate that slaveholding is generated in power, and any one having the means of buying his fellow creature with the paltry dross, can become a slave owner, no matter his color, his creed or country, and that the colored man would as soon enslave his fellow man as the white man, had he the power.[3]

This perceptive observation might well have been lost on many people with whom Baquaqua came in contact, but he made it clear in his published autobiography.

Without knowing it, when the ship arrived in New York in late June 1847,[4] Baquaqua entered the next phase of his remarkable life, a world of abolitionist struggle in North America. The opportunity to achieve his freedom presented itself because slavery had been abolished in New York State for decades. New York City, with its sizable population of African descent, had become a stronghold of the abolitionist movement in the northern states. Its vibrant community of free people of African descent and several organizations that were opposed to slavery provided the context that enabled Baquaqua to escape, something he had unsuccessfully attempted in Brazil. The organization that came to his rescue was the New York Vigilance Society, one of many such associations in northern cities that had opposed slavery and assisted individuals in their flights from bondage since the late 1830s.[5] The Vigilance Society was closely connected to the *National Anti-Slavery Standard*. Despite doctrinal disputes among abolitionists, there was considerable overlap among the different groups, which was particularly relevant in helping Baquaqua and David achieve their freedom. Maria chose to remain in slavery and did not attempt to seek her freedom, apparently a result of considerable intimidation and tighter surveillance of her movements.

The *Lembrança* docked at the foot of Roosevelt Street, on the East River, where the west tower of the Brooklyn Bridge is now anchored, whereupon local stevedores boarded the ship and saw Baquaqua and David unloading coffee. As was the practice at the time, members of the Vigilance Society were informed and approached the *Lembrança*, as they did all foreign ships, to see if there were any enslaved persons on board. Thus was initiated a legal tug-of-war over the fate of Baquaqua and José da Rocha. According to Don Papson and Tom Calarco,[6] African American abolitionist William P. Powell, who operated the Colored Sailor's Home at 61 Cherry Street, was told of those on board the *Lembrança*.[7] Powell immediately went on board and saw two able-bodied Africans hoisting bags of coffee up from the hold. To avoid suspicion, he examined the vessel's rigging, windlass, and pumps. One of the Africans came up to him, and Powell asked him in Portuguese if he was a slave. When Powell learned that he was and that the other man was, too, and that there was also an enslaved woman on board, he informed the man that according to New York law they were not slaves. He told him to go back to work, to say nothing, and before sunset they would be free.[8] Powell, "himself a coloured man, and once a sailor," was therefore an important figure in Baquaqua's life, not only because of his initial contact on board the *Lembrança* but because of the likely subsequent connection between Baquaqua and Powell in England.[9]

Powell had opened the Colored Sailor's Home because African Americans were not welcome in other establishments that catered to sailors in New York City. As Eric Foner has argued, Powell was long forgotten in US history, just as Baquaqua has been overlooked. Born in New York City, Powell was a committed abolitionist who had moved to New York from New Bedford, Massachusetts, in late 1837. His stint as a seaman on whaling expeditions had exposed him to the discrimination that sailors of African origin, including himself, had experienced. When he moved to New York City in 1839, he opened a boarding house, initially on John Street, in association with the American Seaman's Friend Society, a missionary organization dedicated to temperance. Thereafter Powell was a noted champion of the rights of African American sailors, and by extension any sailors of African background who came into New York harbor. He was a founder of the Manhattan Anti-Slavery Society in 1840, serving as its secretary, and was also involved in forming the Vigilance Society. He wrote numerous articles on slavery, petitioned Congress, and sent memorials to legislatures in the northern states. Powell covered most of the expenses of the boarding house through the charges for staying there, as well as subsidies from the Seaman's Friend Society, and he also invested his own money in maintaining the establishment. He never turned sailors away if they could not afford the cost of accommodation, and at mealtime he deliberately promoted abolitionist ideas as well as temperance. He maintained a library for his boarders, as well (figure 4.2).[10]

Powell moved the Sailor's Home to Pearl Street and hence closer to the docks on the East River in 1849, after which he was able to accommodate seventy sailors at a time. Hence, his involvement in Baquaqua's struggle for freedom is not surprising. At the time, it was recognized that Powell

has done much for this class of people, and entertains at his house probably one-fourth of all who come into this port. We know that he is indefatigable in befriending these men, in his efforts to surround them with the best influences, and to protect them from the thousand temptations and evil courses to which sailors are peculiarly exposed. No one, better than he, knows their necessities, their difficulties, and their merits; and though he has never made any appeal for help in his noble effort in behalf of seamen, we know that he has spent a considerable sum of money in rendering them assistance, and in so much has been successful, notwith-

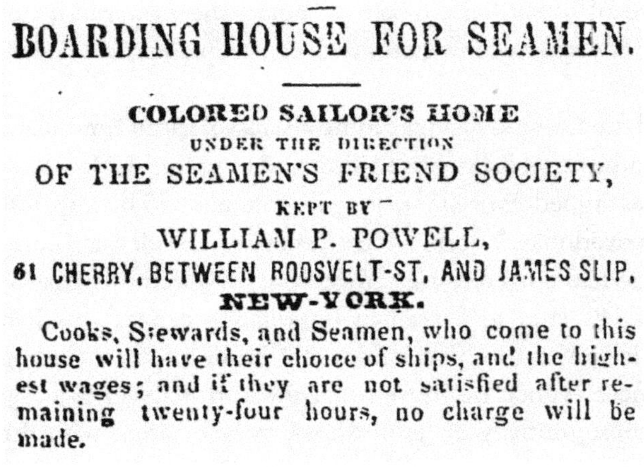

BOARDING HOUSE FOR SEAMEN.

——

COLORED SAILOR'S HOME
UNDER THE DIRECTION
OF THE SEAMEN'S FRIEND SOCIETY,
KEPT BY
WILLIAM P. POWELL,
61 CHERRY, BETWEEN ROOSVELT-ST, AND JAMES SLIP,
NEW-YORK.

Cooks, Stewards, and Seamen, who come to this
house will have their choice of ships, and the highest wages; and if they are not satisfied after remaining twenty-four hours, no charge will be
made.

FIGURE 4.2
William P. Powell,
Boarding House for
Seamen, Organization
of Black Maritime
Graduates.

standing his clients are denied the right of ever aspiring beyond the fore-
castle or galley, and are even virtually deprived of the poor privilege of
shipping for these in vessels bound to all southern ports of this country.
His Home is peculiarly deserving of the attention and assistance of the
friends of—next to the slaves,—the most deserving and most abused
class of our countrymen, and we trust that it may receive it. That Mr. *Powell* perfectly understands, as well as is deeply interested in the work he has
undertaken, our readers will want no better evidence than the series of
very able articles by him, which we published some time since, and which
attracted considerable attention from those who value statistics and other
information upon this subject. We know no other man so conversant with
it, or so able to turn his knowledge to practical account.[11]

Other members of the Vigilance Society who were involved in supporting
Baquaqua's bid for freedom were associated with the American Anti-Slavery
Society, which succeeded the Manhattan Anti-Slavery Society in 1835, with
David Ruggles as secretary. Lydia Maria Child and David Lee Child founded
its newspaper, the weekly *National Anti-Slavery Standard*,[12] in June 1840. In
1843 Sydney Howard Gay (figure 4.3) became its editor and was thereafter a
leading abolitionist who sheltered fugitive Blacks on the Underground Railroad, his newspaper office serving as a way station.[13] Gay devoted much of
his time to freeing enslaved people in North America. He worked closely
with Louis Napoleon (1800–81), an African American furniture polisher and
porter. Napoleon was an associate of several leading abolitionists, including
Gerrit Smith, Arthur and Lewis Tappan, Horace Greeley, Henry Ward

Beecher, George William Curtis, and most importantly Sydney Howard Gay as the editor of the *National Anti-Slavery Standard*. He lived around the corner from Gay's office in lower Manhattan and together the two men are credited with helping some three thousand individuals.[14] In this partnership, Gay would record the donations, expenses, and stories of runaway slaves, and Napoleon was involved in freeing them. Gay corresponded with other Underground Railroad operatives, while Napoleon would meet the fugitives when they arrived in New York from Philadelphia and elsewhere and shelter them in his home before guiding them on their way.

Hence when the *Lembrança* arrived in New York harbor in late June 1847, the Vigilance Committee was ready. The stevedores notified Powell that slaves were being held on board the ship, and "a crowd of colored persons" gathered at the wharf. Powell dispatched Louis Napoleon to obtain a writ of habeas corpus requiring the Africans to be brought before a judge, although Napoleon did not actually obtain the writ. Powell loitered on the dock and even on the deck of the ship while waiting for Napoleon to obtain the writ. Instead, John Inverness, a Black man who operated a restaurant at 63 Mott Street, actually obtained the writ.[15] At the urging of these local abolitionists and prompted by severe beatings, Baquaqua, along with his two fellow slaves, sought the "freedom" that he speaks about so poignantly in his autobiography. On 16 July, the *New York Daily Tribune*, referring to Baquaqua (under the name José da Costa) and his fellow slave José da Rocha, reported: "They declare that they have been cruelly treated during the voyage, having been frequently flogged by the captain; and once stretched at full length upon a gun with hands and feet secured to receive the punishment. In some situations Da Rocha has been compelled to inflict the blows upon his fellow slave."[16] This incident is recalled in the affidavit of Baquaqua (submitted under his Portuguese name José da Costa) and his fellow slave José da Rocha: on 21 July, Baquaqua had asked the captain to let him and his companion go on shore, but they were beaten instead and then confined to the ship's "store-room" for four days, three of them without food. According to his testimony, Baquaqua had merely asked "to go ashore for a short time on Sunday to see the town," rather than explicitly for the purpose of claiming his freedom.[17]

The case of the "Brazilian slaves" first came to the attention of the local press in New York. The case was well covered in the New York *Daily Tribune*, the *Herald*, the *Express*, and especially the *National Anti-Slavery Standard*, whose publisher, Sydney Howard Gay, was closely associated with those who provided the legal and financial support for the fugitives. Gay was a key player in freeing Baquaqua in New York and was involved in reporting the story of enslaved people who had been brought from Brazil to New York City. During the *Lembrança* case that concerned Baquaqua and the other enslaved persons, Judges Charles P. Daly and Henry P. Edwards issued the same ruling in this case that "the treaty of reciprocity between Brazil and the United States governing crew members required them to be returned to their captain." Gay commented that the judges had "prostituted their position on the bench to protect the Foreign Slave-Trade in the port of New-York." Without question, Gay and the other abolitionists were determined that the two "Brazilians" would be freed. During the court proceedings that followed the escape of Baquaqua and his companion, Gay noted that "the public was fully satisfied that, with the assistance of somebody," the Brazilian men had "taken possession of their own bodies, and gone to parts unknown."[18]

Although hardly noticed in the study of the abolitionist movement in the United States and the development of the "Underground Railroad," the code name for the resistance movement that enabled many enslaved African Americans to escape to freedom, the case of the *Lembrança* was well known at the time. During July and August 1847, the fate of the three enslaved individuals was the subject of three court cases held in New York City Hall (figure 4.3) that were reported not only in New York newspapers but in scattered newspapers across the United States from Baltimore to Boston and even in the southern states. In addition, the legal opinions that were rendered in the case were publicized both at the time and in subsequent documentation that chronicled the activities of the judicial system. The case was even followed through newspapers in Brazil.[19] Despite contemporary notoriety, Baquaqua escaped the attention of later scholars who focused on slavery and abolition because of his name. At the time he was still known as José da Costa, the name he had been given in Brazil. Only after he successfully fled the United States for Haiti in September 1847 did he reclaim the name by which he had been known in Djougou.

Attempts by Baquaqua and José da Rocha to jump ship failed, but the writ required their delivery to the Court of Common Pleas at the City Hall of New York. The writ was issued by Judge Daly in the Court of Common Pleas on Saturday 10 July instructing Captain da Costa to deliver the enslaved José da Costa (i.e., Baquaqua), José da Rocha, and Maria da Costa, but the hearing was then adjourned until the following Monday, 12 July, and Daly's judgement delivered only on Saturday, 17 July. The "venerable" Isaac T. Hopper arranged for the initial hearing to be postponed, apparently with the assistance of his son, John Hopper, counsel. There was another legal advisor, Mr. Moffat, who also intervened on behalf of the slaves. Joseph L. White,

FIGURE 4.3 New York City Hall, an illustration of 1838, I. N. Pheleps Stokes Collection, New York Public Library, also in Charles Lockwood, *Manhattan Moves Uptown: An Illustrated History* (Boston: Houghton Mifflin, 1976), 2. Print Collection, New York Public Library.

attorney, helped represent Baquaqua, before the case was turned over to John Jay II (1817–94), a graduate of Columbia College and the son of abolitionist Judge William Jay and grandson of Chief Justice John Jay, who signed the Declaration of Independence and helped draft the US Constitution before becoming the first Chief Justice of the Supreme Court. His son had a well-deserved reputation as a lawyer and was a judge himself, and the grandson carried on the family tradition. For the final hearing on 17 July, John Jay II and Joseph White had replaced the Hoppers, while a Mr. Purroy appeared for Captain da Costa.

John Jay II was well respected and a leading advocate of manumission, defending fugitive slaves in the city in the 1840s and 1850s. As a lawyer, Jay coordinated efforts with the Black community in the city to protect the legal rights of newly manumitted and free Blacks, as well as ensuring the promise of education for Black youth with the establishment of African Free Schools. He took over the case of the *Lembrança* as a defense attorney for the Africans onboard. When brought to court, both Judge Daly and Edwards ordered the two men to be returned to the ship. During the latter part of this case, the captain offered to sell the enslaved people for $300 each; however, before the sale could commence, the enslaved persons escaped. Jay commented on this case stating their escape was "perfectly justifiable," as they were jailed without warrant; however, he made it clear he was not involved.[20]

Counsel for the slaves appealed to a New York State law of 1840, by which slaves brought into the state became free. Purroy cited the US-Brazilian treaty of 1829 that provided for the return of absconding members of ship crews. The "Peace, Friendship, Commerce, and Navigation" agreement had been signed by Brazil on 12 December 1828 and entered in force on 18 March 1829, and would be terminated on 12 December 1841 unless neither party objected to its continuation. Article XXXI declared that

> Consuls shall have power to require the assistance of authorities of the country, for the arrest, detention and custody of deserters from public and private vessels of their country, and for that purpose they shall address themselves to the courts, judges, and officers competent, and shall demand the said deserters in writing providing by an exhibition of the registers of the vessels or ships roll, or other public documents, that those men were part of said crews . . . , the delivery shall not be refused. Such deserters, when arrested, shall be put at the disposal of said Consuls, and may be put in public prison, at the request and expense of those who reclaim them, to be sent to the ships to which they belonged."[21]

Whether or not the treaty was still in force became a matter of dispute in the case of another ship, the *Porpoise*,[22] but Judge Daly ruled that the two male slaves should be returned to the ship, on the grounds that they were crew members, rather than recognizing their status as slaves.[23]

The *Evening Express* declared that the writ had probably been instigated by "the society for the abolition of slavery" because "Mr. Hopper [Isaac Hopper's attorney son, John] and other gentlemen connected to the anti-slavery cause" were at the hearing.[24] On July 12, the case was brought before the Court of Common Pleas, which was held in New York City Hall. Many sympathizers, mostly African Americans, were at the windows, doors, and in the passage leading to the judge's crowded chambers.[25] "There was quite an excitement around the Hall, a large number of colored persons and others assembling in view of the proceedings," reported the *New York Daily Tribune*, referring to the hearing on Monday, 12 July.[26] Daly presided on the bench.

John Jay II and Joseph L. White were retained as defense attorneys for the *Lembrança* slaves. The contemporary newspaper reports confirm that Captain Costa "sent for the Brazilian Consul as his counsel" in the initial hearing on Saturday, 10 July, but he did not arrive in time, causing the postponement of the hearing till Monday, 12 July.[27] The Consul, Luiz Henrique Ferreira de Aguiar, probably attended on 12 July, although this is not explicitly reported, but in any case on the following day, Tuesday 13 July, Costa submitted a letter of protest signed by the Consul.[28]

The captain owned two of the slaves, Maria and José da Costa (i.e., Baquaqua), and the owner of the *Lembrança* owned the third, José da Rocha, who served at least part time as the cook, while Maria was a nurse and servant to the captain's wife and infant child.[29] Maria da Costa disassociated herself from her fellow slaves at this point. After the initial hearing, she opted to return to the ship; on the understanding that the Captain would bring her to court for the hearing; and by the time of the judgement on 17 July, counsel for both parties agreed that she wished to remain in the service of her mistress, and that her status was therefore no longer at issue.[30] It was alleged that she was very attached to them and was allowed to return to the ship. It is not possible to know the reasons for her decision because her testimony has not survived. Other evidence suggests that the captain and his wife were hardly kind to their slaves, and it may be that Maria had personal reasons for wanting to return to Brazil.

Jay demanded that the men be freed in accordance with the state law barring slave transit. The captain insisted that the treaty between Brazil and the United States required each country to respect the property rights of citizens of the other. Unfortunately for the two men, Daly ruled on 17 July that they should be returned to the ship, on the grounds that they were members of its crew, apparently recognizing that the treaty was still in force. The judgement technically ignored their status as slaves.[31] After Daly's judgement, Baquaqua and his fellow slaves were restored to Captain Costa on board his ship, where the men were detained in irons.

The defense appealed Daly's decision to the New York Supreme Court. On Monday, 19 July, a second writ of habeas corpus was issued by another judge, J. W. Edmonds, of the New York Supreme Court (see Appendix A).[32] Jay and White again appeared for the slaves, and Purroy for the Captain. Jay and White argued that, since no interpreter had been provided, the two slaves had not been able to understand the proceedings or instruct their counsel. Through an interpreter and with the assistance of their abolitionist supporters, the two men filed an affidavit on 21 July.[33] The affidavit explained the difficulties that the two men were having in understanding the various hearings. Their lawyers claimed that "they do not understand the English language, and did not, and could not, comprehend what was said and done."[34] They also disputed the description of the status of the two men as crew members, on the grounds that they had received no pay, and counter-charged the captain with assault and false imprisonment of them. After various adjournments, Edwards delivered a judgement on Thursday, 5 August, again in favor of Captain Costa.[35]

Baquaqua and José da Rocha were sent to a jail on Eldridge Street, pending the outcome of the case.[36] The prison (figure 4.4) was a "private establishment." The decision of Judge Edwards did not resolve the case, and a third writ of habeas corpus was issued by Judge Oakley of the New York Supreme Court for hearing on Monday, 9 August. Negotiations were also initiated with Costa about the possibility of his accepting $300 for the redemption of the two men, although he said they were each worth $500 in Brazil.[37] But before the sale could be arranged or Oakley could hear the appeal, the Africans escaped.[38] They broke out of jail on the night of Saturday, 7 August. According to the *New York Daily Tribune* (10 August 1847), "The Keeper of Eldridge st. Jail, in whose custody the two slaves of the L'Emperance [sic] were left, reported, this morning, that they were in the jail last night when he went to bed, but on rising this morning he found that they were gone. He knows nothing about the manner in which they got off." The *National Anti-Slavery Standard* reported on 12 August that the jailer "fell asleep leaving the keys to the cell" on his desk.[39] Joseph Cornell was the keeper and James Lord the deputy jailer. Captain Elias Smith, an antislavery lecturer from New England who worked on the *National Anti-Slavery Standard*, and William H. Leonard, a Black printer at the newspaper, rescued Baquaqua and his fellow crew member from jail.[40]

Jay was gratified. He said their escape was "perfectly justifiable"; as they had been jailed without a legal warrant. However, he made it clear that he had not been involved. While prosecuting attorney Purroy acknowledged that Jay was not at fault, he said he had an understanding with Elias Smith that the slaves would remain in prison until their sale was completed. Smith substantiated Purroy's statement on 7 August in a letter to *Standard* agent Erastus D. Hudson: "I spent half the last night at the prison, to see that they wasn't carried off."[41] According to one account, an unnamed abolitionist debtor who was detained in the house of detention knew the jailer had a taste for brandy, and he drank with him until about midnight, at which time the jailer was dead drunk. The jailer put his prison keys under his pillow and went to sleep. The abolitionist took the keys, let the slaves out, put the keys back, and

FIGURE 4.4 Eldridge Street Jail, from George Hayward—New York Public Library Digital Gallery; *Emmet Collection of Manuscripts Etc. Relating to American History, Booth's History of New York*, Volume 8.

returned to his bunk.[42] Reportedly, Gay and his companions, with the aid of the incarcerated abolitionist, had gotten the jailer intoxicated and freed the prisoners, who were soon on their way to Boston, passing through Springfield. Wesleyan minister Rev. Luther Lee later claimed that he was responsible for organizing the escape (figure 4.5).[43]

When Monday came, the Rev. Lee was a spectator in the courtroom. Lee recalled, "[T]he judge, who was an aged, able and very venerable man, put on a solemn face and said, 'The only conclusion to which the court can come is that the men went out at the key-hole.'"[44] Gay said the public was "fully satisfied that, with the assistance of somebody," the Brazilian men had "taken possession of their own bodies, and gone to parts unknown."[45] As the *New York Tribune* put it, "the birds had flown."[46]

According to Lee, the lawyers who had handled the case had blundered. After repeating his interpretation of what went wrong and asserting that

FIGURE 4.5
Reverend Luther Lee,
abolitionist Methodist
(1800–1889)—
frontispiece of book,
*Autobiography of
The Rev. Luther Lee*
(New York: Phillips &
Hart, 1882).

"I could have made a better reply myself," he then confessed to his role in organizing the escape because he overheard a conversation between Captain Costa and the warden of the jail:

> The captain turned to the keeper of the Eldridge-street jail and said, "It will not pay for me to take these men on board of my vessel to bring them back on Monday; take them and lock them up, and I will pay you for their board." "All right," said the jailer, and led them away. I was in the court room, a silent spectator, hearing the battle between the lawyers. When I had heard the contract between the captain and the jailer I walked out and found a man I happened to know, who had more brains than tongue and more cunning than logic, and said to him, "Those men are not in the custody of the law, and will not be until nine o'clock on Monday. They are private boarders at the jail, and if they can be got out between this time and Monday it will not be jail-breaking."[47]

As it happened, Lee went to court on Monday "to see and hear what might be said and done" because "the men were gone, and no one knew how they got away." "The captain appeared with his attorney and made a return to the writ. It affirmed that the men described in the writ were in his custody on Saturday, that he left them in care of the keeper of the Eldridge-street jail, that when he called for them they were not there, and he did not know how they escaped nor whence they had gone. As no one doubted the truth of his return it relieved him of all responsibility, but his men were gone."[48] The disappearance of the two men caused considerable confusion, needless to say.

The defense then "filed an affidavit that no one had asked counsel of him and that he had given counsel to no person in regard to the men since the last decision by the court." Judge Oakley thereupon sent for the jailer, who

> made oath that the men were in the jail on Sunday night, and that on Monday morning they were gone; that he found the keys in their usual place, and no doors or windows were open or broken, and that there were no marks of violence, and that he had no knowledge of the manner in which they escaped. . . . The facts were as follows: somebody—I never knew who—went in and had a good time with the jailer until a very late hour, and the result was the jailer slept very sound after he was gone. This same person who spent the evening with the jailer put a flea in the ear of a person who was locked up for a day or two for some small offense, and the flea in his ear caused him to wake up at twelve o'clock at night and go and get the keys and open the door and put the two men out, and then lock the door and put the keys in their place and go to his bunk. When the jailer got up in the morning he was doing a loud business in the lien of snoring.[49]

The escape inspired a rare burst of humor in the *New York Evangelist*. A carriage was waiting for the men when they came out of the jail, into which they entered and were driven across the state line into Connecticut and then to Boston. A ship was on the point of sailing for Haiti, and they were put on board and sent to that island.[50] Tongue in cheek, the *Evangelist* quipped that the Underground Railroad "runs directly under the prison in New York, and . . . the slaves let themselves down through a stone trap-door into one of the cars."[51] According to the *Springfield Gazette*, as quoted in the *New York Daily Tribune*, 23 August 1847, "[T]hese victims of oppression arrived in that place [Springfield] a few days since, by the underground railroad, and after a short tarry left for Canada by the same route." In fact, they went to Boston and not Canada. Among the places in Springfield where individuals were secreted was the United States Hotel, owned and operated by Jeremy and Phoebe Werringer, who employed workers of African descent who assisted in hiding temporary visitors. By 1847, it became more of a risk in town, being considered too dangerous, so that several abolitionists, including Rev. Dr. Samuel Osgood, Rufus Elmer, a Mr. Calhoun, and "a negro preacher" organized a house "in the woods at Brightwood, on the north side of the city, for the use of the fugitives," which is most likely where Baquaqua and his friend were taken before being moved on to Boston.

It is not clear who assisted Baquaqua in Boston, but there was a strong network of abolitionists who could have helped.[52] As Wilbur Siebert has demonstrated, "No town on the entire New England coast received a larger number of fugitive slaves than Boston. Most of them came as stowaways on vessels from Southern ports, and some from Plymouth and perhaps other shore towns south of Boston where they had landed," but unlike most stowaway fugitives, Baquaqua came by land.[53] There were several Vigilance Societies or their equivalents such as the Defensive League of Freedom in Boston in the 1840s, usually short-lived and arising from episodic cases in support of individuals whom slave catchers had apprehended or otherwise came to the attention of law enforcement officers and the courts. There was a latent and sometimes open split between supporters associated with William Lloyd Garrison, who published the influential newspaper, *The Liberator,* and other abolitionists, but this did not affect the willingness of residents to help those who were fleeing. There were close connections between abolitionists in New York and Boston, and it seems that Gay of the *National Anti-Slavery Standard* and Garrison were frequently in contact. As Gay's daughter, Mary Otis Willcox, wrote in a biography of her father that was never published, "The Standard Office [in New York] was a station of the 'Under Ground Railroad' of course and there are two account books giving in short paragraphs the history of the runaway slaves who passed through, and the amount of money spent in forwarding him or her to Syracuse, Canada, Albany, Boston or whichever Station was to her next. And at every station there was a faithful abolitionist waiting."[54]

The account books to which Willcox refers were the notebooks that he compiled of those whom Gay helped after 1855, but they indicate the elaborate network of contacts that he had already nourished as early as 1847 when he very well might have assisted Baquaqua and his companion's escape to Boston.[55] Without any concrete evidence, Gay certainly could have helped direct Baquaqua and his companion to Garrison for assistance.

Baquaqua claimed that the two men were given a choice of going to England or Haïti, and they chose the latter. The ship that Baquaqua and David boarded also contained other passengers, most notably a Mr. Jones, an African American who was connected with the American Free Baptist Mission, and who ultimately may have provided Baquaqua and his associate with an invitation to the Mission. Baquaqua quickly endeared himself to the Rev.

William Judd, who was in charge of the mission, and especially to his wife and her sister. Baquaqua was accompanied to Haiti by José da Rocha, who became known to the Baptist Free Mission in Haïti as David, and may have taken that name earlier.[56] Although this Jones was evidently connected with the American Free Baptist Mission and may have introduced Baquaqua to the Rev. Judd,[57] he appears to be a different person than the Rev. William L. Jones, who was pastor of the mission in Port-au-Paix on the north coast of Haiti and was not of African descent. In fact, Rev. Jones was on sick leave in the United States and did not return to Haiti until November 1848.[58]

While this odd chain of events was running its course, Sydney H. Gay—as editor of the *National Anti-Slavery Standard* and fundraiser for the society— appealed to the vestry of St. Philips Episcopal Church, whose parishioners included the elite of the African American community, for a donation to defray legal expenses in the ongoing case. Gay obviously thought this was a reasonable appeal, given the parish's connection to Jay and the number of parishioners active in the Anti-Slavery Society that included William Powell. The vestry, however, rejected the overture, as noted in the minutes of their August 12 meeting that was chaired by James McCune Smith, the secretary: "A letter was received from Gay requesting that this church do join other *colored* churches in this city in raising One Hundred Dollars for carrying on the suit in the case of the Brazilian slaves. *Moved,* that in the opinion of this vestry the question is one that concerns all men regardless of complexion, and that this vestry cannot by word or deed assent to the doctrine that it is a matter particularly pertaining to colored churches. *Agreed.*"[59]

Smith was influential in St. Philip's Church. He was a physician, apothecary, and abolitionist. He was the first African American to hold a medical degree. He graduated top of his class at the University of Glasgow. He practiced at the Colored Orphan Asylum in Manhattan for almost twenty years and was the first African American to run a pharmacy in the United States. He published numerous essays and articles on medical issues, race, and society. He worked closely with Frederick Douglass in founding the National Council of Colored People in 1853 and was prominent in aiding fugitives escaping from slavery. Moreover, Smith opposed emigration schemes. It is not clear if Smith convinced the vestry to take this position or if Gay's appeal truly offended general sentiment that the case of the Brazilian slaves was something only "colored" churches would support. The minutes do not record any discussion, only Smith's summary.

St. Philip's was the place of worship of the African American elite of New York.[60] Philip Lacy was the parish sexton at the time, and thus in charge of collecting the rents on pews. Because he received a commission of six percent on each rental in addition to a yearly salary of $72, he knew every person in the congregation.[61] Lacy lived on Orange Street, in the center of the Five Points slum and close to the African Society Hall, headquarters of the African Mutual Relief Society. Maria Wright was the organist, her husband having died in 1843, the year she started playing for the church. The choir director was Robert Hamilton, who worked as a porter and lived around the corner on Leonard Street.[62] Powell was also in the congregation and one of its more radical members. Details on other prominent personages in the church confirm the profile. The church consisted of the free African American elite, and that elite was wary of racialized politics that considered the plight of fugitives from slavery to be a "Black" problem when it clearly was a national problem. The parishioners were nonetheless at the forefront of the African descendent community in New York, and in the same year that Baquaqua's case was before the courts, were instrumental in founding the New York Society for Promotion of Education among Colored Children.[63]

For several months after Baquaqua escaped, Gay regretted that he had not paid John Jay's associate, Joseph White, for his services on behalf of Baquaqua and the other Brazilians. Gay wrote to Jay apologizing for the delay in paying White. When Jay was about to embark on a trip to England in April of 1848, Gay sent Jay several letters of introduction to British friends and this apology:

> Now that I am writing let me apologize for my dilatoriness in relation to Mr. White's fee in the Brazilian slave-case. We as you know, perhaps have no fund for such cares, & the money was to have been paid out of my own pocket. My only excuse for so long a delay, is that sometimes, increased expenses, & decreased income for the year has straitened me exceedingly. I can only express my regret, & confess my mortification. I consider it still as a debt due to you, to be liquidated the moment I am able. I regret that I can not do so before you leave.[64]

In a blistering response, Jay responded that the onus for reimbursement on that case did not fall on Gay but rather was a national disgrace.[65] "About the Brazilian case let me say that I never regarded you or Smith as responsible for the money I had the pleasure of advancing except some fund be placed in your hands. . . . I fear it is now too late to do anything for the interest of the public in these matters soon dies—But if anything sh^d be raised please remember that I have relinquished all my claims in favor of the New Vigilance Committee."[66]

While he excused Gay's debt, he requested that any money raised for the Brazilian case go to the recently organized New York State Vigilance Committee, which operated separately from Gay. Jay's reference to "Smith" is not clear, but he was probably referring to Gay's associate, Elias Smith, or more likely the secretary of the vestry at St. Philip's Episcopal Church, James McCune Smith.

The news about the *Lembrança* and its slaves caught the attention of numerous newspapers in the United States, including the *Anti-Slavery Bugle* in New Lisbon, Ohio, *The Evangelist* in Oberlin, Ohio, the *Boston Cultivator*, as well as the *National Anti-Slavery Standard, New York Daily Tribune, New York Evening Express, New York Express, New York Herald,* and *New York Independent.* The story also came to the attention of Brazilian newspapers. On 20 September 1847 in Fortaleza, Ceará, the *O Cearense* celebrated the new zero tariffs over Brazilian coffee entering in New York: "[Y]esterday, news arrived informing that the coffee imported in New York, in the Brazilian ship Lembrança was admitted without any payment of taxes."[67] That was a real reason for commemoration. Exportation of coffee was the main economic exchange between the Empire of Brazil and the United States. One of the key partners was Phipps Brothers & Co., which had imported coffee on the *Lembrança.* The news was in Brazilian newspapers within ten days of the official communication from Luis Henrique Ferreira d'Aguiar (figure 4.6), Consul General of Brazil in the United States (1842–75), to his superior in Washington stating that "Brazilian ships continue to be equated to the North-American ships, and the coffee imported under the national flag continue to be admitted free of taxation. Thus, the articles carried and imported from the barques Lembrança, Albini and the brig Pureza were received as if imported from the American pavilion."[68] The bad news for the proslavery Brazilian public arrived a few days after. The slaves embarked were in a trial to be set free.

A translation of an article from 23 July 1847, first written in the *N.Y. Morning Express*, was published in *Diário do Rio de Janeiro* and *O Mercantil* of Minas Gerais. The translation described details of the "Brazilian Slaves Case," still in its development. The article commented on the decision of Judge Daly one week before, for "the blacks to be restituted to their master as part of the crew, having in consideration the Brazilian laws [...] appears to us to be the decision most fair and right" and the risk of changes in the case having abolitionists as lawyers involved in the case. The article ended with a proslavery tone: "If the blacks are here set free among ourselves, the abolitionists will be the last ones to give them what to eat and to dress, and will abandon them immediately as they usually do. Victims of their own ignorance and dumbness, for committing crimes and begging. This is their philanthropy."[69] The next pages were followed by a long comment reiterating proslavery Brazilian

FIGURE 4.6
A portrait of Luís
Henrique Ferreira
d'Aguiar, consul
general of Brazil in
the United States
(1842–75), *O Novo
Mundo* (New York)
5:59, 23 August 1875.

opinion about the case. The article was not signed and combined a discourse about sovereignty, defense of property, and a slight threat to the citizens of United States living in Brazil.

> We do not admit that any country's law (much less from the US where slavery is legal) shall deprive a Brazilian subject from its property of any kind. Being it recognized by Brazilian law, if this deprivation happens (what we do not expect), for the reason of enforcement of particular and local laws of a state [New York] which is only part of an union, neither you, American citizens, should make any claims nor your government should request any reparation because of any loss caused by our courts' decisions and in conformity with the Brazilian law. You shall not make those spiteful comparisons of probity between Brazilian and American authorities. They have the same obligation to show the requested respect to our courts. . . . Actually, according to our understanding, those particular and local laws should be applied only to your citizens and not to foreigners who travel to there with good intentions, seeking their own businesses and the hospitality which is guaranteed by the general law of

nations. They do not like being subject to the fantasies of 15 to 20 states which form the union. However, this case is very serious, not for its own consequences, but for the example for future Brazilian ships which would sail to the United States.[70]

The author of this missive referred positively to the zero taxation for Brazilian coffee but advised that this commercial advantage could not be taken into consideration if the status of slave crews was to be repeatedly questioned. It was argued that Brazilian businessmen of the 1840s would not produce coffee without slave labor and the shipping of coffee could not be done without slaves: "Everyone who knows the Brazilian merchant navy should understand that it is impossible to sail in a Brazilian ship without part of the crew being slaves. Without the continuous flow of conscripts to the navy our ships would be without a single person, being hard to find sailors."[71] The everyday life of a laborer on a Brazilian merchant ship was brutal, and the brutalization was racialized. The argument was made that slaves would comprise the main labor force in merchant marine.

The news about the mysterious escape in New York also took space in the *Jornal do Commercio* in Rio de Janeiro. On 15 October 1847 the *Jornal* reported news obtained in Philadelphia: "The protectors of the slaves, who were decided to free them despite the law, got to make them disappear form the Eldridge street prison leaving no clue. The prison keeper says he locked the prisoners Sunday night among the other inmates and took the keys to his chamber, where he found them again in the morning. But when opening the cages, he realized that the two slaves had escaped during the night. The how they escaped is something completely unknown."[72]

On 23 October 1847, the *Lembrança* was back in business, with two slaves less aboard and a cargo of 94,577 pine logs being sent by Phipps Brothers & Co. to Brazil, and a couple days after was already sailing for its usual coastal trade on southern shores.[73] Shortly thereafter, the *Lembrança* would become involved in the slave trade from Africa, the ship's owners apparently wary of trade with the United States.

For Baquaqua, it meant that he had enacted the first English word he knew, "free," that enabled him to go to Haiti, where he recreated himself as Mahommah Gardo Baquaqua, all names from his youth when he was a free Muslim in a prominent family. From the time he was liberated by the New York Vigilance Society and employed at the Free Will Baptist Mission in Port-au-Prince, he not only successfully asserted his freedom but also moved beyond his Muslim upbringing in his quest to return to Africa. His plight was important in another respect. His escape was a further example to those who owned slaves that the government had to take a more assertive role in preventing those who were enslaved from escaping. One of the judges involved in the case, Judge Edmonds, had been a circuit judge from 1845–47, and then was appointed to the New York Supreme Court. He was involved in several fugitive slave cases, including George Kirk in October 1846, John Lee in December 1848, as well as Baquaqua. Edmonds subsequently had to withstand a reputation for encouraging escapes. His decisions were cited as one of the reasons for passing the Fugitive Slave Act on 18 September 1850, which undoubtedly marked a new stage in the struggle over slavery. Drafted by Democratic Senator James M. Mason of Virginia, the bill effectively undermined the rights of anyone who was Black. The act required the apprehension of anyone who escaped from slavery based only on the sworn testimony of a claimant to ownership. Provision of habeas corpus was denied, and there was no allowance for a trial. An alleged slave owner only had to obtain an affidavit from a federal marshal, which resulted in kidnapping and enslavement without any basis for defense. Officials who did not enforce the law were subject to heavy fines, while officers who captured the person accused of being a fugitive was entitled to a bonus or promotion. The act was a harbinger of civil war to come. It placed those who helped people escape or otherwise survive into a position where they had to break the law if they opposed slavery.

Baquaqua's case indirectly laid the foundation for the passage of the Fugitive Slave Law in 1850. Incidents like his escape prompted proslavery advocates to push for tougher measures in apprehending fugitives, making it easier to seize those who had escaped, and even those who were free and had not run away, and threatening criminal conviction and fines for anyone who assisted in escapes. His daring flight from jail was noticed with indignation and disbelief at the time, drawing extensive commentary in the press, even if his case has been largely overlooked ever since. Baquaqua subsequently remained in contact with leading abolitionists who encouraged resistance to slavery. While it is clear that he had neither the dramatic oratorial skills of Frederick Douglass nor the literary abilities of Gustavus Vassa, his involvement in the abolition campaign uncovers dimensions of resistance to slavery that have been virtually ignored in North America. Baquaqua demonstrates that the experiences of other Muslims in North America are important to study. Baquaqua's bold move in his quest for "freedom," as he expressed it in his limited English, exposes the network of extreme abolitionists who were willing to violate the law to help enslaved persons find ways to escape, as he himself had done.

CHAPTER FIVE

With the Free Will Baptists

Four weeks later, Baquaqua and Rocha left Boston for Haiti, a land where, as the autobiography notes, Blacks were free since the revolution of the 1790s. Baquaqua and his friend David Rocha arrived in Port-au-Prince, the capital of Haiti, sometime before 8 October 1847.[1] It was clearly a magical moment for Baquaqua. As he noted, "When I arrived at Hayti I felt myself free, as indeed I was. No slavery exists there, yet all are people of color who dwell there."[2] Having been assisted in escaping in New York with the help of radical abolitionists, many of whom were also Black, he now was in the only country in the world that had completely abolished slavery. While Baquaqua would not have known the details of the St. Domingue revolution and the establishment of Haiti as an independent country ruled by people of African descent in 1804, he clearly understood that there was no danger of being re-enslaved, whatever other obstacles he had to endure. Port-au-Prince was the capital where he would reside (figure 5.1), and he seems to have met some important government officials, most especially General Alexis Dupuy, who had been minister of war in the short-lived government of Jean-Baptiste Riché in 1846–47 and minister of finance, commerce, and foreign relations under Faustin Soulouque (1847–59).

In Haiti, Baquaqua became associated with the American Baptist Free Mission Society, often referred to as the Free Will Baptists. The Society was passionately opposed to slavery and therefore reflected the polarization of United States society. The Free Will Baptists were particularly outspoken on moral issues, and opposition to slavery was a principal focus. Baquaqua knew Haiti as the Black Republic of the Americas. At the time, it was the only place in the Americas where Blacks were in power. Born in anticolonial struggle and the war of independence that ended slavery, Haiti was known to Baquaqua as a land where there was no slavery.

According to Baquaqua, General Dupuy introduced him to the Baptists. After Baquaqua arrived in Port-au-Prince, he went to the "Emperor's House"—that is, the Palais National—which did indeed become the Emperor's House when Soulouque declared himself emperor in August 1849. It was there that he met Dupuy, according to Baquaqua "De Pe by name" who was "very kind to us." Baquaqua described him as "a mulatto" who gave him "plenty to eat and drink, and at night allowed me to lay down with his horses

FIGURE 5.1 A panorama of Port-au-Prince in 1870 in Samuel Hazard, *Santo Domingo Past and Present with a Glance at Hayti* (London: S. Low, Marston, Low, & Searle, 1873).

in the stables."[3] Dupuy took Baquaqua and his friend to the Baptist mission house and explained to Rev. William L. Judd that the two men were slaves from Brazil "and told him our circumstances, . . . and asked him if he could do something for us, when he agreed to take me into his service, upon which I entered with the most cheerful alacrity."[4]

Dupuy's father, Baron Dupuy, was an officer under Jean-Jacques Dessaline, but he was opposed to his presidency and took his family into exile in Philadelphia until Henri Christophe came into power in 1806. Baron Dupuy then became one of Christophe's closest advisors between 1804 and 1806. Alexis followed in his father's footsteps and was a key member of the regime of Jean-Baptiste Riché during his brief presidency in 1846–47. Indeed, Dupuy was directly involved in the choice of Soulouque, who was a career officer and general in the Haitian army, as president upon Riché's unexpected death. While Dupuy ensured a smooth transition between Riché's and Soulouque's presidencies in hopes of enacting administrative and economic reforms to improve the country's finances, this proved impossible as the government was in disarray. Soulouque was much more temperamental than Dupuy had anticipated, and his emergence allowed the largely disenfranchised poor Black population to become influential, virtually staging a second revolution that some thought consolidated the emergence of Haiti that had been fore-stalled in 1804.

Soulouque began to mistrust Dupuy and his ministers, favoring a darker-skinned minister who detested "mulattoes" and believed that "mulattoes," who held most of the wealth and property in the country and were disliked by much of the darker-skinned population, were conspiring against the president. Soulouque, a dark-skinned man himself, adopted this animosity and began persecuting those considered to be mixed race. Like Dupuy, most of his ministers were of mixed race and were removed from office. The situation quickly developed into an overt massacre on 16 April 1848. Soulouque ambushed the ministers and ordered his army to open fire and kill them. Dupuy narrowly escaped death by jumping over a wall. He fled to San Francisco where he worked at the Royal Mail Steam Packet Company importing coffee from Haiti. He would return to Haiti when Soulouque was finally removed from office in 1859, and Fabre-Nicolas Geffrard (1859–67) appointed him minister of finance.[5]

It was Baquaqua's association with the mission in Port-au-Prince that enabled him to assert his identity as Mahommah Gardo Baquaqua, although he did not assert his adherence to Islam. It is impossible to know for certain, but it is possible that he avoided any public display of Islam, a precaution that he would have been aware of in West Africa that was brought more forcefully to his attention in Brazil because of the recent Muslim uprising in Bahia. Judd and his wife Nancy, who ran the Port-au-Prince mission, apparently had no objections or Baquaqua was insistent in selecting a Muslim name at the time of his conversion and baptism as a Free Will Baptist. He would spend the next six years under the tutelage of the Free Will Baptists, and in that period, he was paraded about as an abolitionist trophy. Was his name questioned? Was his faith challenged?

The Baptist movement traced its origins in North America to the eighteenth century as a reaction to the predominance of the Congregationalists in New England and was strong in the southern states after American independence. The Free Mission Society was an outgrowth of the Free Will Baptist movement, which had broken with other Baptists over the issue of abolition in 1843, only reuniting after the Civil War in 1870.[6] In the 1840s and 1850s, the Free Mission undertook work among Native Americans in the United States and among fugitive slaves in Canada West who had fled on the Underground Railroad, as well as launching the mission in Haiti, to which Baquaqua by good fortune was introduced.[7] As described in an early history of the movement, *Facts for Baptist Churches. Collected, Arranged and Reviewed* by A.T. Foss and E. Mathews, in 1850, Free Will Baptist churches were found throughout New England, upstate New York, and eastern Pennsylvania with missions among African American refugees in Canada. Baquaqua is associated with this book of facts; his photograph is on the frontispiece of the volume, standing next to the Rev. Judd, who introduced Baquaqua to the Baptist faith in Haiti in 1847–48. Judd was born in 1813 and at the age of sixteen was baptized at the Baptist church in Stephentown, New York. He was ordained in Michigan in 1834 and became licensed to preach at the age of twenty-one. He then worked as a missionary in Michigan, Ohio, and Canada. From 1840 to 1847, he was a pastor of the Baptist church in Meredith, New York. He met his wife Nancy A. Lake during his time in Meredith, as she resided in the nearby town of Milford. They had a son during these years who died in 1869.[8]

The convention that founded the Free Mission Society at Tremont Chapel in Boston on 4 May 1843 issued a pledge that became the doctrinal basis of the movement and its commitment to abolition, temperance, and conversion. Its egalitarian ideals rejected discrimination on the basis of either race or gender. As a missionary for the American Free Will Baptists, Reverend William L. Judd opposed slavery and supported foreign missions both in Haiti and Africa. Inadvertently, Baquaqua became attached to the mission, probably not realizing the full significance of the mission's opposition to slavery. Freed from jail by activists, Baquaqua was now associated with the radical Baptists who were in the forefront in the fight to end slavery.

According to Foss and Mathews, the slavery issue came to a head in 1845 and 1846 and resulted in an irreversible split between slave-owning Baptists and their apologists and Baptists who adamantly opposed slavery as an anathema.[9] The northern Baptists were often referred to as Free Will Baptists because of their emphasis on free grace, free salvation, and free will. The Society not only established missions in Haiti with which Baquaqua was associated but frequently discussed opening missions in Africa, the Pacific islands, and elsewhere. Baquaqua's unexpected appearance in Port-au-Prince reinforced interest in a mission to be sent to Africa.

Rev. William M. Jones established the Haïtian mission in Port-au-Prince in 1844. He remained in Haiti until 1850 at the mission in Port-au-Paix on the north coast, which had been the center of sugar production before the revolution in the 1790s.[10] Judd was appointed missionary to Haiti on 8 May 1846 and arrived in Port-au-Prince in on 15 January 1847. His wife Nancy, her sister Electa Lake, and their young son accompanied him. Initially, Judd was not able to preach to many Haitians as he did not speak French, but he learned the language quickly. The mission garnered much public attention, and, during his time there, Judd baptized many people. The church also avidly disseminated translations of religious materials, including the Bible, in French.

The Judds hired Baquaqua as a cook, a position he held until he left Haiti and that he had held onboard the *Lembrança*.[11] Although he was a household servant, his relationship with the family quickly extended far past that. Baquaqua became a disciple of the Judds and admired Rev. Judd highly. Although the family could not communicate with him very well at first because of the language barrier, the Judds provided him with English lessons. Baquaqua, who now had a newfound thirst for knowledge that he had not displayed as a Qur'anic student in Djougou, soon became fluent enough to communicate. He told the family stories about his life in Africa, his enslavement in Brazil, and his desire for conversion. Clearly Baquaqua experienced a spiritual transformation that had been shaped by his misdemeanors in Africa, the roughness of slavery in Brazil, and the unexpected liberation that took place in New York. Judd began to write letters about Baquaqua's experiences, which were eventually published first in the *Christian Contributor and Free Missionary* and then in his autobiography. Baquaqua converted to the Free Will Baptist faith and was baptized by Judd in 1848. A. T. Foss and Edward Mathews were so impressed with the conversion that they used a portrait of Judd and Baquaqua as the frontispiece for their book, published in 1850, only three years after Baquaqua had left Brazil, *Facts for Baptist Churches* (figure 5.2).

The Judd family encouraged Baquaqua to return to Africa as a missionary, which played a big part in his desire to convert. Indeed, a central goal of the Haitian mission was to send converts from Haiti to Africa as missionaries in the belief that missionaries of African descent would facilitate the spread of Christianity. Judd's vision was for Baquaqua to become an interpreter and guide for an American missionary in Africa, and on that basis, he appealed to the society to support Baquaqua. Instrumental to this was securing him education in the United States. As a result of Judd's efforts, and less than two years after his arrival in Haiti, Baquaqua sailed back to the United States to attend school. Through Judd, Baquaqua gained access to the network of the American Baptist Free Mission Society, which allowed him to connect with abolitionists in the United States and Canada West as well as eventually reach a publisher willing to expose his story more widely through print, al-

WILLIAM L. JUDD.

AMERICAN BAPTIST FREE MISSIONARY FOR HAYTI TEACHING MAHOMMAH

FIGURE 5.2 Rev. William L. Judd and Baquaqua, frontispiece in A. T. Foss and Edward Mathews, *Facts for Baptist Churches* (Utica, NY: American Baptist Free Mission Society, 1850).

though in the end his autobiography was scarcely recognized and poorly distributed. While in the north of Haiti, he toured churches to spread the message of the mission. The Haitian mission became well known within the society as it was impressive for its size and its number of native ministers. It was recognized as the Society's principal foreign mission.

Judd returned to the United States numerous times due to health concerns and to garner support and funding from the American members of the mission society for the Haitian mission. Despite his success as a missionary, he was accused of acts of immorality in 1855, details of which are not known. When the accusations were presented to him, he did not deny them and agreed to atone for his sins. The Society suggested he resign voluntarily, but he had a change of heart and revoked his confession of guilt. Finally, his hand was forced, and his resignation was fixed for 17 June 1855. He sent his resignation to the board himself following the recommendations of other members of the Haitian mission. Officially, Rev. Judd was part of the American Baptist Free Mission Society from 1846 to 1853.

Instead of leaving Haiti and his post after his resignation, Judd decided to become an independent missionary, which undermined the Society's role within the mission churches in the country. He kept control of the Port-au-Prince mission and the church's property. The Society tried to regain control by encouraging its church members to turn on him by sending his original admission of guilt. He then filed a lawsuit against the Society, but the suit was ultimately abandoned as the judicial decisions were not in favor of Judd. Eventually, Rev. Judd had to exploit political instabilities to regain possession of the church through the Haitian government. Judd worked around twenty years for the Haitian mission. He ultimately compromised himself to the politics of President Salnave (1867–69) and fled to the Dominican Republic after losing the trust of his followers, where he died in 1869. A Haitian named Lucius Hyppolite, whom he had converted, continued to run the Haitian mission for thirty years following Judd's departure.

The Free Will Baptists were in favor of a mission to Africa; indeed, it had initiated its mission in Haiti, in part in the hope of recruiting personnel there for missionary work in Africa. For this purpose, Baquaqua seemed to be a providential gift. Baquaqua himself quickly warmed to the idea of returning to Africa, which he expressed as early as March 1848, and (as will be seen) frequently repeated thereafter. Baquaqua, of course, responded to the religious commitment of his Baptist mentors, whose reports on his conversion no doubt primarily projected their own concerns and perceptions rather than those of Baquaqua himself. But both his mentors and his own wishes came together on one important point—the return to Africa.

Judd wrote to Cyrus Grosvenor in Utica on 28 October 1847, which reveals that he was fully aware of the situation. It is worth quoting Judd at length because it is the first description of Baquaqua's background, which is fully discussed in chapter 1.

I notice by the papers from New York that the case of the two Brazilian slaves has made some excitement in that ancient city of sober Dutchmen. I suppose that both their friends and enemies would like to know their whereabouts. For the satisfaction of all and especially for Capt. Climente [sic], you are at liberty to say that they are both safe in Port au Prince. One of them is now living in the family of your missionary. He is the younger of the two, and I think by far the most intelligent. He is, as we suppose, about 16 years of age. It appears that they two Africans are not from the same tribe. The one who is with us is so far advanced in English that I have been able to learn from him precisely his former residence in Africa. He is from the city of Kashina, of the tribe Houssa, in the northern or central part of Soudan. He is acquainted with all the cities between there and the coast, in a southerly direction. His native language is Arabic, which he yet remembers and can even write with considerable facility. I suppose his intercourse with other slaves from the same country, has done much to retain it in his memory, which appears also to be remarkably strong. He remembers well the Yaoors, the next nation west of the Houssas. He says he is acquainted with the city of Kano, and appears to be familiar with the term Soudan, the general name of the country, including some five or six states in the very centre of Africa. He says that in all these States the Arabic language is spoken and cultivated in books. I should think that probably his family is one of considerable importance in the Houssa nation. From his account they must have been rich. His father died before he left. He says his oldest brother was well educated, could read and write the Arabic with fluency. He says they put him to his books very closely, but loving play, he used to leave home clandestinely, and it was in one such affray as this that he was taken by some of the tribes nearer the coast, and sold [to] the Portuguese of South America.[12]

Considering that Judd was able to learn this much about Baquaqua's background less than a month after Baquaqua had arrived in Haiti is astonishing. Mrs. Judd noted that Baquaqua spoke Portuguese in addition to one or more African languages, but not English of French, beyond "a very few sentences in broken English, which he learned on his passage here."[13] For this reason, the Judds were initially not able to communicate with him directly, rather they depended on the African American by the name of Jones. Despite some obvious confusion, since the Judds had no knowledge of the interior of West Africa, there is remarkable consistency in what we know about Baquaqua's early life. He was not from Katsina, but his mother was. Kano had become the most important city in the Sokoto Caliphate after

Katsina's decline. Arabic was known, especially within the elite but also among everyone who was Muslim because prayers had to be made in Arabic.

Most astonishing, since Judd baptized Baquaqua, was the recognition that his name was Muhammad, although Judd was not aware that the name was so common in Muslim society that there were variations in rendering and pronunciation, which was necessary to make distinctions in its application as a name.

> His African name is Mahommah (the first and last a sounded like an a in man, and the o like a in what). I presume it is the same name which we call Mahomet. All the Arabic words I can pronounce he at once recognizes, and all the Arabic characters that I have been able to show him from my books, he at once reads and explains as well as he can in broken English, their meaning. So that I am entirely satisfied that he knows the Arabic language. If any friend could send me some Arabic books, it would be of great importance, especially the Bible in Arabic.[14]

Judd probably did not know that Baquaqua had requested that Rev. Lee, who was involved in his escape from jail, send him the Bible in Arabic, which probably only happened after Baquaqua learned that Lee was in Syracuse, close to New York Central College in McGrawville, just to the south. As Lee noted in his autobiography in recounting his own involvement in the escape of Baquaqua and his companion from jail in New York,

> One of the two was a man advanced in life, and the other was a young man and had lately been stolen from Africa. He was a son of one of their petty kings, and was educated in Arabic, and I received a letter from him requesting me to send him an Arabic Bible, which I did. A few years after he returned to New York to improve his English education, and on learning that I had removed to Syracuse he came out and made me a visit, so grateful did he feel for the part I had acted in his behalf.[15]

According to Lee, "[O]n learning that I had removed to Syracuse he [Baquaqua] came out and made me a visit, so grateful did he feel for the part I had acted in his behalf."[16]

Judd immediately grasped the possibility that Baquaqua might be useful to the Free Mission Society in establishing a mission in Africa, and this factor remained central to Baquaqua's ongoing involvement with the Baptists until he realized that their commitment was not as strong as he certainly hoped that it would be.

For I have the most sanguine hopes that the Lord will convert his soul before long, and then he will yet become a missionary to his native land. The circumstances of his escape and final arrival in Port-au-Prince, and his entrance into my family, are so clearly providential that I can not doubt but God has some very glorious object to accomplish through him in this connection. To narrate these would require a long letter, and I have no doubt would be very interesting to others as well as to us. But in writing what I have, I have been obliged to trespass upon the time which seemed almost absolutely demanded for other purposes, and have only done so because duty appeared to call loudest in this direction.[17]

Even at this early date, Judd was prophetic in recognizing that the establishment of a mission in Africa would be difficult. Baquaqua adhered to the Free Will Baptists because of his hope that a mission in Africa would enable him to return to his "native land." The problem was recruiting someone to lead the mission. As Judd asked,

But where is the man, to accompany this young lad to his native land, to bear the gospel of Jesus Christ among the millions of that vast country? Who has faith enough to undertake with the false prophet? I have no doubt but some one will be needed, and whoever goes ought to be a man of extraordinary knowledge of the world and able to endure hardships. I think however, that if a person could reach the spot, he would probably find a healthy place, as the city of Kashina is very probably upon the head waters of the Niger.[18]

In the meantime, Judd saw his role as continuing the dialogue with Baquaqua and ultimately baptizing him. That in itself is a mystery to the extent that Judd allowed Baquaqua to take a name as a Christian that was Muslim and Hausa, Mahommah Gardo Baquaqua. "I hope that while Mahommah is undergoing the necessary preparation, our friends in the States will be upon the qui vive for a man properly qualified to accompany him. A study of the Hebrew and Arabic, would undoubtedly be an essential qualification, while Mahommah could give him the vernacular style."[19] In further astonishment, Judd was told about "the people of Dahomey and Ashantee," of whom he could have known but little, who Baquaqua said "do not speak the Arabic." Judd's intention was "the early conversion of Mahommah." Judd was relaying this information less than two months after taking Baquaqua into his home as a cook and before Baquaqua actually underwent baptism. Judd had already followed up on one of Baquaqua's requests. He had approached Brother W. H. Webley, who "has taken a lively interest in our African boy Mahommah" and was trying to get a copy of the Bible in Arabic. Webley was based at Jacmel in southern Haïti and met Baquaqua in early November 1847, shortly after the latter's installation in the Judd household, when he suggested that, if the American Baptist Free Mission Society could not send Baquaqua as a missionary to Africa, the English Baptists might do so.[20] Baquaqua also accompanied Judd on a visit to Webley at Jacmel in 1849.[21] Judd was fully aware of the "many particulars of his escape from prison, etc." and made it clear that Baquaqua "wishes to express thanks to those kind friends in New York and Boston, who so kindly assisted him."

On arrival in Port-au-Prince, Baquaqua had first worked for an African American émigré, but he was not treated well for reasons that are not explained. Baquaqua was eventually turned out. He claims then to have been at another low point in his ongoing odyssey, hampered as he was by not speaking French, and he sought solace in drink.[22] Thus, his association with the Free Will Baptists transformed his life, resulting not only in his conversion and baptism but also later his education in the United States. His association with the Mission gave him access to a network of Baptist abolitionists in New York, Pennsylvania, and Canada West, ultimately leading to the publication of his autobiography. Soon after meeting the Rev. Mr. and Mrs. Judd, and Mrs. Judd's sister Electa Lake, who shared their home, Baquaqua was living in their house, serving as their cook, and sharing his life with them.[23] From the beginning there was a meeting of minds, and very quickly a strong bond developed, reinforced on Judd's side by the hope that if Baquaqua were converted he might become a missionary in Africa. Although waiting on the Judd household, his relationship with the family quickly extended far past that. Baquaqua became a disciple of the Judds and admired Rev. Judd highly.

Baquaqua was converted to the Free Will Baptist faith and was baptized by Rev. Judd in 1848. While the Judds listened to his stories of his family and his enslavement, and doing a good job of understanding what they were being told, they increasingly encouraged him to return to Africa as a missionary, which played a big part in Baquaqua's own desire to convert. Judd thought that if Baquaqua was to become an interpreter and guide for an American missionary in Africa, the Free Will Baptists should support him, especially in securing him an education in the United States. Through Judd, Baquaqua gained access to the network of the American Baptist Free Mission Society, which allowed him to connect with abolitionists in the United States and Canada West as well as a publisher for his story.

With the Judds's encouragement, Baquaqua also seized the opportunity to acquire an education in English. As Mrs. Judd reported, within a few days of his arrival, he "expresses a very strong desire to obtain an education. . . . He very eagerly embraces every opportunity to read; and among us all, he manages to get several lessons into [a] day, generally."[24] Thereafter, Baquaqua studied English and otherwise ingratiated himself into the hearts of the Judd household. In March 1848, he experienced conversion to Christianity and in July was baptized into the Baptist church.[25] After conversion, he continued his education, concentrating on reading the Bible and learning to write in English.[26] This interest in education soon brought him to the attention of Cyrus Grosvenor, the editor of the *Christian Contributor and Free Missionary*, an organ of the Free Will Baptist movement then being published in Utica, New York, to whom Baquaqua wrote a letter that was printed in that journal in December 1848.[27] Grosvenor was to become president of New York Central College, which Baquaqua would attend. As his letter makes clear, Baquaqua hoped to continue his education in the United States: "I want to go to the United States very much, and go to school and learn to understand the Bible very well," preparatory to going back to Africa as a missionary.[28]

By chance of circumstances, Baquaqua had the opportunity to attend college because of his flight to Haiti in 1847. The Society also founded New York Central College, which opened in 1849 in McGrawville, a small town in the central "finger lakes" region of New York state. Baquaqua experienced harsh winters subjected to the heavy snow of central New York (see figure 5.3).[29]

McGrawville was located along one of the glacial valleys without a lake to the south of Syracuse and its nexus of lakes and canals that formed the hub of the Erie Canal system. Baquaqua became one of the first students at Central College in 1849, identified as "Mahome, a gigantic Negro direct from Africa."[30] It was only four years since he had left Djougou. Grosvenor published an appeal for "one rich man" to sponsor Baquaqua's education in America.[31] That man almost certainly turned out to be Gerrit Smith (1797–1874) of the sleepy village of Peterboro, New York, where Smith made his home. Smith was an ardent abolitionist, a temperance man, and perhaps the richest man in New York state, who invested in canals, railroads, and owned vast tracts of land.[32]

After Baquaqua returned to the United States, Baquaqua visited Smith in Peterboro several times, it seems. When Baquaqua was having difficulties with the Free Mission Society, he wrote to Smith, and when he wanted funds to publish his autobiography, he also approached Smith soliciting a loan to

FIGURE 5.3 Village of McGrawville, New York, circa 1864, as photographed by G. L. Holden, dentist and photographer, Cortland County Historical Society Collections, Cortland, New York; gift of Minne E. Holden Young.

meet the costs of printing. Although Smith had been brought up in a Presbyterian household, as an adult and political activist, he was not affiliated with any religious denomination, consciously fashioning himself as nondenominational and founding a "free" church in Peterboro. Nonetheless, his connections with the Baptist Free Mission were strong. He attended the Baptist-run Hamilton College (1814–18) and supported the Baptist Free Mission in founding New York Central College in McGrawville in 1849. He also hosted the semi-annual meeting of the American Baptist Free Mission at his home in Peterboro in 1851 (which Baquaqua attended). In addition, he maintained strong links with many of the important abolitionists, including those in Canada West, whatever their religious affiliation.

Like McGrawville, Peterboro was isolated from the main transport corridors. The Smith mansion was at one end of the broad tree-lined park that marked the center of Peterboro, with a Temperance Hotel near the Smith mansion and the Baptist church at the opposite end of the square. The village was named after Smith's father who had pioneered the family business into a vast holding of land and extensive investments in banks, canals, and railroads. Gerrit inherited his father's wealth in 1819 and proceeded to consolidate his holdings despite his radical visions that tied him to the abolitionist cause.

He corresponded with most of the abolitionist leaders from Frederick Douglass of *The North Star* in Rochester to William Lloyd Garrison of *The Liberator* in Boston. He was instrumental in placing Baquaqua in touch with other abolitionists and supported his attendance at Central College. Smith almost certainly later helped Baquaqua publish his autobiography.

In addition to his considerable land holdings in upstate New York and his investments in banking, railroads, and canals, Smith was active in various nondenominational reform movements, including temperance, bible and tract societies, and the Sunday school movement, as well as various antislavery organizations. He also granted land to free Blacks of African descent, most of whom lived in Brooklyn, so that they could meet the property requirement under the restrictive voting regulations of New York State. Although elected to the House of Representatives in 1852, he resigned his seat in August 1854, returning to politics in 1856 as the presidential candidate for the Liberty Party, and in 1859 providing clandestine financial support for John Brown's abortive raid on Harper's Ferry in Virginia, now West Virginia.[33] Since Smith was more widely connected than Baquaqua's erstwhile Baptist sponsors, it was perhaps through him that Baquaqua was introduced to his editor and his publisher in Michigan. However, it was Smith whom Baquaqua approached when he found that he could no longer count on the Free Mission Society for financial support in publishing the autobiography.[34]

Fortunately, there are stories, including reports of Baquaqua's own comments, that allow some assessment of how Baquaqua interpreted his commitment to Christianity, considering his Muslim background in Africa. In Djougou, as has been seen, Baquaqua had belonged to a devoutly Muslim family, even if his own commitment to the tenets of Islam was less stringent than that of his father or brother; in addition to dropping out of Quranic school, he also indulged in alcoholic drinks, which was by his own account the occasion of his enslavement, despite his own recognition, stated in the autobiography, that Muslims "use no kinds of intoxicating drinks on any occasion."[35] As a slave in Brazil, he had also received some rudimentary instruction in the Roman Catholic religion, although he was retrospectively dismissive of its superficiality: "[W]e were taught to chant some words which we did not know the meaning of."[36]

Prior to his conversion, in his conversations with Jones on the voyage from Boston to Haiti and after arrival there, they had discussed "his ideas of God, &c., of the soul, of heaven, &c." Baquaqua had apparently indicated his continuing adherence to Islam: "His name for God is Allah"; and tried to convey to Jones his concept of the soul through an analogy with a person's shadow. He also expressed disapproval of alcoholic drinks; "He is, also, strongly opposed to intemperance. When Jones explained to him the object of our Temperance Pledge, he expressed himself very ready to have his name attached to it."[37] Given his own indulgence in alcohol earlier, in Brazil as well as in Africa, and indeed his admitted lapses in this respect in Haiti later, prior to his definitive conversion, this lapse should perhaps be understood in terms of an assertion of the Islamic prohibition, to which Baquaqua as a Muslim in principle subscribed, rather than a statement about his personal conduct. But in any case, a degree of convergence between Islam and Baptist Christianity is evident, which must be presumed to have facilitated his subsequent conversion.

The account of Baquaqua's conversion in March 1848 given by Mrs. Judd is conventional enough in stressing his growing consciousness of his own sinfulness and of the presumed evidence of God's providential intervention in his life hitherto: "Mahomah sin so much, O too much ... God very good for Mahomah—not let him die."[38] Mrs. Judd understood him to be "referring to his sins in Africa, as well as since." The later autobiography indicates that it was specifically his behavior when employed as a palace servant whose "wickedness" he retrospectively repented, referring mainly to his activities in looting provisions from the local peasantry,[39] but perhaps also to his indulgence in alcoholic drinks. It is noteworthy, however, that Baquaqua saw the problem of sin in collective as well as individual terms, as affecting the society in Africa from which he had come as well as himself specifically: "[H]e had been thinking about Africa; and how bad the people were there. (This he would never admit until lately.) 'Now I see the people very bad in Africa.'" In the night after this conversation, "he dreamed of being there [in Africa]," and the next day announced his wish to go back to Africa to preach Christianity. Although the Judds assumed that Baquaqua's dream of home related to his realization of the "wickedness" of African society, and its consequent need of Christian salvation, it is surely not overly cynical to suggest that nostalgia for his homeland, very likely crystallized by the stimulus of the Judds's persistent urging on him of the idea of returning as a missionary, played a central role in his conversion. Certainly, Baquaqua's commitment to education and to the Christian church was consistently linked thereafter to the project of returning home.

After his conversion, Baquaqua seems to have internalized the Christian teaching he received. He thought that the Muslim religion to which he had adhered in Africa was rather a variant of the worship of the same "True God," although nominally at least he now asserted that Islam was a false faith— unless the numerous references in the autobiography to Muhammad as a "false prophet" are to be attributed to his editor Samuel Moore, rather than to

Baquaqua himself. There are, nevertheless, some indications that his attitude to Islam remained ambivalent. One was his retention of the name Mahommah, which oddly is nowhere commented on in the Free Will Baptist sources, despite its obvious (and indeed, recognized) significance as a badge of religious affiliation. It is also noteworthy that reference to his conversion stresses the issue of temperance, on which Baptist and Islamic teaching converged: "[A]fter my conversion to Christianity I gave up drinking and all other kinds of vices."[40] There is also an intriguing story, reported by Mrs. Judd, of a conversation Baquaqua had with someone who was Spanish and Catholic in Haiti, in which he derided the latter's veneration of a crucifix: "[T]his God wood, eh? . . . Well you take e little wood—make a God—go pray for God, eh? . . . Oh! Your God not say be nothing . . . O Mr. [Hepburn] very bad, [to] have wooden God. God not like it."[41] Here again, although the Judds understood Baquaqua's anti-Catholicism as evidence of the strength of his Baptist faith, an alternative reading might be that his commitment to Christianity was sometimes compatible with the retention of things Muslim. Condemnation of wooden idols was a central feature of Islam, which may have influenced the argument that he pursued. In this way, perhaps, Baquaqua was able to find some resolution of the predicament of being born a Muslim but being saved by Christians.

In October 1849, just over two years after arriving in Haiti, Baquaqua departed for New York, arriving there apparently on 25 November. He was accompanied on this voyage by Mrs. Judd and her sister Electa Lake, who was returning to the United States for reasons of health. In the autobiography, Baquaqua says he was sent out of Haiti to avoid being drafted into the militia;[42] and the contemporary account of Mrs. Judd confirms that there were fears that "he might be arrested and pressed into the army."[43] But this circumstance can only have determined the precise timing of his return to the United States; the overriding reason for this return, which had been projected since the previous year, was to advance his education, with a view to returning to Africa as part of a mission. The danger of being drafted related to the protracted war in which Soulouque was currently engaged in his attempt to conquer the Spanish side of the island of Hispaniola.

During this period, Baquaqua lived in a moment of great personal turmoil. He was in an unknown land. Though now free and in a free land, his freedom should not be limited to just not having chains or physical punishment. That too was a time of uncertainty, of sadness, and without any purpose. The interaction with the Judds offered him the possibility of once again dreaming of returning to Africa, even if for that he had to propagate Protestant Christianity. It is quite interesting to think of a connection between the stories of Baquaqua and Haiti. Both trace the quest for freedom. Baquaqua, of course, knew slavery, having been controlled by different masters and indeed one woman in northern Dahomey. These periods of being dominated provide context for the imposition of slavery and the denial of freedom. His journey is a continuous adventure because he never lost interest in freedom, and, when he found a chance, he didn't think twice and ran toward it. Despite Haiti's current conditions, its history was also marked by the experience of suffering domination in different contexts of European colonization, even though freedom, equality, and fraternity were being preached in abolitionist and religious circles. The population in the most prosperous French colony at the end of the eighteenth century had seized the opportunity to obtain freedom from colonization and slavery. Baquaqua would have known this legacy. It must have seemed curious that the polarization of Haiti left no room for him. He wasted no time in Haiti but concentrated on learning English and coming to terms with conversion. There is nothing in his writing or in memoranda about him that show any awareness of the political situation in Haiti in the time he was there.

Baquaqua's stay in Port-au-Prince was during a period of intense political disruption as Soulouque moved to eliminate opposition through detention and execution of the country's educated elite and reliance on *vodun* priests who held considerable sway over the rural, uneducated population. Vodun, or *vodou*, was the Haitian manifestation of religious observation in Ouidah, which focused on temples inhabited by pythons. Soulouque was more in tune with popular belief in vodun than Christianity. According to Emmanuel Lachaud, "Soulouque targeted Protestantism as incompatible with the nation and, thereby, incompatible with his rule."[44] The political situation was hardly conducive to achieving the goals that the Judds were clearly promoting— that is, the establishment of more missions, including one in Africa. Hence Baquaqua's initial introduction to Christianity and the possibility that his commitment in converting was the hope that he would be able to return to Africa. In supporting Baquaqua in this aim, the Judds arranged to take Baquaqua back to the United States.

Upon their arrival in New York City in 1849, as reported by Mrs. Judd, she, her sister, and Baquaqua proceeded by steamer to Albany, from where they "took the cars" to Fort Plain in the Mohawk River valley and then went by stagecoach to the sisters' parental home in Milford. They also visited

Meredith, in nearby Delaware County, where Judd had been pastor for seven years. Baquaqua had now entered the Baptist and abolitionist networks of the United States, and everywhere he visited he was encouraged to solicit donations to support his future educational career. As Mrs. Judd observed, people "manifested a deep interest in Mahommah . . . [in] every family where we visited, and this interest was manifested by giving him money, or substantial articles of clothing, &c."[45] According to his autobiography, Baquaqua remained four weeks in Milford, before moving from there to Meredith, "amongst the Free Missions," where the subject of his further education was discussed, and to his relief, "they agreed at once [to] undertake the task of educating me."[46] This probably refers to a meeting of the Board of the American Baptist Free Mission Society, which was attended by Baquaqua, together with Mrs. Judd and her sister, and where he spoke about his desire to return to Africa as a missionary.[47] Further efforts were made to raise funds for him; in the following year, the Annual Meeting of the Free Mission Society expressed its thanks to the Free Mission Society of Franklin, New York, for having "kindly [come] forward and ministered to his needs."[48] This was not to be Baquaqua's last fundraising mission. Later he also visited other towns where abolitionists were prominent, often for the purpose of raising money for his education and then increasingly to sponsor his return to Africa. Baquaqua's tour of the Free Will Baptist network introduced him to abolitionists throughout upstate New York, especially in Syracuse, Utica, and McGrawville, and later also in eastern Pennsylvania.[49]

Between 1850 and 1853, Baquaqua attended New York Central College in McGrawville, in the finger lakes district of upstate New York (figure 5.4). As an abolitionist institution established by the American Baptist Free Mission Society, Central College admitted women as well as Blacks. Its charter stated the basic commitments of the Free Baptists, "unchangeably pledged to the morality of Anti-slavery; and . . . the unity, equity, and brotherhood of the human race." The College was also committed to "equal advantages in literary, scientific, moral and physical education" for women.[50] Baquaqua, with Mrs. Judd and her sister, arrived at Central College in McGrawville on 16 January 1850; a letter from the latter records the dinner held for their reception, at which the president of the college, Cyrus Grosvenor, and Baquaqua himself both spoke. Grosvenor was already familiar with Baquaqua since he edited the *Christian Contributor and Free Missionary*, and, as has been demonstrated, had been in correspondence with the Judds about Baquaqua. In her presentation, Mrs. Judd's sister, E. C. Lake, praised the commitment to equality,

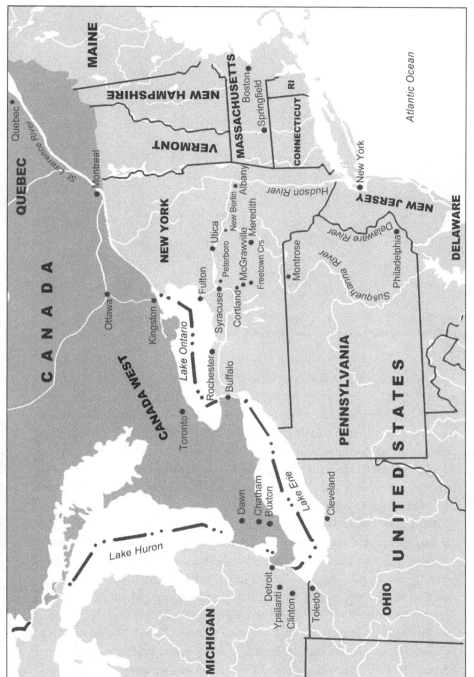

MAP 5.1 Upstate New York and Canada West

FIGURE 5.4 New York Central College, McGraw, New York: Cortland County Historical Society Collections, Cortland, New York; gift of Mrs. Seba Alexander.

without respect to gender, race, or authority, that she witnessed during the event.[51] Brother J. Scott of the Baptist Church, Elgin, Illinois, was in attendance at a prayer meeting in the college on the following night, Saturday, 17 January, and reported that Mrs. Judd and her sister had "brought a colored youth with them, named Mahommah." He understood that "He is a native of Africa, and was kidnapped by some of the natives of America [sic] . . . He is to be a student here; and will probably, some time or other, bear the glad tidings of salvation to central Africa."[52]

Baquaqua joined the college in the middle of its first year in operation. He was enrolled in the Primary Department, the preparatory school for the college.[53] His teacher, Miss Kezia King, wrote a report on her experience teaching his class, although she did not specifically mention Baquaqua.[54] She also wrote a poem that was to be recited by Baquaqua, which is quoted in the autobiography.[55] While he was there, Central College grew to about two hundred students, half of whom were women. There were other Blacks besides Baquaqua, including Joseph Purvis, Robert Purvis, and James Forten, the sons of prominent families of African descent in Philadelphia.[56]

There was one other student who had been born in Africa, John Lom La-grow, from Senegambia, also enrolled in the Primary Department, with whom Baquaqua roomed for a time during 1852.[57] Lagrow is credited as coming from "Senegambia, Africa" in the *Catalogue of the Officers & Students* for 1852/53. He is said to have come from Africa two years earlier "as a cabin boy on a vessel"; he had lived the previous year with a family in Augusta, Maine, but had then been taken by J. E. Ambrose to Utica and then to Syracuse, where Gerrit Smith, the principal benefactor of Central College, "manifested a very deep interest in his welfare" and paid for his fare to McGrawville. On 1 August 1852, Lagrow wrote to Smith asking for money to buy boots and a pair of pants, identifying himself as being "from Africa."[58] In a letter to Ambrose dated 17 July 1852, in *The American Baptist*, Lagrow wrote, "I wish to inform you that I am well, and well pleased with my school and place. I am boarding with Mr. Briggs on the College farm, and at work for him the most of the time that I labor. I think I am doing well in my studies, and think we have very good teachers, and I feel glad that I came here. I room with Mahom-mah, and find him a very pleasant companion." Similarly, Baquaqua's educa-tion continued to be financed by charitable donations, organized through the Free Mission Society. As the Board of the Society reported to its Annual Meeting in 1852: "Eld. B.F. Remington in connection with brethren Silus Hammond and Ezra Thompson are a committee of the Board to oversee and make arrangements for that education which is necessary to prepare him for wider usefulness on his return [to Africa]. Through their exertions, those of some others, and his own labors, enough has been obtained to meet his expenses to the present."[59] However, Baquaqua also contributed to his own living expenses, for at least part of his time at Central College, by leas-ing and cultivating a farm locally.[60]

Baquaqua was exposed to teasing from the other students, and perhaps it was even racially motivated, although it is difficult to distinguish between outright hostility and the types of pranks that school children sometimes had to endure. In May 1850, he wrote to "Sister Cushman," apparently Jose-phine Cushman Bateham, whom he had met in Haiti, to complain about such abuse. Cushman referred to him in unflattering terms herself, calling him "the converted African slave, who was last year in Hayti, in the family of Rev Wm. L. Judd." She condescendingly attributed his letter as being "full of beautiful Christian simplicity, and as coming from a converted heathen slave, administers some admonitions which we would fain [sic] hope will not be in vain."

DEAR SISTER CUSHMAN:

I hope we will meet together again in this world; but if we do not, I hope we will meet in heaven. I almost weep some times when I think about you, and brother Cushman, and his death in Hayti. But we must not be sorry, for he has gone home; we hope we shall meet again in heaven. I came here, to McGrawville, with sister Judd; and I have learned somethings since I have been here, and I think I understand better than I did when I saw you. I wish to study to prepare myself to return to Africa, to teach the poor people of Africa about Christ; that He died for our sins. I hope you will pray for me, that God may make me humble, and deliver me from wicked people. God made the world, and everything in the world; but we are poor creatures; we do not love God enough in our hearts. God has done much good for me; He is very good to me; and I feel very thankful to Him. I find many good friends here; they are very kind to me; some of them give me bed clothes to keep me warm; some of them make me a coat. It is very cold here. There are many good people here, I find, and many bad people, too. The people at Hayti are very bad, but not so bad as some of the people here; for the people here know better; they have the Bible to read; the people at Hayti don' t know how to read the Bible. Some of the people here don't believe the Bible, and don't believe in our Saviour, Jesus Christ. Dear Sister, I staid at Hayti a little more than two years, but I never heard any young man or woman say that they did not believe the Bible. But since I came here to America, I see some who say they don't believe the Bible; some say they don't believe in Jesus. In this College, too, some of them are very good, and some of them are very bad. When I first came here they used me very bad; and I felt very bad, and thought I would not stay here, but would go away. They took out the bell-tongue, and came to me and said that I stole it. I felt very bad. They took the furnace doors, and, the next morning, came and asked me where I put the furnace doors. I said I did not know where they were; they said yes, that I knew. They make much mischief here; it makes me feel very bad, but I try to pray, and read the Bible in my room very much, and God helps me; He is very good to me, and makes me happy always. I hope you will pray for the poor slave, I am very sorry, I am very sorry; because I have been a slave once, myself, five or six years ago; and I know that Slavery is very bad; I suffered much; Slavery was very bad for me; and now I am very sorry for the poor slave; I am very sorry! I am very sorry! And some white people here don't care much about Slavery; some think it is very good.

From your Friend,

MAHOMMAH G. BAYUAYUA [sic][61]

The *Catalogue of Officers and Students* of Central College for the years 1851/52 and 1852/53 lists Baquaqua's place of residence as McGrawville;[62] and the autobiography indicates that he roomed in the college.[63] According to his roommate Lagrow, part of the time Baquaqua lived at the college farm, apparently referring to the building across the street from the main building of the college.[64] However, he resided part of this period at Freetown Corners, a few miles from McGrawville: two letters by him that were published in the *American Baptist* in 1850–51 were both written from Freetown; and later, at least, he was a member of the Baptist Church there.[65] He was also active in wider Free Baptist networks, partly in order to raise funds for his education. In September 1851, he spoke at the Semi-Annual Meeting of the Baptist Free Mission Society, held at Peterboro, New York, the home of Gerrit Smith, where a collection of $2.35 was made for his benefit.[66] And in June 1852, he attended the Annual Meeting of the Society, this time at Montrose, Pennsylvania, where "Mahommah, the converted African, led in prayer," after which a collection in aid of his education was taken up.[67]

At Central College, as earlier in Haiti, Baquaqua seems to have been an assiduous student, in contrast to his own reports of his earlier educational failures in Djougou, where he had dropped out of school. When he spoke to the Board of the Free Mission Society in 1850, it was noted that his English was still poor, although he was nevertheless positively received: "Though imperfectly acquainted with our language, his prayers and exhortations testify to every hearer that he had been truly taught of Christ."[68] During his time at Central College, the autobiography claims that he "made very great progress in learning;"[69] and this is supported by an approving report of the Board of the Free Mission Society in 1853 that "his fidelity to Christ continues unchanged; [and] his progress in knowledge is encouraging."[70] Yet, it is clear that he had continuing trouble with English, perhaps especially with the spoken word, although he wrote (in his extant letters) carefully and intelligibly, if ungrammatically. A report of 1853, after he had left Central College, refers to the "quite broken English" that he still spoke, although it also noted that "he improves [as] rapidly as could reasonably be anticipated in communicating his thoughts"; and he seems to have been an effective speaker, to the extent that audiences liked him and warmed to his story, despite the deficiencies of his English.[71]

According to the autobiography, Baquaqua studied at Central College for "nearly three years," which indicates that he left around the end of 1852 or the beginning of 1853, in the middle of the academic session.[72] The reason for his departure is not given, but it may be suspected that either his performance was judged inadequate to proceed to more advanced study or it was thought that he would be able to raise funds to support a mission to Africa. After leaving Central College, according to the autobiography, he initially continued his education in a school at Freetown Corners, also "under the direction of the missions,"[73] although no confirmation of this has been traced in Free Mission records. At the Annual Meeting of the Free Mission Society in June 1852, a committee was formed to oversee fund raising to support Baquaqua's education: "It is still the desire of Mahommah, the converted African to return to the land of his nativity as a missionary of the Cross. Eld B. F. Remington in connection with brethren Silus Hammond and Ezra Thompson, are a committee of the Board to oversee and make arrangements for that education which it [is] necessary to prepare him for wider usefulness on his return. Through their exertions, those of some others, and his own labors, enough has been obtained to meet his expenses to the present. . . . A collection to aid in the education of Mahommah was taken up."[74]

These efforts may have been sufficient to subsidize Baquaqua's education, although never enough to eliminate his need to work on the college farms or to lease an acre of land to grow food. In the summer of 1853, however, as Baquaqua later complained, his "friends" decided that his education should be discontinued or suspended, so that he could devote his time to fund-raising for the projected African mission in which he was intended to serve.[75] In June 1853, shortly after the Annual Meeting of the Free Mission Society in Utica, New York, which Baquaqua attended, the Society's Board charged him with touring Baptist Churches to solicit donations,[76] though on this, conversely, the autobiography is curiously silent. The fundraising campaign began in eastern Pennsylvania at Montrose, where Albert L. Post, the vice president and a trustee of Central College lived.[77] Post was born in Montrose in 1809, educated at Union College, then read law under Judge William Jessup, at Montrose, and was admitted to the Bar in 1833. He served as a deputy attorney-general of

Pennsylvania in 1836. For a period following 1837, he published the *Specta-tor*, an abolitionist newspaper. He assisted fugitives in making their escape. In 1841 he was ordained and involved in the Baptist church as well as Central College. He died in 1887.

After visiting the small Black community of Brooklyn, south of Montrose, Baquaqua returned to New York State. His surviving letters show that he was again a resident in McGrawville by August 1853, although during August and September he successively visited Syracuse and New Berlin; whether any of these visits were in connection with his fundraising activities for the Free Mission Society is not indicated but can be assumed.[78] The Eleventh Annual Meeting of the American Baptist Free Mission Society, held in June 1854, noted that Mahommah G. Baquaqua had been authorized in 1853 "to visit, under the supervision of a Committee appointed for that purpose, certain pastors, and to seek aid from them and their churches for the purpose of opening a mission in Africa. It is understood that he did thus visit, to some extent; but with what results is not definitely known to us. A resolution was passed by the Board on the 1st of September last, that the same Committee be requested to correspond with several individuals named, in regard to their becoming Missionaries in Africa. No such Missionary, however, has yet been secured."[79] According to Baquaqua, he was expected to raise $5,000 in a year, which may explain the coldness of the 1854 Annual Report. Baquaqua thought that he could "never do it in a year."[80]

The amount he raised by early July 1853 ($200) was clearly a paltry sum in comparison with the amount that was required. It is for this reason, perhaps, that Baquaqua concluded that "I do not think that my friends will do anything in my Mission."[81]

Although Baquaqua moved within the Free Baptist network, he was also exposed to the ugly racist face of upstate New York. In the autobiography he reports a series of incidents of harassment against him by fellow students in McGrawville, which he believed were racially inspired: "I could not tell why they plagued me thus, excepting that they did not like my color."[82] His experience indicates that it was difficult for a Black man even in supposedly abolitionist McGrawville. In a scandal that occurred during the period of his residence, William Allen, a professor who was of partial African descent at Central College, became involved with one of his students, Mary King, a white girl from Fulton, north of Syracuse, whose father was a minister and avowedly an abolitionist.[83] When Allen went to visit her, he found himself exposed to the virulent hostility of the community, including the supposedly abolitionist King family. Only Mary's sister remained loyal to the couple. On

30 January 1853, a mob of local people drove Allen out of town; he was lucky that he was not lynched. He and Mary then arranged to meet in New York City, where they were married on 30 March and sailed from Boston for England on 9 April. In England, the couple was active on the abolitionist lecture circuit, also touring extensively in Ireland.[84] The Allen-King romance was condemned in much of the upstate New York press.[85] In response, Allen published a book about the couple's experiences, *American Prejudice against Colour: An Authentic Narrative, Showing How Easily the Nation Got into an Uproar*, in 1853. As noted below, Baquaqua met up with Allen in London after going to England in 1855.

As one of the students at Central College, King probably had a strong influence on Baquaqua. King's personal crisis that had been racialized provided the context for Baquaqua's experiences at Central College. Because of local prejudice, the Black students at the College were not allowed to go into the village of McGrawville, an atmosphere that the King affair only exacerbated. As a classicist, appointed to teach Greek and rhetoric, Allen publicly was an eloquent speaker whom the *Syracuse Daily Standard* referred to as "a colored gentleman, of brilliant talents, and education" whose lecture "was one of the best ever delivered in this city."[86] Allen gave numerous public lectures and wrote many letters to the abolitionist press. He was preoccupied with lecturing on the "African race," a subject on which he spoke more than on all other topics combined. He argued that "Africans originated the arts and sciences and gave the first impulse to civilization."[87] He gave other talks, including "The Mental Powers and Abilities of the Colored Man" in Boston in 1849; "History, Literature, and Destiny of the Colored Race" in Rochester in 1849; a series of lectures on the "Origin, Literature and Destiny of the African Race" in 1850, Saxonville, Massachusetts in 1850; and "The Origin, History, Characteristics, Condition, and Probable Destiny of the African Race" in Liverpool in 1857.[88]

Although Baquaqua does not mention the Allen-King affair, either in the autobiography or in his extant letters, it seems probable that it had indirect repercussions in his personal life. Like Allen, Baquaqua also became close friends with a white girl, who was a fellow member of the Baptist Church at Freetown Corners and whom he met shortly after his arrival in McGrawville. Around June 1853, rumors began circulating that he intended to marry this girl. As he wrote to George Whipple,

> I did not like to have you think that I have been doing some things very bad. But I did not. This Lady they spoke of, She was very good friends to the colored people. I got acquainted with her about three years ago. She

very good friend to me, about four months ago they began to talk about her and I, that we going to get marry. Her Mother did not allow me to come to her house, so I want [= went] one day and told her that I never say to her daughter that I should like to get Marry with her, but She did not believe me.[89]

Despite his denials, her mother banned him from her household. In October of the same year, after further rumors that the couple intended imminently to marry, Baquaqua was warned not to attend the church at Freetown Corners because persons opposed to the supposed marriage might "do very bad to me." Faced with this explicit threat of violence, he observed that "I have to be very careful, I don't go out much . . . I have a great trouble with these wickit [wicked] people."[90] The pressure thus placed upon him to distance himself from his friend presumably reflected local reaction to the incident involving Professor Allen, which had occurred only a few months earlier.

By the latter half of 1853, indeed, it seems that Baquaqua was increasingly disillusioned with US society. In August of that year, he asserted that if he could not go to Africa, he would not stay in the United States: "I did not like to stay in this country." Again in September, he wrote that "I think I shall not remain in the United States long," Instead, he said he would go to Canada.[91] His letters indicate that he intended to leave McGrawville for Canada in late October,[92] and very likely he did, this being the visit to Canada for "a short time" mentioned in the autobiography.[93] By January 1854, as his letters show, he was back in McGrawville,[94] but he presumably left definitively for Canada West soon afterward. The autobiography reports his very favorable impressions of Canada: "I was kindly received by all classes wherever I went . . . I am thankful to God . . . that I am now in a land . . . where every man acting as a man, no matter what his color, is regarded as a brother, and where all are equally free to do and to say;"[95] the contrast with his experience in the United States, although implicit, is pointed. His experience may have been as pleasant as he portrayed, although in fact refugees fleeing the United States on the Underground Railroad were not always so well received.[96]

In his memoirs, Baquaqua claims that he took out naturalization papers in Canada, which would technically have made him a British citizen.[97] Although no records appear to have survived, it is likely that he was registered, as fugitives and asylum seekers from the United States were, for the purpose of providing him with documentation that could be used to foil would-be bounty hunters from the United States who occasionally tried to kidnap refugees and return them to their masters south of the border.[98] In Canada, he stayed for a

FIGURE 5.5 Chatham, Canada West: King Street, looking west from 5th Street, 1860, Courtesy of the Chatham-Kent Museum, 85.27.2.15, N674, Bk. 2#15.

time in Chatham, from where his only extant letter from Canada was written, in May 1854. Chatham, located on the Thames River and connecting via Lake St. Clair with Detroit, was the center of the largest concentration of Black immigrants in southwestern Canada West.[99] As the commercial and transportation center, Chatham became one of the principal foci for the refugee population (figure 5.5).

Nearby Buxton, located a few kilometers south of Chatham, had been founded in 1849 as an all-Black community of landowning farmers under the patronage of the Rev. William King, a Presbyterian minister and former slave owner. The community at Dawn, to the north of Chatham, was established as refuge for fugitives from the United States and a center of education and training under the leadership of Josiah Henson, allegedly the model for the Uncle Tom of Harriet Beecher Stowe's *Uncle Tom's Cabin*. Rev. William P. Newman, also of the Free Mission Society, became secretary of the settlement. Newman was an African American from Ohio, who wrote "The Colored People of Canada" for the *Christian Contributor and Free Missionary* in its 13 September 1848 issue. He was pastor at the Second Baptist Church in

Detroit in 1849, and otherwise "labored among the colored people of Canada West." Newman became pastor of the Baptist church in Toronto in 1852 and was appointed editor of the *Provincial Freeman* in 1855. He was a frequent correspondent for the *American Baptist* between 1851 and 1855, whereafter he used the *Provincial Freeman* as his voice. Newman was a relentless critic of Josiah Henson and Henson's management of the Dawn Settlement, which was forced into receivership in 1854.[100] Newman arguably can be considered to have undermined the development of the Dawn settlement.

In choosing to stay in Chatham, Baquaqua may have been using his connections in the Free Mission Society, since it was one of the places in Canada West where the Free Will Baptists were to be found, although by 1854, Baquaqua's relations with the Free Mission Society had become somewhat strained. He developed other contacts, perhaps specifically through Gerrit Smith, who at the time was a congressman from upstate New York and well known in Canada West through the Underground Railroad network, and with whom Baquaqua corresponded during his period of residence in Canada.[101] In his letter to Smith in May 1854, Baquaqua confides his anguish over the failure of the Free Will Baptists to fulfill the commitment to an African Mission, with which he had intended to be attached. With his hopes of returning to Africa undermined, he appears to have contemplated settling permanently in North America; he specifically requested assistance from Smith in buying land in Canada (probably at nearby Buxton, which required that settlers be landowners). Alternatively, he suggested that he be granted land in New York State, presumably because he knew that Smith had been granting land to people of African descent and poor whites from his vast holdings in the Adirondack Mountains.[102] The New York Legislature enacted restrictive voting rights to prevent Blacks in New York and elsewhere from voting. Requirements were increased to include ownership of property. Because of his vast land holdings, Smith challenged the discriminatory limitations by giving land to Blacks from Brooklyn and elsewhere. While much of the land in the Adirondacks was poor farmland, and some land grants were actually at the bottom of lakes, Smith's efforts to counteract New York legislation to limit voting rights attracted John Brown, who would later lead the uprising in Kansas against slavery and then the abortive attempt to seize the federal arsenal at Harper's Ferry, and who left Connecticut to reside in the nascent community. Brown knew how to farm, unlike the urban Blacks that had been given land and actually showed up to take possession. The settlers included those who settled at a place named Timbuctoo. Brown quickly became disillusioned with this new venture to teach people how to farm and moved to Kansas with his sons to confront slavery more openly and more violently. For reasons that are not entirely explained, Baquaqua did not take up land in the Adirondacks. Nor did anything become of his request for land in Canada West. He decided instead to pursue his aim to return to Africa.

In July 1854, Baquaqua went to Detroit to arrange publication of his narrative, where he wrote again to Smith, this time soliciting his help in meeting the cost of printing.[103] The role Smith may have played in the publication is not clear otherwise. It was thought that he would attend a convention of emigrationists in Cleveland in August, which Martin Delany and James Whitfield of Buffalo organized. Baquaqua was staying in Chatham at the time that Delany was living there. His autobiography was advertised in the *Cleveland Daily Herald* on 23 August with Baquaqua identified as

> a native of Zoogo, in the interior of Africa [who] has, through amanuensis, written a book of sixty-six pages, giving a history of his rather eventful life, and a description of his country. To the many who are interested in learning of that dark land, the book cannot fail to be of use. The author, Mohammah, is now a resident of Canada, and we learn, is preparing himself to return to do good in Africa. His conversion to Christianity, the value and cheapness of his narrative, (25 cents) his desire to use the proceeds in fitting himself for usefulness, and his presence in the city to sell his work, will no doubt enable him to dispose of many copies here, which will the better enable him to return to bless his "Own—his native land."[104]

As the cover clearly shows, he wanted his identity as an African prominent. As seen in figure 5.6, draped over his shoulder is a garment, while his right shoulder is naked, although this is not the way Muslims dressed in Djougou or elsewhere in the Hausa diaspora, the image clearly was intended to give the impression that he was "African."

He almost certainly did not go to Cleveland. His name is not mentioned in the proceedings of the convention, which are well recorded.[105] If he had been there, he would almost certainly made contact with James Whitfield, who wrote the poem "Prayer of the Oppressed," which blesses Baquaqua's autobiography. The poem was initially published in *America, and Other Poems* in 1853.[106] Similarly, he would have met Martin Delany, who organized the conference and whose interests in returning to Africa were similar to Baquaqua's. A meeting might have consolidated a relationship that would have seen Baquaqua part of Delany's mission to the Niger River and Abeokuta only a few years later.[107] In the absence of further evidence, therefore, it seems that Baquaqua did not actually make it to Cleveland.

AN INTERESTING NARRATIVE.

BIOGRAPHY
OF

MAHOMMAH G. BAQUAQUA,

A NATIVE OF ZOOGOO, IN THE INTERIOR OF AFRICA
(A Convert to Christianity.)

WITH A DESCRIPTION OF THAT PART OF THE WORLD:
INCLUDING THE

Manners and Customs of the Inhabitants.

Their Religious Notions, Form of Government, Laws, Appearance of the Country, Buildings, Agriculture, Manufactures, Shepherds and Herdsmen, Animals, Marriage and Funeral Ceremonies, Dress, Trade and Commerce, Warfare, Slavery, with an Account of Mahommah's early life, Education, Capture and Slavery in Africa and Brazil, Escape, Reception by Rev. W. L. Judd, Baptist Missionary at Port au Prince, Conversion to Christianity, Baptism, his Views, Objects and Aim, &c.

WRITTEN AND REVISED FROM HIS OWN WORDS,

BY SAMUEL MOORE, ESQ,

Late publisher of the "North of England Shipping Gazette," author of several popular works, and editor of sundry reform papers

MAHOMMAH G. BAQUAQUA,
Engraved by J. C. Darby, from a Daguerreotype by Sutton.

DETROIT:
Printed for the Author, Mahommah Gardo Baquaqua,
BY GEO. E. POMEROY & CO., TRIBUNE OFFICE.
1854.

FIGURE 5.6 *Mahommah Gardo Baquaqua, An Interesting Narrative. Biography of Mahommah G. Baquaqua, A Native of Zoogoo, in the Interior of Africa (A Convert to Christianity,) with a Description of That Part of the World; Including the Manners and Customs of the Inhabitants* (Detroit, 1854) showing copyright date, 21 August 1854 (Burton Historical Collection, Detroit Public Library).

What is clear is that when he went to McGrawville, he saw his former teacher, Kezia King, seeking her introduction in a visit to Hillsdale, where she was from. His former teacher wrote to her sisters to explain that the purpose of his visit was to raise money "that he can return to his native land, and tell his countrymen and friends of the Bible of the Saviour and try to assist Missionaries in establishing Missions in Central Africa, where the foot of the white man has never trod."[108] The task of selling his book was difficult because in places like Hillsdale "there was not much sympathy for the colored race." Ms. King herself, in her letter, reveals the depth of such hostility, where Blacks were referred to as "Niggers." Indeed, she introduces the subject of Baquaqua in her letter in a demeaning preface: "Now if you please I want to write a chapter about *Niggers*." Nonetheless, she admonished her sisters: "[D]on't say nigger in his hearing," since he was "perfectly neat, and cleanly in his person and would not dirty a good bed." Despite such blatant racism, by January 1855, Baquaqua seems to have raised enough money to board a ship in New York City and leave for England. Where he got the passage money from is not known. Nor is it entirely clear whether his commitment to abolition, which his relationship with foremost abolitionists confirms, continued to be a significant motivating factor or whether he just wanted to get back to Africa. The attitude of supposed friends and mentors like Kezia King could well have reinforced Baquaqua's desire to return to his mother's home in Katsina.

Hence, the Free Mission Society sent missionaries to Haiti, and Baquaqua benefited from his association with the Free Will Baptists. The Baptists were interested in recruiting Blacks who would evangelize Africa. From their optimistic perspective, their work had begun in Canada West, and New York Central College was started to train workers for Africa. The specific mission to Africa in which Baquaqua was to participate failed because Rev. William P. Newman changed his mind and became a pastor in Toronto rather than traveling to Africa with Baquaqua. Newman eventually went to Haiti in 1859 after laboring eleven years in Canada. Baquaqua became associated with Rev. Chauncey Leonard of the Baptist church in Washington, but other than going to Liberia, nothing is known of any further interaction. The Free Will Baptists ceased to exist after the Civil War. Estranged from the other denominations through insistence on emancipation in their opposition to African enslavement, the Free Mission Society faced new obstacles after the Civil War. Many members withdrew from the Society when Blacks began joining in large numbers. Plans to associate the Free Mission work with one of the Black conventions led to nothing. In 1872, the Free Will Mission Society voted to dissolve, transferring its Japan mission to the Missionary Union.[109]

CHAPTER SIX

Baquaqua's Narrative of Freedom

When Baquaqua was in Detroit in July 1854, he arranged publication of his autobiography with George E. Pomeroy and Co.

Baquaqua's pamphlet was sixty-six pages in length. Its descriptive title, *Biography of Mahommah G. Baquaqua. A Native of Zoogoo, in the Interior of Africa (A Convert to Christianity,) with a Description of that Part of the World; Including the Manners and Customs of the Inhabitants,* might have attracted public attention, given that it was published only four years after the Fugitive Slave Law, but it was virtually ignored, except for limited circulation among Free Will Baptists. We have generally referred to him by his third name, Baquaqua, as this seems to have been recognized as his surname in North America (he himself, for example, signing some of his letters "M.G. Baquaqua"). However, he was regularly addressed and referred to by his first name, Mahommah, although in Africa, from the evidence of the autobiography he was usually called by his second name, Gardo.[1] Following customary practice in West Africa, he did not actually have a surname but would have been identified as the son of his father, who is unfortunately not named, and sometimes his mother, who likewise is not named. Samuel Moore is credited as the editor, although the great majority of the text is either written in the first person as Baquaqua's own words, as in the use of the first person singular, or in paraphrases from Baquaqua's description.[2] Moore's own contributions to the text tend toward religious pronouncements and occasional observations and interjections. It is also possible to suggest context and correct errors of detail that Moore inadvertently introduced in editing Baquaqua's manuscript.

The autobiography, which is the backbone of this study, can be labeled a "freedom narrative," although the literary genre with which it is commonly associated is usually referred to as a "slave narrative." The distinction is important. Those personal accounts that refer to individuals who were born free but were subsequently enslaved and yet sometimes miraculously regained freedom are distinguished from those accounts that relate the life history of a person born into slavery.[3] In many cases these later accounts also involved the quest for freedom, which the surviving narratives recount, often after many years of enslavement. The distinction emphasizes those who were born in Africa as opposed to those born in the Americas with no firsthand experience of life in Africa. In Baquaqua's case, he was enslaved briefly in Africa as a teenager, but then, if his account is to be believed, he was freed only to be enslaved again and taken to Brazil, where he was in slavery for two years. Thus, from his birth in the early 1820s to the last we know about him, circa 1862, he was enslaved only two years and was a free person for at least forty years. Slavery was certainly a significant part of his life, but far more important was what he did as a free person, from his birth until the last we hear of him. A reference to his life story and indeed his autobiography in terms of slavery distorts our understanding of his experiences and inappropriately mislabels his memoirs. Slavery did not define his identity. He clearly always wanted to be free, and he knew what freedom was in contrast to slavery.

His account does make clear an important distinction between those who were brought across the Atlantic into slavery and those who did not experience the Middle Passage but were born in the Americas or who arrived too young to have vivid memories of the horrors of the journey. For Baquaqua, the Middle Passage and the introduction into slavery in Brazil were horrendous experiences that seem to have been fixated in his mind. It would not be surprising if he had nightmares, flashes of remembrance, and paranoid turmoil that his imersion within the Baptist community must have assuaged. Unlike those who were born in slavery and were told about Africa, Baquaqua's account reveals the ongoing trauma caused by the terror of enslavement, the ordeal of treks to the coast, and the brutal discipline of the prison ships.

Baquaqua's autobiography chronicles his life in Africa before he was sent to Brazil. His account reveals a split between trying to tell his compiler Samuel Moore what his life had been like, what the geopolitical and economic setting of his upbringing had been, and details of family, religion, and society. The underlying theme of his desire to return to Africa seems to have been the need to erase the bonds of slavery and regain links of kinship, despite the stresses that familial relations may have had on his fortunes. His father had passed away, and his position at Soubroukou was hardly promising, as indeed his enslavement proved. Yet, amid the personal details of Baquaqua's life and the tragedy of his enslavement, Baquaqua provides perhaps the most detailed description of the African background of someone who was enslaved and sent to the Americas of any of the surviving narratives of slavery. We know more about his travels to the coast than we do for most of the enslaved who were deported from Africa. His discussion of the Middle Passage is one of the most significant testimonies of the Atlantic crossing.[4] These features of his account reinforce the numerous fragments of violence and suffering that the enslaved population had to endure crossing the Atlantic. His life story is distinguishable in another way, too. His odyssey took him from the Muslim commercial interior of West Africa through Dahomey to Ouidah, the largest slave export depot in West Africa. Although during the 1840s, the British Naval blockade off the coast forced the major commercial houses at Ouidah to shift the departure point from the beach at Ouidah further east to Petit Popo, located on a spit of sand sticking out into the ocean where the lagoon system behind the coast emptied into the sea in the west.

The autobiography provides virtually all that we know about Baquaqua's birth, his youth, and his enslavement through the time he spent in Brazil. The first part comprises five brief chapters in the first twenty-five pages. The second part comprises well over half of the whole work, accounting for the last forty-one pages. Also included in the second section are two poems: "Lines Spoken by Mahommah" by his former teacher, Kezia King. In addition there is a poem by African American poet James M. Whitfield (1822–71), "Prayer of the Oppressed."[5] Allan Austin speculates that Baquaqua may have come across the poem when he visited Detroit to get his book published.[6] Baquaqua's publisher, George E. Pomeroy Co., also printed "Arguments, Pro and Con, on the Call for a National Emigration Convention" in 1854, which was written by Whitfield along with Frederick Douglass and W. J. Watkins.[7] The cover of the book also carries an engraving of Baquaqua by Detroit artist and engraver J. G. Darby, who worked in graphic design, printmaking, lithography, etching, and woodblocks. Darby is said to have used the image from a daguerreotype photograph taken by Moses Sutton, whose studio was also in Detroit, almost certainly when Baquaqua was there in 1854.[8]

Apparently, Baquaqua initially thought he could promote his book at the National Emigration Convention of Colored People held in Cleveland on 24–26 August 1854. James Whitfield, the author whose poem Baquaqua quotes in his autobiography, was one of the principal organizers. Whitfield wrote the poem "Prayer of the Oppressed" that blesses Baquaqua's autobiography. The poem was initially published in *America, and Other Poems* in 1853, and its reprint in Baquaqua's volume suggests a close affinity.[9] If they did not know each other before Baquaqua published his autobiography, they certainly would have met in Cleveland.

Baquaqua did not actually go to Cleveland, however. His name is not mentioned in the proceedings of the convention, which are well recorded.[10] If he had been there, he would certainly have been in contact with Whitfield, and he would have met Martin Delany, who was the principal organizer of the conference, and who expressed interests in returning to Africa that were similar to Baquaqua's. A meeting might have consolidated a relationship that would have seen Baquaqua join Delany's mission to the Niger River and Abeokuta only a few years later.[11] In the absence of further evidence, therefore, it seems that Baquaqua missed an opportunity to sell his book in Cleveland and consolidate relationships that might have assisted in his return to Africa. As it was, very few of his pamphlets were sold and can be found today in only a few special collections.

Delany was a foremost spokesman for emigration. He had been born free in Virginia on 6 May 1812, and subsequently had a distinguished career as an abolitionist, journalist, physician, military officer, and writer, and is often considered to have been one of earliest proponents of Black nationalism.[12] He was educated at Harvard and started a weekly newspaper, the *Mystery*, in Pittsburgh before joining Frederick Douglass in the publication of the *North Star* in Rochester, NY between 1846 and 1849. After finishing medical school, he became deeply interested in foreign colonization, living for a time in Canada West, where he finished his novel, *Blake*, and then led an exploratory expedition to the Niger River delta and Yorubaland in anticipation of a settlement scheme. A meeting in Cleveland might have consolidated a relationship that would have seen Baquaqua join Delany's mission to the Niger River and Abeokuta in 1859–60, but Baquaqua was not part of that expedition.[13] Otherwise Baquaqua's relationship with Delaney is unknown, although they almost met in Cleveland in the summer of 1854.

It is possible to determine what portion of the autobiography is Baquaqua's dictation, because there are large parts of the text written in the first person or summarizing what Baquaqua must have said.[14] On the title page, Samuel Moore, Esq. is clearly identified as the person who wrote and revised the text; to be exact, it states: "Written and Revised . . . By Samuel Moore, Esq.," but it also indicates that Moore did this "from his [i.e., Baquaqua's] own Words." Furthermore, it is stated that the text was "Printed for the Author, Mahommah Gardo Baquaqua," and the copyright is taken out in Baquaqua's name "In the Office of the District Court of the United States for the District of Michigan." Besides the sections that are written in the first person, a careful reading of the text establishes with reasonable clarity which sections are Moore's interpretation of what Baquaqua said, or what Moore thought Baquaqua said or meant. And there are insertions, beginning with the short introduction, "Preface and Compiler's Notes," which are certainly Moore's own pronouncements. Moore's introduction consists of 1,071 words covering two pages. The text begins with a list of numbers in Dendi, which was the commercial language of Baquaqua's hometown, Djougou. The numbers include 1–100 and hundreds up to one thousand. The actual "biography" consists of 22,069 words, and includes a short section that was taken from A. T. Foss and E. Mathews, *Facts for Baptist Churches*, published in Utica, New York, in 1850, amounting to 169 words; and a slightly longer section of 320 words that was previously published in the *Christian Contributor* and credited to the Rev. William L. Judd, who was Baquaqua's mentor in Haiti and whose wife and sister-in-law were responsible for enrolling Baquaqua in Central College in McGrawville, New York. In total, at least 80 percent of the text is written in first person singular or is clearly summaries by Moore of what Baquaqua told him.

A major problem arises in attempting to identify the person who is mentioned on the title page as the editor of the manuscript, Samuel Moore. Who was Samuel Moore? The answer is unknown. There are several possibilities, but for one reason or another the identification cannot be established. Baquaqua secured the copyright, and the text makes it clear that he is the author, and Samuel Moore appears on the cover of the pamphlet as the editor. Documentation makes it clear that he was paid for his editorship, which clearly involved recording verbatim what Baquaqua told him and summarizing what he been told otherwise. The authorship is clear, and the extent of editorial intervention can be discerned. The identity of Samuel Moore cannot.

The authenticity of the text is not in doubt. Baquaqua held the copyright. He paid Samuel Moore to help edit the manuscript. Acknowledgment is clearly stated on the cover and in related attributions. No one at the time or since has questioned these details. The question becomes, who was Samuel Moore? He supposedly edited the manuscript and might be expected given the time to have claimed sole proprietorship of the text. Instead, he was relegated to a prominent position on the cover plus repeated evangelical interventions in the text that surely could not have been Baquaqua's. Interjections appear to be from someone who was British, not American, and who was "reform" oriented, which at the time meant the expansion of the electorate for Parliament. Moore claims he was "editor of sundry reform papers," none of which have been identified. Such an emphasis on reform underlined the 1837 rebellion in Upper Canada that was a milestone in Canadian history, and therefore a first guess is to look for someone named Samuel Moore who was reform-oriented and, hence, perhaps involved in the 1837 uprising. Moore also claimed to be the "late publisher" of the *North of England Shipping Gazette* and the author of "several popular works," although a search in Canada and Britain has uncovered nothing that can be attributed to someone named Samuel Moore in the 1840s and early 1850s. The "North of England Shipping Gazette" is another clue, and the *Sunderland Times,* in northeast England, had a supplement to the newspaper exactly in the years that fit Moore's claim that was called the "North of England Shipping and Mercantile Gazette," but none of its editors for the few years that this supplement was added to the *Sunderland Times* was named Samuel Moore. Moreover, the variation in title should be noted.[15]

Efforts to identify Samuel Moore revealed more contradictions than solutions. One man with that name in Nova Scotia moved to Upper Canada. In 1827, Samuel D. Moore, one of the family members descended from the Andrew Moore, Scottish emigrant, and his wife, Mary, together with their family moved to Michigan and in 1850 settled on a large farm in the district south of Ypsilanti. This Samuel Moore was in direct line in the fourth generation from the emigrant ancestor of the family who had moved to Nova Scotia. Baquaqua referred to Moore in a letter as an "English man," which could fit this description.[16] Samuel Moore of Ypsilanti wrote an article titled "Friends' Meeting Houses," in which he argued for the importance of using Friends' meeting houses (which refers to meeting houses of the Religious Society of Friends [Quakers]) to hold antislavery talks. It was this stance that resulted in a backlash among Friends and his expulsion from the Quakers. In a letter of 12 January 1856, Moore published a declaration, "A Protest," in which he stated that he was not paying taxes anymore as a protest against slavery. He was also the local agent of *The Anti-Slavery Bugle* of Salem, Ohio. However, unlike the editor of Baquaqua's text, Samuel Moore of Ypsilanti always used an initial for his middle name, Downing, which was not used on the cover page of the autobiography; and the editor Samuel Moore identified himself as "Esquire," which Quakers in the United States had stopped using a generation earlier.

Moore of Ypsilanti married Miss Elizabeth Moore, of Ypsilanti, and had three sons—Wendell and Walter, who were students at the University of Michigan, and Eli. Our subject was a member of the Golden Rule Chapter of the Free and Accepted Masons. He also belonged to the Royal Arch Masons and the Commandery of the Knights Templar. He was a Republican in politics and in religion a member of the Unitarian Church after his expulsion from the Friends. Samuel Moore was among the most active abolitionists.[17] The proximity to Detroit, though, and the prospect of freedom in Canada, was responsible for the arrival of fugitives in this area as much as the work of local abolitionists. If no abolitionists were there, fugitives from slavery would still have had to travel through Michigan from almost any place west of the Appalachians to get to Canada. According to one abolitionist,

> After leaving Detroit I went to Ypsilanti, and worked in that region. I
> found a good home with Samuel Moore and wife—one of the subscrib-

ers to *The Truth Seeker,* and *Freethinkers' Magazine.* He is an old man, but his letters always seem to give me the feeling of a good hand-shake. His wife, a good woman, has "passed on." Mr. Moore took me around the country and spoke with me, wherever he could find a house open to us. We met with very little hostility. I then went to Ann Arbor. There was a little society there who were mostly Reformed Friends.[18]

It might not have been difficult to find someone willing to earn some money editing the text of an African, but who was the person who agreed to do so? Why did that person claim to be an author of "popular works," when the rich inventories of publications, pamphlets, political tracts, and newspapers from the period are silent on anyone named Samuel Moore. Given Baquaqua's reliance on the Free Will Baptists and funds he had raised for the proposed Baptist mission to Africa, two details stand out. First, Moore clearly did some editing for financial gain, which suggests that he was willing to take money from an African and perform a service that indicates that he was receptive to Baquaqua's story. Second, the transaction indicates that Baquaqua had some funds of his own that he did not pass on to the Free Will Baptists.

Samuel Moore, Esq. is credited with writing and revising the manuscript "from his own words," that is, from Baquaqua's own words. In his correspondence with George Whipple of the American Missionary Association, Baquaqua observed that "the English language has been very hard for me to understand and speak." At this point, Baquaqua decided to approach the American Colonization Society, which began some correspondence with George Whipple, who was secretary of the Society. Gerrit Smith probably provided the introduction. Whipple had attended Oneida Institute in upstate New York and was one of the young men who left Oneida on account of the action of its Board of Trustees denying the right to free speech. He with most of his class soon went to Oberlin, where they pursued their theological studies during 1834–35. Whipple graduated in 1836 and was ordained, but he never assumed pastoral duties. Instead, he was appointed principal of the preparatory department at Oberlin. From 1837 until 1846, Rev. Whipple was professor of mathematics and natural philosophy at Oberlin. He and his wife Alice lived at 231 Clinton Street in Brooklyn, New York, in a house with a large marble staircase that dominated the entry hall. The Whipples were noted for their culture and refinement and generous hospitality.

Baquaqua knew that to become a missionary in Africa, as he told Whipple, "I must understand English language more than I dose [sic] now."[19] His letters themselves, although containing many errors of spelling and syntax, are generally readily intelligible. Moore's reference to "the . . . English spoken by Mahommah" implies that Moore took down the account from Mahommah's dictation as being "from the mouth of a native," rather than editing a written text. According to Moore,

> In compiling the following pages, many difficulties have had naturally to be encountered, in consequence of the imperfect English spoken by Mahommah, but great care has been taken to render the work as readable and clear as possible to the capacities of all classes of readers; the description of the people (their manners and customs) of that country, which is little known to the world at large, will be found highly instructive—the friends of the poor African negro and the colored race generally, will be greatly benefitted by reading the work carefully from beginning to end; they will there see throughout its pages, the horrible sufferings and tortures inflicted upon that portion of God's creatures, merely because "their skin is of a darker hue," notwithstanding their hearts are as soft and flexible as the man of paler cast.

To avoid any doubt, moreover, the cover makes it clear that the text was "Printed for the author, Mahommah Gardo Baquaqua, by Geo. E. Pomeroy & Co., Tribune Office [Detroit], 1854. The publication was entered according to the Act of Congress, in the year 1854, by MAHOMMAH GARDO BAQUAQUA, In the Office of the District Court of the United States for the District of Michigan." The firm of George E. Pomeroy & Co. stated boldly that the pamphlet was "printed for the author," who is identified as Mahommah Gardo Baquaqua.

George Eltweed Pomeroy, born 16 September 1807, founded an express company between Albany and Buffalo, New York, in 1841 that eventually became Wells Fargo, selling out to his brother in 1844. He then founded the Detroit *Tribune*, residing in a palatial home in Clifton, Michigan, to the west of Detroit. In later years, he lived in Toledo, Ohio, where he died on 12 January 1886.[20] However, Moore was a known abolitionist, and Pomeroy did publish at least one other abolitionist tract in 1854, and that tract was coauthored by James Whitfield, whose poem was included in the autobiography.[21] Therefore, it can be supposed that Baquaqua somehow was referred to both Moore and Pomeroy, and perhaps to Whitfield's poem, through the abolitionist network.

As described earlier in this chapter, Law and Lovejoy were able to piece together scattered information that seemed to establish that Samuel Moore came from Ypsilanti, just west of Detroit. Initially it was thought this Moore was the editor, following the lead of Allan Austin, who did not explain how or when Baquaqua and this Moore met nor were Law and Lovejoy able to find out.[22]

The question is, therefore, who was Samuel Moore about whom we know very little other than the claim on the cover of the *Biography* that he had published the *North of England Shipping Gazette*, presumably before moving to North America. Similarly, his claim to have written "several popular works" and edited "sundry reform papers" suggests that he had also undertaken these writings before he left England. The text of the autobiography makes clear that it was completed after Baquaqua had left the United States for Canada, which was probably in late January or February 1854, and the text had been finished by 4 July of the same year, when Baquaqua reported in one of his extant letters that it was "ready for the press," and he was seeking assistance in meeting the costs of printing.[23] It was published by 21 August, when a copy was deposited, for purposes of copyright, in the Clerk's Office of the United States District Court of Michigan, this latter date being recorded in a handwritten note on the cover of this copy, now preserved in the Detroit Public Library. The clerk who recorded the copyright was W. David King.[24] Where Baquaqua and Moore collaborated on the writing—whether in Canada West, or whether Baquaqua traveled to meet Moore in Michigan or in New York or Pennsylvania—is also not known; Baquaqua was in Detroit in early July, as noted above, but this was in order to see an already completed manuscript through the press. As far as is known, Moore and Baquaqua were not otherwise associated with each other.

The question arises, as Law and Lovejoy observed, to what extent was Baquaqua himself responsible for the authorship of the pamphlet? Is it a biography or an autobiography? Whose voice are we in fact hearing? The principal study previously published, by Allan Austin, implicitly treats the book as Moore's rather than Baquaqua's, and is more generally dismissive of Baquaqua's intellectual abilities (though not much less so about Moore's).[25] Austin refers to "the naïveté of both men."[26] This, however, seems to misconceive the process of composition, as indicated by the internal evidence of the book itself. On the title page, it is in fact Baquaqua who is identified as "the author," although the text is also said to have been "written and revised from his own words" by Moore. "Written" here evidently means "written down" rather than "composed," the implication being that Moore put into writing an account given orally by Baquaqua—an inference which is confirmed by the reference to narration in Moore's Preface to the book. This interpretation is also supported by a short review of the book (the only contemporary notice of it that has been traced), which was published in *The American Baptist* in November 1854, and which explicitly credits Baquaqua rather than Moore with authorship, describing it as "an autobiography, but revised and prepared for publication by Samuel Moore."[27]

The review was almost certainly written by the editor of *The American Baptist*, Warham Walker, who must be presumed to have been familiar with the circumstances of the production of the autobiography, since he knew Baquaqua well. He had earlier published two of Baquaqua's letters in his journal, and both men had attended Annual Meetings of the American Baptist Free Mission Society, of which Walker was a Trustee. Walker and Baquaqua also served together on the African Mission Committee of the Society in 1853. It may be noted, however, that in the Preface to the book Moore describes himself as "compiling" the work,[28] seemingly implying a more active role than merely "revising" a dictated text. The resolution of this apparent contradiction is to be found in a study of the contents of the book itself, which as noted above fall into two distinct parts. The first part, which gives a general account of Baquaqua's homeland in Africa, is basically written in the third person, though with occasional illustrative direct quotations from Baquaqua.

The autobiography is divided into seven chapters, the longest being the seventh and constituting three-quarters of the text. Baquaqua's observations of Djougou, his early life, and his first, brief enslavement in Gonja circa 1842–44, amount to 9,220 words. The section on his second enslavement and journey to the coast occupies 3,426 words, so that the portion of the autobiography that relates to Africa reaches 12,646 words, or more than half of the text. His description of the Middle Passage, his time in Brazil, until he reached New York City, which lasted for about two years, is covered in 4,651 words, while the remaining text, which accounts for his trial in New York City, his escape from slavery, his time in Haiti, his attendance at Central College, and subsequent experiences until the publication of the pamphlet, including excerpts from Foss and Mathews, *Facts for Baptist Churches*, and Judd's comments from the *Christian Contributor*,[29] constitutes 4,772 words. Hence, the autobiography is unlike any other published narrative of slavery in that the largest portion relates specifically to his background in Africa rather than his time in the Americas. Besides the autobiography, there is considerably more information about him in the 1840s through the mid-1850s and a trickle of evidence thereafter. The surviving documentation, including letters that he wrote and reports of his activities, particularly in newspaper accounts and the publications of the Free Will Baptists, makes it possible to reconstruct much more than is in the autobiography for the period down to the early 1860s, although after that the trail goes cold.

The account of Baquaqua's own life is mainly written in the first person, although with occasional third-person interpolations. The first-person mode becomes especially dominant when the text arrives at what is signaled as "the most interesting portion of Mahommah's story," namely his enslavement in Africa, sale into export, and subsequent experiences in the Americas, which is explicitly stated to be given "in nearly his own words."[30] It seems reasonable to conclude that Moore was indeed a "compiler" with regard to the first section of the book, organizing material supplied by Baquaqua into a coherent whole, but a "reviser" with regard to the second section, editing a narrative dictated by Baquaqua.

In an entrepreneurial or legal, as opposed to a narrowly literary, sense, the book was clearly Baquaqua's rather than Moore's. The text itself makes clear that Baquaqua took the initiative in its production: "I came to the conclusion that the time had arrived when I might with propriety commit to paper all that has been recounted in this work."[31] The letter Baquaqua wrote reporting the completion of the text in July 1854 indicates that Moore was only a hired assistant, whom Baquaqua paid for his services ("English man [sic] wrote it for me. I pay him for do it").[32] Consistently with this, on the title page of the book, it is explicitly described as "printed for the Author, Mahommah Gardo Baquaqua by Geo. E. Pomeroy and Co.," which suggests that the publisher recognized his authorship; and this legal authorship is confirmed on the reverse page, giving copyright information, where the work is recorded as registered in the United States District Court of Michigan under Baquaqua's own name. This is not to deny that there are particular sections of the text that represent the voice of Moore rather than of Baquaqua. Some passages, including many of the elaborate instances of abolitionist rhetoric, are distinguished by a more pretentiously literary style and embellished with bits of poetry and other quotations, and these almost certainly represent Moore's hand. Moreover, even beyond such straightforward editorial interpolations, there are places where the composite character of the work seems to have resulted in errors and confusion, arising from imperfect communication between Moore and Baquaqua, on points that the latter should have known well. The book is even more interesting because of this ambiguity as to whether it is biography, autobiography, or in fact something else: a coauthored work that is part biography of Baquaqua and part descriptive account of his homeland, in whose production Moore served as scribe, in the process sometimes getting details wrong.

According to Moore, he summarized Baquaqua's account but held out the possibility of an expanded version at some time in the future.

To give more fully a description of the manners and customs of the people, would no doubt be highly interesting to most of our readers, and it would give us great pleasure to do so, would the limits of the present work admit of it; but at present, we must hope they will be contented and pleased, with what has already been written for them, and it is to be hoped, they will profit by its perusal. At some other time, should the public think fit to patronize these few stray sheets, it may be, that a larger and more extensive volume may be issued by the author of the present work, in which will be given more fully everything within his knowledge of Africa and the Africans.[33]

Consideration of authorship of the work should also take account of a collective dimension arising from Baquaqua's close relationship with his mentors in the American Baptist Free Mission Society and its supporting churches. Among those who contributed to Baquaqua's evolution into authorship were the Rev. Mr. Judd, mentioned in the title page of the autobiography, and his wife Nancy, under whose guidance he was converted in Haiti; Warham Walker of *The American Baptist*, as noted above; and also Cyrus P. Grosvenor, editor of the *Christian Contributor and Free Missionary* and president of New York Central College where Baquaqua was educated. The autobiography was preceded, as has been seen, by the publication of letters written by and about Baquaqua in the journals edited by Grosvenor and Walker; and a brief biographical notice of him, including an account of his baptism in Haiti, had been published, together with the photograph of Baquaqua receiving instruction from the Rev. Mr. Judd, in the book *Facts for Baptist Churches*, published for the American Baptist Free Mission Society in 1850.[34] This biographical note is entirely derived from earlier printed accounts, mainly in the *Christian Contributor and Free Missionary*.

His Baptist mentor at Central College, Cyrus Grosvenor, may well have played a role in planning the publication of the autobiography. Grosvenor knew Baquaqua especially well; as editor of the *Christian Contributor and Free Missionary*, Grosvenor had published a series of letters from Judd and his wife on Baquaqua and the Haitian mission, as well as letters by Baquaqua himself, during 1847–50; and as president of New York Central College, he was responsible for admitting Baquaqua as a student in early 1850, and personally welcomed him to the college. He also was well known in Canada West, where Baquaqua traveled. Grosvenor spent "several weeks of missionary service" there for the American Baptist Free Mission Society during the summer of

1853, after the Annual Meeting of the Society in Utica, New York, which both he and Baquaqua attended. His stay would presumably have included a visit to Detroit, where the autobiography was to be published, since the Free Mission in Michigan was linked administratively to the Mission in Canada West.[35] Baquaqua wrote his autobiography in this context, which suggests the possibility that Grosvenor might have played some role at least in the preparatory stages of its production. Whatever Grosvenor's role, it should be noted that during 1853, after completing his education at Central College, Baquaqua himself had been involved in fundraising for a projected Baptist mission to Africa, in which he himself was to serve. His desire to return to Africa as a missionary and his appeal for funds for this purpose are reiterated in the autobiography. Although the book was published in his own name (and thus reflecting a degree of estrangement from the Free Baptists by 1854), it seems likely that it was originally conceived for publication, in effect, on behalf of the American Baptist Free Mission Society, and in particular in support of its efforts to raise funds for the African Mission. Moreover, it is clear that Baquaqua's story of his life had taken shape, in oral if not in written form, over several years prior to being written up for publication in 1854. He had told parts of his story on many occasions. When he arrived in Haiti in 1847, Nancy Judd noted that he remembered not only incidents in his own individual life in Africa but also "the productions and manner of cultivating" their customs and "some of the laws of his country"; and after his conversion in 1848 he delivered an oration of thanks to God at a Baptist prayer meeting, first in his "native tongue" and then in English, which consisted of a summary of his experiences, from enslavement in Africa, through slavery in Brazil and liberation in New York, to conversion in Haiti.[36] As Mrs. Judd reflected, in a letter to Cyrus Grosvenor published in the *Christian Contributor and Free Missionary*, "O how many, many deeply interesting circumstances, I have gathered already of his former history, if I had time to write and you room to publish, which I feel could not fail to be read with the deepest interest."[37] So it may well be that the idea of a book on Baquaqua's life originated with her. Likewise, in the United States, when Mrs. Judd introduced Baquaqua at New York Central College in 1850, she "related some incidents connected with his history and conversion," which one in her audience judged "truly interesting and affecting."[38] Subsequently, Baquaqua took over the role of narrator himself: in 1853, when he was involved in fundraising for the projected African mission in Pennsylvania, he is reported to have "made several attempts to give a sketch of the manners, customs &c. of his native country, and of his being kidnapped and sold into slavery, &c. &c."[39] The autobiography as published may therefore be considered a written version of what Baquaqua had been saying on the Baptist lecture-circuit.

However, although the presumption that the project originated in Baquaqua's involvement with the Baptist Free Mission Society is strong, by the time of its actual publication in the summer of 1854, his relations with the Society had deteriorated. This may account for the fact that the editor whose assistance Baquaqua sought, Samuel Moore, was from outside the Free Mission circles in which he had moved in New York State. Law and Lovejoy initially thought that Moore was not a Baptist but rather a Unitarian from Ireland, although now we know that Moore was a Quaker who was ultimately removed as a Friend and was not from Ireland. Likewise, it is not known how Baquaqua met his publisher, George E. Pomeroy, who among other things was the owner of the Detroit *Tribune*: he had no known connection with the Baptist Free Mission Society and was in fact Presbyterian.

Baquaqua's arrival in New York in 1847 and the ensuing legal proceedings were reported in local newspapers and the abolitionist press elsewhere, while the subsequent period of his residence in Haiti and the United States is extensively documented in American Baptist sources. For this later period, in fact, the supplementary documentation is fuller than the account given in the autobiography; although there are differences of emphasis and nuance, the additional material is complementary to rather than contradictory to the autobiography and tends broadly to confirm its accuracy. For the period in Africa and Brazil before 1847, there is no such additional material relating to Baquaqua's individual life, and the account in the autobiography can be evaluated only in the light of more general, contextual information; but here again, in the view of the present authors, Baquaqua's account is generally consistent with what we think we know of conditions in his homeland of Djougou, in the kingdom of Dahomey through which he was exported, in the Middle Passage across the Atlantic, and in Brazil where he was held in slavery. The question is complicated, however, by the fact that some of the details of Baquaqua's life recorded in the earlier American Baptist sources in Haiti contradict what is said in the later autobiography. In principle, it has seemed that the autobiography is normally to be preferred to the earlier accounts, on the grounds that Baquaqua himself exercised greater control over its contents, which are, therefore, more likely to represent his own perceptions. By contrast, the version of his account recorded by the Judds in Haiti involved problematic processes of translation. When he arrived, as Mrs. Judd noted, Baquaqua spoke Portuguese in addition to one or more African languages, but not English beyond "a very few sentences in broken English,

which he learned on his passage out here." He did not understand French of
the patois spoken in Haiti. The Judds were therefore initially not able to communicate with him directly, but depended on an intermediary, an African
American called Jones, who himself spoke only "but little Portuguese." Because
of this, as Mrs. Judd acknowledged, "he could not, of course, learn so much as
he would have done, had he been able to have conversed with him more
freely."[40] Only three weeks later, admittedly, her husband claimed that
Baquaqua had "so far advanced in English that I have been able to learn from
him precisely his former residence in Africa," but since (as will appear below)
Judd's understanding on this question is among the points contradicted in the
later autobiography, some skepticism seems in order.[41] In these circumstances,
it seems likely that many of the discrepancies between the autobiography and
the earlier statements of the Judds reflect misunderstandings on the latter's (or
Jones's) part. This is not to deny that Baquaqua himself may have changed his
story over time or sought to conceal or obscure certain elements in it, but this
explanation is invoked sparingly, and only when plausible reasons for such
shifts can be adduced.

But there is another Samuel Moore who has to be considered a candidate
for editing Baquaqua's narrative, the father of Hannah Moore, who was a missionary connected with the Mendi Mission inland from Sherbro Island south
of the Sierra Leone peninsula. Hannah had initially been a missionary among
the Cherokee. Encouraged by her father, she had left their small village in
Connecticut near the Massachusetts border and joined the Mendi Mission,
as attested by a letter from her father in May 1853. Samuel Moore wrote to
Lewis Tappan enclosing two dollars, which he included as a "donation for the
Mendi Mission where my daughter Hannah Moore is engaged."[42] It is unlikely that Hannah's father was involved with Baquaqua, however. Moreover,
a man who was donating to the Mendi Mission is hardly likely to have
accepted a payment from someone who wanted to return to Africa with the
Baptists. Moreover, there is no known connection between Baquaqua and
Samuel Moore of Connecticut, although they probably had mutual acquain-
tances in church and abolitionist circles, such as the group that associated
with Lewis Tappan.

Finally, the efforts to locate Samuel Moore in Norwich, Ontario, also
proved futile. The Moores of Norwich were closely connected with the 1837
rebellion in Upper Canada and with abolitionists in Rochester, but nobody
in the family history seems to be a likely candidate for Baquaqua's autobiography. We are left with the conclusion that it is uncertain who the Samuel
Moore who edited Baquaqua's book was.

Nonetheless, Baquaqua's account serves as an example of how biography and autobiography can inform our understanding of the African diaspora and how individuals fit into the history of trans-Atlantic slavery, even if biographical details are incomplete.[43] Identities along the slave route from Africa to the Americas produced very different personal profiles; that of Baquaqua is only one, but it allows some glimpse into the oft impenetrable silence of the enslaved. The details of biography allow the possibility of subjecting ethnic stereotypes, ascribed signs of identity, and the historicism of tradition and memory to the scrutiny of rigorous methodology. To what extent is ethnicity essentialist, existing independently of individuals and resisting the changes of circumstance and situation? What was the relationship between the individual and the collective under racialized slavery? Conducting such biographical research is difficult because data are widely dispersed, but fortunately in the case of Baquaqua there is considerable information available. First, there is the autobiography, whose account was brought to the attention of the scholarly world by Abraham Chapman in 1971[44] and subsequently by other scholars,[45] highlighted and analyzed by Allan Austin in 1984, and more widely spread through various publications in Brazil.[46] Austin's early work should be noted because he published the complete autobiography, although details of his analysis, particularly the sections relating to Africa, are revised here.

The most authoritative critique of the autobiography is that of Robin Law and Lovejoy, initially in 2001 and revised in 2006.[47] The present study corrects some details of the Law/Lovejoy annotated version, while considerably more field work and archival research supplement the Law/Lovejoy analysis. The most important differences in interpretation have been examined in detail. Ciavolella's extensive field work in Djougou has clarified many details that uncovers an anthropological context. Moreover, Ciavolella benefited from extensive papers of Yves Person, who conducted field work in Djougou in the 1950s, publishing several articles arising from that research, although nothing specifically on Baquaqua.[48] Ciavolella, therefore, has added important details on the African portions of Baquaqua's story. The various translations into Portuguese and other publications in English add very little to the autobiography or a more detailed biography, and often overlook or do not acknowledge the detailed research that has otherwise been done, initially by Austin, then by Law/Lovejoy, and finally by Ciavolella.[49] The exception is the translation of Robert Krueger, who relies on Austin's annotations.[50] Other publications draw on the Law/Lovejoy annotated version.[51]

We also do not know how many letters Baquaqua wrote and how many he received, although sixteen have been recovered. We do not know what happened to his personal effects when he went to England, especially his books and letters. How many other letters did he write and to whom? His letters do provide a sense of his moods or at least what he was revealing to his confidants and mentors. His correspondence suggests that he came to appreciate the importance of letter writing when he was in Haiti. Presumably with some coaching, he wrote several letters that were heavily edited because they are cogent and are expressive of his ambitions, or at least what he was willing to claim as his ambitions. Later letters were clearly written without editorship. Those letters are a bit rough but comprehensible. There are enough letters that they provide an important supplement to the autobiography and the reports of the Judds of what they thought he told them.

His last letters show a steady improvement in his command of written English. His letters are not formulaic, other than including predictable religious statements. The tone of the letters depended in part on the identity of the recipient, whether Baquaqua was asking for assistance, advice, or explaining his actions that were being criticized. His standard of composition did not attain the literary levels of Frederick Douglass, noted editor of *The North Star*, or the theatrics of Henry Box Brown, whose fame arose from his miraculous survival in a box in which he was hiding that was turned upside down so that he was on his head for the whole journey of escape to Philadelphia in 1849.[52] Baquaqua slipped through the New York judicial system into a world of oblivion. He reemerged periodically as a refugee in Haiti arriving via the Underground Railroad, and then was one of the first Africans to attend college in the United States at Central College in 1849. He wrote his autobiography. He never claimed to have been anyone other than himself, not a super hero or a model. He was raised with a sense of Islamic modesty and endurance. In none of the surviving documentation is there any indication that he was ever afraid. He portrays a constant sense of purpose that relates to returning to the homeland of his mother. The intention beyond the kinship attraction is not clear. Baquaqua shows no particular interest in Islam, although being called Muhammad was enough to make identification clear. He suggests no pretensions at Islamic scholarship or ambitions at leadership as an imam or teacher. Yet, he leaves the impression that he was someone who had not abandoned his Muslim background. He experienced bouts of drinking, but he presents such lapses as shameful violations of acceptable custom in Muslim society. This focus on abstinence coincided with Baptist prescriptions on drinking.

CHAPTER SEVEN

Return to Africa

From his association with the Free Will Baptists in Port-au-Prince, if not earlier, Baquaqua was destined to return to Africa. Rev. Judd saw in him the prospect of a successful African Mission, and the training and guidance provided to Baquaqua was directed at achieving this end. Shortly after Baquaqua moved into the Judd household in October 1847, Judd expressed his wish for the "speedy conversion of Mahommah," so that he might become "a missionary to his native land," which Judd (as noted earlier) then believed to be Katsina. What Judd had in mind was apparently that Baquaqua would serve as interpreter and local guide for an American missionary; he expressed the hope that the Baptists in the United States would be on the lookout for "a man properly qualified to accompany him," including having some knowledge of "Hebrew and Arabic."[1] Baquaqua jumped at the idea when it was first suggested, although like many others forced to cross the Atlantic in slavery, he already had nostalgic longing to do so. Baquaqua expressed this again and again in reference specifically to missing his mother, which might help explain why he selected his mother's nickname for him as his surname when he was baptized. After his conversion in March 1848, Mrs. Judd reported that, "for the first time since he has lived with us, he expressed a desire to go back to Africa, to tell them about Jesus Christ," wording that leaves unclear whether what was new was his desire to return home, or his intention to preach Christianity there. It is hard not to be skeptical in thinking that teaching Christianity was a means to an end. Again, in July, shortly after Baquaqua's baptism, she observed that, "he appears to have an increasing desire for Africa, which we feel to encourage." Likewise, the Rev. Judd, describing Baquaqua's baptism, enthusiastically reported that he "talks much of Africa, and prays ardently that her people may receive the Gospel—dreams often of visiting Kachna [Katsina], accompanied by 'a good white man,' as he calls a missionary."[2] Samuel Moore noted in his "Compiler's Notes" for the autobiography that

> The cherished object of Mahommah has been for a long time past, indeed ever since his conversion to Christianity whilst at Hayti, to be enabled to return to his native land, to instruct his own people in the ways of the gospel of Christ, and to be the means of their salvation, which it is

to be hoped he will be able to accomplish ere long; in the meantime he has become a subject of the Queen of England, and is at present living under her benign laws and influence in Canada, stirring up the colored population and agitating for the abolition of slavery all over the world, a cause which ought to occupy the hearts and feelings of every benevolent and charitable man and woman throughout the world.[3]

Moore was extrapolating from what had been reported at the Sixth Annual Meeting of the American Baptist Free Mission Society meeting held in Charlestown, Massachusetts, on 2 May 1849 (see Appendix B) and had been published in the *Christian Contributor and Free Missionary* in 1847 and 1848. Baquaqua had declared in a letter to Cyrus Grosvenor in November 1848: "By-and-by I want to go back to Africa, and see my friends and tell all the people about Jesus Christ."[4] Despite his own sustained efforts over several years and some support from the Free Mission Society, his desire to return to Africa was not realized until 1862, when he traveled to Sierra Leone and Liberia, after which he drops out of the historical record.

The project of education for Baquaqua in the United States, as the autobiography notes,[5] was explicitly conceived with the intention of training him for missionary work in Africa; he reiterated his commitment to the latter from time to time during his period of study at New York Central College. At the meeting of the Board of the Free Mission Society in 1850, for example, he spoke to this purpose: "His soul was full of the desire to return as a missionary of the gospel to Africa, the land of his birth and whence he was stolen. He feels that unless his mother and other relatives, of whom he makes frequent, mention, can learn of Christ, they are lost."[6] However, once again, his mother was prominent in his thoughts. In a letter of 1851, he asked for prayers "that God will help me in my studies, and send me back to Africa, that I may tell my poor friends about the Saviour who died for our sins and rose again."[7] In 1852, when he attended the Annual Meeting of the Free Mission Society, he reiterated his desire to return home as a missionary: "how ardently he longed to make known to them the good news of salvation."[8] Given his family's position in Muslim society as successful merchants and the religious leadership of his brother, uncle, and grandfather, it would be naive to think that he could have undermined their commitment to Islam and their association with the scholarly leadership of the Sokoto Caliphate. Baquaqua was neither naive nor uninformed, and he surely would have understood this.

Baquaqua was involved in fundraising almost from the time he joined the American Baptist Free Mission in Port-au-Prince, and after his return to the United States, he was preoccupied with fundraising and earning money. At its annual meeting on 5 June 1850, the Free Mission Society acknowledged the contributions toward Baquaqua's well-being and education. As noted in the autobiography, "the Missions" provided early assistance, which apparently referred to the "Franklin Free Mission Society of this State [i.e., New York], who after Mahommah's arrival in the United States, kindly came forward and administered to his necessities."[9] Baquaqua raised small amounts of money from a great number of people, viz.: "My Dear Brother:—I have received a letter from sister Josephine Cushman Bateham. She gave me one dollar, and her friend one dollar. She lives a great way off, but she remembers me."[10] Baquaqua had met Bateham in Haiti and had sent her condolences on the death of her husband. Mahommah was expected to speak publicly at various Baptist churches, and in this way to raise funds. Sometimes for effect he even spoke in an "African" tongue, whether in Hausa or Dendi is now known, such as at the first Convocation at Central College in 1850 but also at various gatherings elsewhere, including the annual meetings of the American Baptist Free Mission Society. At the 1851 morning session of the Society on 5 September 1851, "Mahomah, a Haitien convert, and Br. Hyde of Wisconsin" both spoke and $2.35 was collected "for the benefit of Mahomah."[11] Considering the paltry amounts that were actually raised and Baquaqua's ongoing living expenses, it was virtually impossible for Baquaqua alone to come up with the money needed to finance a mission in Africa. No significant donor ever materialized, although Gerrit Smith in Peterboro certainly had the means to do so.

At the Annual Meeting of the Free Mission Society in Montrose, Pennsylvania, in June 1852, the Board expressed its support for a mission to Africa: "In reference to an African mission, the Board are of the opinion, that, under existing circumstances, such as the want of means and information, Eld. Newman had better be appointed as a missionary to Africa; that he be recommended to visit the churches in behalf of the contemplated mission, and that he continue to collect funds until enough shall be raised [can't read next few words] ... years after his arrival in Africa. The Board would respectfully recommend this plan to the consideration of the Society at its present session."[12] Hence, in July 1853, in the weeks after the annual meeting that had been held in Utica in June, Baquaqua toured parts of Pennsylvania. As noted previously, Baquaqua was expected to raise $5,000 in a year, which may explain the coldness of the 1854 Annual Report. Baquaqua thought that he could "never do it in a year."[13] In fact, by early July 1853 the $200 he had raised was much less than he was expected to garner. While the amount may seem like a paltry sum, it was significant in terms of potential costs. At the time, it cost 20 guineas (£21) to travel from New York to Liverpool, plus the cost of provisions; at least this was what the United States Mail Steamer of the Collins Line charged for second class accommodation.[14] Baquaqua came to realize that he had been charged to raise funds for a prolonged mission that included the expenses of the clergyman selected to head the mission. It is for this reason, perhaps, that Baquaqua concluded that "I do not think that my friends will do anything in my Mission."[15]

The Eleventh Annual Meeting of the American Baptist Free Mission Society, held in June 1854, noted that Baquaqua had been authorized in 1853 "to visit, under the supervision of a Committee appointed for that purpose, certain pastors, and to seek aid from them and their churches for the purpose of opening a mission in Africa. It is understood that he did thus visit, to some extent; but with what results is not definitely known to us. A resolution was passed by the Board on the 1st of September last, that the same Committee be requested to correspond with several individuals named, in regard to their becoming Missionaries in Africa. No such Missionary, however, has yet been secured."[16] Rev. Albert L. Post of Montrose, Pennsylvania, president of the society and a leader in its affairs throughout this period, assisted fugitives to escape. In 1841, he was ordained and devoted his time to evangelistic work in connection with the Baptist Church. Besides being vice-president of NY Central College and a Trustee, he was pastor of Bridgewater Baptist Church. Bridgewater was the township surrounding the Borough of Montrose. Post was selected as clerk and was responsible for adoption of a resolution: "Resolved that we believe the system of Slavery as it exists in the United States, to be sinful, and ought to be abolished."[17]

Because Baquaqua was appointed to the Society's Committee on the African Mission, together with Post and Warham Walker, the editor of *The American Baptist*,[18] he was systematically involved in the campaign to raise funds for the projected mission, and for his own return to Africa. As reported by Post in July 1853, Baquaqua "has spent a little time in this and a few neighboring places, collecting funds for the contemplated African mission . . . [and] the plan is to send him to such pastors of churches, or other religious persons, as will take an interest in the mission to labor under their general direction." Baquaqua's approach was to talk about his own life and the "manners, customs &c. of his native country," anticipating the content and perhaps the form of the later autobiography; it was probably in this context that the idea of publishing the latter was conceived. According to Post, his talks went down well with his audiences, speaking "uniformly with interest to his hearers," despite the continuing deficiencies of his English, which is how he had already raised $200 in money and pledges.[19]

The Board of the Free Mission Society regularly had discussed the proposed African mission from 1848 onward, and Baquaqua's intended role in it, as recorded in its Annual Reports. These make clear that what was envisaged was that Baquaqua would act as an assistant to an American missionary rather than operate on his own. In 1852, its Committee on the African Mission explicitly recommended that "the return of Mahommah [to Africa] be deferred until a suitable person be obtained to accompany him." During that same year, in fact, this problem appeared to have been solved, when the Rev. William P. Newman came forward. At its June 1852 meeting in Montrose, Pennsylvania, the Board expressed the opinion that "under existing circumstances, such as the want of means and information, Eld. Newman had better be appointed as a missionary to Africa; that he be recommended to visit the churches in behalf of the contemplated mission, and that he continue to collect funds until enough shall be raised to sustain him for at least two years after his arrival in Africa."[20] Both Newman and Baquaqua addressed the semi-annual meeting of the Missionary Society in Utica on 5 September 1851 and were on the committee to establish the Africa Mission. The Board of the Society was pleased that it was "still the desire of Mahommah, the converted African, to return to the land of his nativity as a missionary of the Cross." Newman now offered his services: "If it is the will of God, I am ready to go to Africa with Br. Mahommah and do what I can."[21] Someone who is only referred to as a "sister" also volunteered for the mission to Africa. The proposed appointment of Newman fell through, however, and instead of going to Africa, Newman accepted the pastorate of the First Baptist Church in Toronto, which he took up in December 1852.[22] At the Society's annual meeting in Utica in June 1853, the Board was forced to defer the mission, noting that "no suitable person has yet appeared . . . to be joined with Mahommah in the attempt to introduce Christianity among his people at Zougo [Djougou]."[23]

At the same time, the Society's difficulties in finding anyone to accompany Baquaqua to Africa persisted. On 1 September 1853, the Board instructed the African Mission Committee to "correspond with several individuals named, in regard to their becoming Missionaries in Africa," but as the Board once again reported to the following annual meeting in June 1854, "no such missionary has . . . yet been secured."[24] On 8 October Baquaqua wrote to George Whipple (1805–76) of the American Missionary Association, which sponsored the Mendi Mission in Sierra Leone that had been founded in support of the survivors of the *Amistad* rebellion. Whipple became secretary of the American Missionary Association. A series of letters between Baquaqua and Whipple show the extent of their contact.

> I have just returned home and found a letter from you. I have consulted some of my friends and no objections have been made as yet, to my going to Africa in connexion with the Mendi Mission.
>
> I have just heard that Brother [George] Thompson has returned to the United States on account of his wife's illness.
>
> If that is true, will you not inform me, and where I may direct a letter to him. I know very well that I should be better prepared to go, I ought to have been in school last summer, but my friends thought best, that I should go round and see what I could get to aid me on my mission. I think I can improve my mind some yet, but the English Language has been very hard for me to understand and speak.
>
> I think I shall not remain in the United States long, unless the prospect opens for me to return to my native land. I do not wish to burden your Society. If I could do good by going I should be happy indeed to go but if not I think I shall go to Canada, and then I fear I shall give up going entirely. Please my good brother write me immediately, for I will stay here till I hear from you. I thank you kindly for your good advice and will try and do the best I can. Pray for me my brother that God will direct my steps. This is my prayer.[25]

His relationship with Whipple shows that Baquaqua was attempting to expand his network beyond the Free Will Baptists. His overture demonstrates that he knew about *La Amistad* case and its ongoing trajectory. The captives on board *La Amistad* had come from the interior of Sierra Leone and were being transferred along the northern coast of Cuba in 1839 for sale. The enslaved were able to seize the ship, kill the captain, and begin a journey that was intended to return to Africa but instead ended up off Long Island in the United States. The *Amistad* case became a legal nightmare. The saga received a lot of attention and made its way to the US Supreme Court.[26]

The *Amistad* controversy raises questions about Baquaqua's ordeal, which happened less than a decade after it put into harbor in the United States. The trials associated with the seizure of the ship and the disposition of the enslaved Africans on board eventually resulted in repatriation of the survivors to the area inland from Sierra Leone from where they had come. Thus was founded the Mendi Mission and the corresponding prominence of George Thompson (1804–78), whose radical abolitionism virtually forced him into exile as the principal propagandist for the mission. He wrote *Thompson in Africa: or, An Account of the Missionary Labors, Sufferings, Travels, and Observations of George Thompson in Western Africa, at the Mendi Mission* and *The Palm Land: or West Africa, Illustrated.*[27] He toured parts of North America as well as Britain, and he met Baquaqua through Gerrit Smith when Thompson was visiting Peterboro. Baquaqua by contrast came off a ship with two other slaves, one of whom voluntarily returned to the ship. Rather than stage a revolt on the ship, Baquaqua and his mate were beaten and abused and relied on the intervention of activists who came to their defense to the point of breaking them out of jail.

Baquaqua came to know George Whipple in relation to the Mendi Mission as well, and that association indirectly connected Baquaqua with the abolitionist circle associated with Lewis Tappan, who took the lead in defending the captives on board the *Amistad*. Whipple and other Congregationalists associated with Tappan formed the American Missionary Association.[28] Tappan helped organize over one hundred Congregational churches in support of the *Amistad* refugees, whose case went all the way to the Supreme Court, and whose brother Benjamin was a senator. Initially a Unitarian, he rejoined the Congregationalists, and subsequently was associated with the "immediatists" who were proactive in their opposition to slavery and who included William Lloyd Garrison, Gerrit Smith, Theodore Dwight Weld, and Amos A. Phelps.[29]

Baquaqua contacted Whipple when he was trying to raise money to fund his trip back to Africa. In a letter written in August 1853, Baquaqua declared that he did not think that his "friends"—that is, the Baptists—would do enough to aid his mission. The Baptist leadership made it clear that the $400 he had raised from his lectures at various Baptist churches was inadequate, and Baquaqua was now looking for additional sponsorship. He certainly would have discussed the situation with Gerrit Smith, with whom he was in contact in relation to obtaining land and in subsidizing the publication of his autobiography. Gerrit Smith was in a position to introduce Baquaqua to Whipple. Smith was also closely associated through the American Missionary Association in New York City. At the time, Whipple was secretary of the association. However they came in contact, Whipple and Baquaqua corresponded between August 1853 and January 1854 regarding employment opportunities.

The surviving correspondence suggests that Baquaqua and Whipple became quite close. If this is so, the prospects that Baquaqua would go to the Mendi Mission were enhanced. In August 1853, Baquaqua was in Brooklyn, Pennsylvania, a small community whose inhabitants were of African descent just south of Montrose where Post lived. Baquaqua had visited Montrose at a time when Post was influential in the Free Mission Society movement. Clearly, after discussing prospects with Post, Baquaqua exchanged letters with Whipple: "I have wrote one to you and I did not hear from you. I should like you tell me if you please, if I go with Br. Thompson do you think we can try to found [find] my Mother and Sister and Brother in Africa. Write to me this week and sent to New Berlin N.Y. If vessel ready to go to Africa I am ready to go."[30] Baquaqua reached out to Whipple again when he was facing the racist backlash against him because of his three-year friendship with the girl in Mc-Grawville, whom it was rumored he was planning to marry.[31]

The gloss on their exchange reveals the racism that underlay the sentiments of many of those who opposed slavery. Relationships across gender were racialized as taboo. Baquaqua was not in danger because of bounty hunters enforcing the Fugitive Slave Act but because racism had raised its ugly head, just as it had in the case of William Allen, the classics professor at Central College. Only a few months earlier Allen and his amour had to flee to England, having to arrange meet so that her parents would not intervene and eventually setting sail. The story fulfills a romance that satisfies acts of resistance but at a cost. Allen was a brilliant scholar of race but was never allowed to hold a prestigious position at a university. He wrote several books while he was in exile. His training in classics underlay his achievements and should have generated a senior position in academia.

By the latter half of 1853, Baquaqua was beginning to become disillusioned with the Free Mission Society and was skeptical of its ability to secure his return to Africa. By October, it was clear to Baquaqua that $400 from his lectures at various Baptist churches was far from the amount that the Baptists thought was necessary for a mission. According to Abner Bates, who tried to help Baquaqua retrieve funds that had been raised for the Baptist Mission, whatever the amount that the Baptists thought was necessary: "[I]t is hardly probable he will secure [it] as he has already visited most of the churches which simpathise [sic] with the Movement."[32]

By then, in fact, he had already contacted the American Missionary Association in New York City, whose secretary, George Whipple, appears to have taken notice. In August 1853 Baquaqua wrote to Whipple from Brooklyn, Pennsylvania, a small, all-Black settlement south of Montrose, where Rev. Post was stationed.[33] The American Missionary Association had established the Mendi Mission, led by George Thompson, which returned the surviving members of the successful slave revolt on the *Amistad* to the Sierra Leone hinterland in 1841. This mission had difficulty in maintaining its numbers and had to be reinforced in the early 1850s.[34] Baquaqua offered his services for the Mendi Mission, apparently thinking that he might be able to proceed from Sierra Leone to his home in Djougou, if not Katsina. In one of his letters he asked, "[I]f I go with Br Thompson, do you think we can try to found [= find] my Mother and Sister and Brother in Africa?"[35] But, alas, it does not seem that Baquaqua was successful in his attempt to join the Mendi Mission.

George Thompson was an English member of Parliament, an abolitionist, and a close associate of William Lloyd Garrison. He was well known to anti-slavery activists on both sides of the Atlantic. He visited Gerrit Smith in Peterboro where he possibly met Baquaqua. Thompson was arguably one of the most articulate abolitionists and human rights lecturers in Britain and the United States at the time. He was a powerful orator and fought for abolition throughout his personal and professional career, often risking his life in the process. He grew up with the slave trade. His father worked on ships that transported Africans to the Americas and told him about the barbarities on the slave ships. He became a proponent of emancipation and campaigned for the end of slavery in 1834 and the end of apprenticeship in 1838. He participated in the first World Antislavery Convention in 1840 and was elected MP for Tower Hamlets in 1847. In the United States he was associated with William Lloyd Garrison, Gerrit Smith, and Frederick Douglass, who toured Britain in the 1840s.

Thompson was one of the many people Baquaqua interacted with during the time that he was raising money for his attempted missionary project in Africa. While the American Missionary Association established the Mendi Mission, Thompson provided its direction and hence was involved in the return of the surviving members of the successful slave revolt on the *Amistad* in 1841. Baquaqua offered his services to the Mendi Mission, thinking that he might be able to proceed from Sierra Leone to his home in Djougou to locate his mother, brother, and sister. Although there is no documentation of the American Missionary Association's response to Baquaqua's request, his letters allude to the fact that there were objections or queries raised by Whipple relating to Baquaqua's linguistic competence, personal conduct, and religious affiliation, as well as to the unlikely prospect of financial support from the Baptist Free Mission.[36]

The attitude of the American Missionary Association itself to this approach is not directly documented, since we have only Baquaqua's side of the correspondence, but his letters seem to be responding to these objections. Baquaqua pressed his qualifications as an interpreter, admitting the limitations of his competence in English but stressing his knowledge of the Arabic and "Zogoo [i.e., Dendi]" languages; the phrase of Arabic that he included in one of his letters, noted earlier, was presumably intended to demonstrate his potential usefulness as a translator. However, he also offered, if he was not considered adequately qualified to serve as a teacher or interpreter, to serve Thompson (as he had Judd earlier) as a cook. Despite the evidently luke-warm response of Whipple, Baquaqua initially expected to go to Africa with the Mendi mission before the end of 1853: in August he wrote, "I made my mand [= mind] to go to Africa this fall"; and in September, "Please . . . tell me when the vessel will go to Africa, if it will go in October or December." But by January 1854, his hopes were receding into the remoter future: "I should like to know, if I will go to Africa, this year or next year."[37] In the end, he evidently gave up hope altogether and left for Canada.

It appears from the surviving correspondence that Baquaqua initially ap-proached the American Missionary Association without the knowledge of the Baptist Free Mission Society. As he admitted in August 1853: "I not gone [= going] to say anything about you or anybody else to my friends." Whipple evidently insisted that he should clear the matter with them, and in October he reported: "I have consulted some of my friends and no objection has been made as yet, to my going to Africa in connexion with the Mendi mission."[38] Nevertheless, it appears that some degree of distance now emerged in rela-tions between Baquaqua and his Baptist sponsors. At the Annual Meeting of the Free Mission Society in June 1854, reference was made to the fundraising activities for the projected African mission with which Baquaqua had been charged in the previous year: "At the first meeting of the Board after the An-niversary, in June last, Mahommah G. Baquaqua was authorized to visit, under the supervision of a Committee appointed for that purpose, certain pastors, and to seek aid from them and their churches for the purpose of opening a mission in Africa. It is understood that he did thus visit, to some extent; but with what results is not definitely known to us."[39] This makes clear that communication with Baquaqua, now at Chatham in Canada West, had become tenuous, if not broken altogether. However, the somewhat coy wording of this report, by implication blaming Baquaqua for the lapse of con-tact, appears to conceal a more overt breach. Baquaqua himself, in his letter to Gerrit Smith in May 1854, was more robust in his expression and explicitly blamed the Society: "I am very sorry to inform you that the Free Mission has kill[ed] the Africa Mission, and kill[ed] Mahommah too . . . The Free Mis-sion did not do right by me at this time."[40]

It is not certain when Baquaqua decided to write his autobiography, but he needed to raise money to return to Africa, and somehow he came to realize that he might be able to sell his life's story. The Annual Reports of the Society for 1854 and 1855 make no reference to a possible publication, which suggests that there was no Baptist support for its publication. However, *The American Baptist* published a review in November 1854; hence, it was known to its readership at least and certainly had to be known to the Baptist leadership.[41] Lack of sponsorship evidently explains why he published the autobiography under his own name rather than, as might have been anticipated, under the auspices of the Free Mission Society. It is indicative that when he needed money to finance the printing of the book a few weeks later, he turned to Smith as a potential individual benefactor, rather than the Society.

Baquaqua probably first thought of an autobiography when he was lecturing to Baptist congregations about his youth, his enslavement, and his conversion. These were the details that people wanted to know. It is also possible that he was influenced by Frederick Douglass's autobiography and what he read elsewhere, such as the 18 June 1851 issue of the *Voice of the Fugitive*, which contained a "Story of a Native African," which was an abstract from the autobiography of Gustavus Vassa (aka Olaudah Equiano).[42] The account is introduced as an "extract from the narrative of Gustavus Vassa, who was stolen from his native land when a boy and made a slave; but who afterwards became enlightened and wrote a history of his life, which was first published in England." The quotation establishes that Vassa's "interesting narrative" was circulating in the Underground Railroad network in Canada and easily could have been one of the inspirations for Baquaqua to write his own. Like Baquaqua's experience, Vassa had been kidnapped when he was a boy named Olaudah Equiano, but unlike Baquaqua, Vassa retained his slave name except for purposes for authenticating his birth and childhood in Africa.

Baquaqua presumably hoped that an autobiography would elicit the necessary funds for his return to Africa. Vassa's autobiography certainly achieved financial success for its author, although Baquaqua could not have known that. By contrast, the response to Baquaqua's autobiography must have been disappointing; certainly, the pamphlet did not circulate widely or attract much attention, and Baquaqua apparently did not take many, if any, copies of the autobiography with him when he went to England. In January 1855, evidently in frustration, Baquaqua decided to leave North America in the hope of getting from England to Africa. How he was able to pay for his fare, which must have cost £21, plus provisions, is not known.[43] As subsequent events would demonstrate, he certainly had little money and no clear possibilities of support. The Annual Meeting of the American Baptist Free Mission Society, held in New York City in May 1855, once again noted the lack of progress in realizing the projected African mission, due to the failure to find anybody willing to go after Rev. Newman backed out. There was no real prospect that the Baptists would send a mission, despite Baquaqua's interest.

> In the mean time, Mahommah G. Baquaqua, the African convert, to whom the attention of the Society has been directed in the hope that he might one day become useful to such missionaries, as an interpreter,—yearning for his home and kindred, and weary and heart-sick, of hope long deferred,—has gone, with such slender resources as he could collect, to seek his mother. He sailed from New York about the 30th January last, for Liverpool,—having letters of introduction to several persons in the latter city, from whom he expected counsel and aid in making his way to Africa.[44]

Certainly, one letter must have been to William Powell, who was known to welcome anyone of African descent from the United States. Powell had been heavily involved in helping people to escape from slavery, including Baquaqua himself, before becoming disillusioned and moving his family to England after the passage of the Fugitive Slave Act in 1850. This was the very person who had helped Baquaqua gain his freedom in New York in 1847.

It can be assumed that he was also hoping to receive assistance from the Baptist Free Mission network, whose agent in England was none other than Edward Mathews. Together with Foss, Mathews had published *Facts for Baptist Churches* in 1850, containing information on Baquaqua as well as a frontispiece of Baquaqua with Rev. Judd for the book. Mathews was thus well acquainted with Baquaqua's ambitions, if not also with him personally.[45] Though Mathews was based in Bristol rather than in Liverpool, where Baquaqua landed, Baquaqua probably hoped to contact him.[46] As is clear from Mathews's autobiography, he was one of the most outspoken radical abolitionists, almost getting himself killed in Kentucky for his antislavery activities. Baquaqua was also in touch with Professor Allen and his wife, who it will be remembered had fled to England from New York Central College, and now lived in London. The reference to Professor Allen referred to the instructor at Central College who eloped with one of the female students, Mary G. King. After establishing a residence in London, Allen lectured on antislavery and wrote *The American Prejudice against Colour* about the persecution surrounding his courtship of his wife and their elopement. He corresponded with William Lloyd Garrison and Gerrit Smith, among others, and met visitors of African descent who came to London, including Baquaqua, whom he had known at Central College before he had been forced to flee.

The Allens introduced Baquaqua to other abolitionists in London, including the Ladies Society to Aid Fugitives from Slavery. Baquaqua may have approached the American Missionary Association at this time, hoping to enlist an English-based mission to Africa. He had been in contact with George Thompson of the Mendi Mission, although it seems Baquaqua never went there, despite his assertion that he might try (figure 7.1). He wrote to Whipple on 14 September 1853, "[T]ell me when the vessal will go to Africa,"[47] and he specifically mentioned Thompson's mission among the Mende survivors of the *Amistad*.

It would have been easy for him to approach the Baptist Missionary Society in Britain. Baquaqua had known one if its missionaries, W. H. Webley, earlier in Haiti.[48] These Baptists maintained a mission at Douala, on the coast of Cameroun, where Black personnel from Jamaica were employed since 1841, but Baquaqua was not associated with this Baptist faction. Baquaqua may have approached the English Baptists who backed the Douala mission, but if he did, he was evidently not successful in being enlisted for their Cameroun mission and does not otherwise seem to appear in its records.[49] However, it may be that he was hoping to secure secular assistance, perhaps working for his passage on a commercial shipping service to Africa like Mac-Gregor Laird's African Steamship Company.[50]

Despite his move to England, Baquaqua remained in the thoughts of the American Baptist Free Mission Society, in connection with its continuing discussions of the projected African Mission. At the 1856 Annual Meeting, the Board noted that Baquaqua was a subject of discussion.

> From the first the Society has proposed to itself a mission in Africa. It was hoped, ere long, that the providence of God, which strangely threw upon our hands Mahommah G. Baquaqua, a young native of Africa would open the way for the accomplishment of this much desired object. But hitherto efforts have seemed to be entire failures. Up to very recently, the door has seemed to be shut. It is now, however, evidently opened. Facts which have appeared in the Am. Baptist [American Baptist], proving this, are worthy of a place in our report, and we give them hoping that they may awaken a suitable ardor in all to enter the field through that door.[51]

The new opportunity to which the board referred was a request for assistance from Baptists in Sierra Leone, which was also supported by George Thompson of the Mendi Mission, whom Baquaqua himself had previously approached. John J. Brown, acting pastor of the First Baptist Church in

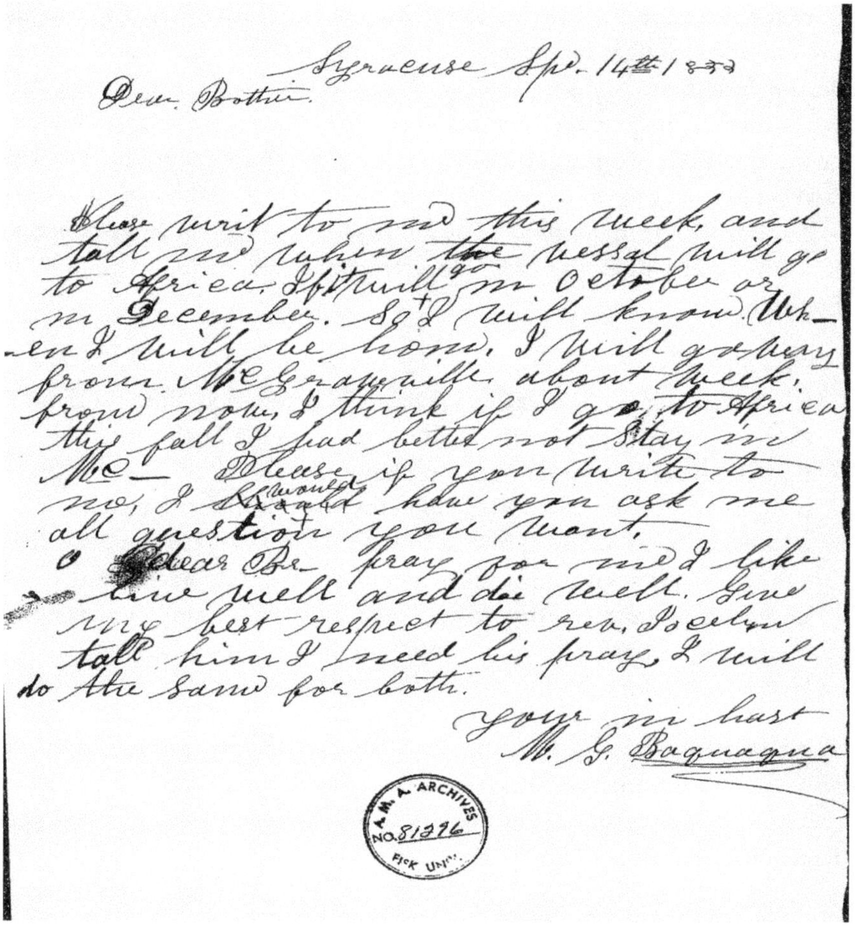
Syracuse Sep. 14th 1853
Dear Brother.

Please writ to me this week, and tall me when the vessal will go to Africa. If it will go in October or in December. So I will know. When I will be home. I will go away from McGrawville about week. from now, I think if I go to Africa this fall I had better not stay in McG— Please if you write to me, I would have you ask me all question you want.
O dear Br pray for me I like live well and die well. Give my best respect to rev. Jocelyn tall him I need his pray, I will do the same for both.

Your in hast
M. G. Baquaqua

FIGURE 7.1 A letter from Baquaqua to George Whipple: "[T]ell me when the vessal will go to Africa," 14 September 1853 (American Missionary Association Archives, Amistad Research Center, Tulane University, New Orleans).

Freetown, Sierra Leone, whose membership consisted of African American immigrants from Nova Scotia, had sent a plea for the Free Mission Society to send "a good minister" to take over leadership of the church. The board expressed its customary hope that "neither the men nor the means may be wanting . . . to establish and carry on this proposed mission," but once again no practical action resulted.[52] Whether the mention of Baquaqua in this context should be read as implying that he was still considered by the Society as a possible member of its African Mission is unclear, but given that the request from the Freetown Baptists was specifically for a minister, lack of the requisite training as well as his current distance may well have sabotaged any opportunity for him.

Meanwhile, Baquaqua's attempts to reach Africa from England were evidently also initially unsuccessful. Sometime after his arrival in Liverpool, he traveled to London, where Prof. Allen introduced him to the Ladies Society to Aid Fugitives from Slavery.[53] The Society was founded in November 1853 "for the special object of extending temporary aid to fugitive Slaves in England."

> Although the number is not considerable of the fugitives from Slavery who reach England, it is extremely difficult, if not impossible, for them to procure employment here, in consequence of their being unaccustomed, generally, to other than the labour peculiar to cotton and sugar plantations. As they reach England in the most destitute condition, it occurred to a few ladies to form a Committee, for the purpose of raising a fund to supply these unfortunate persons with food, lodging, and other necessaries; and thus promote their procuring speedy employment on board ship, or passages to one or other of the colonies, where their labour is in request.[54]

The report was issued *"for private circulation only."* A long list of subscribers was attached. Among the list of eight cases that were included as examples of the assistance that the Ladies Society highlighted was that of "Mohamna Baquaqua, a native of Africa."

> At an early age he was stolen from his home, and conveyed in a slave-ship to Brazil. During his residence of several years in Brazil, he endured great hardships, and was the subject of severe sufferings. After having been sold from one owner to another, he became the property of the captain of a ship, and sailed with him to different ports. At length, New York became the place of their visit; and it was there that he learnt that he might be free if he wished. He eagerly availed himself of the opportunity afforded him, and put himself under the care of "Abolitionists." By them he was placed in the McGranville [sic] Institute, under the tutorship, amongst others, of Professor Allen, by whom he is not only well known but esteemed. Being anxious to return to his mother's house, he came to England, hoping to meet with friends who might be disposed to take up his case. He at length determined on taking a situation as a cook on board a ship, and endeavour to save enough to pay for his passage to Sierra Leone. Being entirely destitute on

his arrival in England, the sum of £8. 19s. 9d. was advanced, for the purpose of obtaining for him suitable clothing, board and lodging. He has now procured employment as a ship's cook, and left for the Mediterranean.[55]

No further details are provided for Baquaqua's enlistment on a ship, other than that he left for the Mediterranean sometime in 1855. What Baquaqua did after returning from the Mediterranean is not known, but it seems unlikely that he was prospering. In 1857, he again wrote to the American Baptist Free Mission Society asking for assistance. In February, the Board of the Society noted that it had received a letter from "Mahommah, the African educated in this country, now in England, expressing his desire to return and labor among his countrymen."[56] The Board discussed the overture but, in the end, decided to defer a decision for a year, and apparently no mission was ever sent. At least there seems to be no evidence in surviving documents to suggest that the proposal was ever discussed again.

Baquaqua's efforts to return to Africa were accompanied and supported by a self-conscious emphasis on his origins in that continent. At a prayer meeting after his baptism in Haiti in July 1848, as reported by Mrs. Judd, after finding his English inadequate to express his feelings, he dramatically switched into his "native tongue," the effect of which Mrs. Judd found "thrilling."[57] Although on this occasion the action was presumably not premeditated, Baquaqua subsequently exploited the dramatic effect of speaking in an African language deliberately: on his introduction to New York Central College in January 1850, as reported by Electa Lake, "Arabic and Indian [i.e., Native American] songs" were sung, the former presumably by Baquaqua, since this was followed by a conversation between him and some "Indian" students of the College, "the former speaking in the Arabic and the latter replying in the Indian tongue, much to the diversion of all present."[58] Whether the language which he spoke on this and other occasions was really Arabic, of which his knowledge was probably limited to religious formulae, may be doubted; more likely, if he made an extended oration, it was in Dendi or Hausa. At the commencement ceremonies at the college later in 1850, Baquaqua again delivered "a speech in one of the African tongues."[59] It may also be noted that in the engraving on the cover of the autobiography, Baquaqua is shown wearing African-style robes, in interesting contrast to the earlier photograph of him with the Rev. Mr. Judd, in which he appears in European dress. This evidently represents a further effort at promoting an exotic image of his African background.

No doubt there was an element of calculation in this emphasis on his identity as an African, since it was precisely his African origins that recommended him for association with the Baptist Free Mission. But his employment and conversion in turn were attractive to Baquaqua precisely because of the prospect of his return to Africa. It may be suggested that a more positive assertion of his African roots was involved, and this is consistent with the fact, noted earlier, that the autobiography emphasizes his life in Africa. His odyssey to some extent was representative of other Muslims in diaspora who also stand out.[60] His continued identity as a Muslim is problematic, nonetheless. There is no sense in the sources that he was a practicing Muslim, praying every day, not eating pork, and not drinking, but he did lead a pious life. Moreover, he was respected in religious circles for over a decade after being a cook for the Free Will Baptist mission in Port-au-Prince. He kept his Muslim name, thereby associating with the Hausa background of his mother, but provided vocabulary in Dendi when asked to speak in his native tongue. He did not refer to the language of the people of Djougou, where he was born and brought up, but surely he must have known some Yom. He referred to Yoruba customs relating to twins even though he was not directly exposed to any Yoruba communities until he passed through several on his trip to the coast. The confusion in his description of *ibeji* figurines and twins is probably a misunderstanding on the part of Samuel Moore, who attributes the practice to a custom that Baquaqua had to perform rather than Baquaqua's attempt to contrast his own background being born after twins, as his name Gardo indicates, with that of Yoruba religious beliefs associate with *orisa* and forms of ritual, which he certainly would have known about.

Despite his determination and his best efforts, Baquaqua seems to have missed several opportunities to return to Africa in the 1850s. The Free Will Baptists had failed him, despite his fundraising and the publication of his autobiography. His efforts to pursue his course back to Africa led him to Liverpool, and although he had letters of introduction, the trip was a gamble. Baquaqua almost certainly met William Powell in Liverpool in 1855, although it is not clear if Powell knew who Baquaqua was. As discussed above, Powell helped Baquaqua escape from jail in New York in 1847 and had moved his family of seven children to Liverpool in 1851 to escape the constant struggle against racism that followed the passage of the Fugitive Slave Law of 1850.[61] Powell educated his children in England. Indeed, one of his sons became a doctor who served in the American Civil War. Powell Sr.'s employment as "a Custom-House clerk" with C. Bushell and Co., marine brokers on Dale Street, enabled him to meet most travelers of African descent who arrived from North America, although as noted above it is not clear if he actually came into contact with Baquaqua at that time. But his home at 50 Great Nelson Street in

Liverpool and afterward at 7 Clifton Street, Everton, from 1852 must have been open to new arrivals, just as his establishment for Black seafarers in New York City had been.[62] It's possible that Powell missed Baquaqua, but the fact that Baquaqua had letters of introduction suggests that one was addressed to Powell. Liverpool was a busy port (figure 7.2), and the fact that Powell never seems to have mentioned Baquaqua may indicate that they did not meet.

In a letter to the *National Anti-Slavery Standard* in August 1853, Powell noted that his position at Bushell and Co. enabled him to spend "part of my time . . . devoted to waiting on passengers often arriving in Liverpool by the Underground Railroad."[63] He claimed that "in these cases, I clean their boots and give them generally a British Liberty polish. No less than five have visited me within the last five months; namely Grandison Boyd, Charles Hill, George Washington, Alexander Everett, and Ananias Smith; the first you know; the second is from Maryland, formerly owned by Dr. Alan; the third is from Georgia; the fourth from Virginia; and the fifth, from New Orleans, was stowed away on board ship there, among the cotton bales, by the sailors."[64] William Allen noted that on arrival in England, he spent two weeks in Liverpool, "rendered more agreeable by the kindness of our mutual friend, Wm. P. Powell, Esq., formerly of New York."[65] It is possible that he also met Baquaqua when he arrived in 1854. Powell renewed his management of the Colored Sailor's Home when he moved back to New York after the outbreak of the Civil War and only escaped with his family during a race riot in 1863 by climbing over the roofs of adjacent buildings, his own home being destroyed in the ensuing fire set by arsonists.[66]

But even with Powell's help, if he got any, Baquaqua was unable to raise further funds that might have helped him reach Africa. Baquaqua came to the attention of the Ladies Society to Aid Fugitives from Slavery in London in 1855, which provided him with some support: "Being entirely destitute on his arrival in England, the sum of £8. 19s. 9d. was advanced, for the purpose of obtaining for him suitable clothing, board and lodging."[67] Their report also indicates that Baquaqua was able to contact one of his former teachers at Central College, Professor Allen, who had been forced to flee Central College with his fiancée, who was the daughter of an abolitionist minister in Fulton, New York, who nonetheless objected to his daughter's engagement to someone who was Black, even if the person was classified as being three-quarters white. The Ladies Society reported that by the time their 1855 report was published, Baquaqua had "procured employment as a ship's cook, and left for the Mediterranean."[68] Otherwise, his letter to the Baptists in 1857 requesting further support seems to indicate an ongoing problem of financial survival.

FIGURE 7.2   The Waterlook Docks, Liverpool, *Illustrated London News*, 1850.

The American Colonization Society was ostensibly a charity for people of African descent that allowed people to relocate from the United States back to Africa on the Kru coast in a newly established colony called Liberia. Wishful thinkers imagined that the foundation of an African American colony would be attractive to former slaves and free Blacks and thereby remove them from United States demography. In fact, the reason for the gradual consolidation of Liberia over twenty-five years before it was first formally recognized as a state in 1847 was the enforced migration of enslaved who were promised their emancipation if they settled in Liberia. In addition, thousands of captives on slave ships were settled there who had no relationship with the Indigenous population. Similar to Sierra Leone, Liberia emerged as a creole-dominated society with strained relations with the Indigenous inhabitants who spoke Kru or a related dialect.[69]

The Mendi Mission that involved the resettlement of survivors of the *Amistad* slave revolt were sent back to West Africa and established a mission in Mende territory on the mainland south of the Freetown peninsula.[70] Baquaqua knew George Thompson, the prominent abolitionist who publicized the efforts of the Mission and is known to have been a correspondent of Baquaqua's mentor, Gerrit Smith, and who visited Smith in Peterboro in 1851 when Baquaqua was at Central College, was in contact with George Whipple, who was in the circle of abolitionists associated with Lewis Tappan.[71] As Baquaqua wrote to Whipple on 8 October 1853:

> I have just returned home and found a letter from you. I have consulted some of my friends and no objections have been made as yet, to my going to Africa in connexion with the Mendi Mission.
>
> I have just heard that Brother Thompson has returned to the United States on account of his wife's illness.
>
> If that is true, will you not inform me, and where I may direct a letter to him. I know very well that I should be better prepared to go, I ought to have been in school last summer, but my friends thought best, that I should go round and see what I could get to aid me on my mission. I think I can improve my mind some yet, but the English Language has been very hard for me to understand and speak.
>
> I think I shall not remain in the United States long, unless the prospect opens for me to return to my native land. I do not wish to burden your Society. If I could do good by going I should be happy indeed to go but if not I think I shall go to Canada, and then I fear I shall give up going entirely. Please my good brother write me immediately, for I will stay here till I hear from you. I thank you kindly for your good advice and will try and do the best I can. Pray for me my brother that God will direct my steps. This is my prayer.[72]

Baquaqua's efforts to join the Mendi Mission appear never to have reached fruition, although Baquaqua probably made additional inquiries when he reached Sierra Leone in 1862. Delany's expedition to several Yoruba cities, especially Abeokuta, in 1859 was another opportunity that Baquaqua seems to have missed.[73] Delany was one of the first African Americans admitted to Harvard Medical School. He was born free because his mother was a free woman even though his father was enslaved. His paternal grandparents were Gola. With this background, Delany was an activist in the Pittsburgh Vigilance Committee and the Young Men's Literary and Moral Reform Society. Similar to Baquaqua, he spent time in Chatham for a period of his life. Delany and his family moved to Chatham in 1856. He had a medical practice located on King Street, and in May of 1858, he attended John Brown's meeting held in Chatham where the raid on Harper's Ferry was organized. Delany even wrote his novel, *Blake,* there. It was reported in the *Chatham Tri-Weekly Planet* in 1861 that Dr. Delany had been the chief commissioner of the Niger Valley Exploring Party, following his return to Chatham on 29 December 1860.

Although Delany and Baquaqua were not in Chatham at the same time, it is very likely that Delany shared the same group of associates in Chatham as Baquaqua did when he was there in 1854. Delany was associated with the Dawn settlement to the north of Chatham. It is also plausible that they shared the same abolitionist group in upstate New York. Delany and Baquaqua have a separate shared associate, as in 1847, Delany worked alongside Frederick Douglass in Rochester in publishing *The North Star*. Baquaqua's relationship to Douglass is unknown although Douglass attended New York Central College to deliver speeches, such as on 5 July 1852, when Douglass addressed the Anti-Slavery Sewing Society. At the time, Baquaqua was a student.

Ironically, Delany's mission to West Africa occurred less than two years after Baquaqua approached the Free Will Baptists for support for the last time. In many ways, Delany's venture to the Niger River and Yorubaland in 1859 was a logical connection for Baquaqua. As noted above, Delany and Whitfield organized the emigrationist conference in Cleveland in 1854, which Baquaqua apparently had intended to attend.[74] His autobiography was advertised as being on sale in Cleveland during the conference, and a co-organizer of the conference was the Buffalo poet James Whitfield, whose poem, "Prayer of the Oppressed," was reprinted in Baquaqua's autobiography. Although it seems that Baquaqua never made it to Cleveland, their mutual interest in emigration, without doubt, was known to each other, as to Whitfield. There is an untold story of how these men with similar interests and persuasions could have missed each other.

Another chance for Baquaqua to return to West Africa was based on his experience as a cook and seaman, which were skills he acquired when he was a slave to Captain Costa in Brazil. William Powell, who had run the hostel for Black seamen and had been a member of the New York Vigilance Society, which freed Baquaqua from jail, had emigrated to Liverpool in 1851, where he was employed at one of the docks and where he looked after Blacks coming from the United States. It is surprising that Powell missed Baquaqua, which it seems he might have, for otherwise he was in a position to help Baquaqua find employment. In 1874, Powell was the corresponding editor of *The Elevator* of San Francisco, and in the 19 December 1874 edition, Powell wrote a long article on the Underground Railroad in which he recounted the Baquaqua episode in 1847, including the escape from jail, but Powell treats the incident in a manner that suggests that he never met Baquaqua again.[75]

How it was that Baquaqua appears not to have come to the attention of Macgregor Laird, the Birkenhead shipbuilder in Liverpool, who operated the African Steamship Company, is not clear. After two disastrous expeditions up the Niger River in 1832 and 1834, Laird designed paddle wheel steamboats that could navigate the river.[76] He then invested in steam navigation in the 1850s, establishing the African Steam Navigation Company, which provided regular mail communication by steamship between England and West Africa after Britain occupied Lagos in 1851. In 1854, the small steamer, *Pleiad,* under command of W. B. Baikie, successfully navigated the Niger, which led to a contract with the British government to send annual steamers up the Niger River, and thereupon Laird's company operated mail steamers for regular shipments to the ports of West Africa.[77] Baquaqua, with or without Powell's help, could have conceivably been in contact with Laird, but there is no evidence that this ever happened. Baquaqua had experience as a cook in Brazil, Haiti, and the Mediterranean and conceivably could have found employment with the African Steam Navigation Company.

Despite these various missed opportunities, Baquaqua was eventually successful in returning to West Africa. The last we hear of him is that he was in Liberia in 1863 in association with the brief expedition of the Rev. Chauncey Leonard of the First Baptist Church in Washington, DC. On 27 October 1862, President Abraham Lincoln received a delegation of nine Black emigrationists at the White House. The delegation wrote a memorial asking Lincoln when emigration support would begin, and Lincoln reassured them of his government's commitment. The enslaved population in Washington had just been emancipated, and Lincoln thought it was possible that many newly freed people would be interested in emigrating to Liberia. Lincoln intended to promote emigration of former slaves from the United States at the end of the Civil War, and he had appointed Senator Samuel C. Pomeroy of Kansas in charge of colonization. A few days later, Lincoln met two other supporters of colonization, including George W. Samson, president of Columbian College (now George Washington University) and Rev. Chauncey Leonard, the "esteemed colored" minister of the First Baptist Church in Washington. Born in 1822 in Connecticut, Leonard was ordained in 1853 and for three years in the mid-1850s ran the Saratoga Street Colored Institute, a school for Black children in Baltimore. In 1858, he moved to Washington as pastor of the 17th Street Baptist Church. In 1861, he opened a school for Black children.

On 1 November 1862, Samson and Leonard went to the White House to meet with Lincoln, who gave them $500 from the colonization fund to send Leonard to Liberia on a scouting mission, if R. R. Gurley, the secretary of the American Colonization Society, thought it was in the interest of the "colored people." In January 1863, Gurley and Philadelphia minister Thomas S. Malcolm met with Lincoln to arrange for Leonard to sail for Monrovia. Lincoln provided another $200 to cover the trip, and Leonard left Boston for Liberia

in the brig *Samuel Cook* on 4 February "to make arrangements for the location of some of his people in that country. He has visited several points of interest on the African coast, and expresses much gratification with the
condition and prospects of Liberia." Among his delegation was "Mahomah,
a native African from Brazil," who was clearly Baquaqua.[78] Leonard and
Baquaqua were linked through the Free Will Baptist movement, although
how they met and who introduced them is not known. After his return in late
1863, Leonard became the hospital chaplain at the Hospital for Colored
Troops for the remainder of the Civil War.[79]

Baquaqua was part of Leonard's delegation in West Africa. Nonetheless,
Miles Mark Fisher claimed in his brief history of the Baptist denomination
that "Chauncey Leonard of Washington and Mahomah, a native African from
Brazil, went to Africa."[80] Mahomah, a native African from Brazil, is clearly
Baquaqua, but in what capacity he was part of Leonard's delegation was not
stated. Leonard's ship, the brig *Samuel Cook*, apparently stopped in Liverpool
before proceeding to Sierra Leone, because Baquaqua must have joined
Leonard in Britain before reaching Liberia. Both Baquaqua and Leonard
were Free Will Baptists, so it is possible that they were part of the same mission. Possibly they could have met through Rev. Edward Mathews who was
in Britain and who coauthored *Facts for Baptist Churches* whose frontispiece
was a photograph of Baquaqua and Judd. He "was aided by our government
early in the year to visit Liberia to see the country, and more particularly to
establish a mission of the Baptist Church within its limits, with the view of
making that Republic a permanent home for himself and a number of his
friends." *The American Baptist*, published in New York, included two letters
from Leonard, the first dated "Freetown, Sierra Leone, March 24, 1863," mentioning his safe arrival, after having encountered "two heavy gales, and entering on the 23d instant the harbor of Sierra Leone."[81] Leonard then toured
Freetown and adjacent villages along Regent Road. On 12 April, he ascended
the "Rochelle river about twenty miles, passing the native villages of Kissey,
Wellington, Hastings, and Waterloo, containing from one to three thousand
inhabitants each."[82] He visited four small Baptist churches and discovered
that there was no ordained minister at any of the churches. He planned to be
in Monrovia during the month of May.

Subsequently, settlers were sent to Liberia. According to *The African Repository* of the Auxiliary State Colonization Societies in 1863

> Eighty-three emigrants and twenty-five cabin passengers were carried to
> Liberia by the packet Mary Caroline Stevens; she having cleared from

Baltimore November 15th, 1862, and May 25th, 1863. Of the latter several were returning Liberians. Efforts have been made by the Board—in this State and in the District of Columbia—to induce emigration, but with little success. Rev. Chauncey Leonard, pastor of a church in Washington City, left Boston in the brig Samuel Cook, February 4th, to examine the Republic, and to make arrangements for the location of some of his people in that country. He has visited several points of interest on the African coast, and expresses much gratification with the condition and prospects of Liberia. His return is looked for at an early day. Several applications have been received for emigration by the Mary Caroline Stevens, to sail about December 1st, next. She has superior accommodations for three hundred passengers, and a free passage and support for six months after their arrival, are granted to all respectable persons of color who may desire to find a home in that Republic. Colored men, of commercial knowledge and skill, with energy and directing capital in Liberia, are destined to rapidly accumulate wealth and strengthen the foundations already laid of African elevation and nationality. Of all places on the earth it is the most promising for the culture of the American people of color.[83]

It is not known if Baquaqua was in Liberia to receive the immigrants. At this point, his trail goes cold. Assuming his continued good health, he had a bright future in Liberia if he had chosen to stay there. There was also nothing to prevent him from continuing his journey home to Katsina, which was very possible in the 1860s.

If Baquaqua was in Liberia, then it was not at all impossible for him to travel on to Lagos and then overland or up the Niger River to the Sokoto Caliphate and his mother's family in Katsina. At the time, the British consulate in Lagos was issuing letters of introduction that were comparable to passports in Arabic for Muslims traveling into the interior, and presumably Baquaqua could easily have obtained one of these if he had made it to Lagos.[84] However, such a measure would have been unnecessary for Baquaqua, who was fluent in Hausa. There was already a well-established Hausa community in Lagos in the 1860s. Hausa merchants had been traveling to Lagos at least since the 1810s, usually overland along routes that were parallel to the one that Hugh Clapperton took into the interior on his second expedition in 1826, or down the Niger River and through the delta to Lagos. By the 1860s, kola nuts were being brought from Freetown and Accra, and probably Monrovia as well. Kola was the backbone of the trade through Djougou, and Baquaqua could easily have tapped into the business. In Lagos, it would have been relatively easy for him to have gained access to the Hausa commercial network that was widespread and well established. The Hausa merchants active in Lagos in the 1860s would have assured him a safe passage to Katsina. Of course, extenuating circumstances may have prevented him from such a journey, and he could have been diverted for any one of many reasons. In any event, efforts to establish his return to Katsina have failed to confirm that he made it there.[85]

It was certainly possible that Baquaqua was able to return. Others were successful. The focus in North America was on Liberia. It can be said that there was regular contact between the United States and Monrovia, often out of Baltimore. For some reason, Baquaqua was not able to avail himself of this passage. There is no evidence that he actually tried, but his associations with leading abolitionists must have meant that he was aware of the opportunities and did his best to apply. In his correspondence with George Whipple between August 1853 and January 1854, he attempted to secure employment. Many Brazilians were able to return to the Bight of Benin.[86] There were enough to form recognizable groups in the coastal ports of Lagos, Badagri, Porto Novo, Ouidah, and Accra. In addition, the return of Liberated Africans to the Yoruba cities, the Niger River, and Calabar reflected the mobility of people to insert themselves back into the societies from which many had actually come.

Conclusion

Biography can provide nuances to historiographical reconstruction by inserting individual people into the narrative. Baquaqua's moment in the narrative reveals the complexities of the trajectories of those who experienced slavery in the Americas. The public interest in better understanding the different historical contexts in the diaspora presents an opportunity for those interested in what happened in the past to tell a human story. Considering the more than thirteen million Africans who boarded ships for the Americas, there are still only a few whom we know enough about to identify by name or even an ethnicity, as unclear what that identification might have meant. Seldom can we discern their interests, their passions, their religion, and their perspectives on how they saw themselves and positioned themselves in the world. Biographical studies are fundamental contributions so that we can have a more contextualized view of the violence that these people experienced during their time of slavery in Africa and the Americas. However, the trajectories of Africans also constitute exemplary narratives of freedom. It is impressive to be able to know the stories of people who lived through enslavement, the violence of crossing the Atlantic, often in deplorable conditions, captive work on plantations, or on the streets of the cities of the European colonies in the Americas. In the face of all the adversities of life, individuals like Baquaqua managed to regain their freedom, reestablish dignity, and rebuild their lives.

Although the trajectory of some enslaved Africans is known, Baquaqua's life was unusual in the different contexts of transatlantic slavery. His biography has the makings of theater, as if his life story were a script for fantastic literature. He was born in the Muslim hinterland of West Africa circa 1820 and was twice enslaved, or at least that is what he claims. The account of his childhood, his family, and the cultures and social habits that lived in the city where he was born offers us new dimensions about what daily life was like in West Africa before being sent to slavery in the Americas. When he was in Brazil, Baquaqua got to know three widely different parts of the country and experienced the haphazard cruelty of master-slave relations. He hardly understood the Catholic rituals he was forced to attend, and his arbitrary baptism upon arrival in Pernambuco had virtually no significance other than giving him a name, unlike his second baptism when he chose his name and understood what he was doing. His story calls attention to the question of the names of Africans in Brazil. He was baptized as José da Costa, demonstrating that the violence of slavery was not limited only to physical punishment but also involved erasure of the culture, memories, and identities of individuals by giving them names that renounced their earlier names and had no cultural context. This deliberate form of subjugation did not undermine Baquaqua's determination to somehow acquire his freedom and then even have the possibility of wanting to return to Africa. Few people had the chance to make the return trip. Surely, every individual dreamed of their lands, their cultures, family ties, sounds, tastes, and traditions that were left in the life they had known before the tragedy of slavery. Baquaqua was one of the few who had the opportunity to return.

Baquaqua's story presents the broad context of slavery in the Muslim states of West Africa. Jihād altered the fabric of society in the interior. His mother's family was part of the commercial network that controlled long-distance trade across the region centered on the Sokoto Caliphate. His initial enslavement took place amid a civil war that questioned Asante's dominance over Muslim populations in the north of its empire. His account is contextualized within the political transformations that occurred in West Africa during the first half of the nineteenth century. Baquaqua's experiences expand our knowledge about the ways of living in the interior towns of West Africa and how a broad commercial context led to the systematic supply of enslaved labor to the Atlantic markets, even at a time when the British Navy was in search of ships to be judged in the Mixed Commissions in Sierra Leone, Rio de Janeiro, Havana, among other places.

The dynamics of trade between the Bight of Benin and Brazil during the eighteenth and nineteenth centuries was an extension of the vibrant trade routes of the interior.[1] Some merchants trading between the Bight of Benin and Bahia were Muslims and spoke Hausa. By the 1860s, there was an active trade along the coast from Sierra Leone to Lagos in kola, thereby reshaping the distribution routes for the popular stimulant among Muslims in the interior. The trade routes radiated outward from the Sokoto Caliphate cities not only across Borgu to Asante but also southward to Lagos, down the Niger River to the delta, and overland beyond the Benue valley southward to the grasslands north of Mount Cameroon. Trade connected with Timbuktu to the northwest, across the Sahara via Ghat and Ghadames, and eastward beyond Lake Chad following the pilgrimage route to the Red Sea and the Hijaz. These routes linked trans-Saharan trails and Asante sources of kola nuts, as well as providing outlets for textiles produced in the Hausa emirates. Muslims dominated this interior trade. Baquaqua's family was part of the mercantile elite that ultimately intersected with different points that connected with slavery in Brazil. There was a shared cultural identity underlying Muslim society and use of Hausa as a language of commerce. The cultural signs reinforced African characteristics since individuals like Baquaqua retained their ethnic identities, even though diverse cultural elements were injected into their experiences.

His remarkable journey took him to many parts of the Black Atlantic, which makes his biography a unique expose of the different dimensions of the daily life of Africans enslaved and freed in the Atlantic world. His trajectory took him to four continents, crossed countless languages, and brokered many experiences of life and death. He understood what it was like to lose everything and recover recognition in the society in which he was forced to live with dignity, even maintaining a deep desire to return to Africa. Baquaqua's odyssey is an example of survival, resistance, and resilience, especially when we realize that he was always a negotiator, a person who had dreams and desires and who pursued small and large opportunities. Baquaqua undertook a long journey of learning, elaborating individual and collective strategies that guaranteed survival. Through persistence, he demonstrated that the objective of returning to Africa might well be achieved.

Baquaqua affirmed his Muslim origins in his autobiography, in different letters that he wrote, and what he told people. Despite the impositions that his first master made, forcing him to attend Catholic prayers in Pernambuco and, later, his conversion to Protestant Christianity in Haiti, Baquaqua still made his Muslim identity evident through choice of his name, which became possible even as he underwent conversion to Christianity. He retained memories of his family's religious and cultural practices, while his Islamic upbringing emerged in the few uses of Arabic that he recorded at different events, the speeches he made in his "native" language, and even the clothes he wore on occasion. Identification with his native Muslim upbringing was maintained, evidenced by the re-adoption of his birth name, Mahommah, and the names he was known in his hometown of Djougou—that is, Gardo, which indicated that he was born after twins, and Ba Ƙwaƙwa, the name his mother gave her favorite son, which he wrote as Baquaqua. His strong desire to return to West Africa, where his family was devoutly Muslim, further confirms the perennial association with his origins. Thus, Baquaqua's trajectory directly informs the debate on identity of Africans in diaspora, their ways of maintaining, adapting, and articulating a self-image on different occasions, being always ready to demonstrate their ethnic and cultural values of life in Africa.

The political context to which he was exposed provides a fresh view on how Africans had to adjust to very different situations once they experienced slavery. Baquaqua came from a respectable Muslim commercial family that was associated with the jihād state of the Sokoto Caliphate and engaged in profitable trade with Asante in the widely consumed stimulant, *C. nitida*, or kola, which consisted of caffeine that was acceptable while smoking and alcohol were not. Sharing kola readily filled social and religious functions of hospitality and were conspicuous expressions of wealth. Wrenched from this setting, Baquaqua began the drudgery of the enslaved march to the coast through the notorious Dahomey and its slave port of Ouidah, from where perhaps one million victims embarked for the Americas over the course of the trans-Atlantic traffic. Because of the British blockade, Baquaqua had to be spirited to another location, most likely Petit Popo, where the Ouidah merchant Felix de Souza and his son had a branch firm. Once again, Baquaqua's experience clearly stands out, providing evidence on the ineffectiveness of the British blockade and the local ability to circumvent ship seizures.

His presence in the Americas began with the illegal slave trade, when Africans disembarked in Brazilian ports after 1831 should have been considered Free Africans or "Liberated Africans." Hence, the period of Baquaqua's slavery was illegal, which should have allowed him to demand his freedom at any time. Baquaqua apparently had no opportunity to take advantage of the law. He did not appeal for Brazilian justice through a civil process of freedom, as many other enslaved Africans were able to do. Nor was Baquaqua able to negotiate a letter of freedom, as some Africans had been able to do in the context of Brazilian society. Baquaqua tried different ways to get his freedom. First, he thought he was being a "good servant," so that mutual trust could offer him room to negotiate his manumission or at least alleviate his condition. When that approach didn't seem to work, he attempted escape and thought about suicide, thinking that distance or death would guarantee his full freedom. His master clearly understood that Baquaqua was not adjusting to slavery and hence sold him to a dealer from Rio de Janeiro who in turn sold him to the captain of the *Lembrança*. Baquaqua's subsequent journeys along the coast of Brazil expanded his horizons. He learned how others had acquired freedom, and as he knew more, he began to see opportunities to secure his freedom. When an opportunity suddenly presented itself upon arrival in New York, Baquaqua did not think twice and risked harsh punishment in escaping from the ship, running through the streets of New York, and seeking help from American abolitionists, without speaking more than one word of English, which was "freedom."

Baquaqua's escape from jail in New York forestalled far more significant consequences legally than it did. His case challenged a fundamental contradiction in international trade. Where did sovereignty reside? The flight of crew members from a foreign ship was covered under the United States-Brazil "Peace, Friendship, Commerce, and Navigation" agreement of 1829. Crew members, if apprehended, had to be returned to the ship. New York State law, however, granted freedom to anyone who was enslaved. There was legally no slavery in the state. The decision to escape wound up short-circuiting a legal trial that might have set an important precedent. His case had the potential to have an international impact on the right to freedom of enslaved Africans in different parts of the Americas. After all, those who were enslaved were being brought into a jurisdiction in the United States where there had been restrictions for over fifty years. Louis Napoleon, who helped him escape, had benefited from reforms in New York. Although Napoleon's mother had been enslaved, he was born free according to New York law. Later, New York passed other legislation that effectively freed anyone who somehow managed to reach the state. We have always been puzzled about the circumstances.

We have asked ourselves what would have led the captain of a Brazilian ship to take enslaved Africans to New York City with its strong abolitionist atmosphere. Perhaps, Brazil's conservative slave culture gave a false sense of security that property would somehow be respected. Presumably, Captain Costa would not have gone anywhere if he thought that his property rights over his slaves were not guaranteed. Captain Costa was not naive in trusting the flag of Brazil, a slaveholding empire, as sufficient protection given the profitable nature of trade in Brazilian coffee and American pine lumber that underlay a strong economic exchange between Brazil and the United States. It seemed that the *Porpoise* affair had established Brazilian commercial rights in the United States. The *Porpoise* incident in 1845 was covered extensively in Brazil and undoubtedly was of intense interest to ship owners and captains. The *Lembrança* case two years later in New York also received widespread press coverage not only in New York, especially in abolitionist newspapers, but also in the southern United States, and not surprisingly in Brazil. The escape of both Baquaqua and his shipmate was dramatic, if for no other reason than it constituted a successful jail break in New York. It was more than that. It occurred in a context of tense diplomatic relations between the United States and Brazil, at least since the dramatic confrontation in Rio de Janeiro over the US Marine seizure of the *Porpoise* and the Brazilian response. The United States was forced to back down, virtually censoring Commodore Turner, the commander of the American Navy in Brazil who was there because of the

Webster-Ashburton Treaty of 1842 that included provisions for British-US co-operation in suppressing the trans-Atlantic slave trade. The confrontation could have led to the renunciation of the 1829 treaty between the United States and Brazil, which was a cornerstone of the US policy toward Latin America devised under President Monroe and subsequently known as the Monroe Doctrine. The evolution of US policy in the face of British dominance of international trade was an uphill battle that reached its imperialist potential many decades later. Nonetheless, the *Porpoise* affair had implications for the *Lembrança* case in New York that dramatized Baquaqua's escape. If Baquaqua and his shipmate had not escaped, Judge Edwards would have had to assess the relative merits of New York laws that ended slavery and the terms of the US-Brazilian accord that required that absconding crew be returned to the ship which they had fled. Nevertheless, the incident further exacerbated tensions between proslavery advocates and abolitionists in the United States, which resulted in the contentious Fugitive Slave Act of 1850.

The details of Baquaqua's life are sufficiently clear to establish the basic chronology and locations of his movements, at least until the early 1860s. His voice clearly can be heard through his own words and through reports of what people said about him. He wrote words in Dendi when asked to give vocabulary terms in his "African" language, and at times there are reports of him speaking Arabic, although it is not clear how competent those who reported his proficiency actually were and if they had ever heard any Arabic, or Dendi for that matter. Yet, despite this allusion to language, he associated with his mother, who was from Katsina, a major city connected with trade to Asante in which Hausa was the common language. His uncle operated a *mai gida* establishment at Salaga that provided accommodation and brokerage services for visiting merchants from the Caliphate, who were overwhelmingly Hausa, as well.

In his autobiography, Baquaqua gives details of his life and the social relations he experienced during his Atlantic voyage. However, many details were suppressed for reasons that can and should be problematized. Thus, it is possible to cross-check the information for the Brazilian context experienced by Baquaqua in considering the details he recalled and those omitted by him in his narrative. Regarding the idea of a biography as the description and contextualization of a personal trajectory—the narrative of a life—Baquaqua provides significant details about the transformations that occurred during most of his life. His perspective on the recollections and omissions delimit his memoirs. As in any autobiographical narrative, there is a selection of episodes and how each is told (or not told). However, there are gaps in his narrative, some spaces where details are not enough for contextualizing the social relations in which he was inserted. Baquaqua's narrative is somewhat elusive with respect to his enslavement, perhaps from a desire to erase memory.

The itinerary of Mahommah Gardo Baquaqua, emphasizing his passage through slavery in Brazil, reveals a struggle for a cultural identity that individuals were more easily able to preserve if they were free. If, for survival, a person needed to reframe existence in face of the condition of slavery through "conversion" to Christianity, the adoption of another name, identification with a particular "nation," and so on, it sometimes created an "ethnic mirage" that could lead to confusing interpretations of identities in the trans-Atlantic diaspora.[2] Before being a slave in Brazil, Baquaqua was someone who had grown up in Djougou and, as such, he bore a series of cultural markers that forged his first and main identity as a person of diaspora. The knowledge of his dispersed family came to his attention while he was a child and was fundamental in marking his personality; the proof is his own autobiographical description. When he had the opportunity to explain his background and then write (and dictate) his memoirs, he emphasized the cultural meanings of his life in Africa to establish his self-identification. His choiice of the name he wanted to be called after regaining his freedom puts a curious gloss on the aspiring Protestant missionary that his devoted patrons had projected onto him. He had already lived as a slave in the Atlantic world, after leaving his familiar Muslim community, and now had been baptized twice, first in Pernambuco and then in Haiti. His African recollections and the experiences he had to endure assumed considerable importance. Turmoil and brutality made their mark. It meant that Baquaqua wished to be identified as African, even more than being a Muslim, because of the experiences lived throughout his relatively short but spectacular personal trajectory. As an African, Baquaqua was an agent of his own history, despite the realities experienced during his Atlantic travels. Thus, the perspective for a historian of the Atlantic diaspora is established. New cumulative cultural experiences, even the most adverse ones, do not replace identifying marks but supplement them. These new experiences are able to reframe some aspects of a person's life, transforming daily actions and perspectives, but the deeper psyche that actually forged the "self" is always preserved, even when little activated for brief periods and perhaps even for extended periods.

Our initial proposition was to contextualize Baquaqua's own memories through an investigation of documents from that period. To this end, we followed the path to freedom of the young "José da Costa," the slave of a maritime captain. His experiences accumulated each year, due to visiting different places in Brazil, which enabled him to conceptualize his own manumission. His conditions provided the opportunity that made escape possible. Some Africans in Baquaqua's position were able to negotiate their freedom in stages as compensation for years of service or for religious reasons, while many others fled to live in *quilombola* communities. Baquaqua is a striking exception, as his escape was transnational. He broke out of the Brazilian theater. The transnational ambiance of his case reverberated in Brazil, the United States, and Canada at least. He seized an opportunity that tested his ability to articulate himself, which he did by inserting himself into the abolitionist struggle by publishing his autobiography.

Baquaqua's path to freedom did not end when he escaped from slavery. On the contrary, his dramatic story exposes the struggle to escape the grasp of slavery. His arrival in Haiti started with hope but soon turned to disillusionment, to the point where he slipped back into alcoholism. Fortunately, he was introduced to a network of religious abolitionists who were fundamental to his salvation. Apparently, Alexis Dupuy, who in late 1847 was politically influential, was somehow involved in the introduction. Shortly thereafter, Dupuy fell out of favor with Soulouque and was a casualty of the first of the massacres that were perpetrated to consolidate Soulouque's position. Despite the political turmoil accompanying Soulouque's presidency, Baquaqua experienced conversion to Protestant Christianity, took advantage of the possibility of studying and began to think about being a missionary or interpreter in Africa. He was clearly presented with a range of opportunities that gave him new chances to express freedom.

It was his memories of freedom in Africa in contrast to the time of slavery in Brazil that made him unique in the United States and Canada. Baquaqua's memories expose the lived experiences in the Black Atlantic. He had been a cook on board a ship in Brazil, and that enabled him to become a cook for the family that had welcomed him in Haiti. Then, upon returning to the United States, he enrolled in New York Central College, which brought him to the attention of important American abolitionists, as with Gerrit Smith. This connection enabled him to travel between different cities and places in the United States and Canada. However, not everything was easy. Baquaqua also experienced racial prejudice, notably when he became friends with a young white woman, but racial perspectives closed any chance of a relationship. Likewise, the awaited funds for financing his trip back to Africa never occurred as he once thought. Despite the suffering of slavery and the adversities of freedom in North America, Baquaqua interacted with major figures in the abolitionist struggle. He corresponded with religious leaders, friends, congressmen, and officials seeking support for his journey back to his homeland. He started writing.

His autobiography has many implications for scholars interested in the histories and cultural and literary expressions of Africans in the Americas. Baquaqua wrote about his personal memories, connecting him directly to his childhood, his family, and ethnic culture in the interior of Africa. No documentary record of colonization of Africans can offer such fundamental dimensions of individuals who experienced slavery and needed to fight for survival and freedom. Even with conversion to Christianity, he chose a name for himself that symbolically connected him with the African continent and his homeland. His name carried religious meaning, but it also carried family traditions representing the fact that he was born after the birth of twins. His name also conveyed his most personal memories, which involved his relationship with his mother. Undoubtedly, his choice of name reminded him of his family and his hometown, but it also represented how he wanted to be seen and remembered throughout his life. Moreover, his autobiography was also a statement of his opposition to slavery. The story of his trials and tribulations reinforced propaganda for abolitionism not only in the United States but throughout the world. It is possible that Baquaqua knew that publishing his story would not only cross Atlantic borders but also cross time. It is common for the stories of enslaved Africans to be seen as examples of defeat. However, Baquaqua clearly demonstrates that slavery was a place of struggle, bequeathing stories of resistance, resilience, and overcoming adversity.

Baquaqua seems not to have been in contact with other Muslims, either in Brazil, North America, or Haiti. He undoubtedly would have been aware of Muslims in Brazil because they were visible in Rio de Janeiro and Rio Grande do Sul, although less so in Pernambuco perhaps. He makes no mention of other Hausa-speaking Muslims in Brazil, even though there were sizable numbers. There were Muslims in the United States, too, but he apparently never met anyone who was Muslim. His level of isolation was a characteristic of slavery, perhaps extreme. He was separated from his religious community and people who knew the same language. He was fortunate in having the opportunity to explain his background to the Judds and others associated with the Free Will Baptist movement. Because Baquaqua appears to have been more isolated than many other enslaved, he had to find alternate ways of bonding. Baquaqua was outside of his community during his period of slavery and only reestablished broader relationships through his association with the Free Will Baptists, with whom he was ultimately disillusioned. He was thrust into the cauldron of North American politics, which slavery made particularly volatile.

As someone from Africa who had come from a commercial and scholarly center on a prosperous caravan route, he had experience as a street vendor, common laborer, shipmate, and cook. He had worked in a blacksmith's shop making needles, and he had been employed in the palace of a local official near Djougou. While he was in McGrawville, he also rented land at nearby Freetown Corners so that he could farm during the summer. He lectured in at least a dozen Baptist churches and at Free Will Baptist conventions. He gave a valedictory address at New York Central College, during which he spoke in his native tongue, which would have been either Dendi or more likely Hausa.

Baquaqua's perseverance provides historical context for Africa and the Americas. Individuals were treated as if they were property, but even so, they often found ways to assert their humanity. This study can serve as methodological inspiration for scholars interested in biographical studies of Africans and their narratives of freedom. Baquaqua's experiences are a good story about survival under slavery and its racialized legacy. His picaresque instincts took him from one setting to another, allowing him to express his opposition to enslavement, and making him willing to risk escape without adequate knowledge of language or a clear understanding of legal proceedings and the plot to break him out of jail and send him to Haiti. Baquaqua's life was dramatic. He expressed his desires, joys, and hopes, but above all, he adhered to his goal to recover his freedom and return to Africa. He did it because he came to know people who could help him, first in escaping in New York City and then in getting an education at Central College. This support reinforced his own agency. He had his personal history and acquired a broad view of the world that was enriched through each social context in which he had lived.

His time in Brazil chronicles a rough period in social history, in which society was basically operating beyond the grasp of the law. Legally, there should have been no more enslaved Africans arriving in Brazil after 1831. Certainly, there were real problems of legal circumvention when Baquaqua arrived in 1845. Legally, he arrived under circumstances in which he could have been declared a "Liberated African" if the British had seized his ship, and there were legal precedents where individuals had their status recognized as Liberated Africans even when the British had not taken them off a ship. How widespread this practice was and how Baquaqua would have learned about the possibility, and then how to realize it, are unclear, but what is certain is that Baquaqua did not act on the possibility. He gives no indication that being recognized as a Liberated African was ever an option.

Baquaqua's chance to express his compelling cry for freedom came as the abolition movement was gaining momentum. There had been a ground swell of popular outrage over the slave trade that led to its legal abolition in Britain and progressively elsewhere. Baquaqua would have become aware of abolition because of his association with the Baptists, if he did not already have vague understandings of the violation of law in Brazil where he might have legally become a Liberated African subject to indenture. It is no coincidence that Baquaqua appears on the frontispiece of Foss and Mathews, *Facts for Baptist Churches*, in 1850, by A. T. Foss and Edward Mathews. While Foss collected much of the antislavery documentation at different Baptist churches in the Northeast and Midwest of the United States. Mathews provided the virulent antislavery rhetoric that exposed him as one of the most radical abolitionists of the 1840s and 1850s. For Mathews, antislavery was doctrine. His blunt pronouncements against slavery almost got him killed in Kentucky and forced him to retreat to Britain to continue his antislavery crusade. Mathews spoke out against the war with Mexico as a cover for expanding territory where slavery would be legal.[3] In his 1853 autobiography, Mathews lists his lengthy curriculum vitae of letters to newspapers, lectures, and publications. After his return to Britain, he continued his efforts, which makes the list of his public pronouncements more impressive. That Baquaqua should grace the volume standing next to Rev. Judd clearly was meant to impress those Baptists who had embraced abolition and chide those who were not willing to commit themselves to the emancipation of slaves and the spread of missionary work to Africa.

The political context in which Baquaqua operated is missing in his autobiography and other documentation. His discussion of West African political history exposes the consolidation of Asante hegemony that included a vibrant export trade in kola nuts and other goods within West Africa. Baquaqua's enslavement in Brazil opened his eyes to discriminatory injustice that was the bedrock of slavery and prompted his escape. In the process of changing locales, he came in contact with many new ideas, some of which prompted him to recoil and some which offered opportunities. He did not react well to imposed Christian worship in Pernambuco. He may have thought he had been a poor student in Djougou, but he had gone to school. He could write phrases in Arabic, and he clearly was fluent in at least Hausa and Dendi. As it happened, the mythical Underground Railroad seemed to operate under the Eldridge Street jail in New York and whisked him away to Boston and on a flight to Haiti. He made his escape in an increasingly hostile environment in the United States that was exacerbated by the war with Mexico and the annexation of Texas, imperial ventures at colonization that were tied to slavery and prompted responses that consciously violated laws that were imposed to reinforce slavery. The Fugitive Slave Law of 1850 lurked in the background while Baquaqua was enrolled in Central College, and plans were afoot to mount a Baptist mission in Africa.

Baquaqua found sanctuary in Haiti, but it was at a time when the Sou-louque government attempted to unite the whole island, which introduced new risks for Baquaqua. Nonetheless, he was in Haiti at a time when it was still considered a pariah because it had emerged in revolution, abolished slavery, and installed governments led by men of African descent. His return to the United States to attend Central College avoided conscription into Sou-louque's army, which failed to conquer the Spanish side of Hispanola. He was fortunate because many Haitian troops died in the disasterous campaign. Baquaqua might have been one of the casualties if he had stayed in Haiti, just as he might well have died if his brother had not rescued him from slavery in Dagomba, as many people who were taken captive did when they reached Kumasi. Instead, he was thrust into the antislavery campaign in the United States, where he associated with some of the most radical abolitionists. He made his way back to Africa, but unfortunately he disappeared for reasons that are unknown. He was not especially old, approximately forty when last documented. Being back in Africa potentially brought him into a commercial network that connected with where he wanted to go. It was feasible, especially considering Baquaqua's knowledge of trade in kola and other commodities in the Muslim interior. Was he reintegrated, or did some tragedy happen that would explain his disappearance?

What would have happened to Baquaqua if the British had seized his ship? He would have been taken to Rio de Janeiro where his ship captain would have been prosecuted before the Mixed Commission. He would have become a Liberated African, which was the term used to characterize those taken off slave ships. As in Sierra Leone and elsewhere, he would not have been actually liberated but instead would have been subjected to a period of indenture. Indeed, many individuals who were not removed from slave ships but who arrived in Brazil after the slave trade was declared illegal in 1831 found ways to assert a claim to being a Liberated African and thereby find some protection from the excesses of slavery. Whereas the Brazilian state was lackluster in stopping the arrival of ships from Africa, despite the law, the treaty with Britain did allow some people to take advantage once they found out about its provisions. Hence there were other cases of Muslims in the same period, roughly 1820–65, who managed to alter their status, as Rufino was able to do. In Rufino's case, he even found employment on illegal slave ships as a cook. Baquaqua appears not to have known about the murkiness of the legal situation, which may have meant that he was unaware of the legal definition of "liberated." A comparison of the opportunities of different individuals, focusing on Muslims, shows that Rufino somehow found a way to take advantage of the legal setting, while Baquaqua did not. Baquaqua is representative of the trajectory of Muslims from the Bight of Benin, but his experiences were divergent from the pattern in that he found another way to escape slavery.

Baquaqua's experiences stand in contrast in his quest to return to Africa to the vast majority of Africans who had no such opportunity. Rufino, by comparison, initially worked on a slave ship that went to Angola, but after his ship was seized by a British vessel, he was taken to St. Helena and then Sierra Leone. When he subsequently returned to Sierra Leone, his purpose was to study under the guidance of resident Muslim clerics and to acquire Arabic texts that would prove useful on his return to Brazil. Unlike Baquaqua, he had no intention of remaining in Africa. Rufino was able to establish a reputation as a learned Muslim scholar in Recife and spent time making and selling amulets containing Qur'anic verses wrapped in leather poaches. Baquaqua too was on a religious mission, at least ostensibly, in accompanying the Baptist mission of Rev. Chauncey Leonard to Liberia, but with a difference. Rufino chose not to remain in Africa among Muslims in the Yoruba community in Sierra Leone, while Baquaqua very specifically intended to reach his mother's hometown of Katsina in the Sokoto Caliphate, whereupon presumably he would have been reintegrated into the commercial network of his family. He had no desire to return to Brazil, unlike Rufino, Osefikunde, and others who were involved in trade between Bahia and West Africa. At the time of his arrest in 1853, Rufino had assembled a considerable library of Arabic texts. Unfortunately, the person whom the authorities relied upon to examine Rufino's manuscripts was a Jew who had lived in Morocco and Egypt and probably could not read texts from West Africa, where written Arabic was much closer to classical Arabic than the colloquial spoken in North Africa. It seems clear that Rufino was making amulets, a skill that he probably fully developed when he was in Sierra Leone. He apparently stayed in Fourah Bay, which was the location of Fula Town and the central mosque of the Muslim community.[4] Whether Baquaqua renounced his allegiance to Christianity, either openly or surrepticiously, is unknown, but if he had been successful in reaching Katsina, he most surely would have reaffirmed his Muslim identity.

Appendix A
Application for Writ of Habeas Corpus

This is an application upon a writ of habeas corpus to discharge Jose da Costa, Jose da Rocha, and Maria da Costa, alleged by the relator, John lnverness, to be restrained of their liberty by Clemente Jos da Costa, master of the Brazilian barque Llembranca [sic].

It is set forth in the return of the master, that the persons above named were brought from Rio de Janeiro to the port of New York, in the barque aforesaid.

That the two first named, Jose da Costa and Jose da Rocha, were shipped on board the Llembranca [sic] at Rio de Janeiro as part of the crew, and as such he is required to take them back by the laws of Brazil. That the woman Maria has come upon the voyage to this port as a servant and nurse to his wife and family, in whose service she now is. It is further set forth in the return, that Jose da Costa and the woman Maria, are slaves, lawfully acquired by the respondent, according to the laws of Brazil, by which laws, slavery is permitted and the acquisition, possession, and transfer of persons as property, allowed, recognized and protected.

That Jose da Rocha is also a slave, and the property lawfully acquired is as aforesaid, of Antonio Jose da Rocha Peresira [sic], of Rio de Janerio [sic], part owner of the barque, and by him committed to the custody of the respondent.

These facts are admitted by the relator, but he denies that they are sufficient to justify the detention of the parties concerned.

The fact that Jose da Costa and Jose da Rocha constitute part of the crew of the Llembranca [sic], is an answer to the application for their discharge. By φ [Article] 31st, of the existing treaty between the United States and Brazil, provision is made for the arrest, detention, and custody of persons composing a part of the crew of any public or private vessel of either nation, who shall desert.

The consuls of the respective nations are authorized to apply to the proper judicial authorities, and upon proving by the exhibition of the ship's roll, register or other document, that the persons claimed were part of the crew, they are required to be delivered up. They are to be put at the disposal of the consul, and may, at his request, be placed in any public prison until sent to the vessels to which they belong, or to others of the same nation. The treaties made under the authority of the United States, are declared by the 6th Article of the Constitution to be the supreme law of the land, to be binding upon the judges of every state, any thing in the constitution or laws of any state to the contrary notwithstanding.

I am bound, therefore, to regard and carry out the provisions of this treaty. And it would be a palpable violation of its obvious meaning and intent, to discharge persons upon a writ of *habeas corpus*, admitted to be part of the crew of a Brazilian vessel. If the two persons should desert, they could be reclaimed as a part of the crew. It would be the duty of the judicial tribunals of this state, in such a case, upon the proper application, to deliver them up.

The right of the master to detain them as a part of his crew, is necessarily implied When a duty is imposed to deliver them to him, should they desert from his service, he undoubtedly has a right to detain them as a part of his crew, if he has a right to reclaim them when they leave his vessel.

That they are slaves does not alter or vary the case, for were I to hold that they are free persons, according to the laws of this state, the master would still be entitled to retain them as members of his crew.

They must, therefore, be returned on board the vessel from whence they were brought in obedience to this writ.

It will not be necessary to determine the principal question argued upon the return, to wit—Whether slaves voluntarily brought into this state, are to be regarded as property within the meaning of that section of the treaty by which the United States has stipulated specially to protect the property of subjects of Brazil.

The point is not material to the matter now before me. Da Rocha and da Costa are left in the custody of the respondent, not upon the ground that they are his property, but because they compose a portion of his crew.

The question could only be material as far as respects the right of the respondent to detain the woman Maria. But she, by her own declaration, is under no restraint. The writ has been sued out without her knowledge, p'rivity or consent. She has expressly declared her unwillingness to leave the service of the respondent, and expressed her desire to return with him to Rio de Janeiro.

As she is on board the respondent's vessel of her free will, she can not be regarded as under restraint. The interposition of this writ, therefore, in her behalf, is not called for. She has elected to remain where she now is, and there is no room to make any order respecting her.[1]

The adjudication of an officer having power to issue and decide upon a writ of *habeas corpus*, may be set up as *res adjudicata* upon any subsequent writ of *habeas corpus* and is conclusive upon the same parties, when the subject matter is the same; and there are no new facts.—

The parties are the same, where the writ is issued on behalf of the same person, against the same respondent, although the relators are different.

The material facts alleged in the return, which are not denied by the party brought up must be taken to be true.

The circumstances under which this application was made, sufficiently appear in the opinion of the court.

John Jay and *J. L. White* for the slaves.

Summary of writs of *habeas corpus* and applicability of the doctrine of *res judicata*

Writ of habeas corpus: the essential value of the writ, as affording "a free, easy, cheap, expeditious and ample"—remedy against infringements of personal liberty, and would tend to place the liberty of the citizen at the disposal of a single judge; which is the very thing the writ is intended to prevent.[2]

The proceeding before Judge Daly was not between the same parties or privies—but a matter *inter alias acta*—between the relator, John Inverness, and the captain—with which the Africans had nothing to do. It was a proceeding instituted without their privity or consent, and by which they are in no way bound. The relator was to them a stranger, the counsel unknown and unauthorized: ignorant of the language, they had no understanding of the matter.

A decision is not *res juaicata*, unless the parties to be affected by it have had an opportunity of being fairly heard, and the decision is made upon due deliberation by the judge. These Africans in the former proceeding, were denied a hearing. The order of the court was based upon an admission on the record made without their authority, knowledge or assent—and the truth of which they positively deny. . . .

In this case, the former decision was based on the admission upon the record, that the Africans were seamen; the present record shows they are not, and can not be, seamen, in the meaning of our law, and it further shows a new imprisonment, manacling, and restraint differing from any that appeared in the first proceeding, and which, of itself, admitting them to have been seamen, was a breach of the contract assumed to exist between them and the captain—and has rendered that compact void, and determined the relationship in which the opinion of Judge Daly declared that they stood.

This writ should not be dismissed on the ground that the case is *res judicata*, even did it possess the essentials which it wants, for the reason that it appears by the opinion of Judge Daly, that the Africans were remanded as seamen, although admitted by the captain to be slaves, and it being an established principle that no slave can either make or assent to a contract, and it being the law of this state that all slaves brought within its borders are free, and that servitude under any possible form, pretence, or circumstances, shall not be recognized by our courts, save in the single case of fugitives held to service in the southern states, it would be a violation of constitutional right, a denial of justice, and an outrage upon personal freedom, were a judge, when appealed to for protection upon habeas corpus, to dismiss that writ upon the strength of a decision shown to be erroneous, and remand these Africans to an imprisonment known to be unlawful, to a condition of servitude which the law abhors, and has peremptorily forbidden, and to the power of a master who has threatened them with violence, the instant he escapes from the jurisdiction of a free state.

EDWARDS, J.—A writ of *habeas corpus* was issued by his honor, Judge Edmonds, on the 17th day of July last, directed to Clemente Jose Da Costa, master of the Brazilian bark Lew Branca, commanding him to have the bodies of Jose da Costa and Jose da Rocha, by him imprisoned and detained, as was alleged, together with the cause of such imprisonment and detention, before him, the said judge, at a time and place therein specified. The respondent appeared before Judge Edmonds, and made his return to the said writ, under oath; to which the said da Costa and da Rocha put in an answer, also under oath. At this stage of the proceedings, by the consent of the counsel for all the parties, the writ was amended in such a manner as to be returnable before me, and, by a similar consent, I allowed the writ *nunc pro tunc*.

The return of the respondent admits the detention of da Costa and da Rocha, and alleges that before the issuing and service of the said *habeas corpus*, to wit: on the 10th day of July last, a writ of *habeas corpus* was allowed and issued, by the Hon. Charles P. Daly, one of the associate judges of the court of common pleas, in and for the city and county of New-York, and of the degree of counsellor of the supreme court, directed to the said respondent, with the object and for the purpose of producing, before the said judge, the persons named in the said first mentioned writ, for the purpose of inquiring into the cause of their detention or imprisonment by the said respondent. That, in obedience to the said writ issued by the said Judge Daly, the respondent produced before the said judge, the persons of the two negro men called Jose da Costa and Jose da Rocha. That upon said writ so issued by said

Judge Daly, and upon the return thereto, proceedings were duly had before said judge, who after mature deliberation, and after hearing the allegations and arguments of counsel on both sides, decided and adjudged, on or about the 16th day of July last, that the said Jose da Costa and Jose da Rocha were legally under the restraint of the said respondent, and that they should be remanded to his custody; which said decision and judgment of said Judge Daly, it is alleged in the said return, are still in force, unreversed, not set aside, nor made void. The return further states, that in pursuance of said decision and adjudication, the persons of said da Costa and da Rocha were committed to the custody of the respondent. The return also sets forth other matters, to which it is not necessary, in this place, to allude.

The answer of da Costa and da Rocha, does not deny the substance of any of the allegations above cited from the return of the respondent.

Upon the said return and answer, the respondent contends that there has been an adjudication of the matter by Judge Daly, and that such adjudication is binding upon me, and precludes any investigation into the facts of the case, unless new matters are shown, which have arisen since the adjudication of Judge Daly, and which renders such investigation proper.

Before the enactment of the Revised Statutes, the law seems to have been settled, that the return of the respondent was conclusive, and that none of the facts contained in it could be controverted. (3 *Hill*, 658, *note* 30.) By the revised statutes, the party brought up may deny any of the material facts set forth in the return, or allege any fact to show either that the imprisonment or detention is unlawful, or that he is entitled to his discharge. (2 *R. S.* 471, *p.* 50.)

If, then, any of the material facts set forth in the return, are not denied by the party brought up, the return, *pro tanto*, has the same effect as before the revised statutes, and those facts must be taken to be true. (3 *Hill*, 658, *note* 28.)

Upon this construction of the law, I am bound to assume that the facts set forth in the return, and not denied in the answer, are true, and that da Costa and da Rocha have heretofore been brought before Judge Daly, upon a writ of *habeas corpus*, and that, after an investigation into the causes of their detention by the respondent, Judge Daly adjudged that they were legally under the restraint of the respondent, and that they should be awarded to his custody; and that said judgment now remains in full force.

It thus appears that there has been an adjudication, upon a writ of *habeas corpus*: that da Costa and da Rocha were at the time of the said adjudication, under the legal restraint of the respondent.

The next question is, does the principle of *res adjudicata* apply to this case, and am I precluded by the above mentioned adjudication from any further inquiry into the subject? In the case of *Mercein v. The People ex rel. Barry*, (25 *Wend.* 64) it was decided by the court of errors of this state, that the principle of res adjudicata was applicable to a proceeding under *habeas corpus*. Two opinions only were delivered; one by the chancellor and the other by Senator Paige. The question under review had been decided by Judge Inglis, then a judge of the court of common pleas, upon a writ of *habeas corpus* issued by him. The chancellor, in delivering his opinion, said that "he concurred in the decision of Judge Inglis, that the principle of *res adjudicata* was applicable to a proceeding upon habeas corpus, and that it could make no difference in the application of the principle, whether the first writ was returnable before a court of record, or a judge or commissioner out of court, for, in neither case, ought the party suing out the writ, to be permitted to proceed *ad infinitum* before the same court or officer, or before another court or officer, having concurrent juris-diction, to review the former decision, while the facts remain the same; but if dissatisfied with the first decision, should appeal to a higher tribunal.

Senator Paige says, that "if a final adjudication upon a habeas corpus is not to be deemed *res adjudicata,* the consequences will be lamentable. This favored writ will become an en-gine of oppression, instead of a writ of liberty." He further says, "I think that the following rule will be found sustained by the cases, viz.: Whenever a final adjudication of an inferior court of record, or of an inferior court not of record, or of persons invested with power to decide on the property and rights of the citizens, is examinable by the supreme court, upon a writ of error, on a certiorari, in every such case, such final adjudication may he pleaded as *res adjudicata,* and is conclusive upon the parties in all future controversies relating to the same matter." And, finally, a resolution was adopted by the court. "That in the opinion of the court, the decision of Judge Inglis upon the question of *res adjudicata* was correct, and in conformity to the law." This decision fully and clearly establishes the rule that the princi-ple of res adjudicate is applicable to proceedings upon *habeas corpus.*

The only question, then, that remains upon this branch of the case is, whether the same subject matter between the same parties, has been adjudged by an officer having power to issue and decide upon a writ of *habeas corpus.*

First. Is the subject matter the same?

The subject matter under the first writ, was the imprisonment and detention of da Costa and da Rocha, and the adjudication of the judge was, that they were "legally under the re-straint of the respondent, and should be remanded to his custody." The subject matter of the present writ, is the detention of the same persons by the respondent; and I am called upon to decide what was decided by Judge Daly, viz: Whether they are legally under the restraint of the respondent?

Second. Are the parties the same?

The proceedings, in both cases, have been in behalf of the same persons, against the same respondent. The fact that the relators are different, does not alter the case.

Third. Had Judge Daly the power to issue the writ and to decide the questions arising under it?

By the law, as it stood under the old constitution, it is not questioned that he had the power. By the new law, it is enacted that the "judges of the court of common pleas for the city and county of New-York, shall have and possess the same powers, and perform the same duties as the first judge and assistant judges of the said court of common pleas now have and possess and perform." (*Laws of 1847, p.* 281, *s.* 7).

There are several matters alleged in the answer of da Costa and da Rocha, for the pur-pose of showing that there was irregularity in the proceedings before Judge Daly. The an-swer to all these allegations is, that I am bound by the adjudication, and can not look behind it. If there has been irregularity, I have no power to decide upon that question, in this collateral proceeding. The remedy must be in a court sitting as a court of review.

But it is contended that new facts have arisen in this case since the decision of Judge Daly. The answer of da Costa and da Rocha, sets forth that since the said adjudication, and on the 17th July last, they were hand-cuffed and put in a store-room, in the forward cabin of the vessel, and there confined, and that the respondent also threatened them with violence when he "got them at sea." These are not new facts of such a character as to change the relations of the parties. If there has been an abuse of the right which it has been adjudged that the respondent had to the custody of the persons held in restraint by him, the remedy is not by *habeas corpus*; much less so as to any threatened violence.

With these views, I am of opinion that the question presented to me under the present writ of *habeas corpus*, is *res adjudicata*, and that I am precluded from going into any investigations of the facts in the case; and that no new facts are set forth in the proceedings which authorize any interference by me. The writ must, therefore, be dismissed, and Jose da Costa and Jose da Rocha remanded to the custody of the respondent.[3] Their identity as crew was confirmed in a second legal decision by Judge Henry P. Edwards, who ruled on 5 August that Judge Daly had been correct in his judgment, and, therefore, remanded the two men to the custody of the captain of the ship.[4]

After Edwards upheld Daly's decision, Howard Gay wrote in the *National Anti-Slavery Standard*, that the judges had "prostituted their position on the bench to protect the Foreign Slave-Trade in the port of New-York."[5]

Appendix B

Haitien Mission 1849–50: Annual Reports of the American Baptist Free Mission Society

Sixth Annual Meeting of the American Baptist
Free Mission Society, Utica, 6 June 1849

HAITIEN MISSIONS.

WM. L. JUDD and family were sent to sustain that mission. On the return of Eld. Jones to Haiti, it was mutually agreed between them that br. JUDD should continue at Port-au-Prince, and that br. Jones should proceed to Port-de-Paix for the establishment of a new station. This has been done and the mission at Port-de-Paix is in operation. The present ability of Mr. and Mrs. Jones, freely to use the language of the country, renders the establishment of their new mission less difficult than their former one at Port-au-Prince. Both of our Haitien ministers now preach with good acceptance, in the French language, the glorious gospel of the grace of God, while their wives and sister LAKE familiarly converse with the people, of Christ and him crucified. Sister LAKE has been and still is usefully occupied in school in imparting religious and literary instruction to the youth and children. We have, therefore, in that field, five missionaries thoroughly qualified to discharge the duties of their stations.

Among the blessings bestowed on the Haitien Mission, we may particularly notice the conversion of Mahommah a fugitive slave and native of Africa. This young man had been stolen from the home and friends of his childhood, and carried into Brazilian slavery; but soon escaped and sought a refuge in this land which boasts of its freedom and philanthropy: but that refuge he sought here in vain. Flying, therefore, from our shores, he was providentially conducted to the city of Port-au-Prince and to the Christian hospitalities of Wm. L. Judd. Our missionary received him gladly; and, while he provided for him a home and temporal comforts, he failed not to instruct him in the religion of the gospel. This instruction was to him as life from the dead, and his heart felt its powers. He saw and acknowledged its adaptedness to his case as a sinner. He bowed to its authority. He rejoiced in its Truth and became a disciple of its divine Author. The conversion and baptism of Mahommah, together with his strong desire and purpose so return in due time to the land of his birth, bearing to his people the good tidings which have been to himself of so great joy, we can not but regard as indications of the will of God that this Society is yet to have opened before it a wide and effectual door into the interior of that continent which others have passed by as unworthy of the attention and labor of elevated white men and only a fitting locality for the missionary service of emancipated slaves. If, then, any shall esteem it a reproach and dishonor to the F. M. Society to be engaged in enlightening Africa and her injured sons and bringing home to our common Father this neglected portion of His children, let that reproach fall upon us and that dishonor be visited upon our heads. This reproach has already attached itself to the Free Mission Society, from the fact of our sympathy with the slaves of our country, and from our refusal to admit into our treasury the avails of their toils and the price of their bodies and souls, which all other Baptist Societies have freely admitted and to this day are admitting into their treasuries. We go forth to the regeneration of Haiti and Africa fully aware that we are bearing this reproach of Christ. Yet none of these things may be allowed to move us, neither may we innocently count even our reputation, our pecuniary interest or our life, so dear unto ourselves as to divert our feet from the known path of duty or to retard our progress in that way. The voice of God calls the Baptist churches of the North to arise to the great and truly noble work of turning the river of the water of life over that vast continent which, instead of being cared for and visited in the affliction of her children and offered the consolations of the gospel, has been robbed of her children by the piratical hands of slaveholders under the connivance of the nominal churches. This anti-christian practice has been so long continued and so pervading, that any manifestation of zeal on the behalf of the African race awakens the ridicule and prompts the contemptuous smile of the majority of American Christians; and they have said to us—why turn away from Burmah and the Karens and the inhabitants of China to evangelize a handful of negroes? We reply that we behold one-sixth of all the inhabitants of the world within the circle which encompasses the African race; and we can not esteem these a number too inconsiderable for our regard. A higher proportion of these one hundred and fifty millions are destitute of the gospel than of any other race. We see them unjustly and cruelly treated above all other races; and that which most of all secures our sympathies for them, is found in the humiliating and shameful fact, that the churches in general have taken sides with their oppressors and have come to regard the salvation of a blackman's soul with comparative indifference and, therefore, to put forth little or no effort to make known to him the unsearchable riches of the grace which is in Christ Jesus. This undervaluing of the colored man appears on every hand, in the church as well as in the world. It has even controlled and repressed the action of Bible Societies in their purpose of supplying the inhabitants of these United States with the word of God; and out of it has sprung that Protestant anomaly that oral instruction will suffice for negroes, whereas the damnation of the Papal church is sealed by her refusal to allow a free circulation of the printed Bible among any portion of white people. The slaveholder avows his determination to confine the religious teaching of slaves within the safe limit of oral instruction, and the non-slaveholding abettor of slavery acquiesces in the wisdom of the device and in its innocence. All ranks of Northern Christians with the exception of Free Missionists, Seventh Day Baptists and Free Will Baptists, consent to this God-dishonoring practice. If our opponents raise a demurer here, we ask of them an act of their own, or even one serious and earnest avowal of their purpose, to place in the hands and beneath the eyes of the three millions of American slaves the printed Bible. We are ignorant of any such fact, if it has taken place. These considerations evince the necessity of a Society whose members understand them and feel their power, and are thus prepared to sympathize with the despised colored man and to stand with unshrinking firmness by his side, asserting his right in all respects to be regarded and trusted as a man, pleading on his behalf and defending him against injustice and wrong so generally and lavishly measured out to him.

Seventh Annual Meeting of the American Baptist
Free Mission Society, Bristol, NY, 5–7 June 1850

THE HAITIEN MISSION

Port-au-Prince.—The following is a brief outline of the condition of the mission station at Port-au-Prince.

During the early part of 1849, Eld. Judd labored under great disadvantage, having found it necessary to reside in the country, at some distance from the city of Port-au-Prince. Afterwards, however, he was able to remove into the city. In his annual report to the Board, he says: "After becoming fully settled in town, I found myself in more immediate contact with the people, and resolved to hold meetings more frequently." Besides preaching three times on the Sabbath, twice in French and once in English, he frequently holds meetings every evening in the week, except Saturday evening. The Lord has appeared in mercy, owning and blessing the labors of His servant. Ten have been added by baptism within the past year, to the little church in Port-au-Prince. On the 15th of last October, Br. Judd writes as follows: "Sunday, the 7th inst., was to us a very happy day. I baptized five persons, two men with their wives, Haitiens, and one American woman, the wife of one of the members of this church, and who at the last baptism said she felt she was left behind."

Of the influence these baptismal scenes have upon the people, Br. Judd writes: "It causes much excitement among the people, to see these per sons not only renounce their religion, but even their baptism. The baptism of repentance seems to them a very serious affair. But I judge from what I can hear, that we have the conscience of the greater portion of the people with us. But many think it a very severe test. Indeed, one of the men baptized, in conversation with a member of the church, a few months since, on the subject of baptism, told him that he saw no particular objection to the principle of it, but he thought a person ought to be bien decide (very decided) to go and be immersed in such a public manner." Our brother assured him that decision is the very thing we seek after in those who wish to attach themselves to this church. And, thank God, we have good evidence that he himself has become "bien decide." He gives us great hope. He is an industrious mechanic, and a man of considerable talent. He also speaks very well in public."

On the 19th of last January, Br. Judd again writes: "We are enjoying an interesting work of grace here, which manifests itself chiefly among the natives. There have been some conversions here, exceedingly interesting. I baptized five persons last Sunday, three men and two women. One of them has been a chanter at a Catholic church, and an ardent devotee. He enjoyed his baptism very much. Himself and one of the others, had never seen a baptism before. The baptism was at sunrise, and was very numerously attended, and, I think, was the most solemn of any that we have had. Several Catholics stood and wept; and many said, this is truly the way in which our Savior himself went—this is the true religion."

In the same letter, Br. Judd writes:—"There are already more applicants than there were before the last baptism." Among the applicants for baptism, he says, there "is a very intelligent man, about fifty years old, and who has been a remarkable devotee." The manner of his conversion is also very remarkable, and an interesting example of the utility of Bible distribution. For several years he has had a bible which he has read very thoroughly. But he has had the idea that he must read it before the cross.

It appears that there is in Haiti, as there was in England and Scotland, while they were Roman Catholic countries, and as there is now on the continent of Europe, in every town and village a public cross. In European countries, the crosses are generally as near as possible to the center of the town or village, but in Haiti, they are generally a little on one side of the town. One portion of Port-au-Prince, is situated on a hill, called Bel Air. Upon this hill, is a place, the inhabitants call Calvary. Here are three crosses, the middle one of which is covered; and upon it is suspended, a figure of Christ, in imitation of the crucifixion. The man, the circumstances of whose conversion, Br. Judd is relating, said, that he had on his knees, and in front of the cross, read all the New Testament, and the Psalms two or three times. He says, he continued to do this, until from the working of the truth upon his own mind, he felt that he could go there no more. He said to Br. Judd, "I felt in my soul in disgust for it, and since that I have went there no more." In examining him afterwards upon his change, Br. Judd says, he "found it to be very clearly a work of divine grace in his heart. . . . . was astounded at his conversation, for in all the Haitien converts I have seen, I have not found one who could give so interesting a Christian experience." He has, doubtless, by this time, united with the church. The church at Port-au-Prince numbered forty at the time Br. Judd made out his annual report. It has already begun to contribute towards the support of the gospel. A translation has been made of the Confession of Faith originally issued by the N. H. State Convention. Five hundred copies have been printed.

It is with great pleasure that the Board are able to inform the Society that a most interesting missionary meeting was held in January with the Baptist Mission church in Port-au-Prince. It was the first attempt of the kind on the part of the Baptists there. The meeting continued two days. The exercises were in French and English. Br. Judd writes that it was a feast of fat things. And thus at no very distant day, the Lord continuing to bless our missionaries with the influences of the Holy Spirit, this Society may expect to see Haiti herself performing missionary labor, and in turn sending her sons and daughters as missionaries among the sable children of Africa.—In the last Annual Report of this Board, mention was made of the fact that Mahommah, one of "the two Brazilian slaves" whose escape from a Brazilian vessel at New York was noticed in the papers some three years ago, had taken refuge in Haiti, and, under the instructions of Br. Judd, had been hopefully converted to Christianity. It gives the Board great pleasure to be able to inform the Society, that this young brother has continued to exhibit a godly walk and conversation. When our sisters Judd and Lake visited this country the past winter for the benefit of the latter's health, they brought him with them, for the purpose of having him placed where he could gain such an education as would fit him, so far as education can do so, as a missionary for Africa. He was present, as were also sisters Judd and Lake, at a meeting of the Board. His soul was full of the desire to return as a missionary of the gospel to Africa, the land of his birth, and whence he was stolen. He feels that unless his mother and other relatives of whom he makes frequent mention, can learn of Christ, they must be lost. Though imperfectly acquainted with our language, his prayers and exhortations testify to every hearer that he has been truly taught of Christ.

The Board feel that they would be doing injustice, did they not in behalf of benighted Africa, return their thanks to those brethren and sisters of the Franklin Free Mission Society of this State, who after Mahommah's arrival in the United States, kindly came forward and ministered to his necessities. That Being who blesses him who in Christ's name gives a cup of cold water to one of his disciples, will reward those who have remembered the wants of Mahommah.

Mahommah is now in N. Y. Central College. The importance of this young brother's education can be felt—only when we call to mind how many of the whites who go as missionaries to Africa are sacrificed. One after another is struck down. About the time of our Anniversary last year, intelligence arrived that Br. Carter had scarcely been permitted to set foot on the African continent before he was swept into the grave. And since this report was commenced, we are called to mourn the loss of Sister Brooks, formerly Fidelia Coburn, of the Canada Mission. She was taken sick during her voyage to Africa, and died soon after landing. Doubtless the climate hastened the death of both, if it was not itself the active cause. How much depends upon the African race for the conversion of Africa, we can not say, but doubtless much. On this account, the education of Mahommah becomes more important.

Glossary

"Gates [Quarters] of Zoogoo"

Ajaggo-co-fa • unidentified
Bah-lah-mon-co-fa • Ba-Leman, that is, Imam; probably the ward now known
    as Limamande
Bah-pa-ra-ha-co-fa • Bakparakpey
Bah-too-loo-co-fa • Batoulou
fo-ro-co-fa • Foro-[Magazi] (lit. "farm of the Magazin")
u-boo-ma-co-fa • yobume (lit. "behind the market")

Journey to the Coast

Ar-oo-zo [?=Ar-oo-go] • Alejo
Cham-mah • Tchamba
Chir-a-chur-ee • Krikri
Dohama • Dahomey
Efau • Ifè, the local term referring to the Yoruba-speaking communities west of Savalou as
    far as Aktpamè to the south of Djougou, including Djalloukou in the north of Dahomey.
Gra-fe • Glehue (Ouidah)

Personal Names/Titles

Baquaqua • Mahommah's last name; ba, not (Hausa) kwakwa, inquisitive (Hausa)
Gardo • Mahommah's middle name (Hausa); Gado/Gardo, son born after twins
Ma-ga-zee • senior title, from Hausa, ward head in Djougou, magazi
massa-sa-ba • title of rulers of neighboring towns subordinate to Djougou, massasawa =
    title of ruler of Soubroukou[1]
Name • (Hausa)
Sa-bee • form of addressing king; sabeni, majesty (Dendi)
Wa-roo • name; see Woo-roo
Woo-roo • name of fellow slave; Woru, first-born son (Dendi)

Place Names

Bergoo, Berzoo • Borgu [=Nikki]
Da-boy-ya • Daboya
Sa-ba • [source of salt, unidentified]
Sal-gar • Salaga

Zar-ach-o • Yarakeou
Zoogoo, Zoozoo • Djougou

Words and Phrases

bah • father *ba*, father (Baatonu); *bàabá*, father (Dendi)
bah-gee • alcoholic drink *bádyi*; Guinee corn beer (Dendi)
bah-she • antilope, *béésè* (Dendi)
bon-ton • type of tree, *bántàn*, silk cotton tree (Dendi)
che-re-choo • bodyguard, *tyiriku*, royal slave (Baatonu)
cofa • gate, *kofa*, gate (Hausa)[2]
gan-ran • "fruit" = kola, *goro*, kola (Hausa)
gardowa • command for Baquaqua; Baquaqua's middle name, with command[3]
goo-noo • "leopard" in "Efau"; *gúnnù*, lion (Dendi)
gui-ge-rah • place of Muslim worship; *dyiŋgìré*, mosque (Dendi)
harnee • corn, *háánì*, millet (Dendi)
harnebee • "fine grain," *háánì bi*, "black corn," sorghum • (Dendi)
in-qua-hoo-noo- • "out today"—invitation to marriage; "ah-dee-ze" = Adiza, personal name
"haw" = *hóŋ* = today (Dendi)
ka-fa • elephant tusk musical instrument; possible Hausa (*kɛfo* = horn)
loch-a-fau • measure of distance, probably "loka[ci] fɔ," i.e., a day's trip, e.g., "mile"[4]
my-ache-ee-ah-dee-za • "the bride and groom are coming; "my-ache-ee" = Mahiachi, personal name
nya-wa-qua-foo • house where bride lodges not identified, but includes *fúù*, prior to marriage house (Dendi)
salla, • prayer; ceremony at end of Ramadan (Hausa)
sarrah • sacrifice at end of Ramadan, *sárà*, alms (Dendi)
unbah • medicine man [non-Muslim] unidentified
wal-la • writing board, *allo*, writing board (Dendi/Hausa)
yah-quim-ta-ca-ri • large elephant, • *térékúnté*, elephant (Dendi)
yah-quin-ta-cha-na • small elephant, elephant + *tyéénè*, small (Dendi)
yo-haw-coo-nah • "hoo-noo" = *hùnú* = go out (Dendi)

Notes

Introduction

1. Baquaqua, *Biography*, which was edited by Samuel Moore.
2. Smith, *Life and Adventures of Venture Smith*; Lovejoy, "African Origins of Venture Smith."
3. Vassa, *Life of Olaudah Equiano*, extract reprinted in *Voice of the Fugitive*, 18 June 1851.
4. Law and Lovejoy, *Biography*.
5. Baquaqua, *Autobiography*, 39.
6. Curtin, *Africa Remembered*.
7. Austin, *African Muslims Sourcebook*.
8. Wilks, "Abu Bakr al-Siddiq of Timbuktu," 159–60; and Wesley, "Abou Bekir Sadiki," 52–55.
9. Smith et al., "Ali Eisami Gazirmabe of Bornu"; Koelle, *African Native Literature*; Koelle, *Grammar of the Bornu*; Lovejoy, "Ali Eisami's Enslavement."
10. Koelle, *Polyglotta Africana*.
11. Koelle, *Pollyglota Africana*, 17.
12. For gender and age ratios of the deported slave population in the nineteenth century, see Eltis and Engerman, "Fluctuations in Sex," and SlaveVoyages, Database.
13. Lander, *Clapperton's Last Expedition*, 204, 206; Lander, "Interior of Africa"; Lupton, *Pascoe, Prince*. For other accounts, see Drumond, "Lettres."
14. Castelnau, *Renseignements*. Also see Dantas, "Francis de Castelnau."
15. All ten biographies in Curtin's volume (*Africa Remembered*) are male; half are Muslims, one of whom was free. The collection is not representative of the slave trade, and Muslims are disproportionately included beyond their actual numbers.
16. Austin, *African Muslims Sourcebook*.
17. Gomez, *Exchanging Our Country Marks*, 59–87.
18. Sylviane A. Diouf draws on Baquaqua's life in her study of enslaved Muslims in the Americas; see *Servants of Allah*, 42–45, 53, 203.
19. Lovejoy, "Jihad e escravidao," which updates "Background to Rebellion."
20. Law and Lovejoy, "Borgu and the Slave Trade."
21. Lovejoy, "Polanyi's 'Ports of Trade.'"
22. Verger, *Trade Relations*, 186–90; Adams, *Remarks on the Country*, 82–87, 188; Akindele and Aguessy, *Contribution a l'étude*, 73.
23. Lupton, *Pascoe, Prince*, which draws on "A short Account of Houssa, a Kingdom in the interior of Africa, situated on the Banks of the Niger," obtained from Abou Bouker, alias William Pasco, "a native of that country [Hausa] and a seaman now belonging to H.M.S Owen Glendower Commander Sir Robert Mends Capn, Coast of Africa April 1823, drawn up by John Evans Admiralty Clerk"; and details on Pascoe in Anon., "Interior of Africa."

24. Schön, *Magána Hausa*; Kirk-Greene and Newman, *West African Travels*. Also see Winckler, "Regards Croises."

25. Mahmadee, *Prince of Kashna*, edited by C. M. with introduction by Richard B. Kimball in the introduction notes that someone identified as C. M. gave him the manuscript. The note is dated Glen Park, November 1865, which locates the estate in Jamaica. We wish to thank Camille Lefebvre for details on the Mahmadee manuscript.

26. These have not been located.

27. Mahmadee, *Prince of Kashna*, ix.

28. Said, *Autobiography of Nicholas Said*; Said, "A Native of Bornou"; Dabovic, "Out of Place"; Calbreath, *The Sergeant*; Lovejoy, "Mohammed Ali Nicholas Sa'id; Austin, "Mohammed Ali Ben Said"; Muhammad, *Autobiography of Nicholas Said*.

29. Bilali of Sapelo Island: Austin, *African Muslims Sourcebook*; Austin, *Transatlantic Stories*; Curtis, *Muslims in America*; Diouf, *Servants of Allah*; Gomez, *Exchanging Our Country Marks*; Martin, "Sapelo Island's Arabic Document."

30. Curtin, "Ayuba Suleiman Diallo of Bondu"; Bluett, published in 1734 under the title *Some Memoirs of the Life of Job*.

31. For Sambo Makumba, see Truman et al., *Visit to the West Indies*, 108–12.

32. *Anais do Arquivo Público*.

33. Mott, *Rosa Egipcíaca*.

34. Sweet, *Domingos Álvares*.

35. Reis, *Domingos Sodré*.

36. d'Avezac-Macaya, "Notice sur le pays"; Santana, "A extaordinária odisseia"; Lloyd, "Osifekunde of Ijebu"; Ojo, "Osifekunde of Ijebu."

37. Castillo and Parés, "Marcelina da Silva."

38. Castillo, "Bamboxê Obitikô."

39. Reis et al., *O Alufá Rufino*; and Reis et al., *The Story of Rufino*, 205. It should be noted that Reis, Gomes, and Carvalho assume that Rufino/Abuncare was "Yoruba" or "Nago" since he was from Oyo, but his Muslim name could well have been Hausa. Reis, Gomes, and Carvalho assert that Rufino was Nago in origin, although he may have been Hausa.

40. See, for example, Cavalheiro, "'I Am Not a Slave'"; Bezerra, "Africans in Diaspora; and Mann and Castillo, "Biography, History, and Diaspora"; Costa and Gomes, "Dos tripulantes da História"; Ferreira and Reginaldo, "Vida e morte"; Soares, *Diálogos Mahis de Francisco Alves de Souza*.

41. See d'Avezac-Macaya, "Notice sur le pays," 1–44; and Santana, "A Extraordinária Odisseia.

42. Reis et al., *O Alufá Rufino*; Said, *Autobiography of Nicholas Said*; Calbreath, *The Sergeant*.

Chapter One

1. Baquaqua, *Autobiography*, 21.

2. Letter of Mrs. N.A.L. Judd, 8 October 1847. In the autobiography, Baquaqua stresses that Muslims did not drink alcohol (p. 24).

3. Baquaqua, *Autobiography*, 26.

4. Baquaqua, *Autobiography*, 27–28.

5. Wilks, "Abu Bakr al-Siddiq" 159–160; and Austin, *African Muslims Sourcebook*, 553, 555.

6. See Barth, *Travels and Discoveries*, 479.

7. Personal communication, Abubakar Babajo Sani, Katsina, 12 December 2014.

8. Brégand, *Commerce caravanier*. Also see Law, "'Central and Eastern Wangara,'" and Lovejoy, "Role of the Wangara."

9. Lovejoy, "Kola in the History"; Lovejoy, "Kola Nuts."

10. Details on the history of Djougou revise Law and Lovejoy, *Biography of Baquaqua*, based on the research of Riccardo Ciavolella, whose study of Djougou has greatly supplemented the earlier field work of Law and Lovejoy. See Ciavolella, "La biographie."

11. British diplomats Edward Bowdich and Joseph Dupuis both recorded some details of the town when they were in Kumasi, the capital of Asante, in 1818 and 1820, respectively; see Bowdich, *Mission*, and Dupuis, *Residence in Ashantee.*

12. Richard Brent Turner concludes erroneously that Baquaqua was born in northern Ghana; see *Islam in the African-American Experience*, 41. Appiah and Gates, *Microsoft Encarta Africana 2000*, have his birthplace as Angola. Similarly, Robert Edgar Conrad proposes that "Zougou" is to be identified with Soulougou in Burkino Faso; see *Children of God's Fire*, 23. This was also initially the opinion of Robert Krueger; see "Milhões de Vozes," 214, although corrected in Krueger, *Biografia e narrative*, 11.

13. "Zugu" remains the local pronunciation of the name of Djougou. There is a village near Kandi in Borgu that is referred to as Zougou Kpantorosi to distinguish it from Djougou, which is known as Djougou Wangara (personal communication, Elisée Soumonni).

14. Austin, *African Muslims Sourcebook*, 15.

15. Baquaqua, *Autobiography*, 14.

16. Baquaqua, *Autobiography*, 14.

17. Baquaqua, *Autobiography*, 14.

18. Ciavolella, *Biographie de Baquaqua.*

19. Baquaqua, *Autobiography*, 14–15.

20. Marco Aime, "Djougou," 481; and Ciavolella, *Biographie de Baquaqua.*

21. See the report of the colonial administrator, Feuille, *Monographie*. We wish to thank Riccardo Ciavolella for sharing this manuscript with us. Also see Ciavolella, *Biographie de Baquaqua.*

22. Baquaqua, *Autobiography*, 15.

23. Ciavolella, *Biographie de Baquaqua*, citing Bassitou Inoussa.

24. See Brégand, *Commerce caravanier*, 93. The current quarters in Djougou include the first district: Gah, Kilir, Madina, Pétoni-Poho-Gorobani, Pétoni-Poho-Partago, Sassirou, Taïfa and Zongo; the second district: Alfa-Issa, Angaradébou, Bassala, Bonborh, Kakabounou-béri, Lémam-Bogou, Lémam-Mandè and Kpatougou; and the third district: Baparapéï, Batoulou, Batoulou-Moula, Foromagazi, Zémbougou-Béri, Timtim- Bongo and Zountori.

25. Baquaqua, *Autobiography*, 15.

26. Person and Person, "Zugu, ville musulmane." Ba-Kparakpe bears some resemblance to Karauka ward in Kano City, wherein Bakarapke could refer to a person from Karauka.

27. Letter of Mrs. N.A.L. Judd, 8 October 1847.

28. Baquaqua, *Autobiography*, 9.

29. For a discussion of shurfa in Borgu and Hausaland in the late eighteenth and early nineteenth centuries, see Lovejoy, *Caravans of Kola*, 58–59, 68–69, 70–71, 73n. Also see Wilks, "Abu Bakr al-Siddiq," 152–69.

30. Baquaqua, *Autobiography*, 15.

31. Letters of Mrs. N.A.L. Judd, 8 October 1847; Rev. W. L. Judd, 28 October 1847.

32. We wish to thank Ibrahim Kankara, Ibrahim Jumare, and Yusufu Yunusa for explaining the use of the name Muhammad and the avoidance of using the name within the family when a son was named after his grandfather; discussion in Katsina, 27–28 November 2017.

33. For its use in Hausa, see Bargery, *A Hausa-English Dictionary*, 341. Also see Harris, "Some Conventional Hausa Names." We wish to thank Obarè Bagodo for information on the use of Gado as a name in Borgu. Also see the report of Feuille, *Monographie*.

34. Baquaqua, *Autobiography*, 26.

35. Baquaqua, *Autobiography*, 40. There is a popular tradition in Brazil that connects Islam, the Catholic Church, and Candomblé in relation to middle names, although Baquaqua probably did not know this. Cosme and Damião, two saints who arrived from Europe in Brazil, received a brother who was born after them. This brother was "Doum." Baquaqua's nickname Gardo indicates that he was born after twins, which in this Brazilian tradition of Doum meant that he should have received donations and gifts as a favorite brother or son. See Verellen, "Cosmas and Damian"; and Thompson, "Sons of Thunder."

36. Bargery, *Hausa/English Dictionary*, 671. This meaning emerged during a group meeting in Katsina during a conference at Umaru Musa Yar'adua University in November 2017. The meeting included Paul Lovejoy, Bruno Véras, Ibrahim Jumare, Yusufu Yunusa, and Ibrahim Kankara. The significance of the meanings has been confirmed with Ibrahim Hamza.

37. Baquaqua, *Autobiography*, 10.

38. The phrase, *allahu akbar* (Arabic: الله أكبر), called Takbir, means "God is the greatest" or "God is great."

39. Baquaqua, *Autobiography*, 11.

40. Levtzion, *Muslims and Chiefs*, 173–78.

41. Dupuis, *Residence in Ashantee*, xlvii. According to Person, "Zugu, ville musulmane," the first king of Djougou to declare himself a Muslim was Atakora II (1899–1921), although in the 1890s Heinrich Klose reported that "the royal family and a large part of the population [of the city of Djougou] are mahometans." The surrounding villages were still "essentially pagan;" see Klose, *Togo sous drapeau allemand*, 390. Austin assumed that the king was nevertheless not Muslim; see *African Muslims Sourcebook*, 646, n. 12–13, 16; and Austin, *Transatlantic Stories*, 162.

42. The wording seems to imply that the king did not reside within the "city," but Baquaqua makes clear that the king's palace, although separate from "the principal part of the city," was situated within the city walls (*Autobiography*, 13).

43. That is, the imam.

44. On 2 June 1830, the Lander brothers noted communal prayers at Kaiama in eastern Borgu, which were led by the "chief mallam" who was assisted in reciting prayers by "two priests of inferior order [who] knelt beside him to hold the hem of his tobe [robe], and a third, in the same position, held the skirts from behind" (Lander and Lander, *Journal of an Expedition*, vol. 1, 213).

45. Baquaqua, *Autobiography*, 10–11.

46. Ciavolella, *Biographie de Baquaqua*, 8 n. 22.

47. Moumine, *Sur la trace*, document on Facebook for the royal family of Djarra of Sasirou, 2018–20. Allan Austin's conclusion that Djougou was "a pre-mosque community" is incorrect; see *African Muslims Sourcebook*, 646 n. 10; and *Transatlantic Stories*, 162. It is possible that Baquaqua's uncle was one of the imams in a list provided by Zakari Dramani-Issifou, but unfortunately the *Autobiography* does not give the names of his father, uncle, or grandfather. See also the discussion in Ciavolella, *Biographie de Baquaqua*.

48. Baquaqua, *Autobiography*, 10.

49. Baquaqua, *Autobiography*, 26.

50. Baquaqua, *Autobiography*, 27.

51. Baquaqua, *Autobiography*, 26.

52. Baquaqua, *Autobiography*, 27.

53. Baquaqua, *Autobiography*, 26.

54. Baquaqua, *Autobiography*, 26.

55. Baquaqua, *Autobiography*, 26.

56. Person, "Note sur les Nyantruku."

57. For a discussion, see Lovejoy, *Caravans of Kola*; Lovejoy, "Polanyi's 'Ports of Trade'"; and Brégard, *Commerce caravanier*. Lovejoy did not refer to Baquaqua's account, nor did Brégard in her study of the Wangara merchants of Borgu. Nonetheless, Baquaqua fully amplifies the analysis of both interpretations.

58. Wilks, "Abu Bakr al-Siddiq," 159–60; and Austin, *African Muslims Sourcebook*, 553, 555.

59. Dupuis, *Residence in Ashanti*, 245, and discussed in Wilks, "Abu Bakr al-Siddiq," 153, and Wilks, *Northern Factor*, 22–24.

60. Madden, *A Twelvemonth's Residence*, vol. 2, 183–89; Renouard, "Routes in North Africa"; and discussed in Wilks, "Abu Bakr al-Siddiq," 152.

61. Lovejoy, *Caravans of Kola*, 48, fn 36. Early nineteenth-century commercial expansion of Asante was first argued by Wilks, "Asante Policy," 129–30. Also see Levtzion, *Muslims and Chiefs*, 22, 27. For a discussion of trade routes and commercial settlements in the region northeast of the Volta, see Berberich, "Locational Analysis." In the late eighteenth century, the Africa Association in London referred to Imhammad of Kafaba; Beaufoy, "Mr Lucas's Communications," vol. 1, 189. In 1887, Louis-Gustave Binger also referred to people at Salaga who had been to Mecca; see *Du Niger au Golfe*, vol. 2, 86; Dupuis, *Residence in Ashantee*, 97; Wilks, "Muslims in Ashanti," 323; Levtzion, "Arabic Manuscripts."

62. Bowdich, *Mission to Ashantee*, 341. See Lovejoy, *Caravans of Kola*, 38; Mahmnd b. Abdallah, *Qissat Salagha*, 25; Wilks, "Abu Bakr al-Siddiq," 167; and Wilks, "Asante Policy," 127. Imhammed's route from Katsina to Kafaba and Nkoranza was as follows: Kashna (Katsina), Youri (Yauri), Gangoo (?), Domboo (?), Nykee (Nikki), Zeggo (Djougou), Kottokolee (Kotokoli, i.e., Dedaure), Kombah (Kpembe), Kaffaba; see Rennell, *A map shewing the progress of discovery & improvement, in the geography of North Africa*. Since Rennell's map underwent several revisions between 1790 and 1810, the 1810 edition of his work is unreliable except for information that is directly attributable to Imhammed, who was the source of the information. There Imhammed does not mention his itinerary, but a German translation of the 1790 edition of the *Proceedings of the African Association*, published in 1791, confirms the above route; see Sotzmann, "Skizze des nordlichen." The map dates to 1791.

63. Lovejoy, *Caravans of Kola*, 38; ʿAbdallah, *Qissat Salagha Ta'rikh Ghunja*, 26, 28; Levtzion, *Muslims and Chiefs*, 28; Dupuis, *Residence in Ashantee*, 248.

64. Bowdich, *Mission to Ashantee*, 341; Dupuis, *Residence in Ashantee*, xl. Also see Daaku, *Oral Traditions of Gonja*, on the early nineteenth-century growth of Salaga. See especially the interview with Hajj Imoru, the Imam of the Salaga Friday mosque, p. 113; and ʿAbdallah, *Qissat Salagha Ta'rikh Ghunja*, 40–41.

65. For a discussion of this trade, see Lovejoy, *Caravans of Kola* and Lovejoy, *Salt of the Desert Sun*. The most authoritative study of the textile industry is Shea, "Export-Oriented Dyed Cloth Industry"; Shea, "Big Is Sometimes Best."

66. Richardson was referring to trade at Zinder, to the northeast of Katsina, but his comments would have applied to Katsina, too; see Richardson, *Mission to Central Africa*, vol. 2, 203.

67. Said, *Autobiography of Nicholas Said*; Said, "A Native of Bornou"; Dabovic, "Out of Place"; Calbreath, *The Sergeant*; Lovejoy, "Mohammed Ali Nicholas Sa'id."

68. There is an extensive literature on the jihād, but see Lovejoy, *Jihād in West Africa*.

69. For a discussion of the jihād and its aftermath in Katsina, see Usman, *Transformation of Katsina*. Also see Meunier, *Voies de l'islam*.

70. According to Barth, *Travels and Discoveries*, vol. 1, 476: "The town, if only half of its immense area were ever tolerably well inhabited, must certainly have had a population of at least a hundred thousand souls, for its circuit is between thirteen and fourteen English miles."

71. Addoun and Lovejoy, "Commerce and Credit"; and Sani, *Trade Diplomacy*. Also see Barth, *Travels and Discoveries*, vol. 1, 479.

72. Baquaqua, *Autobiography*, 2

73. In an early analysis of Baquaqua's autobiography, Austin (*Transatlantic Stories*, 161) stigmatized the general ethnographic data in it as "usually unreliable."

74. Austin, *African Muslims Sourcebook*, 27.

75. Baquaqua, *Autobiography*, 14–15.

76. Dupuis, *Residence in Ashantee*; Law, "'Central and Eastern Wangara.'"

77. Klose, *Togo sous drapeau allemand*, 367–69. Even recent ethnographic literature on Djougou is limited; a major study of the town was undertaken by Yves Person, but it was never published. His rough drafts and notes for this work are preserved, but they are in a fragmentary and disorganized condition, for the most part very difficult both to read and interpret. Riccardo Ciavolella has continued this research.

78. Baquaqua, *Autobiography*, 9.

79. Bruce Lockhart and Lovejoy, *Hugh Clapperton*; Lander, *Clapperton's Last Expedition*; Lander and Lander, *Journal of an Expedition*. Also see Lander Diary.

80. Baquaqua, *Autobiography*, 24.

81. A hinny is the offspring of a male horse and a female donkey. It is the reciprocal cross to the more common mule, which is the product of a male donkey and a female horse.

82. Baquaqua, *Autobiography*, 23.

83. According to Person, "Zugu, ville musulmane," Djougou imported its salt from the coast, from the Petit Popo area, but this seems unlikely. Other accounts suggest that the main source of salt in the Borgu region was from the valley of Dallol Fogha, to the north: Lovejoy, *Salt of the Desert Sun*, 5, 17, 39, 46–47; Brégand, *Commerce caravanier*, 67–69; Debourou, "Commerçants et chefs," 127; Arifaro Bako, "Question du peuplement," 111.

84. FO 97/434, Niger Expeditions, No. 19, Baikie to Lord Russell, 22 March 1862.

85. Dupuis, *Residence in Ashantee*, xcix. "Callio Makaro" is unidentified.

86. Lovejoy, *Salt of the Desert Sun*.

87. Baquaqua, *Autobiography*, 24.

88. Lovejoy, *Caravans of Kola*, citing numerous oral accounts that were conducted in Kano, Katsina and elsewhere.

89. Baquaqua, *Autobiography*, 23.

90. Baquaqua, *Autobiography* 18.

91. Baquaqua, *Autobiography*, 18.

92. Baquaqua, *Autobiography*, 3–4. See especially Brégand, *Commerce caravanier*. For the Wangara in a broader historical and geographical context, see also Lovejoy, "Role of the Wangara," and Law, "Central and Eastern Wangara."

93. For a discussion of the Yowa and their diverse origins, see Person, "Zugu, ville musulmane."

94. Not Bariba (Baatonu), as assumed by Austin, *Transatlantic Stories*, 162.

95. Baatonu (pl. Baatombu) is the indigenous name for the people of Borgu; Bargawa (people of Borgu) is the Hausa name for the people and the region, while Bariba is the Yoruba and Dahomey term. In eastern Borgu (Bussa and Wawa) a distinct language, Boko, is spoken. See Moraes Farias, "Letter from Ki-Toro Mahamman Gaani."

96. Klose, *Togo unter deutscher Flagge*, 1, 390.

97. Letter of Baquaqua to George Whipple, 22 January 1854.

98. Lovejoy, "Cerner les identités," and Lovejoy, "Identidade e a Miragem."

99. Letter of Rev. W. L. Judd, 28 October 1847.

100. Letter of Rev. W. L. Judd, 21 July 1848.

101. American Baptist Free Mission Society, Tenth Annual Meeting, Utica, New York, 1–2 June 1853.

102. Noted in Baquaqua, *Autobiography*, 26.

103. Letter of Rev. W. L. Judd, 28 October 1847, where it is stated that "his father died before he left." For reference to Baquaqua's feelings for his mother, see Baquaqua, *Autobiography*, 35, 39; also for example, letter of Baquaqua to Hepburn, n.d. [November 1848]. On some occasions, he referred to his brother and sister(s) as well as his mother; see letters of Baquaqua to Cyrus Grosvenor, 14 November 1848, and to George Whipple, 25 September 1853; letter of A. L. Post, July 1853, in *The American Baptist*, 21 July 1853.

104. Some slaves from Borgu are documented (under the name "Bariba") in Brazil, in the province of Bahia: for references, see Law and Lovejoy, "Borgu in the Atlantic Slave Trade." But the Bariba are not included among the "nations" of African-born slaves in Rio de Janeiro, listed by Karasch, *Slave Life in Rio de Janeiro*, 11–21, 371.

105. Letter of Rev. W. L. Judd, 28 October 1847. For the Hausa community in Rio de Janeiro, see Karasch, *Slave Life in Rio de Janeiro*, 284–85; and for the preservation of the Arabic language among Muslims in Rio, see *Slave Life in Rio de Janeiro*, 219; Costa e Silva, "Buying and Selling Korans"; Guimarães, "Cidade do feitiço"; Farias et al., *No labirinto das nações*.

Chapter Two

1. Judd, Letter from Mrs. Mary A. L. Judd to Grosvenor, 24 March 1848.

2. Judd, Letter from Mrs. Mary A. L. Judd to Grosvenor.

3. Foss and Mathews, *Facts for Baptist Churches*, 392.

4. Law and Lovejoy, *Biography of Baquaqua*, 35, 36, and repeated subsequently in other publications.

5. Wilks, *Wa and the Wala*, 100; Wilks, *Asante in the Nineteenth Century*, 275–79.

6. Baquaqua, *Autobiography*, 30.

7. The itineraries in Bowdich, *Mission to Ashantee*, 177, 179, 208, give a total of nineteen days' journey between Djougou and Daboya: eight days from Daboya to Yendi, eleven days from Yendi to Djougou.

8. Baquaqua, *Autobiography*, 29.

9. Wilks, *Asante in the Nineteenth Century*, 277.

10. Baquaqua, *Autobiography*, 31.

11. Baquaqua, *Autobiography*, 30.

12. Baquaqua, *Autobiography*, 30.

13. Baquaqua, *Autobiography*, 31.

14. Wilks, *Asante in the Nineteenth Century*.

15. Baquaqua, *Autobiography*, 30.

16. For a discussion, see Law, *Oyo Empire*, 292–95. The jihād in Yoruba country is also discussed in Lovejoy, *Jihād in West Africa*.

17. Mercier, "Histoire et légende, " 94.

18. Baquaqua, *Autobiography*, 29.

19. Mercier, "Bataille d'Illorin," 94. For the provision of religious services, including divination, by Muslim clerics (*alfa*) to rulers in Borgu, see Brégand, *Commerce caravanier*, 140–48.

20. Ciavolella, *Biographie de Baquaqua*.

21. Baquaqua, *Autobiography*, 31.

22. Baquaqua, *Autobiography*, 31.

23. This seems to imply that "massa-sa-ba" was a generic title for the rulers of towns subordinate to Djougou, but in Djougou, Masasawa is considered the title only in Soubroukou: Law/Lovejoy fieldwork, April 1999.

24. See Feuille, *Monographie*.

25. Baquaqua, *Autobiography*, 31.

26. Baquaqua, *Autobiography*, 31.

27. When Ciavolella conducted interviews in Soubroukou, the "palace" of the Massasawa displayed paintings representing scenes of punishment reminding subjects of the royal sanctions for crimes and infidelities, as well as scenes of hunting, lions, and panthers, "fetish" sacrifices, musicians and bards serving the king, which were located beside the front door. The scenes of historical events were unfortunately unrecognizable because of their decay.

28. Baquaqua, *Autobiography*, 31.

29. Dupuis, *Residence in Ashantee*, Appendix No. 4, cxxv. In 1820, Dupuis was able to reconstruct the geography of the region of "Wangara" based essentially on the accounts of local informants who used the idea of a day's journey as a measure of time-distances between places (Dupuis, *Residence in Ashantee*, chapter 16, xix). As Dupuis noted, "[T]hey described [. . .] by day's journey the distance which separated one inner realm from another, confirming all that they argued on the basis of their travel manuscripts, and the tes-

timony of those of them who had visited the places they mentioned. The number of sixteen British miles, three-fourths of which is to be made up in horizontal distance, seems to me, from my own experience, equivalent to a day's journey, where the country is interspersed with forest or thicket; or where the surface is interrupted by hills and mountains. A reduction of a quarter of the effective distance from the path is certainly not overestimated given the vagaries of roads, such as those I have traveled; and I have been credibly assured that the southern roads present, more or less, the same aspect, while those which slope south from the east and north from the west are elsewhere greatly hampered by hills, mountains and ravines." Dupuis based his construction of routes and places defined distances between the small "kingdoms" of the region as one day of travel, such as "from Yarako to Zoogoo."

30. Law and Lovejoy, *Biography of Baquaqua*, 32fn.

31. Ciavolella fieldwork, April 1999, as discussed in *Biographie de Baquaqua*.

32. Lombard, "Quelques notes," 4–5; Lombard, "La vie politique"; Lombard, *Structures de type "féodal"*, 121, 125. Also see Baldus, "Responses to Dependence, 438, 457. Baldus refers to *tkiriku* as "slave servants of wanangari." Technically, these palace servants were slaves in status, which may account for the statement of Mrs. Judd in 1848 that "It seems, from what he has informed us lately, that he was several years a slave in Africa." See letter of Mrs. N.A.L. Judd, 24 March 1848; and Foss and Mathews, *Facts for Baptist Churches*, 392.

33. Baldus, "Social Structure and Ideology."

34. A colonial intelligence report described their role at Nikki as the "krikous" or "king's emissaries" within the royal government; see Anon., "Le Royaume du Borgou," 7.

35. Baquaqua, *Autobiography*, 31.

36. Baquaqua, *Autobiography*, 31.

37. See Pliya, *Afrique Occidentale*, 38, and Sheet 1919: 108, as discussed in Ciavolella, *Biographie de Baquaqua*.

38. Levtzion, "Salaga," 215.

39. Person, "Les grandes compagnies," 127–44. It should be noted that the village, Babanzaure, seems to be derived from Hausa, *baban zaure*, which refers to the big or large entrance room to a compound, which is surrounded by a wall or stockade.

40. Baquaqua, *Autobiography*, 33.

41. Baquaqua, *Autobiography*, 33.

42. Beacham, "Phonology and Morphology," 115.

43. Law and Lovejoy, *Biography of Baquaqua*, 135.

44. The letters "sab-" could derive from the term saawa ("king"), because the sound w in Yom is halfway between the "ou" and the "b" suffixes "-i" and "-ii." See Beacham, "Phonology and Morphology," 111.

45. "Le Royaume du Borgou," 6–7.

46. Brégand, *Commerce caravanier*, 93.

47. Ciavolella interview with Ouorou Komsa Aboubacar, October 2018, in *Biographie de Baquaqua*.

48. Ciavolella interview with Ouorou Komsa Aboubacar, October 2018, in *Biographie de Baquaqua*.

49. Ciavolella interview, October 2018, in *Biographie de Baquaqua*.

50. Feuille, *Monographie du cercle de Djougou*, 54.

51. Ciavolella interview with Ouorou Komsa Aboubacar, October 2018, in *Biographie de Baquaqua.*

52. Ciavolella interview with Ouorou Komsa Aboubacar, October 2018, in *Biographie de Baquaqua.*

53. In 1919, Feuille's map of the territorial distribution of royal powers made a clear distinction between the area under the authority of Kilir—that is, Djougou—and that under the authority of Soubroukou; see Feuille, *Monographie*, and it is also discussed in Ciavolella, *Biographie de Baquaqua*. In 1919, Feuille observed that the notables who surrounded each king outside of Kilir lost their importance in the face of Zarma intervention, which had "led to war and plunder" (*Monographie*, 82–83). As Person has demonstrated, the king of Soubroukou recruited Zarma mercenaries later in the century ("Grandes compagnies zarma").

54. Ciavolella interview with Ouorou Komsa Aboubacar, October 2018, in *Biographie de Baquaqua.*

55. Ciavolella interview with the king of Soubroukou, Ouorou Komsa Aboubacar, October 2018, as cited in Ciavolella, *Biographie de Baquaqua.*

56. Ciavolella interview with the king of Soubroukou, Ouorou Komsa Aboubacar, October 2018, as cited in Ciavolella, *Biographie de Baquaqua.*

57. Colonial impoverishment was enhanced through forced labor, "to which no one dared say no; we were whipped and mistreated" in the construction of the road linking Djougou to Bassila in the territory of Soubroukou (Ciavolella interview with Ouorou Komsa Aboubacar, October 2018). See the maps of "indigenous" and colonial territorial organization in Feuille, *Monographie du cercle de Djougou*, and Auchère 1956, as cited in Ciavolella, *Biographie de Baquaqua.*

58. Baquaqua, *Autobiography*, 32.

59. Clapperton, *Interior of Africa*, 65, 115–16.

60. Dupuis, *Residence in Ashantee* ciii–civ; Klose, *Le Togo*, 398; and Springade 1907, as cited in Ciavolella, *Biographie de Baquaqua.*

61. Klose, *Le Togo*, 395–402.

62. Yves Person, "Note sur les Nyantruku"; Parrinder, "Yoruba-Speaking Peoples," 122, 127.

63. According to Cornevin, "A Propos des Cotoli," but disputed by Alexandre, "L'organisation politique," and Tchagbalé, "Les sept origines possibles."

64. Alexandre, "L'organisation politique," 273.

65. Klose, *Le Togo*, 398.

66. Ciavolella, fieldwork between 2010 and 2018 and cited in *Biographie de Baquaqua*. Person, "Grandes compagnies zarma," in his work at Soubroukou and Djougou referred to raids in the 1880s, but not earlier.

67. In his discussion of enslavement, Moore noted, "We will now, at once, turn to the more interesting portion of Mahommah's history, which treats of his capture in Africa and subsequent slavery. We will give the matter in nearly his own words." See Baquaqua, *Autobiography*, 34–35.

68. Baquaqua, *Autobiography*, 35.

69. Baquaqua, *Autobiography*, 35.

70. Baquaqua, *Autobiography*, 35.

71. "Arjou" in Dupuis, *Residence in Ashantee*, civ; also identified in Law and Lovejoy, *Biography of Baquaqua*, n. 157.

72. Levtzion, *Muslims and Chiefs*, 178; and Delval, *Musulmanes au Togo*, 108.

73. Law and Lovejoy, *Biography of Baquaqua*, 142fn.

74. Law and Lovejoy initially thought that Efau was a corruption of "Fon," the Gbe language of Dahomey, but Ciavollela's research has established that Yoruba/Nago communities to the south of Djougou from the area west of Savalou as far as Aktpamè are known as Ifè. See *Biographie de Baquaqua*.

75. According to John Duncan, *Travels in Western Africa*, vol. 2, 243–44, the first town in Dahomey was Djalloukou, about 40 km northwest of Abomey. Duncan himself took just over three days (21–24 August 1845) to reach Abomey from Djalloukou: Duncan, *Travels in Western Africa*, ii, 253–60.

76. Baquaqua, *Autobiography*, 38.

77. Baquaqua, *Autobiography*, 39.

78. Duncan, *Travels in Western Africa*, vol. 1, 257–58.

79. For a discussion of Dahomey in this period, see Bay, *Wives of the Leopard*, 166–92.

80. Duncan, *Travels in Western Africa*, I, 64, 185–86.

81. Slave Voyages Database (https://www.slavevoyages.org/).

82. For details on da Souza's life, see Costa e Silva, *Francisco Félix de Souza*, and Araujo, "Forgetting and Remembering."

83. Lockhart and Lovejoy, *Hugh Clapperton into the Interior of Africa*, 35–36.

84. Law, "Francisco Felix de Souza."

85. Duncan, *Travels in Western Africa*, vol. 1, 110–11.

86. Duncan, *Travels in Western Africa*, vol. 1, 110–11.

87. Duncan, *Travels in Western Africa*, vol. 1, 142–43.

88. Baquaqua, *Autobiography*, 41.

89. Baquaqua, *Autobiography*, 43.

90. Baquaqua, *Autobiography*, 43.

91. Baquaqua, *Autobiography*, 42–43.

92. Duncan, *Travels in Western Africa*, vol. 1, 143; Hurston, "Cudjo's Own Story," 657. Cudjo was interviewed in Mobile, Alabama, in the 1920s.

93. Fett, *Recaptured Africans*; Forbes, *Six Months' Service*, 95; Forbes, *Dahomey and the Dahomans*.

94. Forbes, *Six Months' Service*, 87.

95. Hurston, "Cudjo's Own Story," 657.

96. Walvin, *Black Ivory*, 48–50.

97. Klein, *Atlantic Slave Trade*, 93–94; Forbes, *Six Months' Service*, 98.

98. Baquaqua, *Autobiography*, 43.

99. Rediker, *Slave Ship*; Fett, *Recaptured Africans*.

100. Forbes, *Six Months' Service*, 99.

101. Letter of Mrs. N.A.L. Judd, 8 October 1847.

102. Klein, *Atlantic Slave Trade*, 95.

103. Eltis, *Economic Growth*, 133; Klein, *Atlantic Slave Trade*, 130.

104. Carvalho, *Liberdade*, 117–42.

105. Carvalho, *Liberdade*, 43.

Chapter Three

1. Details and documentation on Liberated Africans in Brazil can be accessed at https://www.liberatedafricans.org, under the direction of Henry B. Lovejoy. Also see Cavalheiro, "Da liberdade para a emancipação," and Mamigonian, "To Be a Liberated African in Brazil."

2. Baquaqua, *Autobiography*, 44.

3. PP (Parliamentary Papers), Slave Trade 1846, Class B, n°361, sr. Goring to Conde de Aberdeen, Pernambuco, 16 May 1846.

4. Baquaqua, *Autobiography*, 42–44.

5. According to the Portuguese consul in Recife, these ships flew Brazilian flags and had documents showing trade with São Tomé and Príncipe, but in reality, they were going to "Benin, Omin [Lagos] and Ajudá [Ouidah]." The ships were described as "small," in comparison to the large ships, which transported enslaved Africans from Angola (Torre do Tombo, Consulate of Portugal in Pernambuco, box 3, Joaquim Batista Moreira to the minister of foreign affairs, 10 December 1844). According to Carvalho, the Portuguese consul did not mention any ships coming from the Bight of Benin in 1845. However, the consul was mainly concerned with tracking Portuguese flagships, not Brazilian ships, despite his observations made in 1844. Therefore, the fact that no transit of Brazilian ships in 1845 appears in the report does not mean that there was none. Also see Carvalho, "O desembarque nas praias," 223–60.

6. Parliamentary Papers, Slave Trade 1846, Class B, n°173, Consul Cowper to the Count of Aberdeen, Pernambuco, 2 March 1846, with annex 1, List of arrival of vessels suspected of being employed in the Slave Trade from the Coast of Africa to the province of Pernambuco, during the year ending 31 December 1845. Listed as Voyage ID 3592 in https://www.slavevoyages.org/; see Irish University Press, IUP,ST,33/B/293—that is, Great Britain, Irish University Press Series of British Parliamentary Papers: Slave Trade, vols. 1–90 (Shannon, 1969–74). Initially 181 enslaved Africans were on board.

7. Baquaqua, *Autobiography*, 44.

8. Carvalho, *Liberdade*, 102–3.

9. Parliamentary Papers, Slave Trade 1845, Class B, no. 361, Mr. Goring to Earl of Aberdeen, Pernambuco, 16 May 1846.

10. Correspondence on the Slave Trade with Foreign Powers (Class B), 1 January—31 December 1845, vol. 33, Brazil (Consular)—Pernambuco, p. 293.

11. Baquaqua, *Autobiography*, 44.

12. Parliamentary Papers, Slave Trade 1846, Class B, no. 173, Consul Cowper to Earl of Aberdeen, Pernambuco, 2 March 1846, with enclosure 1, List of arrival of vessels suspected of being employed in the Slave Trade from the Coast of Africa to the Province of Pernambuco, during the Year ending 31 December 1845. An earlier description of ships landing off Itamaracá is to be found in "Slavery and the Slave Trade in South America," *The Preston and Lancashire*, 22 July 1843.

13. Baquaqua, *Autobiography*, 44–45.

14. Baquaqua, *Autobiography*, 44.

15. Morel, *O Período das Regências*.

16. Carvalho, *A Construção da Ordem*; Mattos, *Tempo Saquarema*.

17. Chalhoub, *A força da escravidão*; Mamigonian, *Africanos Livres*.

18. Carvalho, "Cavalcantis e Cavalcades," 36; Carvalho, *Movimentos sociais*, 124–26; Mello, *Apreciação da Revolta*.

19. Parliamentary Papers, Slave Trade 1844, Class B, annex n°265, "Probable Amount of the Population of the Province of Pernambuco—1844." According to Vergolino, the majority of African-born slaves listed in post-mortem inventories in Pernambuco, in the nineteenth century, were recorded as coming from West Central Africa, and only a small percentage designated as "gentio costa," apparently referring to West Africa in general, and including "nago," "mine," or "benin"; see Vergolino, "A demografia excrava," 20. On slavery in Pernambuco, see Carvalho, *Liberdade*, 73–90; Carvalho, "Le 'Divin Maître.'"

20. Sweet, "Mistaken Identities?"

21. See Law and Lovejoy, *Biography of Baquaqua*; Carvalho, *Liberdade*, 21–22; and Carvalho, "Negros Canoeiros no Recife."

22. Baquaqua, *Autobiography*, 45.

23. Baquaqua, *Autobiography*, 45.

24. Lovejoy, *Jihad in West Africa*.

25. Baquaqua, *Autobiography*, 45.

26. Baquaqua, *Autobiography*, 46.

27. Baquaqua, *Autobiography*, 46–47; Law and Lovejoy, *Biography of Baquaqua*, 160–61.

28. Canario, *É mais uma cena da escravidão*.

29. Baquaqua, *Autobiography*, 47.

30. See Carvalho, "Negros Canoeiros no Recife," 78–93. On the severity of the slavery regime in the 1840s, see also Eisenberg, *The Sugar Industry in Pernambuco*, 172, 173. As noted in Law and Lovejoy, *Biography of Baquaqua*, 159–60, the urban enslaved in Pernambuco as elsewhere in Brazil generally worked for their masters for wages; see Carvalho, *Liberdade*, 21–22, 26–40, 51–54, 82–91.

31. Santos, *Além das senzalas*.

32. As noted in Law and Lovejoy, *Biography of Baquaqua*, 160fn, "Fugitive slaves were a particularly serious problem in Pernambuco in the mid-1840s. Slaves were often 'stolen,' and many forced a change in masters in a manner suggested here." See Carvalho, *Rotinas e Rupturas do Escravismo*, 202–11. Numerous slaves named José are listed in *Diário do Pernambuco* for 1845 and 1846, but none fit the description of Baquaqua, either because the region of origin was Angola and not West Africa, or because of physical traits that rule out Baquaqua. Several fugitives named José worked for bakers, but the location or other details also preclude a positive identification. (We wish to thank Maciel Henrique Carneiro, Rogério Ribau Ferandes, Clarice Sales de Albuquerque, and Otto Cabral Mendes Filho for searching *Diário do Pernambuco* for 1845 and José Cairus for searching *Diário do Pernambuco* for 1846, which may have been too late anyway.)

33. "Desapareceu da rua da Cruz até o aterro-da-Boa-Vista, um preto de nome José, de nação da Costa Bua, com três riscas na testa; tem três marcas de ferro no rosto; sendo uma na testa e outra em cada face, peito todo riscado, com alguns dentes quebrados, estatura regular, cheio do corpo, bem parecido de figura; levou calça de riscado de algodãozinho, camisa de algodãozinho de mangas curtas; tendo sabido a vender pão pelas ruas, com um panacum grande, e toalha de algodãozinho trançado novo, com franja, fugiu no dia 28 do passado, quem o pegar leve ao aterro da Boa Vista, padaria n° 66 que será recompensado," *Diário de Pernambuco*, 2 October 1845.

34. "Fugiu no dia 23 do corrente um preto da costa, de nome José, padeiro, do que tem as mãos grossas de calo, estatura regular, cheio do corpo, um tanto barrigudo, cor pouco preta, talhos no rosto, de sua nação, e marcas pretas de feridas, tem em um dos pés o dedo do meio cortado; tem sido visto na boa vista, ponte-de-uchoa e nos apipucos; quem o pegar, leve a rua Direita, padaria n° 82, que será recompensado," *Diário de Pernambuco*, 29 October 1845.

35. Feuille, *Monographie du cercle de Djougou*.

36. Baquaqua, *Autobiography*, 47.

37. Silva, *Negro na rua*.

38. Arquivo Histórico do Rio Grande do Sul. Série Marinha. Maço 24. At this time, the most important port in Rio Grande do Sul was at the entrance to the Lagoa dos Patos at the old port of Rio Grande, not at Porto Alegre, at the interior end of the lagoon and subsequently the capital of the state. We thank Vinicius Oliveira for this source.

39. Baquaqua, *Autobiography*, 48–49.

40. Reis et al., *O alufá Rufino*, 30–31.

41. Rodrigues, *De costa a costa*, 162.

42. Baquaqua, *Autobiography*, 48.

43. Baquaqua, *Autobiography*, 48.

44. Karasch, *Slave Life in Rio de Janeiro*, 36.

45. Soares, *Zungú*.

46. Karasch, *Slave Life in Rio de Janeiro*, 44.

47. al-Baghdadi, *Tasliyat al-gharib*; Ribeiro, "Negros Islâmicos"; Farah, "Relato de Viagem."

48. Today, the site is the location of an archaeological project, a laboratory, and a museum.

49. Gomes et al., *No Labirinto das Nações*.

50. Holloway, *Polícia no Rio de Janeiro*.

51. Florentino, "Alforria e etnicidade."

52. Faria, "Damas mercadoras," 110.

53. See testimony by Clemente da Costa, New York, 12 July 1847, published in the *National Anti-Slavery Standard*, 2 November 1847. Law and Lovejoy (*Biography of Baquaqua*, 44) mistakenly indicated that Costa was a part owner in the ship, but he was not.

54. Arquivo Nacional, *Junta do Comércio*.

55. Rocha Pereira married Maria Roza Leite in 1837. We wish to thank Manolo Florentino for this reference.

56. Arquivo Nacional, *Junta do Comércio*.

57. Arquivo Histórico do Rio Grande do Sul. Série Marinha, Maço 24. We wish to thank Vinicius Oliveira for references from Rio Grande do Sul.

58. Rodrigues, *De costa a costa*, 163.

59. Arquivo Histórico do Rio Grande do Sul. Rio Grande, 2°, Tabelionato, Transmissão e Notas, Livro 21, fls 73.a.

60. Kunioch, "Ter escravo no Rio Grande."

61. Arquivo Histórico do Rio Grande do Sul, Carta de Liberdade de Teresa, filha de Rufina, Data de Concessão: 26-03-1866. Data de registro: 03-04-1866, Livro 24, página 28.

62. Law and Lovejoy, *Biography of Baquaqua*, 163–64.

63. Kunioch, "Ter escravo no Rio Grande."

64. Dreys, *Notícia Descriptiva*, 191.

65. Reis et al., *O alufá Rufino*, 45.

66. Baquaqua, *Autobiography*, 48.

67. Baquaqua, *Autobiography*, 48–49.

68. Baquaqua, *Autobiography*, 51.

69. Baquaqua, *Autobiography*, 51.

70. Law and Lovejoy, *Biography of Baquaqua*, 166.

71. Reis et al., *O alufá Rufino*, 80–81, 49.

72. *Jornal do Comércio*, 26 de fevereiro de 1843, 4.

73. Baquaqua, *Autobiography*, 49.

74. Soares, *Devotos da cor*; Bezerra, *Escravidão*; Rodrigues, *De costa a costa*.

75. Baquaqua, *Autobiography*, 50–51.

76. Baquaqua, *Autobiography*, 51.

77. Arquivo Histórico do Itamaraty, Rio de Janeiro: 258-3-5, p. 81. We are grateful to Manolo Florentino and Alberto da Costa e Silva for this reference.

78. Baquaqua, *Autobiography*, 54.

79. For details on the trip, see, in addition to the *Autobiography*, the testimony of Clemente José da Costa, [12] July 1847; and for news of the arrival of the *Lembrança*, see *New York Daily Tribune*, 28 June 1847.

Chapter Four

1. Arquivo Histórico do Itamaraty, Rio de Janeiro: 258/3/5, p. 81.

2. *Diario do Rio de Janeiro*, Rio de Janeiro, Brazil, 23 October 1847.

3. Baquaqua, *Autobiography*, 47–48. For the ownership of slaves by freed men (and by other slaves) in Rio de Janeiro, see Karasch, *Slave Life in Rio de Janeiro*, 207.

4. Affidavit of Clemente José da Costa, New York, 20 July 1847, in *National Anti-Slavery Standard*, 2 September 1847; also, see the announcement of the ship's arrival in *New York Daily Tribune*, 28 June 1847.

5. See *First Annual Report of the New York Committee of Vigilance*, 1837, Wilbur H. Siebert Collection; MSS116AV BOX51 F02 002, Library of Congress. According to the *New York Herald* (12 July 1847), "On Saturday last the fact [that there were three slaves on board the *Lembrança*] leaked out, and in a few moments quite a collection of negroes and abolitionists assembled at the foot of Roosevelt street, where the vessel was lying." For the Vigilance Society, see Perlman, "Organizations of the Free Negro"; Pease, *They Who Would Be Free*; Olsavsky, "Fugitive Slaves"; and Papson and Calarco, *Secret Lives of the Underground Railroad*. There is a brief discussion in Townsend, *Faith in Their Own Color*, 147, and Foner, *Gateway to Freedom*, although Foner did not recognize that the individual in question was Baquaqua. Austin (*Sourcebook*, 653, n. 91; *Transatlantic Stories*, 165) correctly identified those who came on board as members of the New York Vigilance Society.

6. Papson and Calarco, *Secret Lives of the Underground Railroad*, 59.

7. See the advertisements "Sailor's Home" and "Colored Sailor's Home." Also see Foner and Lewis, *Black Worker*.

8. Papson and Calarco, *Secret Lives of the Underground Railroad*, 60. Also see Powell, "Underground Railroad."

9. *National Anti-Slavery Standard,* 24 October 1850.

10. Foner, "William P. Powell."

11. *National Anti-Slavery Standard,* 24 October 1850.

12. Foner, *Gateway to Freedom,* 54–61, 85–97, 128–30, 171–76.

13. Gay later became editor-in-chief of Horace Greeley's *New York Tribune,* as well as the *Chicago Tribune* briefly and then the *New York Evening Post.* Gay is noted for helping as many as 3,000 fugitives, including Henry "Box" Brown, who was smuggled in a box that was mistakenly placed upside down so that he traveled on his head, and most famously Harriet Tubman, whose own exploits in helping people to escape earned her the nickname of General Tubman.

14. Gronningsater, "'On Behalf of His Race."

15. "Reported for the Express," *New York Evening Express,* 13 July 1847.

16. "Reported for the Express," *New York Evening Express,* 13 July 1847; and *New York Daily Tribune,* 16 July 1847.

17. *New York Daily Tribune,* 16 July 1847.

18. "The Brazilian Slaves," *National Anti-Slavery Standard,* 16 September 1847.

19. *Diário do Rio de Janeiro,* 4 October 1847, translating a report from the *New York Evening Express.* Robert Edgar Conrad notes this reference to the *Lembrança* incident in New York but does not identify Baquaqua as one of the slaves on board; see Conrad, *World of Sorrow,* 117.

20. Baquaqua, *Biography;* Foner, *Gateway to Freedom,* 112; Odessky, "'Possessed of One Idea Himself,'" 10–12; Papson and Calarco, *Secret Lives of the Underground Railroad;* and Columbia University and Slavery, "John Jay II: Columbia Abolitionist."

21. See Bevans, *Treaties and Other International Agreements,* vol. 5, 792–803, 801–2.

22. Kelley, *American Slavers,* 348.

23. *New York Daily Tribune* 13, 14, 15, 16, 17, and 19 July 1847, with text of Daly's judgement in *National Anti-Slavery Standard,* 12 August 1847. The prison (a "private establishment) where Baquaqua and his companion were lodged was on Eldridge Street; see *New York Daily Tribune,* 21 July, 12 August 1847, and affidavit of José da Costa and José da Rocha, 21 July 1847, in *National Anti-Slavery Standard,* 2 September 1847.

24. "Reported for the Express," *New York Evening Express,* 13 July 1847.

25. "Reported for the Express," *New York Evening Express,* 13 July 1847.

26. Cf. the report of the *New York Daily Tribune,* 13 July 1847; and *New York Herald,* 13 July 1847.

27. The contemporary newspaper reports confirm that Captain Costa "sent for the Brazilian Consul as his counsel" in the initial hearing on Saturday, 10 July, but he did not arrive in time, causing the postponement of the hearing till Monday, 12 July. Probably the consul attended on 12 July, although this is not explicitly reported, and on the following day, Tuesday 13 July, Costa submitted to the court a letter of protest signed by the Consul: *New York Daily Tribune,* 12 and 14 July 1847. The Brazilian Consul was Luiz Henrique Ferreira de Aguiar.

28. *New York Daily Tribune,* 12 and 14 July 1847; and Rogers, *Sketches of Representative Men,* 287–305.

29. Affidavit of Clemente José da Costa, New York, 20 July 1847, in *National Anti-Slavery Standard,* 2 September 1847; *New York Daily Tribune,* 14 July 1847.

30. *New York Daily Tribune,* 12, 16, and 17 July 1847.

31. *National Anti-Slavery Standard,* 15 July 1847. For Daly's ruling that the three fugitives had to return to the ship, see *National Anti-Slavery Standard,* 22 July 1847.

32. Their affidavit, together with a second one by Captain Costa submitted on this occasion, were published in the *National Anti-Slavery Standard,* 2 September 1847.

33. Their affidavit, together with a second one by Captain Costa submitted on this occasion, were published in the *National Anti-Slavery Standard,* 2 September 1847.

34. "The Brazilian Slave Case - Escape of the Slaves," *National Anti-Slavery Standard,* 12 August 1847.

35. *New York Daily Tribune,* 19, 20, 21, 22 and 27 July, 2 August 1847; with speeches of Jay and White, and affidavits of Clemente José da Costa, 20 July 1847, and of José da Costa (Baquaqua) and José da Rocha, 21 July 1847, in *National Anti-Slavery Standard,* 12 August and 2 September 1847.

36. *National Anti-Slavery Standard,* 29 July 1847.

37. "Brazilian Slave Case."

38. *National Anti-Slavery Standard,* 12 August 1847.

39. *New York Daily Tribune,* 10 August 1847, and *National Anti-Slavery Standard,* 12 August 1847.

40. Foner, *Gateway to Freedom,* 107.

41. Elias Smith to Dr. Hudson, 7 August 1847, Hudson Family Papers, 1807–1963, Special Collections and University Archives, University of Massachusetts Amherst Libraries.

42. Powell, "Underground Railroad."

43. Lee, *Autobiography,* 322–24.

44. Lee, *Autobiography,* 322–24.

45. "The Brazilian Slaves," *National Anti-Slavery Standard,* 19 August 1847.

46. *New York Tribune,* 5, 6 August 1847.

47. Lee, *Autobiography,* 322–25.

48. Lee, *Autobiography,* 322–25.

49. Lee, *Autobiography,* 325.

50. Lee, *Autobiography,* 325.

51. *New York Evangelist,* 23 August 1846.

52. The most authoritative study of fugitives escaping slavery in Massachusetts is Siebert, "Underground Railroad." Also see Bearse, *Reminiscences;* Bartlett, "Abolitionists"; Grodzins, "'Constitution or No Constitution,'"

53. Siebert, "Underground Railroad," 39.

54. Willcox, "A Gay Life," which was to be published by Willcox & Maloney in New York, Sydney Howard Gay Collection, Manuscript Collections, Columbia University Libraries. Willcox was a leading women's rights advocate and later served as Borough Chairman for the City Party of Staten Island, where the Gay home was located.

55. See Papson and Calarco, *Secret Lives of the Underground Railroad,* 117–205 and online by Columbia University Libraries, https://exhibitions.library.columbia.edu/exhibits /show/fugitives.

56. Letters of W. L. Judd, 28 October 1847; Mrs. N.A.L. Judd, 24 March 1848. Baquaqua landed at Port-au-Prince, the Haitian capital, probably by mid-September 1847.

57. Letter of Mrs. N.A.L. Judd, 8 October 1847.

58. Letter of Rev. W. L. Judd, 19 November 1848, in *Christian Contributor and Free Missionary*, 13 December 1848.

59. *Vestry Minutes of St. Philips Episcopal Church*, St. Philips Episcopal Church Records, Manuscripts, Archives, and Rare Books Division, Schomburg Center for Foundations, box 74, 12 August 1847 (italics in original). For further discussion, see Townsend, *Faith in Their Own Color*, 148–53; and Walker, *Afro-American in New York City*.

60. Townsend, *Faith in Their Own Color*.

61. "Financial Report," *Vestry Minutes*, 9 January 1844, and subsequent years.

62. Information about the addresses and/or occupations of individuals is taken from the city directors from the relevant years, unless otherwise noted. In addition to the *Vestry Minutes*, the other source for individuals who considered themselves members of St. Philip's is the open letter written to John Jay in 1845, as the letter states that all the signatories are parishioners: undated newspaper clipping, John Jay II Scrapbook, John Jay Homestead, Katonah, NY.

63. See the discussion in Townsend, *Faith in Their Own Color*, 153. Also see Quarles, *Black Abolitionists*, 198; Walker, *Afro-American in New York City*, 37, 56, 77, 117, 125, 151, 156–59, 173–74; James Abajian, *Blacks in Selected Newspapers*, vol. 1, 145–49, vol. 3, 95.

64. Sydney Howard Gay to John Jay, April 22, John Jay Papers, Rare Book and Manuscript Library, Columbia University.

65. Baquaqua, *Autobiography*; North Country Underground Railroad Historical Association, "Lake Champlain"; Papson and Calarco, *Secret Lives of the Underground Railroad*.

66. John Jay to Sydney Howard Gay, 22 April 1848, Sydney Howard Gay Papers, Rare Book and Manuscript Library, Columbia University.

67. *O Cearense*, Ceará, Brazil, 20 September 1847. Portuguese original: "Os receios tinhão (sic) algumos (sic) pessoas, fundadas na letra da tarifa americana, de que o café (sic) do Brasil importado nos Estados-Unidos, em bandeira brasileira, pagaria direitos, achão (sic)-se felizmente desvanecidos. Hontem chegou a noticia (sic) de que o café (sic) importado em New-Yok (sic), na barca brasileira (sic) Lembrança, foi admitido livre de direitos."

68. Souza, *Relatorio da Repartição*, 63–64. Portuguese original: "[N]avios brasileiros continuão a ser equiparados aos navios norte-americanos, e que o café importado debaixo da bandeira nacional continua a ser admittido livre de direitos; tendo os carregamentos do mesmo artigo importados pelas barcas Lembrança, Albini e brigue Pureza sido recebidos como se tivessem sido importados debaixo do pavilhão americano."

69. *Diário do Rio de Janeiro*.

70. *Diário do Rio de Janeiro*, 8 August 1847; and *O Mercantil*, Minas Gerais, 2 August 1847. Portuguese original: "Não admittimos (sic) direito nas leis de paiz(sic) algum (e muito menos nos Estados-Unidos, onde a escravidão é admittida (sic) para privar o súbdito (sic) brasileiro, por esta maneira, da sua propriedade, seja esta de que natureza for, uma vez que esteja reconhecida pelas leis do Brasil, e si (sic) acontecer (o que não esperamos) de que por motivo das leis particulares de um estado que apenas forma parte da união americana, se pretendesse a título de execução (sic) da lei, privar-nos da nossa propriedade, não se venhão (sic) queixar depois os cidadãos americanos, nem venha o seu governo reclamar- nos indemnizações (sic) de prejuízos que se dizem causados aos

seus súbditos (sic), quando por qualquer sentença de nossos tribunaes (sic), e em conformidade das leis do Brasil, seus reclamos forem rejeitados. Não nos venhão com essas odiosas comparações de honradez entre magistrado americano e magistrado brasileiro. A mesma obrigação tem elles (sic) de respeitar as decisões de nossos tribunaes (sic), que de nós exigem a seu respeito. . . . Na realidade parece-nos que estas leis locaes (sic) e parciais (sic) devião (sic) entender-se unicamente com seus próprios cidadãos, e não com os estrangeiros que na melhor boa fé ali se dirigem, a fazer seu negocio (sic), calculando encontrar o acolhimento que lhes garante a lei geral das nações, e não achar-se sujeito à fantasia de 15 a 20 estados separados que formão (sic) um só corpo. Este caso porém é muito sério, não pelas consequências particulares que em si existem, porém pelo exemplo que abriria para embarcações brasileiras que para o futuro fossem aos Estados-Unidos."

71. Portuguese original: "Todos os que conhecem a marinha mercante brasileira, sabem que não é possivel (sic) navegar nossas embarcações sem ter parte da tripulação de escravos. As continuadas levas para a marinha de guerra deixaria muitas vezes nossas embarcações sem uma unica (sic) pessoa a bordo, e por esse motivo é difícil (sic) obter maruja até ao proprio (sic) acto (sic) de matricula (sic)."

72. *Jornal do Commercio*, 15 October 1847. Portuguese original: "Quando recebemos a noticia(sic) de que o nosso café era ali admittido (sic) em embarcações brasileiras no mesmo pé que si fosse em embarcação americana, lisonjeamo- nos que a nossa navegação mercante de longo curso tivesse mais esta aberta para o seu melhoramento, porém com simelhante(sic) obstaculo(sic) não é possivel(sic) aproveitar nos das vantagens que deviamos(sic) esperar."

73. *Diário do Rio de Janeiro*, 23 October 1847 and 3 November 1847.

Chapter Five

1. *Christian Contributor and Free Missionary*, 19 January 1848.

2. Baquaqua, *Autobiography*, 57.

3. Baquaqua, *Autobiography*, 57.

4. Baquaqua, *Autobiography*, 58.

5. Baur, "Faustin Soulouque"; Lachaud, "The Emancipated Empire"; Hoffmann, *Faustin Soulouque d'Haïti*; and MacLeod, "Soulouque Regime in Haiti."

6. See Mathews, *American Baptist Free Mission Society*. The pledge is published in *The American Baptist*, 29 April 1850.

7. See "Appointments of the A. B. Free Mission Society, 1844–1862," *Nineteenth Annual Meeting of the American Baptist Free Mission Society*, Nicetown, Philadelphia, 7–9 June 1862, 23; and *Seventh Annual Report*, 1850, Bristol, NY, 5–7 June 1850.

8. For details of Judd's involvement with the Free Will Baptists, see *Annual Report, Volume 1* (Utica, NY: American Baptist Free Mission Society, 1847); Foss and Matthews, *Facts for Baptist Churches*; Johnson, *Global Introduction to Baptist Churches*; and Anon., "Le Protestantisme en Haiti."

9. Foss and Mathews, *Facts for Baptist Churches*.

10. "Journal of Wm. M. Jones," 28 November 1846, in *Christian Contributor and Free Missionary*, 10 February 1847; and 29 January 1847, in *Christian Contributor and Free Missionary*,

31 March 1847. Also see *Christian Contributor and Free Missionary*, 20 June 1848; William M. Jones is mentioned in the Eighteenth Annual Report of the American Baptist Free Mission Society, 1861, and the Nineteenth Annual Meeting of the American Baptist Free Mission Society, Nicetown, Philadelphia, 7–9 June 1862, p. 23, which includes a list of appointments of the American Baptist Free Mission Society, 1844–62.

11. Baquaqua hired as a cook, see Mrs. Judd to Grosvenor, 24 March 1848, *Christian Contributor and Free Missionary*, 17 May 1848.

12. Judd to Cyrus Grosvenor, 28 October 1847, *Christian Contributor and Free Baptist Missionary* 4, no. 12 (December 22): 1847.

13. N.A.L. Judd to Grosvenor, Port au Prince, Haiti, (8 October 1847), *Christian Contributor and Free Baptist Missionary* 4, no. 47 (19 January 1848).

14. Judd to Grosvenor, Port au Prince, Haiti, 8 October 1847.

15. Lee, *Autobiography*, 322–25.

16. Lee, *Autobiography*, 322–25.

17. Judd to Grosvenor, Port au Prince, Haiti, 28 October 1847.

18. Judd to Grosvenor, Port au Prince, Haiti, 28 October 1847.

19. Judd to Grosvenor, Port au Prince, Haiti, 28 October 1847.

20. See postscript, dated 5 November 1848, in letter of Rev. W. L. Judd, 28 October 1847.

21. "Haitien Mission: W.L. Judd, Visit to Jacmel," in *Christian Contributor and Free Missionary*, 7 March 1849.

22. Baquaqua, *Autobiography*, 58. Mrs. Judd, writing on 8 October, says that he had been taken into the protection of the mission "within a few days": letter of Mrs. N.A.L. Judd, 8 October 1847.

23. Mrs. Judd to Grosvenor, 24 March 1848, *Christian Contributor and Free Missionary*, 17 May 1848.

24. Letter of Mrs. N.A.L. Judd, 8 October 1847.

25. Baquaqua's conversion is described in the letter of Mrs. N.A.L. Judd, 24 March 1848, and also noted in American Baptist Free Mission Society, Fifth Annual Meeting, Utica, New York, 10–11 May 1848. His baptism is described in the letter of the Rev. W. L. Judd, 21 July 1848 (quoted in Foss and Mathews, *Facts for Baptist Churches*, 393; and from there also in the autobiography, pp. 50–51); apparently it took place on Sunday, 16 July. His conversion was reported in the *Sixth Annual Report of the Trustees of the American Baptist Free Mission Society* (Utica, NY, 1849), 17.

26. Letter of Mrs. N.A.L. Judd to Cyrus Grosvenor, 13 November 1848, in *Christian Contributor and Free Missionary*, 27 December 1848.

27. P. T. Young to Grosvenor, 22 September 1847, *Christian Contributor and Free Missionary*, 20 October 1847.

28. Letter of Baquaqua to Cyrus Grosvenor, 14 November 1848.

29. So called because five lakes (Canandaigua, Cayuga, Honeoye, Keuka, and Seneca) in central New York State are long lakes in north/south valleys formed during glacier times that form the shape of five fingers. McGrawville was not on one of the lakes but was on a valley that was parallel to the lakes and whose river draining the valley flowed southward into the Susquehanna River, which entered the Chesapeake Bay at Baltimore.

30. "New York Central College at M'Graw First Admitted Negro," *Cortland Tribune*, 18 August 1849.

31. "Remarks," appended to letter of Mrs. N.A.L. Judd, 13 November 1848, in *Christian Contributor and Free Missionary*, 27 December 1848.

32. For a discussion of Gerrit Smith, see Stauffer, *Black Hearts of Men*, and Dann, *Practical Dreamer*.

33. See Tanner, "Gerrit Smith: An Interpretation"; and Harlow, *Gerrit Smith*. Also see Winks, *Blacks in Canada*, 179–80, 254.

34. Letter to Gerrit Smith, dated Chatham, Canada West, 25 May 1854.

35. Baquaqua, *Autobiography*, 24.

36. Baquaqua, *Autobiography*, 45.

37. Letter of Mrs. N.A.L. Judd, 8 October 1847.

38. Letter of Mrs. N.A.L. Judd, 24 March 1848.

39. Baquaqua, *Autobiography*, 32.

40. Baquaqua, *Autobiography*, 58.

41. Letter of Mrs. N.A.L. Judd, 21 July 1848.

42. Baquaqua, *Autobiography*, 58–59.

43. Letter of Mrs. N.A.L. Judd, 4 December 1849, in *Christian Contributor and Free Missionary*, 3 January 1850. In late 1849, the *Journal of Commerce* (as reported in the *New York Daily Tribune*, 13 December 1849) noted that Emperor Faustin Soulouque had "almost unlimited power for increasing the military," thereby providing confirmation that such fears of conscription were widespread and well founded.

44. Lachaud, "Emancipated Empire," 152.

45. Letter of Mrs. N.A.L. Judd, 28 March 1850, in *Christian Contributor and Free Missionary*, 18 April 1850.

46. Baquaqua, *Autobiography*, 62.

47. American Baptist Free Mission Society, Seventh Annual Meeting, Bristol, Ontario County, New York, 5–7 June 1850.

48. American Baptist Free Mission Society, Seventh Annual Meeting, Bristol, Ontario County, New York, 5–7 June 1850.

49. For a discussion of Abolitionist efforts to raise funds to support their cause, see Quarles, "Sources of Abolitionist Income."

50. The quotation is from "Miscellaneous Scrap Book and McGraw Schools and Central College," McGraw Historical Society. Central College closed its doors in 1861, primarily because its benefactor, Gerrit Smith, refused to provide additional financing unless the college was reorganized, but efforts to appoint suitable candidates to run the institution failed. For a history of the college, see Short, "New York Central College"; Dunn, "Early Academies of Cortland County"; Wright, "Cornell's Three Precursors"; Hanchett, "'Dedicated to Equality.'"

51. Letter of E. C. Lake, 18 February 1850, in *Christian Contributor and Free Missionary*, 7 March 1850.

52. Letter of J. Scott, 22 January 1850, in *Christian Contributor and Free Missionary*, 7 March 1850.

53. Various documents that mention Baquaqua at Central College are on deposit in the New York Central College Collection, Cortland County Historical Society, Cortland, New York, specifically "Labor Lists of Males and Females," for January–June, September, and October 1850; the Commencement Program, 4 July 1850; and the Catalogues of the Officers and Students 1851–52 and 1852–53, which both list him as a student in the Primary De-

partment. Unlike the advanced program, which was organized in three terms, instruction in the Primary Department was given in four sessions of twelve weeks each in the year, with a one-week vacation between terms, the tuition fee being $4 per term. It should be noted that Frederick Douglass addressed commencement on 2 September 1853, although whether Baquaqua was in attendance is not clear. His surviving correspondence suggests that he was not in McGrawville at the time.

54. Kezia King is listed as a teacher in the Primary Department in the *Catalogue of the Officers and Students of New York Central College* for 1851–52 and 1852–53. Her report to the Board of Trustees, Central College, 11 July 1853, is in Miscellaneous Scrapbook & McGraw Schools and Central College, unpublished, vol. 108, Cortland County Historical Society, Cortland, New York.

55. Baquaqua, *Autobiography*, 62–63.

56. For references to the students who attended Central College, see Hanchett, "New York Central College Students," and Hanchett, "After McGrawville"; on the Forten family, see Winch, "'You Know I Am a Man of Business,'" and Nash, *Forging Freedom*.

57. J. E. Ambrose to W. Walker, 27 July 1852, in *The American Baptist*, 5 August 1852.

58. Gerrit Smith Collection, Special Collections, Syracuse University Library, Syracuse, New York.

59. Ninth Annual Meeting, Montrose, Pennsylvania, as reported in *The American Baptist*, 24 June 1852.

60. Letter of Baquaqua to George Whipple, 6 January 1854.

61. *The Evangelist*, Oberlin, Ohio, vol. 12, June 1850.

62. The *Catalogue of Officers and Students* for these years are to be found in the Cortland County Historical Society, Cortland, New York.

63. Baquaqua, *Autobiography*, 63.

64. Letter from Lagrow to Gerrit Smith, 1 August 1852 (Gerrit Smith Collection, Special Collections, Syracuse University Library, Syracuse, New York).

65. Letters of Baquaqua to Warham Walker [?], 28 September 1850, 21 February 1851; and to George Whipple, 26 October 1853. The last letter states that he had been friendly with a white girl who was also a member of the Freetown Baptist Church, since "about three years ago"—that is, since autumn 1850, around the time of his first letter from Freetown Corners.

66. *The American Baptist*, 11 September 1851.

67. American Baptist Free Mission Society, Ninth Annual Meeting, Montrose, Pennsylvania, 2–4 June 1852.

68. American Baptist Free Mission Society, Seventh Annual Meeting, Bristol, New York, 5–7 June 1850.

69. Baquaqua, *Autobiography*, 62.

70. American Baptist Free Mission Society, Tenth Annual Meeting, Utica, NY, 1–2 June 1853.

71. Letter of A. L. Post, July 1853, in *The American Baptist*, 28 July 1853.

72. Baquaqua, *Autobiography*, 62.

73. Baquaqua, *Autobiography*, 63.

74. Ninth Annual Meeting of the A.B.F.M. Society, at Montrose, Pennsylvania, in *The American Baptist*, Utica, NY, 24 June 1852.

75. Letter of Baquaqua to George Whipple, 8 October 1853.

76. This decision is reported retrospectively in American Baptist Free Mission Society, Eleventh Annual Meeting, Albany, NY, 7–8 June 1854.

77. Letter of A. L. Post, July 1853, in *The American Baptist*, 28 July 1853; *Commemorative Biographical Record of Northeastern Pennsylvania, including the counties of Susquehanna, Wayne, Pike, and Monroe* (Chicago: J. H. Beers, 1900), 266.

78. Letters of Baquaqua to George Whipple, 10 August 1853 (from Brooklyn, PA), 14 September 1853 (from Syracuse); to unnamed recipient, 18 September 1853 and to George Whipple, 25 September 1853 (both from New Berlin); and to George Whipple, 8 October 1853 (from McGrawville).

79. Eleventh Annual Report of the American Baptist Free Mission Society, 7–8 June 1854, in *The American Baptist*, Utica, NY, 20 July 1854.

80. Letter to George Whipple [?], 10 August 1853, Brooklyn, PA.

81. Letter to George Whipple [?], 10 August 1853, Brooklyn, PA.

82. Baquaqua, *Autobiography*, 63.

83. For Allen's story, see Allen, *American Prejudice*; Allen, *A Short Personal Narrative*; Elbert, "Inter-Racial Love Story"; and Allen's letters in Woodson, *Mind of the Negro*, 282–90. Various letters and speeches of Allen and his wife are also published in Ripley, *Black Abolitionist Papers. Volume I*, 355–82; 423–26, 453–56. For an analysis, see Mabee, *Black Education*, 85–92. Also see Hanchett, "New York Central College and Its Three Black Professors." Allan Austin confuses Mary King, the woman whom Prof. Allen married, and Baquaqua's teacher, Miss Kezia King; see *Transatlantic Stories*, 167.

84. Allen, *American Prejudice*, 2, 86.

85. For a sample of press coverage, see the *Syracuse Star*, 1 February 1854; *Oswego Daily Times*, 3 February 1854; both cited in Allen, *American Prejudice*, 53–56, 71–74.

86. Syracuse *Daily Standard*, 19 April 1851; also included in *New York Central College 1849–1860*, ed. Marlene K. Parks, vol. 2, part 1, p. 1 (McGrawville, New York: CreateSpace Independent Publishing Platform,).

87. "Wm. G. Allen," *The Liberator*, 30 August 1850, 4.

88. "Meetings of the Friends of Equal School Rights," *The Liberator*, 9 November 1849, 4; *The North Star*, 6 July 1849.

89. Baquaqua to George Whipple, McGrawville, 26 October 1853.

90. See Baquaqua's letter to George Whipple, 26 October 1853.

91. Letters of Baquaqua to Whipple, 10 August and 8 October 1853.

92. Letter of Baquaqua to Whipple, 26 October 1853.

93. Baquaqua, *Autobiography*, 64.

94. Letters of Baquaqua to Whipple, 6 and 22 January 1854.

95. Baquaqua, *Autobiography*, 64.

96. For various accounts of individuals who arrived in Canada, especially Canada West, see Still, *The Underground Railroad*. Still was a successful merchant in Philadelphia, running a coal business, and head of the Vigilance Committee in Philadelphia. He was born free in New Jersey, but his parents had been enslaved.

97. Baquaqua, *Autobiography*, 64.

98. Winks, *Blacks in Canada*, 244–71.

99. Letter of Baquaqua to Gerrit Smith, 25 May 1854. At the time, there were approximately 800 Blacks living in Chatham, and perhaps another 1,200 or more living in Buxton

and other neighboring communities; see Drew, *North-Side View of Slavery*, 234, 291; Winks, *Blacks in Canada*, 245; and Wayne, "Black Population of Canada West," 73. Also see Farrell, "History of the Negro Community."

100. *Christian Contributor and Free Missionary*, 20 June 1849; also see the *Kent Advertiser*, 4 July 1850.

101. For the Free Mission in Canada West, see American Baptist Free Mission Society, Annual Reports; and Winks, *Blacks in Canada*, 231, 238. For Gerrit Smith's influence in Canada West, see Winks, *Blacks in Canada*, 179–80, 254.

102. On Smith's land grants to Blacks, see Tanner, "Gerrit Smith," 29–30.

103. Letter of Baquaqua to Gerrit Smith, 4 July 1854.

104. *Cleveland Daily Herald*, vol. XX, Issue 195, 23 August 1854.

105. *Proceedings of the National Emigration Convention of Colored People*, Cleveland, 24–26 August 1854 (Pittsburgh: A. A. Anderson, 1854).

106. Sherman, "James M. Whitfield," 173, and Bell, "Introduction," 6, 11.

107. Delany, *Official Report of the Niger Valley*.

108. Kezia King to sisters, 23 October 1854.

109. Fisher, *Short History*, 73–74.

Chapter Six

1. Baquaqua, *Autobiography*, 33, 40.

2. See Ciavolella, "La biographie de Mahommah Baquaqua."

3. For a discussion of "freedom" narratives and the distinction of such accounts from "slave" narratives, see Lovejoy, "Freedom Narratives." Also see the Freedom Narratives website, https://www.freedomnarratives.org. For the genre "slave narratives," see "North American Slave Narratives," in Documenting the American South, https://www.docsouth.unc.edu/neh.

4. There are numerous studies of the Middle Passage, but see Rediker, *Slave Ship*.

5. Whitfield, *America, and Other Poems*, 61–63. Also see Levine and Wilson, *Works of James M. Whitfield*; Sherman, "James M. Whitfield," 173. Also see Bell, "Introduction," 6, 11.

6. Austin, *African Muslims Sourcebook*, 643–44.

7. The pamphlet was edited by Rev. Mathew T. Newsome, who was also African American.

8. Austin, *African Muslims Sourcebook*, 645n.

9. Originally published in Whitfield, *America, and Other Poems*, 61–63. For Whitfield's contribution to African American literature, see Sherman, "James M. Whitfield," 173, and Bell, "Introduction," 6, 11.

10. *Proceedings of the National Emigration Convention of Colored People*, Cleveland, 24–26 August 1854 (Pittsburgh: A. A. Anderson, 1854).

11. Delany, *Official Report*.

12. Griffith, *African Dream*.

13. Delany, *Official Report*.

14. Ciavolella, *Biographie de Baquaqua*, first attempted to determine which portions of the autobiography can be identified with Baquaqua and which comments must have been the comments of Samuel Moore, who is credited on the cover as being Baquaqua's editor.

15. There is no reference to Samuel Moore in the *Sunderland Times*. See G. Barnes, Proprietor, "Prospectus of the Sunderland Times, and North of England Shipping and Mercantile Gazette," *Newcastle Courant*, 22 August 1851, p. 2.

16. Letter of 17 January 1854.

17. For Moore's abolitionist activities, see the account of the Anti-Slavery Convention at Ypsilanti, as reported in the *Anti-Slavery Bugle*, 17 January 1854 and Moore's response to a letter from Jerid Comstock of the Friends Meeting congregation of Michigan restricting Quaker involvement in abolition. Also see Moore's letter addressed to "Friends in Michigan," dated 25 March 1854, Ypsilanti, in the *Bugle*. Moore was in fact an agent for the *Bugle* in Michigan, as noted in the issue of 18 November 1854. Moore was subjected to "Quaker Excommunication," according to the *Bugle*, 24 February 1855.

18. Colman, *Reminiscences*, 28.

19. Letters of 8 October 1853 and 20 January 1854, McGrawville.

20. Pomeroy, *Genealogy of the Pomeroy Family*, 453–54; Palmer, *Early Days in Detroit*, 194–97.

21. Newsome, *Call for a National Emigration Convention*.

22. For Austin's identification, see *African Muslims Sourcebook*, 590, 645n; also see Law and Lovejoy, *Baquaqua*, 7–8.

23. Letter of Baquaqua to Gerrit Smith, 4 July 1854.

24. The copy in the Detroit Public Library was brought to our attention by Silvia Hunold Lara. Another copy is in the Library of Congress.

25. Austin, *Transatlantic Stories*, 160–61.

26. Austin, *Transatlantic Stories*, 160.

27. *The American Baptist*, 2 November 1854.

28. Baquaqua, *Autobiography*, 5.

29. Foss and Mathews, *Facts for Baptist Churches*.

30. Baquaqua, *Autobiography*, 34.

31. Baquaqua, *Autobiography*, 65.

32. Letter to Gerrit Smith, Detroit, 4 July 1854.

33. See Law and Lovejoy, *Biography*, 136.

34. Foss and Mathews, *Facts for Baptist Churches*, 392–93 (most of which is reproduced in the *Autobiography*, 59–60); also reprinted by Austin, *African Muslims Sourcebook*, 638–39.

35. See ABFMS, 11th Annual Meeting, Albany, New York, 7–8 June 1854; for the administrative link between the Free Mission in Detroit and Canada West, see ABFMS, Ninth Annual Meeting, Montrose, Pennsylvania, 2–4 June 1852.

36. Letters of Mrs. N.A.L. Judd to Cyrus Grosvenor, 8 October 1847 and 21 July 1848, in *Christian Contributor and Free Missionary*, 19 January and 30 August 1848.

37. Letter of Mrs. N.A.L. Judd to Cyrus Grosvenor, 24 March 1848, in *Christian Contributor and Free Missionary*, 17 May 1848.

38. Letter of J. Scott, McGrawville, 22 January 1850, in *Christian Contributor and Free Missionary*, 7 March 1850.

39. Letter of A.L.P [Albert L. Post], Montrose, Pennsylvania, July 1853, in *The American Baptist*, 28 July 1853.

40. Letter of Mrs. N.A.L. Judd, 8 October 1847. In the *Biography* (p. 57), Baquaqua actually says that Jones spoke Spanish, rather than Portuguese, implying a further linguistic obstacle.

41. Letter of Rev. W. L. Judd to Cyrus Grosvenor, 28 October 1847, in *Christian Contributor and Free Missionary*, 22 December 1847.

42. Samuel Moore to Lewis Tappan, 16 May 1853.

43. Lovejoy, "Biography as Source Material."

44. Chapman, *Steal Away.*

45. Hogg, *Atlantic Slave Trade*; Pescatello, *African in Latin America*, 186–94; Conrad, *Children of God's Fire*, 23–29.

46. Austin, *African Muslims Sourcebook*, 585–654; Conrad, *Children of God's Fire*, xix, 23–29; Lara, "Biografia de Mahommah G. Baquaqua"; Krueger, "Milhões de Vozes. Also see "Baquaqua Project," https://www.baquaqua.org/Public/.

46. Law and Lovejoy, *Biography of Baquaqua.*

47. See, for example, Person, "Brève note"; "Note sur les Nyantruku"; "Le système des classes"; "Les grandes compagnies"; "Tradition orale et chronologie"; and "*La dynastie de Tyilixa (Djougou)."*

48. See, for example, Neto, *Biografia de Mahommah Gardo Baquaqua*; Araujo, *Biography of Mahommah Gardo Baquaqua*; and in Portuguese as *Biografia de Mahommah Gardo Baquaqua*, where Araujo attributes the text to Samuel Moore.

49. Krueger, *Mahommah Gardo Baquaqua.*

50. Law, "Individualising the Atlantic Slave Trade"; Lovejoy, "Identidade e a Miragem da Ethnicidade"; Bezerra, "Trajectory of Mahomman Gardo Baquaqua in Brazil"; Véras, "Slavery and Freedom Narrative"; and Bicknell, "Atlantic Abolition in the Borderlands."

51. Brown, *Life of Henry Box Brown*; and Chater, *Henry Box Brown.*

Chapter Seven

1. Letter of Rev. W. L. Judd, 28 October 1847.

2. Letters of Mrs. N.A.L. Judd, 24 March & 21 July 1848; Rev. W. L. Judd, 21 July 1848; Rev. W. L. Judd, 21 July 1848.

3. Baquaqua, *Autobiography*, 5.

4. Letter of Baquaqua to Cyrus Grosvenor 14 November 1848. For a discussion of emigrationist objectives, see Bell, *Search for a Place.*

5. Baquaqua, *Autobiography*, 59.

6. American Baptist Free Mission Society, Seventh Annual Meeting, Bristol, New York, 5–7 June 1850.

7. Letter of Baquaqua to W. Walker [?], 21 February 1851.

8. This speech is referred to retrospectively in the report of the following year's meeting: ABFMS, Tenth Annual Meeting, Utica, New York, 1–2 June 1853.

9. Seventh Annual Report of the Board of Trustees of the American Baptist Free Mission Society, 5 June 1850, in *The American Baptist*, Utica, 11 July 1850.

10. Letter from Mahommah, Freetown Corners, 21 February 1851, in *The American Baptist*, Utica, 6 March 1851.

11. Semi-Annual Meeting of the American Baptist Free Mission Society, Peterboro, 4–5 September 1851, in *The American Baptist*, Utica, 11 September 1851.

12. Ninth Annual Meeting of the A.B.F.M. Society, at Montrose, Pennsylvania, in *The American Baptist*, Utica, 24 June 1852.

13. Letter to George Whipple [?], 10 August 1853, Brooklyn, Pennsylvania.

14. *The Liverpool Mercury and Double Supplement*, 5 March 1855, p. 4.

15. *The Liverpool Mercury and Double Supplement*, 5 March 1855, p. 4.

16. Eleventh Annual Report of the American Baptist Free Mission Society, 7–8 June 1854, in *The American Baptist*, Utica, 20 July 1854.

17. Anon., *Commemorative Biographical Record*, 266.

18. For Rev. Albert L. Post, see Merriam, *History of American Baptist Missions*, 92.

19. Letter of A. L. Post, July 1853, in *The American Baptist*, 28 July 1853.

20. American Baptist Free Mission Society, Ninth Annual Meeting, Montrose, Pennsylvania, 2–4 June 1852; also reported in *The American Baptist*, 24 June 1852.

21. *The American Baptist*, 11 September 1851; *Christian Contributor and Free Missionary*, 20 June 1849; and the *Kent Advertiser*, 4 July 1850.

22. Newman's letter of 4 January 1853, in *The American Baptist*, 20 January 1853.

23. American Baptist Free Mission Society, Tenth Annual Meeting, Utica, New York, 1–2 June 1853; *The American Baptist*, 28 July 1853.

24. American Baptist Free Mission Society, Eleventh Annual Meeting, Albany, New York, 7–8 June 1854.

25. Baquaqua to George Whipple, 8 October 1853.

26. Rediker, *Amistad Rebellion*; Lawrance, *Amistad's Orphan*; Yannielli, *Mendi Mission*.

27. Thompson, *Thompson in Africa* and *The Palm Land*. Also see Rice, "Anti-Slavery Mission"; Yannielli, "George Thompson among the Africans."

28. Whipple, "Illustrated History of the Whipple Family."

29. Wyatt-Brown, *Lewis Tappan and the Evangelical War*.

30. Letter to George Whipple, New Berlin, 25 September 1853.

31. Letter to George Whipple, McGrawville, 26 October 1853.

32. Letter of Baquaqua to George Whipple, 10 August 1853. Abner Bates to George Whipple, Syracuse, 7 October 1853, Ms 81341 (American Missionary Association Archives, Amistad Research Center, Tulane University). Also see Bates to Whipple, 15 November 1853. Both letters are reproduced in Law and Lovejoy, *Biography*, Appendix 4.

33. Baquaqua to Whipple, 10 August 1853; and Bates to Whipple, Syracuse, 7 October 1853.

34. Fyfe, *History of Sierra Leone*, 222–23, 246, 285.

35. Letter of Baquaqua to George Whipple, 25 September 1853. Baquaqua's handwriting is not clear in this letter, and he could have written "sisters" rather than "sister"; in the autobiography (p. 24), he reported that he had three sisters. Abner Bates, Baquaqua's friend in Syracuse, thought that Baquaqua should return to Africa with the Mendi Mission, and advised Whipple accordingly. Bates talked with Professor Campbell, one of the teachers at Central College, who concurred that Baquaqua was fit to go. Whether or not efforts to retrieve the funds that Baquaqua had raised while lecturing were successful is not clear. See Bates to Whipple, 7 October 1853 and 15 November 1853. Bates was a dealer in hides, oil, and leather, with a shop at No. 17, East Water Street, opposite the post office (No. 81535, AMA Archives).

36. Papson and Calarco, *Secret Lives of the Underground Railroad*; and Rice, "Anti-Slavery Mission."

37. Letters of Baquaqua to George Whipple, 10 August & 14 September 1853, 6 January 1854.

38. Letters of Baquaqua to George Whipple, 10 August & 8 October 1853.

39. American Baptist Free Mission Society, Eleventh Annual Meeting, Albany, New York, 7–8 June 1854.

40. Letter of Baquaqua to Gerrit Smith (text of letter in Law and Lovejoy, *Biography of Baquaqua*, Appendix 3, no. 14).

41. *The American Baptist*, 2 November 1854 (text of review in Law and Lovejoy, *Biography of Baquaqua*, Appendix 5).

42. Vassa, *Life of Olaudah Equiano*. For a discussion, see Lovejoy, "Olaudah Equiano"

43. For the cost of second-class passage from New York to Liverpool, see *Liverpool Mercury and Double Supplement*, 2 March 1855, 4.

44. American Baptist Free Mission Society, Twelfth Annual Meeting, New York City, 9 May 1855. The board reported that there had been further correspondence with "different brethren, on the question of their becoming, at some future time, missionaries to Africa, but nothing has been done with a view to present action."

45. Mathews had been involved in the abortive Southern Mission of the ABFMS, retreating to England when conditions became unbearable in Kentucky in 1850; Mathews, *Autobiography of the Rev. E. Mathews*, 1–28; and Blackett, "William G. Allen." Also see *The American Baptist*, 20 October 1853.

46. Mathews's appointment as the Society's agent in Britain had been renewed on an annual basis. At its 28 December 1854 meeting, the Board of Society "invited" Mathews "to return to this country early in the Spring," which means that it was possible for Baquaqua to have met him in England in early 1855; see the report of the ABFMS, Twelfth Annual Meeting, New York City, 9 May 1855.

47. Baquaqua to Whipple, 14 September 1853, American Missionary Association Archives, Amistad Research Center.

48. Webley was based at Jacmel in southern Haiti and met Baquaqua in early November 1847, shortly after the latter's installation in the Judd household, when he suggested that, if the American Baptist Free Mission Society could not send Baquaqua as a missionary to Africa, the English Baptists might do so; see postscript, dated 5 November 1848, to letter of Rev. W. L. Judd, 28 October 1847. Baquaqua also accompanied Judd on a visit to Webley at Jacmel in 1849; see "Haitien Mission: W.L. Judd, Visit to Jacmel," in *Christian Contributor and Free Missionary*, 7 March 1849.

49. There is no reference to Baquaqua in Stanley, *History of the Baptist Missionary Society*.

50. Unfortunately, the company's records for the relevant years do not seem to have survived, although such logs do exist for later years.

51. American Baptist Free Mission Society, Thirteenth Annual Meeting, Norristown, Pennsylvania, 21–22 May 1856.

52. American Baptist Free Mission Society, Thirteenth Annual Meeting, Norristown, Pennsylvania, 21–22 May 1856.

53. Anon., *Ladies Society*.

54. Anon., *Ladies Society*, 6–7.

55. Anon., *Ladies Society*, 6–7.

56. *New York Free Mission Record*, 13 February 1857, which reports the meeting of the Board of the American Baptist Free Mission Society. We wish to thank Silvia Lara for this reference.

57. Letter of Mrs. N.A.L. Judd, 21 July 1848.

58. Letter of E. C. Lake, 18 February 1850, in *Christian Contributor and Free Missionary*, 7 March 1850. On 14 March 1850, the *Cortland County Express* of McGrawville noted that Baquaqua, who was referred to as "Mahoni" (i.e., Mahommah), spoke in "the Arabic" at public functions. Our thanks to Anita Wright for this reference.

59. *The American Baptist*, 18 July 1850.

60. Gomez, *Black Crescent*, and Diouf, *Servants of Allah*.

61. He first went to Liverpool in 1849, apparently to make arrangements in case he decided to move there; *National Anti-Slavery Standard*, 12 April 1849.

62. *National Anti-Slavery Standard*, 22 July 1852; 2 September 1852.

63. *National Anti-Slavery Standard*, 6 August 1853. Powell wrote a number of letters to the *Anti-Slavery Standard*.

64. *National Anti-Slavery Standard*, 6 August 1853.

65. Green, "Two Liverpool Families."

66. Foner, "William P. Powell," 88–111.

67. Anon., *Ladies Society*, 6. The Society was "instituted on the 4th of November, 1853, for the special object of extending temporary aid to fugitive Slaves in England, and the report is issued *for private circulation only*, amongst the subscribers." The Society noted that for "the fugitives from Slavery who reach England, it is extremely difficult, if not impossible, for them to procure employment here, in consequence of their being unaccustomed, generally, to other than the labour peculiar to cotton and sugar plantations. As they reach England in the most destitute condition, it occurred to a few ladies to form a Committee, for the purpose of raising a fund to supply these unfortunate persons with food, lodging, and other necessaries; and thus promote their procuring speedy employment on board ship, or passages to one or other of the colonies, where their labour is in request." Baquaqua was one of eight individuals who were singled out for further discussion.

68. Anon., *Ladies Society*, 6.

69. Tomek and Hetrick, *New Directions*; Seeley, "Beyond the American Colonization Society"; Staudenraus, *African Colonization Movement*; Shick, *Behold the Promised Land*.

70. Rediker, *Amistad Rebellion*; Lawrance, *Amistad's Orphans*; Yannielli, *Mendi Mission*; Yannielli, "George Thompson among the Africans"; Thompson, *The Palm Land*; Thompson, *Thompson in Africa*.

71. Friedman, "Confidence and Pertinacity."

72. Baquaqua to George Whipple, McGrawville, 8 October 1853.

73. McClish, "African Missionary Narrative"; Blackett, "Martin R. Delany and Robert Campbell"; Rosenfeld, "Martin Robison Delany"; Delany, *Condition, Elevation, Emigration*.

74. *Proceedings of the National Emigration Convention of Colored People*, Cleveland, 24–26 August 1854 (Pittsburgh: A.A. Anderson, 1854); *Cleveland Daily Herald*, 23 August 1854.

75. Powell, "Underground Railroad."

76. Laird and Oldfield, *Expedition into the Interior of Africa*.

77. "The African Steam Ship Company from 1852 to 1868," http://www.historic-shipping.co.uk/african/africanindex.html, accessed 30 December 2022. Davies, *Trade Makers*; Goldsmith, "River Niger."

78. *The African Repository* 3, No. 11 (November 1863), 387.

79. Jonathan W. White, *A House Built by Slaves: African American Visitors to the Lincoln White House* (Lanham: Rowman & Littlefield, 2022); *The African Repository* 39, no. 11 (November 1863): 350–51; *The Life of William J. Brown of Providence, R.I.* (Nashville, TN: Fisk University, 1883), 204.

80. Miles Mark Fisher, *A Short History of the Baptist Denomination* (Nashville, TN: Sunday School Publishing Board, 1933), 73–74; and *The African Repository* 39, no. 11 (November 1863): 349–51.

81. *The American Baptist*, March 1863.

82. "The Rev. Chauncey Leonard," *The African Repository* (1863), 350.

83. *The African Repository* (1863), 337.

84. For an example of such a passport in Arabic, see Consul Campbell, 4 February 1859, CO 2/28. We wish to thank Kristin Mann for drawing attention to the British policy of issuing passports to returning Muslims from Brazil.

85. We wish to thank Ibrahim Kankara, Department of History, Bayero University, for attempting to discover if anything is remembered about Baquaqua's return in the Wangarawa wards in Katsina City.

86. Castillo, "Exodus of 1835"; Castillo, "Nineteenth-Century Brazilian Returnee Movement."

Conclusion

1. Verger, *Flux et Reflux*. Soares, *Rotas Atlânticas*; Adamu, *Hausa Factor*; Lovejoy, *Caravans of Kola*; Lovejoy, *Ecology and Ethnography*.

2. Lovejoy, "Identidade e a miragem."

3. See Mathews, *Autobiography of the Rev. E. Mathews*, where he lists his lengthy curriculum vitae of letters to newspapers, lectures, and publications.

4. Fourah Bay derives its name from the location where Fula merchants from the interior established a settlement known as Fula Town. A comparison with the Kru settlement at Kru Town on Kru Bay in Freetown suggests the allegedly ethnic designations for different parts of Freetown, including Fourah and Fula are to be equated, the phonemes "r" and "l" often gliding into each other. Reis, Gomes, and Carvalho (in *The Story of Rufino*) suggest the name "fourah" comes from the Hausa word, *fura*, which is the name for the balls of millet dough that are boiled and served with sour milk, often in the afternoon. This speculation clearly has no basis in fact; the settlement, which at the time was on the immediate outskirts of downtown Freetown on the road to Kissi was a Fula settlement, not Hausa. Fula was the local name for Fulbe and in this context referred to merchants, cattle herders, and others from Fuuta Jalon, just as Fulani was the Hausa name for Fulbe far to the east. The various terms for Fulbe can be confusing.

Appendix A

1. Amasa J. Parker, *Reports of Decisions in Criminal Cases made at Term, at Chambers and in the Courts of Oyer and Terminer of the State of New York* (New York: Banks & Brothers, Law Publishers, 1860).

2. Parker, *Reports of Decisions in Criminal Cases*, 130–34.

3. Parker, *Reports of Decisions in Criminal Cases*, 134.

4. Samuel Owen, ed., *New York Legal Observer, Containing Reports of Cases*, vol. 5 (New York, Office Legal Observer, 1847), 299. Also see the case of George Kirk, a fugitive slave, heard before the Hon. J. W. Edmonds, circuit judge, and the argument of John Jay, counsel for Kirk, Supplement to the *New York Legal Observer*.

5. "The Brazilian Slaves," *National Anti-Slavery Standard*, 27 January 1848.

Glossary

1. According to informants in Djougou.

2. According to informants, *kofa* designates the bush beyond the town limits in Dendi, but it is not in Zima, *Lexique Dendi*. The word for ward in Dendi is *frani*, and the word for gate, *fùù mèè*.

3. Perhaps a corruption of Dendi *káá* (take away, remove).

4. The term probably derives from *lokaci*, which in Hausa and the Dendi languages means "time" or "duration," while *afɔ* means "one" (elsewhere transcribed by Moore as "a-faw").

Bibliography

Archives

American Baptist Samuel Colgate Historical Library, Rochester, NY
  Reports of the Annual Meetings of the American Baptist Free Mission Society
American Missionary Association Archives, Amistad Research Center, Tulane University
Archives d'Outre Mer, Aix-en-Provence
  Marcel Feuille, Monographie du cercle de Djougou, 1918, FR CAOM 18 APOM 1 à 9
Arquivo Histórico Diplomático do Itamaraty, Rio de Janeiro
Arquivo Histórico do Rio Grande do Sul
  Carta de Liberdade de Teresa, filha de Rufina, Data de Concessão: 26-03-1866
  Data de registro: 03-04-1866, Livro 24, página 28
  Rio Grande, 2º, Tabelionato, Transmissão e Notas, Livro 21, fls 73.a
Bibliothèque de Centre du Recherches Africaines, Paris
  Fonds Person, Yves Person, "Zugu, ville musulmane"
Chatham-Kent Museum, Chatham, Ontario
Columbia University Libraries, Manuscript Collections
  John Jay Papers
  Sydney Howard Gay Papers
Cortland County Historical Society, Cortland, NY
  Miscellaneous Scrapbook & McGraw Schools and Central College, vol. 108
  New York Central College Collection
Detroit Public Library
  Burton Historical Collection
Lamont Memorial Free Library, McGraw, NY
  Cortland County Sesquicentennial, 1958
  Facts, Fotos and Folklore of McGraw, 1976
  McGraw, N.Y. Illustrated
  McGrawville Centennial, 1969
North Country Underground Railroad Historical Association
Schomburg Center for Foundations, New York Public Library
Syracuse University Library, Special Collections, Syracuse, NY
  Gerrit Smith Papers
The National Archives, UK
  FO 84/886, Slave Trade Correspondence, Journal of Louis Frazer, 30 July 1851
  FO 97/434, Niger Expeditions, No. 19, Baikie to Lord Russell, 22 March 1862
University of Massachusetts Amherst Libraries, Special Collections and University Archives
  Hudson Family Papers, 1807–1963
Wellcome Institute, London
  Lander Diary, Books 1–3 and Richard Lander Text, Acc. 56076 MS 3159

Newspapers

Acton Free Press (Acton, ON)
American Baptist
Anti-Slavery Bugle (New Lisbon, OH)
Boston Cultivator
Christian Contributor and Free Missionary
Church Missionary Gleaner
Church Missionary Intelligencer
Cleveland Daily Herald
Cortland County Express
Cortland Standard
Cortland Tribune
Detroit Tribune
Diário do Pernambuco
Diário do Rio de Janeiro
Evangelist (Oberlin, OH)
Freedom's Journal
Jornal do Commercio
Kent Advertiser
Liberator

Liverpool Mercury
National Anti-Slavery Standard
Newcastle Courant
New York Daily Tribune
New York Evening Express
New York Express
New York Herald
New York Independent
North Star
O Cearense (Ceará, Brazil)
O Mercantil (Minas Gerais)
Oswego Daily Times
Preston and Lancashire (Preston, UK)
Provincial Freeman
San Francisco Elevator
Signal of Liberty (Ann Arbor, MI)
Springfield Gazette
Syracuse Star
Voice of the Fugitive

Correspondence of Mahommah Gardo Baquaqua (1848–54)

Baquaqua to C. P. Grosvenor, Port-au-Prince, Haiti, 14 November 1848, *The American Baptist*, Utica, NY, October 10, 1850.

Baquaqua to Hepburn, Port-au-Prince, Haiti, undated [November 1848], *The American Baptist*, Utica, NY, March 6, 1851.

Baquaqua to Cushman, McGrawville, NY, 18 May 1850, *The Oberlin Evangelist*, 18 May 1850.

Baquaqua to Warham Walker [?], Freetown Corners, NY, 28 September 1850, *The American Baptist*, Utica, NY October 10, 1850.

Baquaqua to Walker [?], Freetown Corners, NY, 21 February 1851, *The American Baptist*, Utica, NY, March 6, 1851.

Baquaqua to George Whipple, Brooklyn, PA, 10 August 1853, No. 81228, American Missionary Association Archives, Amistad Research Center, Tulane University.

Baquaqua to Whipple, Syracuse, NY, 14 September 1853, No. 81296, American Missionary Association Archives, Amistad Research Center, Tulane University.

Baquaqua to unnamed recipient, New Berlin, NY, 18 September 1853, No. 81308, American Missionary Association Archives, Amistad Research Center, Tulane University.

Baquaqua to Whipple [?], New Berlin, NY, 25 September 1853, No. 81322, American Missionary Association Archives, Amistad Research Center, Tulane University.

Baquaqua to Whipple, McGrawville, NY, 8 October 1853 No. 81343, American Missionary Association Archives, Amistad Research Center, Tulane University.

Baquaqua to Bro, Freetown Corners, 14 October 1853, Letter F1–6645, Sierra Leone Box 201, American Missionary Association Archives, Amistad Research Center, Tulane University.

Baquaqua to Whipple [?], McGrawville, NY, 26 October 1853, No. 81362, American Missionary Association Archives, Amistad Research Center, Tulane University.

Baquaqua to Whipple [?], McGrawville, NY, 6 January 1854, No. 81457, American Missionary Association Archives, Amistad Research Center, Tulane University.

Baquaqua to Whipple [?], McGrawville, NY, 22 January 1854 No. 81449, American Missionary Association Archives, Amistad Research Center, Tulane University.

Baquaqua to Gerrit Smith, Chatham, Canada West, 25 May 1854; Gerrit Smith Papers, Syracuse University.

Baquaqua to Gerrit Smith, Detroit, MI, 4 July 1854, Gerrit Smith Papers, Syracuse University.

Unpublished Theses and Papers

'Abd al-Rahman al-Baghdadi. *Tasliyat al-gharib: The Foreigner's Amusement by Wonderful Things*. Translated by Yacine Daddi Addoun, with the assistance of Reneé Soulodre-La France.

Bako, Nassirou Arifari. "La question du peuplement dendi dans la partie septentrionale de la République du Bénin: Le cas du Borgou." Mémoire de maîtrise, Université Nationale du Bénin, 1989.

Beacham, Charles G., Jr. "The Phonology and Morphology of Yom." PhD thesis, Hartford Seminar Foundation, 1968.

Berberich, Charles William. "A Locational Analysis of Trade Routes of the Northeast Asante Frontier Network in the Nineteenth Century." PhD thesis, Northwestern University, 1974.

Bicknell, Alexandra. "Atlantic Abolition in the Borderlands: The Interesting Narrative of Mahommah Gardo Baquaqua." Undergraduate thesis, Western Michigan University, 2020.

Brégand, Denise. "Anthropologie historique et politique du Borgou; Wangara et Wasangari." Thèse de Doctorat Nouveau Régime, Université de Paris 8, 1997.

Cavalheiro, Daniela Carvalho. "Da Liberdade para a Emancipação: Trabalho, Gênero e Identidades de Africanas Livres no Rio de Janeiro Oitocentista." PhD thesis, Universidade Estadual de Campinas, 2020.

Columbia University and Slavery. "John Jay II: Columbia Abolitionist." Accessed 11 October 2024. chrome-extension://efaidnbmnnnibpcajpcglclefindmkaj/https://columbiaandslavery.columbia.edu/content/dam/cuandslavery/about/Eric-Foner-Preliminary-Report.pdf.

Costa e Silva, Alberto da. "Buying and selling Korans in nineteenth century Rio de Janeiro." Paper presented at the conference Rethinking the African Diaspora: The Making of a Black Atlantic World in the Bight of Benin and Brazil, Emory University, Atlanta, 1998.

Daaku, K. Y. *Oral Traditions of Gonja*. Institute of African Studies, University of Ghana, 1969.

Debourou, Djibril Mama. "Commerçants et chefs dans l'ancien Borgu (des origines à 1936)." Thèse de Doctorat du 3ᵉ cycle, Université de Paris I, 1979.

Farrell, John Kevin Anthony. "The History of the Negro Community in Chatham, Ontario." PhD thesis, University of Ottawa, 1955.

Green, Jeffrey. "Two Liverpool Families: The Christians and the Powells." Presented at *What's Happening in Black British History? II* at the Leggate Theatre, Victoria Gallery and Museum, University of Liverpool, 19 February 2015.

Guimarães, Thamires. "A cidade do feitiço: Perseguição e resistência na Belle Époque Carioca. Dissertação de Mestrado em Educação, Cultura e Comunicações." PhD thesis, Universidade do Estado do Rio de Janeiro, 2020.

Hanchett, Catherine M. "After McGrawville: The Later Careers of Some African American Students from New York Central College." Paper presented before the Cortland County Historical Society, 26 February 1992.

———. "'Dedicated to Equality and Brotherhood': New York Central College, C.P. Grosvenor, and Gerrit Smith." Manuscript, Madison County Historical Society, Oneida, NY, 16 February 1989.

———. "New York Central College and Its Three Black Professors, 1849–1857." Paper presented at the conference A Heritage Uncovered: The Black Experience in New York State, Elmira, NY, 22 April 1989.

———. "New York Central College Students." Manuscript, New York Central College Collection, Cortland County Historical Society, Cortland, NY.

Haas, Astrid. "Black, Muslim, Brazilian, Slave: Mahommah Gardo Baquaqua's Interesting Narrative and Its Challenges to Latinidad and to the Slave Narrative in the 21st Century." 36th International Congress of the Latin American Studies Association, Barcelona, Spain, 26 May 2018.

Idris, Musa Baba. "The Role of the Wangara in the Formation of the Trading Diaspora in Borgu." Paper presented at the Conference on Manding Studies, SOAS, London, 1972.

Lachaud, Emmanuel. "The Emancipated Empire: Faustin I Soulouque and the Origins of the Second Haitian Empire, 1847–1859." PhD thesis, Yale University, 2021.

Lovejoy, Paul E. "Slavery and Memory in an Islamic Society: Whose Audience? Which Audience?" Paper presented at the conference Historians and Their Audiences: Mobilizing History for the Millennium, York University, Toronto, 13–15 April 2000.

Mamigonian, Beatriz Gallotti. "To Be a Liberated African in Brazil: Labour and Citizenship in the Nineteenth Century." PhD Thesis, University of Waterloo, 2002.

Mello, Priscilla Leal. "Leitura, Encantamento e Rebelião o islà negro no Brasil." PhD thesis, Universidade Federal Fluminense, 2009.

Odessky, Jared. "'Possessed of One Idea Himself': John Jay II's Challenges to Columbia on Slavery and Race." Seminar Paper, Columbia and Slavery, Spring 2015.

Ouorou-Coubou, Osséni. "L'Islam en pays baatonu au XIX siècle." Memoire de Maîtrise en Histoire, Université Nationale du Bénin, 1997.

Santana, Aderivaldo Ramos. "Destins d'Osifekunde, né et mis en esclavage au Nigeria, déporté au Brésil, transporté en France, revenu au Brésil et assassiné à Recife (1793–1842)." Thèse de doctorat, Sorbonne Université, 2022.

Short, Kenneth Richard. "The Widening Gap: The Story of Abolition within the Ranks of the Baptist Denomination, 1830–1850." Thesis, Colgate Rochester Divinity School, 1958.

Tanner, E. P. "Gerrit Smith: An Interpretation." Paper presented at the annual meeting of the New York State Historical Society, Lake Placid, NY, 1923.

Vergolino, José Raimundo Oliveira. "A demografia excrava no nordeste do Brasil: O caso de Pernambuco—1800/1888." Texto para discussão No. 383, Departamento de Economia, Universidade Federal de Pernambuco, March 1997.

Willcox, Mary Otis. "A Gay Life from the Letters of Sydney Howard Gay." Sydney Howard Gay Collection, Manuscript Collections, Columbia University Libraries.

Winch, Julie. "'A Gentleman of the Pave': James Forten and the Issue of Race in Philadelphia's Antebellum Business Community." Department of History, University of Massachusetts at Boston, 1999.

Published Books and Articles

Abajian, James. *Blacks in Selected Newspapers, Censuses, and Other Sources: An Index to Names and Subjects.* Boston: G. K. Hall, 1977, 3 vols.

Abubakir Sadiki. "Abou Bekir Sadiki, Alias Edward Doulan, Discovered by Dr. Charles H. Wesley." *Journal of Negro History* 21, no. 1 (1936): 52–55.

Adams, John. *Remarks on the Country Extending from Cape Palmas to the River Congo.* London: Whitaker, 1823.

Adamu, Mahdi. *The Hausa Factor in West African History.* Zaria: Ahmadu Bello University Press, 1978.

Aime, Marco. "Djougou, una chefferie sulla rotta della cola." *Africa: Rivista trimestrale di studi e documentazione dell'istituto Italiano per l'Africa e l'Oriente* 49, no. 4 (1994): 481–91.

Akindele, A., and C. Aguessy. *Contribution a l'étude de l'histoire de l'Ancien Royaume de Porto Novo.* Dakar: Mémoire no 25 de l'IFAN, 1953.

Alexandre, Pierre. "L'organisation politique des Kotokoli du Nord-Togo." *Cahiers d'études Africaines* 4, no. 14 (1963): 228–75.

Allen, William G. *American Prejudice against Colour: An Authentic Narrative, Showing How Easily the Nation Got into an Uproar.* London: W. and F. G. Cash, 1853.

———. *A Short Personal Narrative.* Dublin: William Curry and J. Robertson, 1860.

Anais do Arquivo Público do Estado da Bahia. Salvador: Secretaria da Cultura e Turismo, vol. 50, 54, 1992, 1996.

Andrews, William L., ed. *African American Autobiography: A Collection of Critical Essays.* Englewood Cliffs, NJ: Pearson, 1993.

———. *To Tell a Free Story: The First Century of Afro-American Autobiography.* Urbana: University of Illinois Press, 1986.

Andrews, William L., Frances Smith Foster, and Trudier Harris, eds. *The Oxford Companion to African American Literature.* New York: Oxford University Press, 1997.

Anon. 3rd Congress, Second Session, House of Representatives, Correspondence between the Consuls of the United States at Rio de Janeiro, &c., with the Secretary of State, on the Subject of the African Slave Trade, *United States, Congressional Series Set*, Executive Document No. 61, 2 March 1849.

———. "The African Steam Ship Company from 1852 to 1868." http://www.historic -shipping.co.uk/african/africanindex.html.

———. *Blue Book of American Shipping: Marine and Naval Directory of the United States.* Cleveland, OH: The Marine Review Publishing, 1899.

———. *The Centennial Record of Freewill Baptists.* Dover, NH: The Printing Establishment, 1881.

———. "Colored Sailor's Home." *The North Star,* 11 May 1849.

———. *Commemorative Biographical Record of Northeastern Pennsylvania, including the counties of Susquehanna, Wayne, Pike, and Monroe.* Chicago: J. H. Beers, 1900.

———. *Dendi Cine tila Bukatante/Livre du dendi pratique,* n.d.

———. "In Continuation of Intelligence Respecting the Interior of Africa" *The Quarterly Review* 29 (1823): 597–98.

———. *Ladies Society to Aid Fugitives from Slavery.* London: R. Barrett, 1855.

———. "Le Protestantisme en Haiti." *Les Griots: La revue scientifique et littéraire d'Haiti* 3, no. 3 (1939): 384–97.

———. *The Renascence of City of Hall; Commemorative Presentation Rededication of City Hall, The City of New York, July 12, 1956.* New York, 1956.

———. "Le Royaume du Borgou." *Bulletin d'informations et de renseignements de l'Afrique occidentale française* (août 1934), 7.

———. "Sailor's Home." *National Anti-Slavery Standard,* 19 August 1841.

Appiah, Kwame Anthony, and Henry Louis Gates, eds. *Microsoft Encarta Africana 2000.* Redmond, WA: Microsoft Corp., 2000.

Araujo, Ana Lucia. "Forgetting and Remembering the Atlantic Slave Trade: The Legacy of Brazilian Slave Merchant Francisco Félix de Souza." In *Crossing Memories: Slavery and African Diaspora,* edited by Ana Lucia Araujo, Mariana P. Candido, and Paul E. Lovejoy, 79–103. Trenton, NJ: Africa World Press, 2011.

Araujo, Fabio R. de. *The Biography of Mahommah Gardo Baquaqua.* Charlotte, NC: IAP, 2018.

Arquivo Nacional. *Junta do Comércio.* Caixa 394, Pacote 1., Rio de Janeiro, 1809–50.

Austin, Allan. *African Muslims in Ante-Bellum America: A Sourcebook.* New York: Garland Publishing, 1984.

———. *African Muslims in Antebellum America: Transatlantic Stories and Spiritual Struggles.* New York: Routledge, 1997.

———. "Mohammed Ali Ben Said: Travels on Five Continents." *Contributions in Black Studies* 12 (2008): 129–58.

Bailey, Anne C. *African Voices of the Atlantic Slave Trade: Beyond the Silence and the Shame.* Boston: Beacon, 2004.

Bako, Nassirou Arifari. "Routes de commerce et mise en place des populations du Nord du Bénin." In *Le sol, la parole et l'écrit. Mélanges en hommage à Raymond Mauny,* 655–72. Paris: Bibliothèque d'Histoire d'Outer-Mer, 1981, vol. 2.

Baldus, Bernd. "Responses to Dependence in Servile Groups: The Machube of Northern Benin." In *Slavery in Africa: Historical and Anthropological Perspectives,* edited by Suzanne Miers and Igor Kopytoff, 435–57. Madison: University of Wisconsin Press, 1977.

————. "Social Structure and Ideology: Cognitive and Behavioral Responses to Servitude among the Machube of Northern Dahomey." *Canadian Journal of African Studies* 8, no. 2 (1974): 355–83.

Baquaqua, Mahommah Gardo. *Biografia e narrativa do ex-excravo afro-brasileiro*, trans. Robert Krueger. Brasília: Editora UNB, 1997.

————. *Biography of Mahommah G. Baquaqua. A Native of Zoogoo, in the Interior of Africa (A Convert to Christianity,) with a Description of that Part of the World; Including the Manners and Customs of the Inhabitants*. Detroit: George Pomeroy, 1854.

Bargery, G. P. *A Hausa-English Dictionary and English-Hausa Vocabulary*. London: Humphrey Milford, 1934.

Barth, Heinrich. *Travels and Discoveries in North and Central Africa, Being a Journal of an Expedition Undertaken under the Auspices of H.B.M.'s Government in the Years 1849–1855* (London: Harper and Brothers, 1859), 3 vols.

Bartlett, Irving H. "Abolitionists, Fugitives, and Imposters in Boston, 1846–1847." *New England Quarterly* 55 (1982): 97–110.

Bassett, Thomas J., and Philip W. Porter. "'From the Best Authorities': The Mountains of Kong in the Cartography of West Africa." *Journal of African History* 32 (1991): 367–413.

Baur, John E. "Faustin Soulouque, Emperor of Haiti, His Character and His Reign." *The Americas* 6, no. 2 (1949): 131–66.

Bay, Edna G. *Wives of the Leopard: Gender, Politics, and Culture in the Kingdom of Dahomey*. Charlottesville: University of Virginia Press, 1998.

Bearse, Austin. *Reminiscences of Fugitive-Slave Law Days in Boston*. Boston: Warren Richardson, 1880.

Beaufoy, Henry. "Mr Lucas's Communications." In *Proceedings of the Association for Promoting the Discovery of the Interior Parts of Africa*, edited by Robin Hallet. London: Dawson, 1967.

Beeson, Harvey Childs. *Beeson's Marine Directory*. Ann Arbor: The University of Michigan, 1935.

Bell, Howard H. "The Negro Emigration Movement, 1849–1854: A Phase of Negro Nationalism." *Phylon* 20 (1959): 132–42.

Benedict, David. *A General History of the Baptist Denomination in America and Other Parts of the World*. New York: Sheldon, Lamport & Blakemar, 1855.

Bethell, Leslie M. *The Abolition of the Brazilian Slave Trade: Britain, Brazil and the Slave Trade Question 1807–1869*. Cambridge: Cambridge University Press, 1970.

Bevans, Charles I., compiler. *Treaties and Other International Agreements of the United States of America 1776–1949*, vol. 5. Washington, DC: Department of State Publications, 1970.

Bezerra, Nielson Rosa. "Biographies of Africans in Diaspora: Individual Trajectories and Collective Identities." In *UNESCO General History of Africa*, vol. 10, 843–54. Paris: UNESCO, 2023.

————. *As chaves da liberdade: Confluências da escravidão no Recôncavo do Rio de Janeiro, 1833–1888*. Niterói: EdUFF, 2008.

————. *Escravidão, farinha e comércio no Recôncavo do Rio de Janeiro, século XIX*. Rio de Janeiro: APPH-CLIO, 2011.

———. "The Trajectory of Mahomman Gardo Baquaqua in Brazil: Slavery, Freedom and Emancipation in the Atlantic World." In *Another Black Like Me: The Construction of Identities and Solidarity in the African Diaspora*, edited by Bezerra and Elaine Pereira Rocha, 156–70. Cambridge: Cambridge Scholarly Publishing, 2015.

Bezerra and Elaine Pereira Rocha, eds. *Another Black Like Me: The Construction of Identities and Solidarity in the African Diaspora*. Cambridge: Cambridge Scholarly Publishing, 2015.

Bicalho, Gustavo. "Identidades narrativas transatlânticas: Mahommah Gardo Baquaqua e Gustavus Vassa, ou Olaudah Equiano." *Experiências literárias* (2028): 2325–36, https://abralic.org.br/anais/arquivos/2016_1491265277.pdf.

Binger, Louis-Gustave. *Du Niger au Golfe de Guinee par le pays de Kong et le Mossi*. Paris: Librairie Hachette, 1892.

Blackett, Richard. "Martin R. Delany and Robert Campbell: Black Americans in Search of an African Colony." *Journal of Negro History* 62, no. 1 (1977): 1–25.

———. "William G. Allen: The Forgotten Professor." *Civil War History* 26 (1980): 39–52.

Blassingame, John W., ed. *Slave Testimony: Two Centuries of Letters, Speeches, Interviews, and Autobiographies*. Baton Rouge: Louisiana State University Press, 1977.

Blight, David W. *Frederick Douglass: Prophet of Freedom*. New York: Simon & Schuster, 2020.

———, ed. *Passages to Freedom: The Underground Railroad in History and Memory*. Washington: Smithsonian Books, 2006.

Bluett, Thomas. *Some Memoirs of the Life of Job, the Son of Solomon the High Priest of Boonda in Africa, Who Was a Slave about Two Years in Maryland; and Afterwards Being Brought to England, Was Set Free, and Sent to His Native Land in the Year 1734*. London: Richard Ford, 1734.

Borghero, Francesco. "Relation sur l'établissement des missions dans le Vicariat du Dahomé (1863)." In *Journal de Francesco Borghero, premier missionnaire au Dahomey (1861–1865)*, edited by Renzo Mandirola and Yves Morel. Paris: Karthala, 1997.

Bowdich, T. E. *Mission from Cape Coast Castle to Ashantee*. London: John Murray, 1819.

Bowen, T. J. *Central Africa: Adventures & Missionary Labours*. London: Southern Baptist Publication Society, 1857.

Brégand, Denise. *Commerce caravanier et relations sociales au Bénin: Les Wangara du Borgou* Paris: L'Harmattan, 1998.

Brown, Henry Box. *Narrative of the Life of Henry Box Brown, Written by Himself*. Boston: Brown and Stearns, 1849.

Brown, William J. *The Life of William J. Brown of Providence, R.I.* Nashville: Fisk University, 1883.

Bruce Lockhart, Jamie, and Paul E. Lovejoy, eds. *Hugh Clapperton into the Interior of Africa: Records of the Second Expedition, 1825–1827*. Leiden: Brill, 2005.

Buckmaster, Henrietta. *Let My People Go: The Story of the Underground Railroad and the Growth of the Abolition Movement*. Boston: Beacon Press, 1941.

Burton, Richard. *Mission to Gelele, King of Dahome*. London: Tinsley Brothers, 1864.

Calbreath, Dean. *The Sergeant: The Incredible Life of Nicholas Said: Son of an African General, Slave of the Ottomans, Free Man under the Tsars, Hero of the Union Army*. Cambridge, UK: Pegasus Books, 2023.

Canario, Ezequiel David do Amaral. *É mais uma cena da escravidão: Suicídios de escravos do Recife (1850–1888)*. Recife: EDUFPE, 2011.

Castro de Araújo, Ubiratan. "1846: Um ano na rota Bahia-Lagos: Negócios, negociantes e outros parceiros." *Afro-Ásia* 21–22 (1998–99): 83–110.

Carretta, Vincent. "Olaudah Equiano or Gustavus Vassa? New Light on an Eighteenth-Century Question of Identity." *Slavery and Abolition* 20, no. 3 (1999): 96–105.

———, ed. *Unchained Voices: An Anthology of Black Authors in the English-Speaking World of the Eighteenth Century*. Lexington: University of Kentucky Press, 1996.

Carvalho, José Murilo de. *A Construção da Ordem: A elite política. Teatro das Sombras: A política imperial*, 5th ed. Rio de Janeiro: Civilização Brasileira, 2010.

Carvalho, Marcus J. M. de. "Cavalcantis e Cavalcades: A formação das alianças políticas em Pernambuco, 1817–1824." *Revista Brasileira de História* 18, no. 36 (1998): 331–66.

———. "Le 'Divin Maître': Esclavage et liberté à Recife dans les années 1840." In *Pour l'histoire du Brésil*, edited by François Crouzet and Denim Rolland, 435–49. Paris: L'Harmattan, 2000.

———. *Liberdade: Rotinas e rupturas do escravismo, Recife, 1822–1850*. Recife: Editora Universitária da UFPE, 1998.

———. *Movimentos sociais: Pernambuco (1831–1848). O Brasil Imperial*, volume II: 1831–70. Rio de Janeiro: Civilização Brasileira, 2009.

———. "O desembarque nas praias: O funcionamento do trágico de escravos depois de 1831." *Revista de História* 167 (2012): 223–60.

———. "Os caminhos do rio: Negros canoeiros no Recife na primeira metade do século XIX." *Afro-Ásia* 19–20 (1997): 75–93.

Castelnau, Francis de. *Renseignements sur l'Afrique centrale et sur une nation d'hommes a queue qui s'y trouverait, d'après le rapport des Négres du Soudan, esclaves a Bahia*. Paris: P. Bertrand, 1851.

Castillo, Lisa Earl. "Bamboxê Obitikô e a expansão do culto aos orixás (século XIX): Uma rede religiosa afroatlântica." *Tempo* (Niterói) 22, no. 39 (2016): 126–53.

———. "The Exodus of 1835: Agudá Life Stories and Social Networks." in *The Vile Trade: Slavery and the Slave Trade in Africa*, edited by Abi Alabo Derefaka, Wole Ogundele, Akin Alao, and Augustus Babajide Ajibola, 211–24. Durham, NC: Carolina Academic Press, 2015.

———. "Mapping the Nineteenth-Century Brazilian Returnee Movement: Demographics, Life Stories and the Question of Slavery." *Atlantic Studies* 13, no. 1 (2016): 25–52.

Castillo, Lisa Earl, and Luís Nicolau Parés. "Marcelina da Silva: A Nineteenth-Century Candomblé Priestess in Bahia." *Slavery & Abolition* 31 (2010): 1–27.

Cavalheiro, Daniela Carvalho. "'I Am Not a Slave': Liberated Africans and Their Usage of the Judicial System in Nineteenth Century Rio de Janeiro." In *UNESCO General History of Africa*, vol. 10, 891–900. Paris: UNESCO, 2023.

Chalhoub, Sidney. *A força da escravidão: Ilegalidade e costume no Brasil oitocentista*. São Paulo: Companhia das Letras, 2012.

Chapman, Abraham. *Steal Away: Stories of the Runaway Slaves*. New York: Praeger, 1971.

Chater, Kathleen. *Henry Box Brown: From Slavery to Show Business*. Jefferson, NC: McFarland, 2020.

Ciavolella, Riccardo. "La biographie de Mahommah Baquaqua: Traduction et édition critique et commentée." *Hyper Article en Ligne—Sciences de l'Homme et de la Société*. ID: 10670/1.25gs1e, 2021.

Clapperton, Hugh. *Journal of a Second Expedition into the Interior of Africa*. London: John Murray, 1829.

Colman, Lucy Newhall. *Reminiscences*. Buffalo, NY: H. L. Green, 1891.

Conrad, Robert Edgar, ed. *Children of God's Fire: A Documentary History of Black Slavery in Brazil*. Princeton, NJ: Princeton University Press, 1984.

———. *World of Sorrow: The African Slave Trade to Brazil*. Baton Rouge: Louisiana State University Press, 1986.

Cornevin, Robert. "A Propos des Cotoli du Moyen-Togo." *Notes Africaines* 101 (1964): 27–28.

Costa, Valéria, and Flavio Gomes. "Dos tripulantes da História: O africano Duarte José Martins da Costa entre a 'rede miúda' do Tráfico Atlântico (Rio de Janeiro—Angola—Recife—Benim, século XIX)." *Afro-Ásia* 65 (2022): 203–45.

Costa e Silva, Alberto da. *Francisco Félix de Souza, mercador de escravos*. Rio de Janeiro: EdUERJ, 2004.

Curtin, Philip D., ed. *Africa Remembered; Narratives by West Africans from the Era of the Slave Trade*. Madison: University of Wisconsin Press, 1967.

———. "Ayuba Suleiman Diallo of Bondu." In *Africa Remembered: Narratives of Africans from the Era of the Slave Trade*, edited by Philip D. Curtin, 22–59. Madison: University of Wisconsin Press, 1967.

Curtis, Edward E., IV. *Muslims in America: A Short History*. New York: Oxford University Press, 2009.

d'Alaux, Gustave. *L'Empereur Soulouque et son Empire*. Paris: Michel, Levy Frères, 1856.

d'Avezac-Macaya, Marie Armand Pascal. "Notice sur le pays et le people des Yébous en Afrique." *Mémoires de la Société Ethnologique* 2, no. 2 (1845): 1–44.

Dabovic, Safet. "Out of Place: The Travels of Nicholas Said." *Criticism* 54, no. 1 (2012): 59–83.

Daddi Addoun, Yacine and Paul E. Lovejoy. "Commerce and Credit in Katsina in the Nineteenth Century." In *Africa, Empire and Globalization: Essays in Honor of A.G. Hopkins*, edited by Emily Brownell and Toyin Falola, 111–24. Durham, NC: Carolina Academic Press, 2010.

Dann, Norman K. *Practical Dreamer: Gerrit Smith and the Crusade for Social Reform*. Hamilton, NY: Log Cabin Books, 2009.

Dantas, Luis. "Francis de Castelnau e o relato de um grupo de escravos de Salvador da Bahia em 1851 ou Carater Simiesco dos Indesejaveis." *Remate de Males* (Campinas) 12 (1992): 45–55.

Davies, Peter N. *The Trade Makers: Elder Dempster in West Africa, 1852–1972, 1973–1989*. Liverpool: Liverpool University Press, 2000.

Delany, Martin R., and Robert Campbell. *Search for a Place: Black Separatism and Africa, 1860*. Ann Arbor: University of Michigan Press, 1969.

Delany, Martin. *The Condition, Elevation, and Destiny of the Colored People of the United States, Politically Considered*. Amherst, NY: Academic Books, 2004 (1852).

———. *Official Report of the Niger Valley Exploring Party*. Leeds: Thomas Hamilton, 1861. Reprinted in Delany and Campbell, *Search for a Place*, 23–148.

Delval, Raymond. *Les Musulmanes au Togo*. Paris: Publications Orientalists de France, 1981.

Diouf, Sylviane A. *Servants of Allah: African Muslims Enslaved in the Americas*. New York: NYU Press, 1998.

Dixon, Chris, *African America and Haiti: Emigration and Black Nationalism in the Nineteenth Century*. Westport, CT: Greenwood Press, 2000.

Douglass, Frederick. *Narrative of the Life of Frederick Douglass, an American Slave, Written by himself*. Boston: Anti-Slavery Office, 1845.

Drew, Benjamin. *A North-Side View of Slavery. The Refugee: Or the Narratives of Fugitive Slaves in Canada, Related by Themselves, with an Account of the History and Condition of the Colored Population of Upper Canada*. Boston: J. P. Jewett, 1856.

Dreys, Nicolau. *Notícia Descriptiva da Província do Rio Grande de São Pedro do Sul*. Porto Alegre: Livraria Americana, 1927.

Drumond, Menèzes de. "Lettres sur l'Afrique ancienne et modern." *Journal des Voyages* 32 (1826): 203–5.

Duncan, John. *Travels in Western Africa, in 1845 & 1846: Comprising a Journey from Whydah, through the Kingdom of Dahomey, to Adofoodia, in the Interior*. London: R. Bentley, 1847, 2 vols.

Dunn, Seymour B. "The Early Academies of Cortland County." *Cortland County Chronicles* 1 (1957): 57–76.

Dupuis, Joseph. *Journal of a Residence in Ashantee*. London: H. Colburn, 1824.

Eisenberg, Peter L. *The Sugar Industry in Pernambuco, 1840–1910*. Berkeley: University of California Press, 1974.

Elbert, S. "An Inter-Racial Love Story in Fact and Fiction: William and Mary King's Marriage and Louisa May Alcott's Tale." *History Workshop Journal* 53, no. 1 (2002): 17–42.

Eltis, David. *Economic Growth and the Ending of the Transatlantic Trade*. Oxford: Oxford University Press, 1987.

Eltis, David, and Stanley Engerman. "Fluctuations in Sex and Age Ratios in the Transatlantic Slave Trade, 1663–1864." *Economic History Review* 46 (1993): 308–23.

Farah, Paulo Daniel. "Relato de Viagem de um erudito Muçulmano ao Brasil do oitocentos: A exeperiência e o prisma de um viajante do século XIX." *Mestrado em Letras: Linguagem, Cultura e Discurso* 6, no. 2 (2009).

Faria, Sheila de Castro. "Damas mercadoras: As pretas minas no Rio de Janeiro, século XVIII a 1850." In *Rotas Atlânticas da Diáspora Africana*, edited by Mariza Carvalho Soares, 219–32. Niterói: EdUFF, 2007.

Farias, Juliana Barreto, Carlos Eugênio Líbano Soares, and Flávio dos Santos Gomes. *No labirinto das nações: Africanos e identidades no Rio de Janeiro*, Volume 20 of Prêmio Arquivo Nacional de Pesquisa. Rio de Janeiro: Arquivo Nacional, 2003.

Ferreira, Roquinaldo, and Luciene Reginaldo. "Vida e Morte de um Príncipe do Congo: Nicolau de Água Rosada e o fim do Tráfico de Escravizados na África Centro-Ocidental." *Afro-Ásia* 65 (2022): 246–80.

Ferrez, Gilberto. *Photography in Brazil*, trans. Stella de Sá Rego. Albuquerque: New Mexico University Press, 1984.

Fett, Sharla M. *Recaptured Africans: Surviving Slave Ships, Detention, & Dislocation in the Final Years of the Slave Trade*. Chapel Hill, NC: University of North Carolina Press, 2017.

Fisch, Audrey, ed. *The African American Slave Narrative*. Cambridge: Cambridge University Press, 2007.

Fisher, Miles Mark. *A Short History of the Baptist Denomination*. Nashville: Sunday School Publishing Board, 1933.

Florentino, Manolo. "Alforria e etnicidade no Rio de Janeiro oitocentista: Notas de pesquisa." *Topoi* 5 (2002): 25–40.

———. *Em costas negras: Uma história do tráfico de escravos entre a África e o Rio de Janeiro*. São Paulo: Companhia das Letras, 1997.

Foner, Eric. *Gateway to Freedom; The Hidden History of the Underground Railroad*. New York: Norton, 2015.

———. "William P. Powell: Militant Champion of Black Seamen." In *Essays in Afro-American History*, 88–111. Philadelphia: Temple University Press, 1978.

Foner, Philip S., and Ronald L. Lewis. *The Black Worker, Volume 1: The Black Worker to 1896*. Philadelphia: Temple University Press, 1978.

Forbes, Frederick E. *Dahomey and the Dahomans, Being the Journals of Two Missions to the King of Dahomey and Residence at His Capital in the Years 1849 and 1850*. London: Longman, Brown, Green, and Longmans, 1851, 2 vols.

———. *Six Months' Service in the African Blockade, from April to October, 1848*. London: Bentley, 1849.

Foss, A. T., and Edward Mathews. *Facts for Baptist Churches*. Utica, NY: American Baptist Free Mission Society, 1850.

Friedman, Lawrence J. "Confidence and Pertinacity in Evangelical Abolitionism: Lewis Tappan's Circle." *American Quarterly* 31, no. 1 (1979): 81–106.

Frothingham, Octavius Brooks. *Gerrit Smith: A Biography*. New York: G. P. Putnam's sons, 1878.

Fyfe, Christopher. *A History of Sierra Leone*. London: Oxford University Press, 1962.

Gates, Henry Louis, Jr., ed. *The Classic Slave Narratives*. New York: Penguin, 1987.

Gilroy, Paul. *The Black Atlantic: Modernity and Double Consciousness*. London: Verso Books, 1993.

Goldsmith, H. S. "The River Niger; MacGregor Laird and Those Who Inspired Him." *Journal of the Royal African Society* 31 (1932): 383–93.

Gomez, Michael. *Black Crescent: The Experience of African Muslims in the Americas*. Cambridge: Cambridge University Press, 2005.

———. *Exchanging Our Country Marks: The Transformation of African Identities in the Colonial and Antebellum South*. Chapel Hill: University of North Carolina Press, 1998.

Goulart, Maurício A. *A Escravidão Africana no Brasil*. São Paulo: Editora Alfa-Ômega, 1975.

Greene, Sandra E. *West African Narratives of Slavery: Texts from Late Nineteenth- and Early Twentieth-Century Ghana*. Bloomington: Indiana University Press, 2011.

Griffith, Cyril E. *The African Dream: Martin R. Delany and the Emergence of Pan-African Thought*. University Park, PA: Pennsylvania State University Press, 1975.

Grodzins, Dean. "'Constitution or No Constitution, Law or No Law': The Boston Vigilance Committees, 1841–1861." In *Massachusetts and the Civil War: The*

Commonwealth and National Disunion, edited by Matthew Mason, Katheryn P. Viens, and Conrad E. Wrigth, 47–73. Amherst: University of Massachusetts Press, 2015.

Gronningsater, Sarah L. H. "'On Behalf of His Race and the Lemmon Slaves': Louis Napoleon, Northern Black Legal Culture, and the Politics of Sectional Crisis." *Journal of the Civil War Era* 7, no. 2 (2017): 206–41.

Gunn, Jeffrey. *Outsourcing African Labor: Kru Migratory Workers in Global Ports, Estates and Battlefields until the End of the 19th Century.* Berlin: De Gruyter Oldenbourg, 2021.

Hammond, Charles, and Harvey M. Lawson. *The History of Union, Conn.* New Haven, CT: Price, Lee & Adkins, 1893.

Harlow, Ralph Volney. *Gerrit Smith, Philanthropist and Reformer.* New York: H. Holt, 1939.

Harris, Leslie M. *In the Shadow of Slavery: African Americans in New York City, 1626–1863.* Chicago: University of Chicago Press, 2003.

Harris, Percy G. "Some Conventional Hausa Names." *Man* 31 (1931): 272–74.

Hazard, Samuel. *Santo Domingo Past and Present with a Glance at Hayti.* London: Sampson Low, Marston, Low, and Searle, 1873.

Hodgson, W. B. "The Gospels: Written in the Negro Patois of English, with Arabic Characters." Ethnological Society of New York, 13 October 1857.

Hoffmann, Léon-François. *Faustin Soulouque D'Haïti dans l'histoire et la littérature.* Paris: L'Harmattan, 2007.

Hogg, Peter C. *The African Slave Trade and Its Suppression: A Classified and Annotated Bibliography of Books, Pamphlets and Periodical Articles.* London: Frank Cass, 1973.

Holloway, Thomas H. *Polícia no Rio de Janeiro: Repressão e resistência numa cidade do século XIX.* Rio de Janeiro: FGV, 1997.

Horton, James Oliver, and Lois E. Horton. *In Hope of Liberty: Culture, Community and Protest among Northern Free Blacks, 1700–1860.* New York: Oxford University Press, 1997.

Hunwick, John. "'I Wish to Be Seen in Our Land Called Afrika': 'Umar b. Sayyid's Appeal to Be Released from Slavery (1819)." *Journal of Arabic and Islamic Studies* 5 (2003–4): 62–77.

Hurston, Zora Neale. "Cudjo's Own Story of the Last African Slaver." *Journal of Negro History* 12, no. 4 (1927): 648–63.

Johnson, Marion. "News from Nowhere: Duncan and Adofoodia." *History in Africa* 1 (1974): 55–66.

Johnson, Robert E. *A Global Introduction to Baptist Churches.* New York: Cambridge University Press, 2010.

Jones, Howard. *The Mutiny on the Amistad: The Saga of the Slave Revolt and Its Impact on American Abolition, Law and Diplomacy*, rev. ed. Oxford: Oxford University Press, 1988.

Judd, Nancy A. L. "Letter from Mrs. Mary [*sic*] A. L. Judd to Grosvenor, 24 March 1848." *Christian Contributor and Free Missionary* 5, no. 12 (May 17, 1848).

Karasch, Mary. *Slave Life in Rio de Janeiro 1808–1850.* Princeton, NJ: Princeton University Press, 1987.

Karp, Matthew. *This Vast Southern Empire: Slaveholders at the Helm of American Foreign Policy.* Cambridge, MA: Harvard University Press, 2016.

Kelley, Sean. *American Slavers: Merchants, Mariners, and the Transatlantic Commerce in Captives, 1644–1865.* New Haven, CT: Yale University Press, 2023.

Kirk-Greene, Anthony, and Paul Newman, eds. *West African Travels and Adventures: Two Autobiographical Narratives from Northern Nigeria.* New Haven, CT: Yale University Press, 1971.

Klein, Herbert. *The Atlantic Slave Trade.* Cambridge: Cambridge University Press, 1999.

Klose, Heinrich. *Le Togo sous drapeau allemand (1894–1897).* Translated by Phillippe David. Lomé: Halo, 1992.

Koelle, Sigismund Wilhelm. *African Native Literature, or Proverbs, Tales, Fables, & Historical Fragments in the Kanuri or Bornu Language, to Which Are Added a Translation of the Above and a Kanuri-English Vocabulary.* London: Church Missionary House, 1854.

———. *Grammar of the Bornu or Kanuri Language.* London: Church Missionary House, 1854.

———. *Polyglotta Africana or A Comparative Vocabulary.* Freetown, Sierra Leone: Fourah Bay College, 1963 (1854).

Krueger, Robert. "Milhões de vozes, umas pàginas preciosas. As narrativas dos escravos Brasileiros." in *Imàgenes de la Resistencia Indígena y Esclava,* edited by Roger Zapata, 183–232. Lima: Editorial Wari, 1990.

———, tradução. *Mahommah Gardo Baquaqua: Biografia e narrative do ex-excravo afro-brasileiro.* Brasília: Editora Universidade de Brasília, 1997.

Kuba, Richard. *Wasangari und Wangara: Borgu und seine Nachbarn in historische Perspectif.* Hamburg: Perspektive LIT Verlag, 1996.

Kunioch, Márcia N. "Ter escravo no Rio Grande." *Anais do III Encontro Escravidão e Liberdade no Brasil Meridional.* Florianóplis: UFSC, 2007.

Laird, MacGregor, and R.A.K. Oldfield. *Narrative of an Expedition into the Interior of Africa by the River Niger in 1832, 1833, 1834,* 2 vols. London: Richard Bentley, 1837.

Lander, John. *Records of Captain Clapperton's Last Expedition to Africa.* London: John Murray, 1830.

Lander, Richard, and John Lander. *Journal of an Expedition to Explore the Course and Termination of the River Niger.* London & New York: J. and J. Harper, 1832.

Lara, Silvia Hunold. "Biografia de Mahommah G. Baquaqua." *Revista Brasileira de História—São Paulo* 16 (1988): 269–84.

Law, Robin. "Between the Sea and the Lagoons: The Interaction of Maritime and Inland Navigation on the Pre-colonial Slave Coast." *Cahiers d'études africaines* 29 (1989): 209–37.

———. "'Central and Eastern Wangara': An Indigenous West African Perception of the Political and Economic Geography of the Slave Coast, as Recorded by Joséph Dupuis in Kumasi, 1820." *History in Africa* 22 (1995): 281–305.

———. "The Evolution of the Brazilian Community in Ouidah." *Slavery & Abolition* 22 (2001): 22–41.

———. "Francisco Felix de Souza in West Africa, 1800–1849." in *Enslaving Connections: Western Africa and Brazil during the Era of Slavery,* edited by Jose C. Curto and Paul E. Lovejoy, 189–213. Amherst, NY: Humanities Books, 2003.

———. *The Horse in West African History.* London: Cambridge University Press, 1980.

———. "Individualising the Atlantic Slave Trade: The Biography of Mahommah Gardo Baquaqua of Djougou (1854)." *Transactions of the Royal Historical Society* 12 (2002): 113–40.

————. "On Pawning and Enslavement for Debt on the Pre-colonial Slave Coast." In *Pawnship, Slavery and Colonialism in Africa,* edited by Paul E. Lovejoy and Toyin Falola, 55–70. Trenton, NJ: Africa World Press, 2003.

————. *The Oyo Empire c.1600-c.1836.* Oxford: Oxford University Press, 1977.

Law, Robin, and Paul Lovejoy. *The Biography of Mahommah Gardo Baquaqua: His Passage from Slavery to Freedom in Africa and America,* 2nd ed. Princeton, NJ: Marcus Wiener Publishers, 2005.

————. "Borgu in the Atlantic Slave Trade." *African Economic History* 27 (1999): 69–92.

————. "The Changing Dimensions of African History: Reappropriating the Diaspora." In *Rethinking African History,* edited by Simon McGrath et al., 181–200. Edinburgh: Centre of African Studies, University of Edinburgh, 1997.

Lawrance, Benjamin N. *Amistad's Orphans: An Atlantic Story of Children, Slavery, and Smuggling.* New Haven, CT: Yale University Press, 2014.

Lee, Luther. *Autobiography of The Rev. Luther Lee.* New York: Phillips & Hart, 1882.

Lefebvre, Camille. *Frontières de sable, frontières de papier: Histoire de territoires et de frontières, du jihad de Sokoto à la colonisation française du Niger, XIXe–XXe siècles.* Paris: Publications de la Sorbonne, 2015.

————. "Hausa Diasporas and Slavery in Africa, the Atlantic, and the Muslim World," 2023. https://doi.org/10.1093/acrefore/9780190277734.013.917.

Levine, Robert S., and Ivy G. Wilson, eds. *The Works of James M. Whitfield: America and Other Writings by a Nineteenth-Century African American Poet.* Chapel Hill: University of North Carolina Press, 2011.

Levtzion, Nehemiah. "Early Nineteenth Century Arabic Manuscripts from Kumasi." *Transactions of the Historical Society of Ghana* 8 (1965): 113–14.

————. *Muslims and Chiefs in West Africa: A Study of Islam in the Middle Volta Basin in the Pre-colonial Period.* Oxford: Oxford University Press, 1968.

————. "Salaga: A Nineteenth Century Trading Town in Ghana." *Asian and African Studies* 2 (1966): 207–45.

Leyburn, James G. *The Haitian People.* New Haven. CT: Yale University Press, 1966.

Lloyd, P. C. "Osifekunde of Ijebu." In *Africa Remembered: Narratives by West African from the Era of the Slave Trade,* edited by Philip D. Curtin, 217–88. Madison: University of Wisconsin Press, 1967.

Lockwood, Charles. *Manhattan Moves Uptown: An Illustrated History.* Boston: Houghton Mifflin, 1976.

Logan, Rayford W., and Michael R. Winston, eds. *Dictionary of Negro Biography.* New York: W. W. Norton, 1982.

Lombard, Jacques. "Aperçu sur la technologie et l'artisanat bariba." *Etudes dahoméennes* 18 (1957): 7–55.

————. "La vie politique dans une ancienne société de type féodal: Les Bariba du Dahomey." *Cahiers d'études africaines* 1, no. 3 (1960): 5–45.

————. "Quelques notes sur les Peuls du Dahomey." *Notes africaines* 73 (1973): 4–5.

————. *Structures de type "féodal" en Afrique noire: Étude des dynamismes internes et des relations sociales chez les Bariba du Dahomey.* Paris: Mouton, 1965.

Lovejoy, Henry B. "Liberated Africans." https://www.liberatedafricans.org.

Lovejoy, Paul E. "Ali Eisami's Enslavement and Emancipation: The Trajectory of a Liberated African." In *Liberated Africans and the Abolition of the Slave Trade, 1807–1896,* edited by Richard Anderson and Henry B. Lovejoy. Rochester, NY: University of Rochester Press, 2019.

———. "Background to Rebellion: The Origins of Muslim Slaves in Bahia." In *Unfree Labour in the Development of the Atlantic World,* edited by Paul E. Lovejoy and Nicholas Rogers (London: Frank Cass, 1994), 151–82.

———. "Biography as Source Material: Towards a Biographical Archive of Enslaved Africans." In *Source Material for Studying the Slave Trade and the African Diaspora,* edited by Robin Law, 119–40. Stirling: Centre of Commonwealth Studies, University of Stirling.

———. *Caravans of Kola: The Hausa Kola Trade, 1700–1900.* Zaria: Ahmadu Bello University Press, 1980.

———. "Cerner les identités au sein de la diaspora africaine, l'islam et l'esclavage aux Amériques." *Cahiers des Anneaux de la Mémoire* 1 (1999): 249–78.

———. *Ecology and Ethnography of Muslim Trade in West Africa.* Trenton, NJ: Africa World Press, 2005.

———. "Freedom Narratives of Trans-Atlantic Slavery." *Slavery and Abolition* 32, no. 1 (2011): 91–107.

———. "Identidade e a miragem da ethnicidade: A jornada de Mahommah Gardo Baquaqua para as Américas." *Afro-Ásia* 27 (2002): 9–39.

———. "Jihad e escravidão: As origens dos escravos Muçulmanos de Bahia." *Topoi: Revista de História* 1 (2000): 11–44.

———. *Jihād in West Africa during the Age of Revolutions.* Athens: Ohio University Press, 2016.

——— "The Kambarin Beriberi: The Formation of a Specialized Group of Hausa Kola Traders in the Nineteenth Century." *Journal of African History* 14, no. 4 (1973): 633–51.

———. "Kola in the History of West Africa." *Cahiers d'Études Africaines* 20, no. 77/78 (1980): 97–134.

———. "Kola Nuts: The 'Coffee' of the Central Sudan." In *Consuming Habits: Drugs in History and Anthropology,* edited by Jordan Goodman, Paul E. Lovejoy, and Andrew Sherratt. London: Routledge, 1993, 103–25.

——— . "Mohammed Ali Nicholas Sa'id: From Enslavement to American Civil War Veteran." In *Millars: Microhistoria de esclavas y esclavas,* vol. 42 (2017): 219–34. Edited by Vicent Sanz Rozalen and Michael Zeuske.

———. "Olaudah Equiano or Gustavus Vassa—What's in a Name?" *Atlantic Studies* 9, no. 2 (2012): 165–84.

———. "Polanyi's 'Ports of Trade': Salaga and Kano in the Nineteenth Century." *Canadian Journal of African Studies* 16 (1982), 245–78.

———. "The Role of the Wangara in the Economic Transformation of the Central Sudan in the Fifteenth and Sixteenth Centuries." *Journal of African History* 19 (1978): 173–93.

———. *Salt of the Desert Sun. A History of Salt Production and Trade in the Central Sudan.* Cambridge: Cambridge University Press, 1986.

———. "Speculations on the African Origins of Venture Smith." In *Venture Smith and the Business of Slavery and Freedom,* edited by James B. Stewart, 35–55. Amherst: University of Massachusetts Press, 2009.

Lovejoy, Paul E., and Toyin Falola, eds. *Pawnship, Slavery and Colonialism in Africa*. Trenton, NJ: Africa World Press, 2003.

Lupton, Ken. *Pascoe, Prince of Gobir*. London: AuthorHouse, 2009.

Mabee, Carleton. *Black Education in New York State*. Syracuse: Syracuse University Press, 1979.

MacLeod, Murdo J. "The Soulouque Regime in Haiti, 1847–1859." *Caribbean Studies* 10, no. 3 (1970): 35–48.

Madden, R. R. *A Twelvemonth's Residence in the West Indies, during the Transition from Slavery to Apprenticeship*. Westport, CT: Negro University Press, 1970 (1835).

Mahmud b. ʿAbdallah. *Qissat Salagha Ta'rikh Ghunja*, translated by Mahmoud EI-Wakkad, "Qissatu Salga Tarikhu Gonja: The Story of Salaga and the History of Gonja," *Ghana Notes and Queries* 3 (1961), 8–31; 4 (1962), 6–25.

Mamigonian, Beatriz. *Africanos Livres: A abolição do tráfico de escravos no Brasil*. São Paulo: Companhia das Letras, 2017.

Mann, Kristin. *Slavery and the Birth of an African City*. Bloomington: Indiana University Press, 2007.

Mann, Kristin, and Lisa Earl Castillo. "Biography, History, and Diaspora: The Bight of Benin and Bahia." in *UNESCO General History of Africa*, vol. 10, 901–12. Paris: UNESCO, 2023.

Martin, B. G. "Sapelo Island's Arabic Document: The 'Bilali Diary' in Context." *Georgia Historical Quarterly* 77, no. 3 (1994): 589–601.

Mathews, Edward. *The Autobiography of the Rev. E. Mathews, The "Father Dickson," of Mrs. Stowe's "Dred"*. London: Houlston and Weight, 1853.

———. *Review of the Operations of the American Baptist Free Mission Society*. Bristol, NY: Mathews Brothers, 1851.

Mattos, Ilmar R. O. *Tempo Saquarema: A formação do Estado Imperial*. São Paulo: Hucitec Edição, 5th ed., 2004.

McClish, Glen, "Transforming the African Missionary Narrative: Rhetorical Innovation in Martin Delany's Official Report of the Niger Valley Exploring Party," *Advances in the History of Rhetoric* 16, no. 2 (2013): 107–40.

Mello, Urbano Sabino Pessoa de. *Apreciação da Revolta Praieira em Pernambuco*. Brasília: EdUFB/Senado Federal, 1978.

Mercier, P. "Histoire et légende: La bataille d'Illorin." *Notes africaines* 47 (1950): 92–95.

Merriam, Edmund F. *A History of American Baptist Missions*. Philadelphia: American Baptist Publication Society, 1900.

Meunier, Olivier. *Les voies de l'islam au Niger dans le Katsina indépendant du XIXe au XXe siècle (Maradi, pays hawsa)*. Paris: Muséum d'histoire naturelle, 1998.

Misrah, Mahomed. "Narrative of a Journey from Egypt to the Western Coast of Africa, by Mahomed Misrah. Communicated by an Officer Serving in Sierra Leone, April 8, 1821." *The Quarterly Journal of Science, Literature and the Arts* 14 (1823): 1–16.

Mitchell, W. M. *The Underground Railroad*. London: William Tweedie, 1860.

Moraes Farias, P. F. de. "A Letter from Ki-Toro Mahamman Gaani, King of Busa (Borgu, Northern Nigeria) about the 'Kisra' Stories of Origin (c. 1910)." *Sudanic Africa* 3 (1992), 109–32.

Morel, Marco. *O Período das Regências (1831–1840)*. Rio de Janeiro: Jorge Zahar Editor, 2003.

Mott, Luis. *Rosa Egipcíaca: Uma Santa Africana no Brasil*. Rio de Janeiro: Bertrand, 1993.

Moumine, Abdoul, *Sur la trace des DJARRA fondateurs du royaume et de la ville de Djougou*. Facebook document.

Muhammad, Precious Rasheeda, ed. *The Autobiography of Nicholas Said: A Native of Bornou, Eastern Soudan, Central Africa*. Cambridge, MA: Journal of Islam in America Press, 2000.

Muir, Ramsay. *A History of Liverpool*, 2nd ed. London: University Press of Liverpool, 1907.

Nash, Gary B. *Forging Freedom: The Formation of Philadelphia's Black Community, 1720–1840*. Cambridge: Harvard University Press, 1988.

Neto, Egidio Trambaiolli. *Biografia de Mahommah Gardo Baquaqua um Nativo de Zoogoo, no interior da África*. São Paulo: Editora Uirapuru, 2017.

Newsome, M. T., ed. *Arguments, Pro and Con, on the Call for a National Emigration Convention, to be held in Cleveland, Ohio, August, 1854, by Frederick Douglass, W.J. Watkins, and James M. Whitfield, With a Short Appendix of the Statistics of Canada West, West Indies, Central and South America*. Detroit: Geo. Pomeroy, 1854.

North Country Underground Railroad Historical Association. "Lake Champlain: Gateway to Freedom." Accessed 1 October 2019. https://northcountryundergroundrailroad.com/lake-champlain.php?page=4-publisher=North.

Nunez, Benjamin. *Dictionary of Afro-Latin American Civilization*. Westport, CT: Greenwood, 1980.

Ojo, Olatunji. "Osifekunde of Ijebu (Yorubaland)." in *UNESCO General History of Africa*, vol. 10, 993–1048. Paris: UNESCO, 2023.

Olsavsky, Jesse. "Fugitive Slaves, Vigilance Committees, and the Abolitionists' Revolution, 1835–1859." https://geopoliticaleconomy.org/wp-content/uploads/2017/10/Olsavsky-Paper.pdf.

Palmer, Friend. *Early Days in Detroit*. Detroit: Hunt and June, 1906.

Papson, Don, and Tom Calarco. *Secret Lives of the Underground Railroad in New York City: Sydney Howard Gay, Louis Napoleon and the Record of Fugitives*. Jefferson, NC: McFarland, 2015.

Parker, Amasa J., *Reports of Decisions in Criminal Cases made at Term, at Chambers and in the Courts of Oyer and Terminer of the State of New York* (New York: Banks & Brothers, Law Publishers, 1860).

Parrinder, G. "Yoruba-Speaking Peoples in Dahomey." *Africa* 17, no. 2 (1947): 122–29.

Pease, Jane H., *They Who Would Be Free: Blacks' Search for Freedom, 1830–1861*. New York: Atheneum, 1974.

Perham, Margery, and Mary Bull, eds. *The Diaries of Lord Lugard*. London: Faber, 1959, 3 vols.

Perlman, Daniel. "Organizations of the Free Negro in New York City, 1800–1860." *Journal of Negro History* 56 (1971): 181–97.

Person, Yves. "Brève note sur les Logba et leurs classes d'âge." *Études Dahoméennes* 17 (1956): 35–49.

———. "La dynastie de Tyilixa (Djougou)." In *Perspectives nouvelles sur le passé de l'Afrique noire et de Madagascar. Mélanges offerts à Hubert Deschamps*, edited by AA.VV., 201–12. Paris: Publications de la Sorbonne, 1974.

————. "Les grandes compagnies zarma au Dahomey et au Togo (1875–1896). Région de Djougou et de Sokodé." *Le mois en Afrique: Revue française d'études politiques africaines* 18, no. 203/204 (1982–1983): 100–117, 127–44.

————. "Note sur les Nyantruku: Note sur les Ide et Nee, dits Nyantruku ou Oku-Oku (Yoruba des cercles de Djougou et Sokode)." *Études Dahoméennes* 16 (1956): 21–45.

————. "Le système des classes d'âge chez les Tangba et les Yoowa (cercle de Djougou)." *Cahiers d'Études Africaines* 19, no. 73/76 (1979): 25–53.

————. "Tradition orale et chronologie." *Cahiers d'études africaines* 2, no. 7 (1962): 462–76.

Pescatello, Ann M., ed. *The African in Latin America*. New York: Praeger, 1975.

Pliya, Jean. *Afrique Occidentale, Civilisations du Monde. Première partie. Le Dahomey.* Cotonou: République de Dahomey, 1967.

Polk, R. L. *Polk's Detroit City Directory*. Detroit: R. L. Polk, 1855.

Pomeroy, Albert A. *Geneology of the Pomeroy Family: Colateral Lines in Family Groups, Normandy, Great Britain and America; Comprising the Ancestors and Descendants of Eltweed Pomeroy from Beaminster, County Dorset, England, 1630*. Toledo, OH: Franklin Printing & Engraving, 1912.

Powell, Willian P. "Underground Railroad." *San Francisco Elevator*, 19 December 1874.

Quarles, Benjamin. *Black Abolitionists*. New York: Oxford University Press, 1969.

————. "Sources of Abolitionist Income." *Mississippi Valley Historical Review* 32, no. 1 (1945): 63–76.

Read, Ian, and Kari Zimmerman. "Freedom for Too Few: Slave Runaways in the Brazilian Empire." *Journal of Social History* 48, no. 2 (2014): 404–26.

Rediker, Marcus. *The Amistad Rebellion. An Atlantic Odyssey of Slavery and Freedom*. New York: Penguin, 2013.

————. *The Slave Ship: A Human History*. New York: Viking Press, 2007.

Reis, João José. *Domingos Sodré, um Sacerdote Africano: Escravidão, Liberdade e Candomblé na Bahia, século XIX*. São Paulo: Companhia das Letras, 2008.

Reis, João José, Flávio dos Santos Gomes, and Marcus J. M. de Carvalho. *O alufá Rufino. Tráfico, escravidão e liberdade no Atlântico negro (c.1822—c.1853)*. São Paulo, Companhia das Letras, 2011.

————. *The Story of Rufino: Slavery, Freedom, and Islam in the Black Atlantic*. New York: Oxford University Press, 2019.

Rennell, James. *A map shewing the progress of discovery & improvement, in the geography of North Africa*. London: The Association for Promoting the Discovery of the Interior Districts of Africa, 1798.

Renouard, G. C. "Routes in North Africa, by Abu es Siddik." *Journal of the Royal Geographical Society* 6 (1836): 100–13.

Ribeiro, Lidice Meyer Pinto. "Negros Islâmicos no Brasil escravocrata." *Cadernos Ceru* 22, no. 1 (2011): 287–304.

Richardson, James. *Narrative of a Mission to Central Africa Performed in the Years 1850–51*. London: Chapman and Hall, 1853.

Rice, C. Duncan. "The Anti-Slavery Mission of George Thompson to the United States, 1834–1835." *Journal of American Studies* 2, no. 1 (1968): 13–31.

Ripley, C. Peter, ed. *The Black Abolitionist Papers. Volume I. The British Isles, 1830–1865*. Chapel Hill: University of North Carolina Press, 1985.

————. *The Black Abolitionist Papers. Volume II. Canada, 1830–1865.* Chapel Hill: University of North Carolina Press, 1985.

Rodrigues, Jaime. *De costa a costa: Escravos, Marinheiros e Intermediários do Tráfico negreiro de Angola ao Rio de Janeiro (1780–1860).* São Paulo: Companhia das Letras, 2005.

Rogers, Augustus C., ed. *Sketches of Representative Men, North and South,* 3rd ed. New York: Atlantic Publishing, 1874.

Rosenfeld, Louis. "Martin Robison Delany (1812–1885): Physician, Black Separatist, Explorer, Soldier." *Bulletin of the New York Academy of Medicine* 65, no. 7 (1989): 801–18.

Rugendas, J. M. *Viagem Pitoresca através do Brasil.* Belo Horizonte: Itatiaia, 1986.

Said, Nicholas [Mohammad Ali Sa'id]. *The Autobiography of Nicholas Said; A Native of Bornou, Eastern Soudan, Central Africa.* Memphis: Shotwell, 1873.

————. "A Native of Bornou." *The Atlantic Monthly* 19 (October 1867): 485–95.

Sani, Abubakar Babajo. *Trade Diplomacy, Banking and Finance in the Trans-Saharan Trade: An Interpretation of Ahmad Abu al-Ghaith's ledger, a Trade Consul in Katsina, 1824–1870.* Kaduna: Pyla-mak Publishers, 2012.

Sanneh, Lamin. *Abolitionists Abroad: American Blacks and the Making of Modern West Africa.* Cambridge, MA: Harvard University Press, 1999.

Santana, Aderivaldo Ramos de. "A extraordinária odisseia do comerciante Ijebu que foi escravo no Brasil e homem livre na Franca (1820–1842)." *Afro-Asia* 57 (2018): 9–53.

Santos, Ynaê Lopes dos. *Além das senzalas: Arranjos escravos de moradias no Rio de Janeiro (1808–1850).* Rio de Janeiro: HUCITEC, 2010.

Schön, James Frederick. *Magána Hausa. Native Literature, or Proverbs, Tales, Fables and Historical Fragments in the Hausa Language, to Which Is Added a Translation in English.* London: Society for Promoting Christian Knowledge, 1835.

Schön, James Frederick, and Samuel Crowther. *Journals of the Rev. James Frederick Schön and Mr Samuel Crowther, Who . . . Accompanied the Expedition up the River Niger in 1841.* London: Hatchard and Sons, 1842.

Scribner, Harvey. "George Eltweed Pomeroy, Sr." *Memoirs of Lucas County & City of Toledo,* vol. 2. Madison, WI: Western Historical Society, 1910.

Seeley, Samantha. "Beyond the American Colonization Society." *History Compass* 14, no. 3 (2016): 93–104.

Shea, Philip. "Big Is Sometimes Best: The Sokoto Caliphate and Economic Advantages of Size in the Textile Industry." *African Economic History* 34 (2006), 5–21.

————. "The Development of an Export-Oriented Dyed Cloth Industry in Kano Emirate in the Nineteenth Century." PhD diss., University of Wisconsin, 1975.

Sherman, Joan R. "James M. Whitfield: Poet and Emigrationist: A Voice of Protest and Despair." *Journal of Negro History* 57, no. 2 (1972): 169–76.

Shick, Tom W. *Behold the Promised Land: A History of Afro-American Settler Society in Nineteenth-Century Liberia.* Baltimore: Johns Hopkins University Press, 1980.

Short, Kenneth R. "New York Central College: A Baptist Experiment in Integrated Higher Education, 1848–61." *Foundations: A Baptist Journal of History and Theology* 1 (1962): 250–56.

Sidi Mahmadee. *The Prince of Kashna: A West Indian Story.* New York: Carleton, 1866.

Siebert, Wilbur H. "The Underground Railroad in Massachusetts." *American Antiquarian Society* (April 1935): 25–100.

Silva, Marilene Rosa Nogueira da. *Negro Na Rua. A Nova Face da Escravidão.* São Paulo: Hucitec, 1988.

Slave Voyages Database. https://www.slavevoyages.org/voyage/database#statistics.

Smith, H.F.C. [Abdullahi], Last, D. M., and Gubio, Gambo, eds. "Ali Eisami Gazirmabe of Bornu." In *Africa Remembered*, edited by Phillip Curtin, 199–216. Madison: University of Wisconsin Press, 1967.

Smith, Robert. "The Canoe in West African History." *Journal of African History* 11, no. 4 (1970): 515–24.

Smith, Venture, *The Narrative of the Life and Adventures of Venture Smith, a Native of Africa.* New London, CT: C. Holt, 1798.

Soares, Carlos Eugênio Líbano. *Zungú: Rumor de muitas vozes.* Rio de Janeiro: Arquivo Público do Estado do Rio de Janeiro, 1998.

Soares, Mariza de Carvalho. *Devotos da cor: Identidade étnica, religiosidade e escravidão no Rio de Janeiro, século XVIII.* Rio de Janeiro: Civilização Brasileira, 2000.

———. *Diálogos Mahis de Francisco Alves de Souza: Manuscritos de uma Comunidade Católica de Africanos Minas (1786).* Rio de Janeiro: Chão, 2019.

———, ed., *Rotas Atlânticas da Diáspora Africana.* Niterói: EdUFF, 2007.

Sotzmann, D. F. "Skizze des nordlichen Theils von Afrika nach den Geographischen Nachrichten welche die Afrikanische Gesellschaft gesammelt hat zusammengetragen von L Rennell, 1790." *Magazin von merkwurdigen neuen Reisebeschreibungen* 10 (1792), end map.

Souza, Paulo José Soares. *Relatorio da Repartição dos Negocios Estrangerios.* Rio de Janeiro: Typ. dp Diario de A & L. Navarro, 1853.

Spradling, Mary Mace. *In Black and White: A Guide to Magazine Articles, Newspaper Articles, and Books Concerning More than 15,000 Black Individuals and Groups,* 3rd ed. Detroit: Gale Research, 1980.

Stanley, Brian. *The History of the Baptist Missionary Society, 1792–1992.* Edinburgh: T. & T. Clark, 1992.

Staudenraus, P. J. *The African Colonization Movement, 1816–1865.* New York: Columbia University Press, 1961.

Stauffer, John. *The Black Hearts of Men: Radical Abolitionists and the Transformation of Race.* Cambridge, MA: Harvard University Press, 2001.

Sternett, Milton C. *North Star Country: Upstate New York and the Crusade for African American Freedom.* Syracuse, NY: Syracuse University Press, 2002.

Stewart, I. D. "The Anti-Slavery Record of the Freewill Baptists." *The Freewill Baptist Quarterly* 16 (1868): 41–68.

Stewart, Marjorie H. *Borgu and Its Kingdoms: A Reconstruction of a Western Sudanese Polity.* Lewiston, NY: E. Mellen Press, 1993.

Still, William. *The Underground Railroad: A Record of Facts, Authentic Narratives, Letters, &c., Narrating the Hardships, Hair-Breadth Escapes and Death Struggles of the Slaves in Their Efforts for Freedom, As Related by Themselves and Others, or Witnessed by the Author.* Philadelphia: Porter & Coates, 1872.

Stouffer, Allan P. *The Light of Nature and the Law of God: Anti-Slavery in Ontario, 1833–1877.* Montreal: McGill-Queen's University Press, 1992.

Sweet, James. *Domingos Álvares, African Healing, and the Intellectual History of the Atlantic World.* Chapel Hill: University of North Carolina Press, 2011.

————. "Mistaken Identities? Olaudah Equiano, Domingos Alvares, and the Methodological Challenges of Studying the African Diaspora." *American Historical Review* 114, no. 2 (2009): 279–306.

Taylor, Yuval, ed. *I Was Born a Slave: An Anthology of Classic Slave Narratives*, 2 vols. Chicago: Chicago Review Press, 1999.

Tchagbalé, Zakari. "Les sept origines possibles de l'ethnonyme Kotokoli." 11 June 2011. http://linguistiqueetlanguesafricaines.blogspot.com/2011/06/les-sept-origines -possibles-de.html.

Thomas, Hugh. *The Slave Trade: The History of the Atlantic Slave Trade 1440–1870*. New York: Simon and Schuster, 1997.

Thompson, George. *The Palm Land: or West Africa, Illustrated*. Cincinnati: Moore, Wilstach, Keys, 1859.

————. *Thompson in Africa, or an Account of the Missionary Labors, Sufferings, Travels, Observations of George Thompson in Western Africa at the Mendi Mission*. Cleveland, OH: D. M. Ide, 1852.

Thompson, Robert Farris. "Sons of Thunder: Twin Images among the Oyó and Other Yoruba Groups." *African Arts* 4, no. 3 (1971): 8–80.

Tomek, Beverly C., and Matthew J. Hetrick. *New Directions in the Study of African American Recolonization*. Gainesville: University Press of Florida, 2017.

Tomich, Dale. "The Second Slavery and World Capitalism: A Perspective for Historical Inquiry." *International Review of Social History* 63, no. 3 (2018): 477–501.

Townsend, Craig D. *Faith in Their Own Color. Black Episcopalians in Antebellum New York City*. New York: Columbia University Press, 2005.

Trimingham, J. Spencer. *Islam in West Africa*. Oxford: Oxford University Press, 1959.

Truman, George, John Jackson, and Thos. B. Longstreth, *Narrative of a Visit to the West Indies, in 1840 and 1841*. Philadelphia: Merrihew and Thompson, Printers, 1844.

Turner, Richard Brent. *Islam in the African-American Experience*. Bloomington: Indiana University Press, 1997.

Ullman, Victor. *Look to the North Star: A Life of William King*. Boston: Umbrella Press, 1969.

Usman, Y. B. *The Transformation of Katsina, 1400–1883*. Zaria: Ahmadu Bello University Press, 1981.

Vassa, Gustavus. *The Life of Olaudah Equiano, or Gustavus Vassa, the African, Written by Himself*. London: private printing, 1789.

Véras, Bruno Rafael. "The Slavery and Freedom Narrative of Mahommah Gardo Baquaqua in the Nineteenth-Century Atlantic World." *UNESCO General History of Africa*, vol. 10, 1025–38. Paris: UNESCO, 2023.

Verellen, Till. "Cosmas and Damian in the New Sacristy." *Journal of the Warburg and Courtauld Institutes* 42 (London: The Warburg Institute, 1979): 274–77.

Verger, Pierre. *Flux et Reflux de la traite des nègres entre le golfe de Benin et Bahia de Todos os Santos*. The Hague: Mouton, 1968.

————. *Trade Relations between the Bight of Benin and Bahia from the 17th to the 19th Century*. Ibadan, Nigeria: University of Ibadan Press, 1976.

Walker, George E. *The Afro-American in New York City, 1827–1860*. New York: Garland, 1993.

Walvin, James. *Black Ivory: A History of British Slavery*. London: Fontana Press, 1993.

Wayne, Michael. "The Black Population of Canada West on the Eve of the American Civil War: A Reassessment Based on the Manuscript Census of 1861." In *A Nation of Immigrants: Women, Workers, and Communities in Canadian History, 1840s–1960s*, edited by Franca Iacovetta, Paula Draper, and Robert Ventresca, 58–82. Toronto: University of Toronto Press, 1998.

Weir, L. C., J. J. Henderson, and F. Clark. "Early History of the Express Business in the United States." *Expressman's Monthly Journal* 1 (1876): 107–10.

Wesley, Charles H. "The Life and History of Abou Bekir Sadiki, Alias Edward Doulan, *Journal of Negro History* 21 (1936): 52–55.

Whipple III, George. "The Illustrated History of the Whipple Family in America, 1631–1987." Accessed 11 February 2019. https://www.whipple.org/george /whipplehistory/revgeorge.html.

White, Jonathan W. *A House Built by Slaves: African American Visitors to the Lincoln White House*. Lanham, MA: Rowman & Littlefield, 2022.

White, Sophie, and Trevor Burnard, eds. *Hearing Enslaved Voices: African and Indian Slave Testimony in British and French America, 1700–1848*. New York: Routledge, 2020.

Whitfield, James M. *America, and Other Poems*. Buffalo, NY: Leavitt, 1853.

Wilks, Ivor, ed. "Abu Bakr al-Siddiq of Timbuktu." In *Africa Remembered: Narratives of West Africa during the Era of the Slave Trade*, edited by Philip D. Curtin, 159–60. Madison: University of Wisconsin Press, 1967.

———. *Asante in the Nineteenth Century*. Cambridge: Cambridge University Press, 1975.

———. "Asante Policy towards the Hausa Trade in the Nineteenth Century." In *The Development of Indigenous Trade and Markets in West Africa*, edited by Claude Meillassoux (London: Oxford University Press, 1971), 124–41.

———. *The Northern Factor in Ashanti History*. Legon: Institute of African Studies, University of Ghana, 1961.

———. *Wa and the Wala*. Cambridge: Cambridge University Press, 1989.

Winch, Julie. *A Gentleman of Color: The Life of James Forten*. Oxford: Oxford University Press, 2002.

———. "'You Know I Am a Man of Business': James Forten and the Factor of Race in Philadelphia's Antebellum Business Community." *Business and Economic History* 26, no. 1 (1997): 213–28.

Winckler, Julia. "Regards Croises: James Henry Dorugu's Nineteenth-Century European Travel Account." *Journeys* 10, no. 2 (2009): 1–30.

Winks, Robin. *The Blacks in Canada*, 2nd ed. Montreal: McGill-Queen's University Press, 1997.

Wolf, W. "Dr Ludwig Wolfs letzte Reise nach Barbar (Bariba oder Borgu)." *Mitteilungen aus den Deutsche Schutzgebieten* 4 (1891): 1–22.

Woodson, Carter G., ed. *The Mind of the Negro as Reflected in Letters Written during the Crisis, 1800–1860*. New York: Negro University Press, 1970 (1926).

Wright, Albert Hazen, ed. *Cornell's Three Precursors: I. New York Central College*. Ithaca, NY: Studies in History No. 23, Pre-Cornell and Early Cornell VIII, 1960.

Wyatt-Brown, Bertram. *Lewis Tappan and the Evangelical War against Slavery*. New York: Athenaeum, 1971.

Yannielli, Joseph L. "George Thompson among the Africans: Empathy, Authority, and Insanity in the Age of Abolition." *Journal of American History* 96, no. 4 (2010): 979–1000.

————. *The Mendi Mission: Africa and the American Abolition of Slavery.* New Haven, CT: Yale University Press, 2015.

Yetman, Norman R., ed. *Voices from Slavery: 100 Authentic Slave Narratives.* Mineola, NY: Dover Publications, 2000.

Zakari, Dramani-Issifou. "Routes de commerce et mise en place des populations du Nord du Bénin actuel." In *2000 ans d'histoire africaine. Le sol, la parole et l'écrit. Mélanges en hommage à Raymond Mauny.* Tome II, 655–72. Paris: Société française d'histoire d'outre-mer, 1981.

Zima, Petr. *Lexique Dendi (Songhay) (Djougou, Bénin).* Köln: Rüdiger Köppe, 1994.

Index

Page numbers in *italics* refer to illustrations.

Abeokuta, 156, 190

Abomey, Dahomey, 7, 63

Aboubacar, Ouorou Komsa, 53, 56–57

Accra, Ghana, 194, 195

Adamawa, 10

African Free Schools, 108

African Steam Navigation Company, 191

African Steamship Company, 183, 191

Africa Remembered (Curtin), 8

Agades, 37

Agaja, king of Dahomey, 14

Agalawa, 38, 39, 85

Aime, Marco, 26

Aktpamè, 63

al-Baghdadi, 'Abd al-Rahman, 89

alcohol, 22, 62, 68–69, 82

Alédjo-Koura, 59, 60

al-Ghaith, Ahmad Abu, 38

Alkalawa, 37

Allen, William, 145–47, 178, 182, 184, 185, 188

al-Siddiq, Abubakar, 9, 35

Álvares, Domingos, 14

Ambriz, 16

Ambrose, J. E., 143

American Anti-Slavery Society, 104

American Baptist Free Mission Society (Free Will Baptists), 162; and abolition, 121; Baquaqua's involvement in, 2, 5, 7, 8, 18, 23, 45, 121–54, 164–66, 169, 171, 174, 178–79, 185, 203, 204, 205; in Canada, 149, 152, 164–65; dissolution of, 152; in Haiti, 2, 7, 8, 123; theology of, 124

American Colonization Society, 189, 192

American Missionary Association, 159, 175–80, 182

American Prejudice against Colour (Allen), 146, 182

Amistad rebellion (1839), 175–76, 178, 179, 182, 189

Angola, 16, 64, 75–76, 81

Angola, Januario, 92

Antiga Igreja da Sé, 90

Apipucos, 85

Asante, 1, 2, 20, 32; conquests by, 48, 49, 196; kola trade in, 12, 22, 198, 205; Muslim trade restricted in, 35; slave trade and, 37; Sokoto trade with, 40, 43

Atakora-Donga, 24

Atakora-Kusa (bakparakpey), 27

Atakora Mountains, 20, 23

Austin, Allan, 8, 10, 158–59, 160, 161, 168

Australia, 10

Baatonu (Bariba) language, 43

Babanzauré, 55

Badagry, 64–65, 195

Bagazere (head of court musicians), 56

Bagirmi, 10

Bahia, Brazil, 10, 13–15, 196

Baikie, W. B., 41, 191

Bandama River, 66

Baparapé (ward in Djougou), 27

Baquaqua, Mahommah Gardo: as abolitionist, 4, 101, 102, 121–22, 152, 204–5; autobiography of, 4, 5, 6–7, 8, 16–17, 19, 44, 126, 135, 150–71, 180, 203; birth and birthplace of, 20, 23–24; in Brazil, 74–99; in Canada, 147–48, 164; Christian conversion of, 7, 8, 44, 125, 131–36, 170, 195–96, 197, 201, 202, 203; on Djougou, 4–5, 23–25, 40; on double enslavement,

Baquaqua, Mahommah Gardo (cont.)
47–50, 61–73; drinking habits of, 97–98, 99, 131, 134, 135, 136, 169, 202; editor's misunderstandings of, 1, 26–27, 29, 32, 33, 42, 155, 187; on emigration, 156; escape to freedom of, 2–3, 5, 7, 16–17, 18, 84, 94, 96, 98, 100, 106, 113–20; family of, 20–22, 31–34, 44, 171; Free Will Baptists and, 2, 5, 7, 8, 18, 23, 45, 121–52, 164–66, 169, 171, 174, 178–80, 185, 203, 204, 205; on Fulbe shepherds and herdsmen, 42–43; fund-raising by and for, 138, 143–45, 165, 171–74, 176–77, 179, 180, 187, 188; on Gonja civil war, 49–50; Hausa self-identification of, 45–46; image of, 126; itinerary of, 6, 7, 13, 18; on kidnapping, 51–52; languages spoken by, 43–44, 47, 131, 143–44, 159–60, 166–70, 174, 179, 186, 200, 205; as Muslim, 7, 29–31, 32, 82, 101, 121, 123, 134, 136, 186, 197, 207; at New York Central College, 3, 18, 129, 132, 134, 138, 140–44, 146, 157, 164, 169, 171, 186, 202, 204, 206; in New York City, 100–122, 136; nicknames of, 28–29, 56; as palace servant, 25, 54–61, 135; on political system, 52–53; and ransom, 50–51; on slavery, 47, 50; return to Africa, 170–95; on Soubroukou, 57–58; on Wangara, 27–28
Barkly, Henry, 13
Barra de Catuamá, 77
Barth, Heinrich, 12, 21, 37, 38
Bassila, 57
Bateham, Josephine Cushman, 141, 172
Bates, Abner, 178
Batoulou (ward in Djougou), 27
Ba Warakpè, 56
Bebenji, 39
Beberibe River, 78
Beecher, Henry Ward, 104
Bello, Muhamman, 37
Benguela, 81
Bénin, 1, 24
Benue River, 10, 37
Berrinio, Jacob, 100
Bida, 2

Bight of Benin, 2, 8, 11, 18, 195; biographical accounts from, 9; Brazilian trade with, 196; British expedition in, 10; lagoon system in, 65; Oyo domination of, 51; slave trade in, 66, 68, 72, 76, 79–80, 89, 90
Bight of Biafra, 72
Bilad al-Sudan, 10
Bilali, 13
Birnee Yawoori (Birnin Yauri), 9
Birni Ngazargamu, 9, 13
Birnin Kebbi, 36
Biromaté, 57
Boa Vista district (Pernambuco), 84
Bodi, 57
Bonduku, 35
Borgu, 10, 20, 23, 24, 40, 41; Oyo backed by, 51
Borno, 9, 10, 12, 31, 37, 38
Boston, 114
Bouker, Abou (Abubakar; Pascoe [Pasko], William), 10, 12
Bouloum (Brum), 57
Boydm Grandison, 187
Brazil: abolitionism in, 5; coast of, 75; coffee production in, 2, 3; and desertion agreement, 108–9, 199, 200; Muslims in, 7, 46, 203; political strife in, 79; slave trade in, 3, 4, 66, 74, 199, 204, 206; sugar production in, 3
Brown, Henry Box, 169
Brown, John (abolitionist), 18, 134, 149–50, 190
Brown, John J. (pastor), 184
Bugaje, 39
Buna, 9, 35
Bunkure, 39
Bussa, 20, 23, 41

Cabinda, 16
Cabo de Santo Agostinho, 77, 81
Calabar, 195
Calarco, 102
Calhoun (abolitionist), 114
California, 100
Campos de Goytacazes, 92

Canada, 5, 123, 147–48, 152, 157, 164–65
Candomblé, 15
Capibaribe River, 78, 81, 84, 85
cassava, 17, 81, 95, 97
Castelnau, François de, 10
Catuamá, 77
Caxias, Luís Alves de Lima e Silva, Duque
    de, 79
Cazneau, Jane Maria Eliza McManus (Cora
    Montgomery), 13
Chapman, Abraham, 168
Child, David Lee, 104
Chinchorro da Gama, Antonio, 80
Christophe, Henri, 122
Ciavolella, Riccardo, 51–52, 56–57, 168
Clapperton, Hugh, 10, 12, 41, 59, 194
clothing, 36
coffee, 2, 3, 79, 84, 100, 117–18, 199
Colored Sailor's Home, 102, 103
Cornell, Joseph, 111
Costa da Mina, 80
cotton, 36, 42
Cuba, 3, 13
Culcurxu district (Djougou), 25
Curtin, Philip D., 8, 10
Curtis, George William, 104

Daboya, 41, 44, 49–50
da Conceiçao, Maria Delfina, 15
da Costa, Clemente José, 87, 92, 101, 112, 191,
    199; as Baquaqua's master, 7, 86, 95, 96,
    97; in "Brazilian slaves" case, 107–10
da Costa, Maria, 99, 100, 101, 108, 109–10
Dagomba, 1, 206
d'Aguiar, Luiz Henrique Ferreira, 99, 109,
    117, 118
Dahomey, 2, 7, 14, 20, 57; salt trade in, 42;
    slave trade in, 1, 60, 62, 198
Dallol Fogha, 36, 41
Dallol Maouri, 39
Daly, Charles P., 106–10, 117–18
Damagaram, 9, 37
Danga, King, 48
Dan Toga, 39
Darby, J. G., 169

da Rocha, José, 99, 100, 105, 109
da Silva, Madalena, 15
da Silva, Marcelina, 15
Dawn Settlement, 149
de Andrade, Rodolhpho Manoel Martins
    (Otikô, Bamboxé), 15
Delany, Martin, 148, 155, 190–91
Dendi language, 22–23, 26, 29, 31, 43–45,
    53–54, 81, 156, 186
Dendi people, 21, 26, 32, 35, 39, 52
de Oliveira, Lourenço, 93
de Souza, Francisco Felix, 66, 198
de Souza e Oliveira, Saturnino, 99
Dessaline, Jean-Jacques, 122
Diário Novo, 79
Diouf, Sylviane, 10
Dioula, 21. *See also* Juula
Ditamari people, 26
Djalloukou, 63–64, 73
Djarra, Abdoulaye Bindiga, 31
Djarra dynasty, 22, 26, 31
Djatchi, 57
Djérakam (Yarakéou), 59
Djougou city, 20, 45; Baquaqua's descrip-
    tions of, 4–5, 23–25, 40; bifurcation of,
    22; Borgu's influence on, 41, 54; ethnic
    diversity in, 22–23, 43–44; kola trade
    in, 37; as mercantile hub, 1, 19, 31, 34, 57;
    regional links of, 41, 43, 54; subdivisions
    of, 24, 25–26
Djougou language, 43
Djougou region, 24
donkeys, 35, 39, 41
Dorugu, 12
Douglass, Frederick, 4, 5, 115, 134, 156, 156,
    181; in Britain, 179; as *North Star* editor,
    169, 190
Doula, Cameroun, 182–83
Dreys, Nicolau, 96
Duncan, John, 64, 67–69
Dupuis, Joseph, 30, 40
Dupuy, Alexis, 121–23, 202
Dupuy, Baron, 122
dyeing, 36
Dyula merchants, 39. *See also* Juula

Edmonds, John W., 121
Edwards, Henry P., 106, 108, 200
Egyptian Rose, 13–14
Eisami, Ali, 9
Elmer, Rufus, 114
Engenho da Torre, 85
Engenho São Pantaleão do Monteiro, 85
Equiano, Olaudah (Vassa, Gustavus), 4, 181
Everett, Alexander, 187
Ewe, 62

Facts for Baptist Churches (Foss and Mathews), 156–57, 164, 182, 193, 205
Fada Ngurma, 22
Faria, Sheila, 90
Feuille, Marcel, 85
Fisher, Miles Mark, 192
Florentino, Manolo, 89, 90
Foner, Eric, 103
Forbes, Frederick, 64, 71
Foromagazi ward (Djougou), 27
Forten, Robert, 140–41
Foss, A. T., 124, 125, 157, 205
Fourah Bay, 207
France, 3
Frazer, Sergeant, 9
Freetown, 9, 16, 194
Freetown Corners, 143, 144, 146, 147, 204
Free Will Baptists. *See* American Baptist Free Mission Society
Fugitive Slave Act (1850), 3, 5, 17, 133, 182, 187, 200, 206
Fula Town, 16, 64, 207
Fulbe (Fulani), 42–43

Gabankare, 39
Garrison, William Lloyd, 114, 134, 178, 179, 182
Gay, Sydney Howard, 104–5, 106, 111, 114, 115–17
Gazeri (kpey), 26
Geffrard, Fabre-Nicolas, 123
Ghana, 65, 89
Ghezo, king of Dahomey, 64
Glehue (Ouidah), 7, 64, 66, 156, 195, 198

Gobir, 9, 10, 37
Goiana, 77
gold, 35, 36, 79
Gold Coast, 1, 9, 34, 66
Gomez, Michael, 10
Gonja, 1, 7, 9, 21, 31, 35, 48, 51, 52, 73
Goulart, João Alípio, 89
Gourmantché people, 25
Grand Popo, 62, 65, 67, 70
Great Britain, 3, 5, 74, 79
Greeley, Horace, 104
Grey, Charles Edward, 13
Grosvenor, Cyrus P., 127, 132, 138, 164–65, 171
Gummi, 38
Gurley, R. R., 192
Gurma people, 22, 25, 52, 61
Gurungu (kpey), 25–26
Gwandu, 36

Habu (Aba; Sam Jackson), 9
Haiti, 3, 5, 18, 39, 115, 121, 206; European domination of, 137; Free Will Baptists in, 2, 7, 8, 123; revolution and emancipation in, 121
Hamilton, Robert, 116
Hammond, Silus, 143
Hausa language, 10, 12, 20–21, 23, 26, 28–29, 34, 38–39, 42, 53–55; Baquaqua's proficiency in, 43, 172, 186, 204, 205; as commercial lingua franca, 43, 197, 200
Hausa people, 9, 10, 31–32, 34, 37, 54, 150, 196; Asante trade with, 20, 200; Baquaqua's knowledge of, 44–46; in Brazil, 89, 90, 203; kola trade in, 36; in Lagos, 194; scarification among, 85; in Wangara ward, 52
Havana, 196
Henson, Josiah, 148, 149
Hill, Charles, 187
Holloway, Thomas, 90
Hopper, Isaac T., 108
Hopper, John, 108, 109
horses, 35, 41
Hudson, Erastus D., 111
Hyppolite, Lucius, 125

ibn Suleiman, Ayuba, 13
Ibura (district of Recife), 84
Idrisu, Alhaji, 36
Ifá traditions, 15
Ifè, 63
Igarassu, 81
Ilê Axé Iyá Nassô Oká, 15
Ile Oyo (Katunga), 51
Ilorin, 2, 9, 51
indigo, 36
Itamarcá, 77
Ivo da Silveira, Pedro, 79

Jamaica, 4, 12
Japan, 152
Jardim, Manoel Pereira, 93
Jay, John, 108
Jay, John, II, 108, 111, 115, 116–17
Jay, William, 108
Jega, 39
Jenne, 8, 9
jerk meat, 94, 97
Jerry case (1851), 3
Jessup, William, 144
jihād, 9, 10, 31, 32, 196; of Sokoto Caliphate,
    1, 3, 12, 20, 37–38, 51, 198
Jones (Baquaqua's travel partner), 27, 115, 134
Jones, William L., 115, 124–25
Judd, Nancy A. Lake, 1, 23, 25, 28, 39, 71, 72,
    115, 123, 124, 128, 135–38, 157, 164–65, 170,
    186; Baquaqua's accounts misunderstood
    by, 32, 44–48, 166–67; Baquaqua's first
    meeting with, 20
Judd, William L., 1, 23, 25, 28, 39, 46, 115,
    122, 125–31, 157, 164, 182, 186; Baquaqua's
    accounts misunderstood by, 32, 44–48,
    166–67; on Baquaqua's conversion, 170;
    early career of, 124
Juula (Muslim network), 21, 39

Kaiama, 20, 23, 41
Kali, 48–49
Kambarin Beriberi, 38, 39, 85
Kano, 2, 9, 28, 31, 37, 44; Gummi merchants
    in, 39; Katsina eclipsed by, 129; textile
    production in, 36

Kano, Dan, 9
Karasch, Mary, 89
Katsina, 2, 8, 9, 12, 21, 31, 45, 129, 152, 194;
    decline of, 3, 35, 37–38; as frontier town,
    37; during jihād, 37; kola trade in, 36;
    naming customs in, 28; slave trade in, 37;
    Wangara merchants in, 32–33
Katunga, 9
Ketu, 15
Kilir (section of Djougou), 22, 25, 31, 52,
    55, 57
King, Kezia, 140, 152, 156
King, Mary G., 145–47, 182
King, W. David, 161
King, William, 148
kingship, 52–53, 57
Kirk, George, 121
Klose, Heinrich, 40, 43, 60
Koelle, Sigismund, 9
kola and kola trade, 10, 12, 194; donkeys
    used in, 41; growth of, 36, 37, 196–97;
    Hausa merchants in, 38, 39; types of, 22
Komodugu Yo River, 13, 36
Kotokoli, 56, 60
Kpé Lafia, 51
Kpembe, 35
Kpera, Siru, 51
Krikri (Ajéide), 62
Krueger, Robert, 168
Kru language, 189
Kukawa, 13
Kumasi (Asante capital), 30, 40, 41, 206;
    epidemic in, 50
Kura language, 60
Kurungu (bakparakpey), 27

Lachaud, Emmanuel, 137
Lacy, Philip, 129
Ladies Society to Aid Fugitives from
    Slavery, 182, 184–85, 188–89
Lagos, 9, 12, 64, 191, 194, 195
Lagrow, John Low, 141, 143
Laird, Macgregor, 183, 191
Lake, Electa C., 125, 131, 136, 137–38, 140,
    157, 186
Lake Chad, 31, 34, 37, 42

Lake Nokoue, 12

Lander, John, 41

Lander, Richard, 41

Law, Robin, 5, 18, 160, 166, 168

leather goods, 1, 12, 22, 36

Lee, John, 121

Lee, Luther, 111–12, 129

Lembrança (ship), 86, 97, 119, 125, 198; in "Brazilian slaves" case, 106–9, 117, 199, 200; in New York, 99–102, 105; offices for, 90, *91*; owner of, 92; size of, 92, 95

Leonard, Chauncey, 152, 192–93, 207

Leonard, William H., 111

Lewis, Cudjo, 71

Liberia, 5, 171, 189, 192, 194

Lincoln, Abraham, 192

Lokpa people, 26

Lombard, Jacques, 54

Lopes, Francisco Gonçalves, 13

Lord, James, 111

Lovejoy, Paul, 5, 18, 160, 166, 168

Luanda, Angola, 16, 64

Macaro, 76

Mair, Dan, 37–38

Makudawa ward (Katsina), 21

Makumba, Sambo, 13

Malcolm, Thomas S., 192

Male uprising (1835), 13, 16, 64

Malwa (community of Muslim merchants), 62

Mamprussi, 22

Mandinga, 80

Mangari district, 36

manifest destiny, 3, 13

Maradi, 37

Masanawa (ward of Katsina), 21

Mason, James M., 121

Mathews, Edward, 124, 125, 157, 182, 193, 205

Mendi Mission, 18, 175–80, 182, 184, 189–90

metalworking, 21

"Mexican Cession," 100–101

Mexico, 3, 13, 100, 205

Mina, 62, 89, 90

Mina, Felicidade, 92

Mina, Fernando, 92

Minas Gerais, 13, 80, 84

Moffat (lawyer), 108

Mohammadu (Jacob Brown), 9

Mono River, 62, 66

Monroe, James, 200

Monroe Doctrine, 200

Monrovia, Liberia, 194

Monteira, 81

Montgomery, Cora (Cazneau, Jane Maria Eliza McManus), 13

Moore, Andrew, 158

Moore, Hannah, 167

Moore, Mary Elizabeth, 158

Moore, Samuel (Canadian activist), 167

Moore, Samuel (Connecticut abolitionist), 167

Moore, Samuel, 23–27, 32–34, 44, 45, 51, 53–54, 57–58, 101, 135–36; as Baquaqua's editor, 1, 26–27, 29, 32, 33, 42, 155–66, 166, 170–71

Moore, Samuel D. (Michigan abolitionist), 158–59

Morocco, 39

Mozambique, 80

Muhammad, Prophet, 27, 39

mules, 35

Muniyo district, 36

Musa, Kara, 35

Nago people, 89. *See also* Yoruba

Napoleon, Louis, 104–5, 199

National Anti-Slavery Standard, 102, 106, 111

Nevada, 100

Newman, William P., 148–49, 152, 174, 181

New Mexico, 100

New York City, 2, *101*; abolitionism in, 18, 102; Underground Railroad in, 5

New York Vigilance Society, 102–5

Niger River, 9, 20, 34, 37, 38, 39, 44, 64, 191, 194, 195; Delany's mission to, 150, 157, 156, 190

Nikki people, 20, 23, 27, 39, 41, 54

Nyanyakyi, Saidu, 49

Oakley, Thomas J., 110, 113
Olinda, Brazil, 80, 81
onion leaves, 36
Osei Tutu Kwame (Osei Bonsu), 35
Osgood, Samuel, 114
Osifikunde, 15, 19
Otikô, Bamboxé (de Andrade, Rodolhpho Manoel Martins), 15
Ouidah (Glehue), 7, 64, 66, 156, 195, 198
Overweg, Walter, 12
Oyo, 12, 15, 51, 64

Paço Imperial, 90
Pan Amarelo, 77
Papson, Don, 102
Parakou, 23
Pascoe (Pasko), William (Abubakar; Bouker, Abou), 10, 12
Passéré, 57
Pedro I (emperor), 78, 79
Pedro II (emperor), 78, 79
Pélébina, 57
Pereira, Maria Roza Leite, 92
Pereira Sodré, Jerônimo, 14
Pernambuco, 14, 17, 97, 203, 205; political strife in, 79; slave trade in, 74, 76, 77; sugar cane production in, 1
Person, Yves, 25, 27, 52, 55
Petit Popo, 64–65, 156
Phipps Brothers & Co., 100, 117, 119
Pila (village), 57
Pila Pila (Yom) language, 22, 43, 52–53, 54, 186
Pila Pila (Yoowa) people, 22, 43, 55
Poço da Panela, 81
Polyglotta Africana (Koelle), 9
Pomeroy, George Eltweed, 160, 166
Pomeroy, Samuel C., 192
Porpoise affair (1845), 199, 200
Port-au-Paix, Haiti, 48
Port-au-Prince, Haiti, 1, 8, 121, 122
Porto Alegre, 15
Porto de Galinhas, 77
Porto Novo, 12, 66, 195
Portugal, 78

Post, Albert L., 144–45, 173–74, 177
Powell, William P., 102–5, 115, 116, 182, 187, 188, 191
Praieiros movement, 79
Purroy (prosecutor), 108, 111
Purvis, Joseph, 138
Purvis, Robert, 138

Rabba, 9
ransoming, 50–51
Recife, Brazil, 16, 74, 76–79, 85
Recôncavo da Guanabara, 92
Recote do Parto, 13
Remington, B. F., 141
Richardson, James, 37
Riché, Jean-Baptiste, 121, 122
Rio de Janeiro, 1–2, 13–17, 79, 87, 91, 196; Africans in, 89, 203
Rio Grande do Sul, 2, 5–6, 17, 18, 74, 86, 92, 94–96, 203
Rocha Pereira, Antonio José da (David), 92–93, 99, 100, 101, 115, 121–22
Rocha Pereira, Antonio José, 92
Royal Geographical Society, 64
Rufino, Jose Maria, 15–16, 19, 206–7
Ruggles, David, 104
Russia, 13

Saba, Alfa, 36
Saddiku, Abubakar, 37
Safo, 48–49
Sagrada Teologia do Amor Divino das Almas Peregrinas (Egyptian Rose), 13
Sahara, 37
Sahel, 24
Said, Nicholas, 13, 19, 37
Salaga, 12, 20, 21, 32, 55; as mercantile hub, 35–36
Salifa, Alfa, 51
Salnave, Sylvain, 127
salt, 1, 22, 41–42, 62; types of, 36
Samson, George W., 192
Santa Catarina, 86, 88, 96
Santo Amaro, Brazil, 14
Santos, Brazil, 86

São José, Agostinho de, 13
São Paulo, Brazil, 84, 92
São Pedro de Rio Grande, 94–97
Sasirou (Culcurxu), 52, 57, 59
Sawa Maloum, King, 53
Saw-Monni people, 53
Saw-Sowra people, 53
scarification, 38–39, 85
Schon, J. F., 12
Scott, J., 140
Senegambia, 9
Shibdawa, 39
Shurfa, 27
Sibuko (diviner), 51
Siebert, Wilbur, 114
Sierra Leone, 3, 9, 10, 15, 171, 196, 207; Mendi
    Mission in, 18, 175–80, 182, 184, 189–90
silks, 35
silversmithing, 21
Smith, Ananias, 187–88
Smith, Elias, 111, 117
Smith, Gerrit, 3, 5, 104, 150, 179–80, 182, 189,
    202; as Baquaqua's benefactor, 143, 159,
    176, 177, 178; as congressman, 149; as
    presidential candidate, 18; as radical, 18,
    132; wealth of, 132–34, 141, 172
Smith, James McCune, 115–16, 117
Soares, Carlos Eugenio, 89
Sodré, Domingos, 14
Sodré Pereira, Francisco Maria, 14
Sokoto, 1, 2, 36, 39
Sokoto Caliphate, 3, 12, 20, 129, 171, 197, 198;
    Asante trade with, 40, 43; consolidation
    of, 21, 37, 39; founding of, 1; and Katina,
    38; in kola market, 36; languages of, 23
Sokoto River, 39
Songhay Empire, 39
Songhay language, 22–23
Soubroukou, 52, 54–59, 73, 156
Soulouque, Faustin, 121, 122–23, 136, 137,
    202, 206
South Africa, 10
Springfield, MA, 114
St. Helena, 15, 16
Stowe, Harriet Beecher, 148

Sudan, 32
sugar, 3, 79, 125
suicide, 83
Sutton, Moses, 155
Sweet, James, 80

Tamandaré, 77
Tamata, Pierre, 12
Tanéka people, 26
Tapâ, Frederico, 98
Tappan, Arthur, 104
Tappan, Lewis, 104, 167, 176, 189
Tchallaha people, 53, 57
Temba people, 60
temperance, 103, 134–35, 136
Teresa Cristina, Princess of the Two
    Sicilies, 79
Texas, 3, 100, 205
textiles, 1, 22, 36
Thompson, Ezra, 143
Thompson, George, 176, 178–89, 182,
    184, 189
Timbuktu, 39, 196
tobacco, 22, 42
Tokarawa, 38, 39, 85
Trinidad, 13
Tripoli, 37
Tuareg, 37, 39
Tuat, 37
Tubman, Harriet, 5
Turner, Daniel, 199–200

Uchôa, Antônio Borges, 85
Umarun Dallaji, 37
Una, 77
Uncle Tom's Cabin (Stowe), 148
Underground Railroad, 3, 5, 104–6, 114, 123,
    169, 205
Unguwar Madugu, 21
US-Mexican War, 3, 100, 205
Utah, 101
'Uthman dan Fodio, 37

Várzea, 81
Vassa, Gustavus (Olaudah Equiano), 4, 181

Vodun (*vodou*), 137
Volta River, 1, 9, 21, 33–42, 65–66
voting rights, 149

Wa, 49, 50
Walker, Warham, 162, 164, 173
Wangarawa, 21, 25–28, 31, 32, 39, 43, 52, 85
Wasangari people, 54
Washington, George (African traveler), 187
Watkins, W. J., 155
Wawa, 41
Webley, W. H., 131, 182
Webster-Ashburton Treaty (1842), 200
Werringer, Jeremy, 114
Werringer, Phoebe, 114
whale oil, 94, 96, 97
Whipple, Alice, 159
Whipple, George, 146, 159, 175–80, 189, 194
White, Joseph L., 108, 116
White Volta River, 49
Whitfield, James M., 148, 156–57, 160, 190–91
Willcox, Mary Otis, 114
Wright, Maria, 116

Xwla, 62

Yagbum, 49
Yarakéou (Nyantruku; Oku-Oku), 59–60, 73
Yaramé (toll station), 26, 31
Yauri, 41, 44
Yom (Pila Pila) language, 22, 43, 52–53, 54, 186
Yoowa (Pila Pila) people, 22, 26, 43, 55
Yoruba culture, Yoruba people, 186–87; in Brazil, 14, 15; in Djougou, 34; Moore's misunderstanding of, 33, 34; in Sierra Leone, 16, 207
Yoruba language, 64, 90

Zamfara, 36
Zamfara River, 38
Zaria, 2, 31, 36
Zarma people, 55, 56
Zinder, 37
Zougou, 23

www.ingramcontent.com/pod-product-compliance
Lightning Source LLC
LaVergne TN
LVHW092349010825
817679LV00030B/579